face2face

Intermediate Student's Book

SECOND EDITION

Chris Redston & Gillie Cunningham

Contents

Lesson			Vocabulary	Grammar	Real World
1A	Be happy!	p6	weekend activities	question forms	
1B	Love it or hate it	p8	likes and dislikes	positive and negative verb forms, words and phrases	
1C	Join the club!	p10	adjectives (1): feelings prepositions with adjectives		
1D	Nice to meet you	p12			question tags
Extra Practice 1 and Progress Portfolio 1		p115			
2A	Slow down!	p14	collocations (1): work	be able to, be supposed to, be allowed to, modal verbs (1)	
2B	Street food	p16	food and ways of cooking	Present Continuous and Present Simple	
2C	Sleepless nights	p18	sleep; gradable and strong adjectives; adverbs		
2D	What's the matter?	p20			showing concern, giving and responding to advice
Extra Practice 2 and Progress Portfolio 2		p116			
3A	The tourist trade	p22	phrasal verbs (1): travel	Present Perfect Simple: experience, unfinished past and recent events	
3B	Lonely Planet	p24	phrases with travel, get and go on	Present Perfect Continuous and Present Perfect Simple	
3C	Voluntourism	p26	word building (1): suffixes for adjectives and nouns		
3D	A trip to India	p28			asking for and making recommendations
Extra Practice 3 and Progress Portfolio 3		p117			
4A	Musical experiences	p30	collocations (2): music	Past Simple and Past Continuous; used to	
4B	Modern adventurers	p32	adjectives (2): character	Past Perfect	
4C	Unusual days out	p34	guessing meaning from context		
4D	It's only a game!	p36			softening opinions and making generalisations
Extra Practice 4 and Progress Portfolio 4		p118			
5A	Our new home	p38	homes	making comparisons: comparatives, superlatives, (not) as … as, etc.	
5B	A load of old junk	p40	phrasal verbs (2)	the future: will, be going to, Present Continuous	
5C	Birthdays	p42	verb patterns (1)		
5D	Things I need	p44	materials		explaining what you need
Extra Practice 5 and Progress Portfolio 5		p119			
6A	Make up your mind	p46	make and do	first conditional and future time clauses	
6B	Fear of failure	p48	reflexive pronouns	zero conditional; conditionals with imperatives and modal verbs; in case	
6C	Touch wood	p50	synonyms		
6D	The village festival	p52			discussion language
Extra Practice 6 and Progress Portfolio 6		p120			

VIDEO See Teacher's DVD

Speaking	Listening and Video	Reading	Writing
My weekend activities Things that make me happy	What makes me happy? **Help with Listening** Questions with *you*	The secret of happiness	Questions with prepositions at the end; subject questions
How do you feel about … ? Things I like and don't like		Love it or hate it	Sentences with a negative meaning Things I like and don't like
The last time I felt like this Starting a club	Four clubs **Help with Listening** Sentence stress (1)	Laughter is the best medicine	
The last party I went to Conversations at a party	**VIDEO** Nice to meet you		Questions with question tags
HELP WITH PRONUNCIATION *-ed* adjectives p13		**Reading and Writing Portfolio 1** Describing a holiday Workbook p64	
How hard do they work? Our rules	In praise of slow Working conditions		Rules at my place of work, school or university
Food I often/never eat Find someone who …		Steve's Street Food blog The L.A. Street Food Festival	Eating habits in my country
My sleep habits A sleep survey	Interview with a sleep scientist **Help with Listening** Weak forms (1)	It's a nightmare!	Sentences with adjectives and adverbs A sleep survey
Problems and advice What should I do?	**VIDEO** What's the matter? **Help with Listening** Intonation (1): sounding concerned		Two conversations
HELP WITH PRONUNCIATION Strong and weak forms p21		**Reading and Writing Portfolio 2** Notices at work Workbook p66	
Questions about travel My experiences	Your holiday, my job **Help with Listening** Present Perfect Simple or Past Simple	Lewis and Veronica's restaurant	
Guide books A timeline of my life		The world's greatest travellers A guide book writer in Kenya	Questions in the Present Perfect Simple or Continuous
My holidays Choosing the best holiday	An interview with a travel expert **Help with Listening** Linking (1): consonant–vowel links	Two voluntourism holidays Holiday factfiles	
Recommendations about a place that I know well	**VIDEO** A trip to India		Three conversations
HELP WITH PRONUNCIATION The schwa /ə/ in suffixes p29		**Reading and Writing Portfolio 3** Holiday arrangements Workbook p68	
My music My best ever musical experience		Three people's best ever musical experiences	Questions with *used to*
People I know An interesting journey	Ed Stafford's amazing journey **Help with Listening** Past Simple or Past Perfect Big River Man	Big River Man	Notes on an interesting journey
Top five museums or art galleries in my country My free time activities	**Help with Listening** Linking (2): /w/, /j/ and /r/ sounds Free days out in London	The world's weirdest museums	
Football Giving your opinion	**VIDEO** It's only a game!		Softening opinions about children
HELP WITH PRONUNCIATION The letters *or* p37		**Reading and Writing Portfolio 4** Reviewing a novel Workbook p70	
Five things to look for in a new home Three houses/flats I know well	A new place to live	Three places to rent	Sentences that make comparisons Comparing houses/flats I know well
Questions with phrasal verbs Discussing future plans Getting rid of things	Give away, throw away, keep? **Help with Listening** Future verb forms What about these curtains?	Just get rid of it! What about these curtains?	
Birthdays My most memorable birthday	Four memorable birthdays **Help with Listening** Fillers and false starts	Happy birthday to you!	Notes on a memorable birthday
Conversations in a department store Four things I need	**VIDEO** Things I need		Conversations in a department store
HELP WITH PRONUNCIATION /dʒ/, /j/ and /juː/ p45		**Reading and Writing Portfolio 5** Emails with news Workbook p72	
Find someone who … Discussing problems	Two big decisions		Sentences with *if, unless, might* Sentences about me
When I was a child Top tips for language learners	**Help with Listening** Zero or first conditional	How to measure success	Top tips for language learners
Superstitions in my country How lucky are you?	The history of superstitions **Help with Listening** Sentence stress (2)	The secrets of luck	British superstitions
Traditional festivals Organising our own festival	**VIDEO** The village festival		
HELP WITH PRONUNCIATION Words ending in *-ate* p53		**Reading and Writing Portfolio 6** Letters to a newspaper Workbook p74	

Lesson			Vocabulary	Grammar	Real World
7A	Have a go!	p54	goals and achievements	ability: be able to, manage, be useless at, etc.	
7B	What would you do?	p56	computers (1)	second conditional	
7C	Social networking	p58	computers (2) articles: a, an, the, no article		
7D	Can you tell me … ?	p60			indirect and direct questions
Extra Practice 7 and Progress Portfolio 7 p121					
8A	Angry planet	p62	bad weather and natural disasters	the passive	
8B	Recycle!	p64	containers	quantifiers: a bit of, too much/many, (not) enough, plenty of, etc.	
8C	Dangers at sea	p66	word building (2): prefixes and opposites, other prefixes and suffixes		
8D	A hiking trip	p68			warnings and advice
Extra Practice 8 and Progress Portfolio 8 p122					
9A	Get healthy!	p70	health	relative clauses with who, that, which, whose, where and when	
9B	Good news, bad news	p72	collocations (3): the news	Present Perfect Simple active and passive for recent events	
9C	Human behaviour	p74	body movements and responses connecting words		
9D	At the doctor's	p76			what doctors say; what patients say
Extra Practice 9 and Progress Portfolio 9 p123					
10A	The anniversary	p78	contacting people	was/were going to, was/were supposed to	
10B	Who's that?	p80	describing people	modal verbs (2): making deductions	
10C	I do!	p82	phrasal verbs (3)		
10D	Do you mind if I … ?	p84			asking for, giving and refusing permission
Extra Practice 10 and Progress Portfolio 10 p124					
11A	Any messages?	p86	things people do at work	reported speech: sentences	
11B	How did it go?	p88	adjectives (3): jobs	reported speech: questions, requests and imperatives	
11C	Undercover	p90	verb patterns (2): reporting verbs		
11D	It's my first day	p92			checking information
Extra Practice 11 and Progress Portfolio 11 p125					
12A	I wish!	p94	informal words and phrases	wishes	
12B	Important moments	p96	phrases with get	third conditional	
12C	Superheroes	p98	word building (3): word families		
	End of Course Review	p101			
Extra Practice 12 and Progress Portfolio 12 p126					

Pair and Group Work p102   **Language Summaries** p127   **Audio and Video Scripts** p156

VIDEO See Teacher's DVD

Speaking	Listening and Video	Reading	Writing
Goals and achievements Things I can and can't do		Three competitors on a new reality TV show	Sentences about ability True or false sentences
My computer What would you do if …? Important possessions	Life without the internet **Help with Listening** First or second conditional Two conversations	Two conversations	Questions about computers
Social networking My class and the internet	Our social networking habits **Help with Listening** Weak forms (2)	The lonely generation?	A survey on social networking and the internet
Indirect questions	**VIDEO** Can you tell me … ? **Help with Listening** Intonation (2): being polite		Indirect questions
HELP WITH PRONUNCIATION Natural rhythm p61		**Reading and Writing Portfolio 7** Giving instructions Workbook p76	
My weather experiences The passive quiz	Hit by lightning	Q&A – Natural disasters Hit by lightning	Questions in the passive
Things in my kitchen Good/bad things about my town/city	How much do you recycle? **Help with Listening** Quantifiers		Sentences with quantifiers
At the beach An exciting or frightening experience	Dead zones **Help with Listening** Linking (3): review	Saving Jesse's arm	Notes on a frightening or an exciting experience
Hiking and camping Visiting my country/city	**VIDEO** A hiking trip	Going sailing Advice for visitors to the UK	Warnings and advice for people visiting my country or city
HELP WITH PRONUNCIATION /ɪə/, /eə/ and /ɜː/ p69		**Reading and Writing Portfolio 8** Problems and solutions Workbook p78	
My diet		Just juice	Sentences with relative clauses
Where I get my news A news summary	Here is today's news **Help with Listening** Present Perfect Simple active or passive	Four news stories	
Body movements and responses Are you a good liar?	How to tell if someone's lying **Help with Listening** British and American accents	Why do we …?	Sentences with connecting words
Doctor and patient role-plays	**VIDEO** At the doctor's	Dinner plans	A conversation at the doctor's
HELP WITH PRONUNCIATION the letters *ough* p77		**Reading and Writing Portfolio 9** Applying for a job Workbook p80	
Secrets of a successful marriage I was going to, but …	The wedding anniversary		Sentences with *was/were going to* and *was/were supposed to*
Describing wedding guests Who does this belong to?	Where's Peggy's husband?		Making deductions
Weddings in my country A wedding I've been to	Wedding traditions **Help with Listening** /t/ and /d/ at the ends of words	For better, for worse	Notes on a wedding
Staying with relatives and friends Asking for permission role-plays	**VIDEO** Do you mind if I … ? **Help with Listening** Intonation (3): asking for permission		
HELP WITH PRONUNCIATION Linking in phrasal verbs p85		**Reading and Writing Portfolio 10** Describing people Workbook p82	
Things people do at work Reporting true or false sentences	I've had an accident Here are your messages **Help with Listening** /h/ in *he, his, him, her*		Reported sentences True or false sentences
Jobs I would/wouldn't like to do Job interviews Reporting questions	Eva's audition I've got the job!	What NOT to ask at an interview!	Reported questions Reported requests and imperatives Questions to ask your partner
My TV habits What happens at the end?	Episode 5 of *Undercover* **Help with Listening** Missing words	*Undercover*'s success is no secret Conversations from Episode 4	Sentences with reporting verbs
My phone habits Phone conversation role-plays	**VIDEO** It's my first day **Help with Listening** Contrastive stress	Ella's messages Four conversations	Taking messages
HELP WITH PRONUNCIATION Words ending in *-tion, -age* and *-ture* p93		**Reading and Writing Portfolio 11** Telling a story Workbook p84	
Sentences about me My wishes and how life would be different	Five conversations with wishes		Sentences with *I wish …* Personal wishes and second conditionals
True or false sentences with *get* Important moments in my life	Turning points **Help with Listening** Third conditional		True or false sentences with *get* Third conditional sentences
Superheroes Create your own superhero!	The life of Stan Lee **Help with Listening** Sentence stress and weak forms: review	The real Spider-Man	
HELP WITH PRONUNCIATION Review quiz p100		**Reading and Writing Portfolio 12** Life changes Workbook p86	

Phonemic Symbols p175   **Irregular Verb List** p175

1A Be happy!

Vocabulary weekend activities
Grammar question forms

QUICK REVIEW **Meeting new people** Talk to three other students. Introduce yourself and find out two things about each person. Then tell the class about one person you spoke to.

Vocabulary and Speaking
Weekend activities

1 a Match the verbs in A to the words/phrases in B. Then check in Language Summary 1 **VOCABULARY 1.1** p127.

A	B
visit have go to	a lie-in relatives concerts/gigs/festivals
chat have do	a quiet night in yoga to friends online
meet up tidy up go to	museums/art galleries with friends the house/the flat
do have go out	people round for dinner for a drink/meal exercise

b Work in pairs. Ask questions with *How often do you … ?*, *When did you last … ?* or *Do you ever … ?* about the activities in **1a**. Ask follow-up questions if possible.

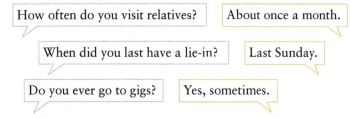

How often do you visit relatives? — About once a month.
When did you last have a lie-in? — Last Sunday.
Do you ever go to gigs? — Yes, sometimes.

Reading and Speaking

2 a Read the beginning of the article about happiness. How did the scientists make their top ten list?

b Look at these reasons for happiness. Put them in order from 1–10 (1 = the most important).

- friends and family
- money
- being married
- helping others
- your genes
- being attractive
- growing old
- religion
- intelligence
- not wanting more than you've got

c Work in pairs. Compare lists. Explain the order you chose.

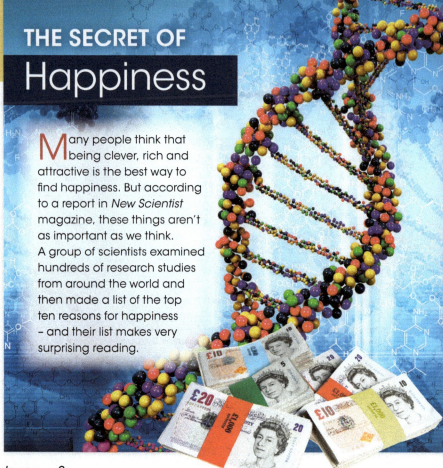

THE SECRET OF Happiness

Many people think that being clever, rich and attractive is the best way to find happiness. But according to a report in *New Scientist* magazine, these things aren't as important as we think. A group of scientists examined hundreds of research studies from around the world and then made a list of the top ten reasons for happiness – and their list makes very surprising reading.

3 Turn to p112. Read the rest of the article and answer the questions.

Listening and Speaking

4 a Look at the photos of Fiona, Maxie and Caroline. What makes them happy, do you think?

b CD1 ▶1 Listen and write two things that make each person happy.

c Listen again. Answer these questions.

1 How often does Fiona teach yoga classes? *Three times a week.*
2 What is Fiona's son doing at the moment?
3 What did Fiona do last Sunday?
4 How many songs has Maxie written?
5 What did he put on YouTube last month?
6 How many countries has he been to?
7 Who does Caroline go to art galleries with?
8 What makes her husband happy?
9 Who visits them most weekends?

Fiona
Maxie
Caroline

HELP WITH GRAMMAR Question forms

5 a Match questions 1–4 in **4c** to these verb forms.

Present Simple 1   Past Simple
Present Continuous   Present Perfect Simple

b Write questions 2–4 from **4c** in the table.

question word	auxiliary	subject	verb	
How often	does	Fiona	teach	yoga classes?

c Look at questions 5–9 in **4c**. Answer these questions.
1 Is the question word the object or the subject in each question?
2 Why don't questions 8 and 9 have an auxiliary?

d Find two questions in **4c** which have a preposition at the end.

e Check in **GRAMMAR 1.1** p128.

6 Fill in the gaps in these questions with *do*, *are*, *have*, *did* or – (= no auxiliary).
1 Whereabouts *do* you live?
2 How long _____ you lived there?
3 Who _____ lives with you?
4 What time _____ you get up on Sundays?
5 Why _____ you studying English?
6 Where _____ you go on holiday last year?
7 How many countries _____ you visited?
8 Who _____ emails you the most?
9 What _____ you do yesterday evening?
10 What _____ you planning to do next weekend?

HELP WITH LISTENING
Questions with *you*

7 a Work in pairs. How do we usually say the auxiliaries and *you* in the questions in **6**?

b CD1 ▸2 Listen to the questions in **6**. Notice how we say *do you* /dəjə/, *have you* /həvjə/, *are you* /əjə/ and *did you* /dɪdʒə/.

8 a CD1 ▸2 **PRONUNCIATION** Listen again and practise. Copy the weak forms.

Whereabouts do you /dəjə/ *live?*

b Work in pairs. Ask and answer the questions in **6**. Ask follow-up questions.

9 Work in new pairs. Student A p102. Student B p107.

Get ready … Get it right!

10 Write a list of five things you do that make you happy.
1 *writing my blog*
2 *going for walks in the park*

11 a Work in groups of three. Take turns to tell the group about each thing on your list. Ask one or two questions about each thing your partners tell you about.

> Writing my blog makes me happy.

> How often do you write it?

> What do you write about?

b Tell the class about one thing that makes you happy.

1B Love it or hate it

Vocabulary likes and dislikes
Grammar positive and negative verb forms, words and phrases

QUICK REVIEW Question forms Choose a partner, but don't talk to him or her yet. Write four questions to ask your partner. Work in pairs. Ask and answer your questions. Then tell the class something interesting you found out about your partner.

A

flying

Vocabulary and Speaking
Likes and dislikes

1 Work in pairs. Match these phrases to groups 1–3. Then check in **VOCABULARY 1.2 ▶ p127**.

1 saying you love or like something
2 saying something is OK
3 saying you don't like something

> I (really) love … 1   I (really) hate … 3
> I don't like … at all.   I can't stand …
> I'm (really/very/quite) interested in …
> I think … is/are all right.
> … (really) get(s) on my nerves.
> I can't bear …   I (really) enjoy …
> I don't mind …   I'm not (very) keen on …
> I'm (really/very/quite) keen on …
> … (really) drive(s) me crazy.
> I think … is/are great/brilliant/wonderful.
> I think … is/are awful/terrible/dreadful.

2 a Decide how you feel about these things. Choose a different phrase from **1** for each thing.

- watching sport on TV
- buying new shoes
- waiting in queues
- getting up early
- cooking
- doing the washing-up
- going to weddings
- tidying up the house or flat

b Work in groups. Compare ideas. Explain why you feel like this.

Reading

3 Read the comments on the internet forum. Then fill in gaps 1–4 with the things in photos A–D. Do the people love or hate these things?

Things we LOVE 😊 and HATE 😠

1 _____ really drives me crazy. You have to listen to this terrible music while you're waiting, and then a woman's voice says, "you're 93rd in the queue". Sometimes you can wait for over an hour and no one answers – and you can't put the phone down because you don't want to lose your place. Then when you finally speak to someone they hardly ever solve your problem, so you have to start again anyway.
MICHAEL

I think ² _____ are brilliant, but I know a lot of people can't stand them. I've got two sisters and neither of them can watch one for more than 5 minutes. I've seen loads of different shows over the years. The ones with celebrities are the best because you can see that none of them are any different to us – they're all just normal people really. But I wouldn't like to be on one myself because I know all my friends would laugh at me!
CORINNE

I really hate ³ _____ . The trains are always really crowded and they're often late or get cancelled for no reason. Yesterday I waited nearly half an hour for a train, and then I didn't get a seat so I had to stand all the way home. I don't think that's right, not when we pay so much for our tickets. And I can't bear listening to other people's phone conversations on the train. How can people talk about hospital visits or relationship problems in public? I don't think I could do that, I'd be too embarrassed.
MARCELA

I really love ⁴ _____ , but my wife doesn't like it at all. I can't understand why – it's much safer than driving and there are no traffic jams. She hasn't flown for years, but as far as I'm concerned, there's no better way to travel. I love just sitting back and watching the clouds go by or chatting to the person next to me. And if I'm not feeling very sociable I can always watch a film, which I never have time to do at home.
HASSAN

phoning call centres

commuting

reality TV programmes

4 a Read the comments on the internet forum again. Are these sentences true (T) or false (F)?

1 Michael doesn't mind talking to call centres. *F*
2 He thinks call centres usually solve your problems.
3 Corinne's sisters can't bear reality TV programmes.
4 Corinne doesn't like programmes with celebrities.
5 Marcela had a difficult journey home yesterday.
6 She enjoys listening to other people's phone conversations.
7 Hassan's wife isn't keen on flying.
8 Hassan often watches films when he's at home.

b Work in groups. Discuss how you feel about the things in the photos. Use phrases from **1** and your own ideas.

HELP WITH GRAMMAR
Positive and negative verb forms, words and phrases

5 a Look at the comments on the internet forum again. Match the phrases in blue to these verb forms. Which phrases are negative?

Present Simple   Present Perfect Simple
Present Continuous   Past Simple

b Look at Marcela's comment again. Find the negative forms of these sentences. Which verb do we usually make negative?

I think that's right.   I think I could do that.

c Look at Hassan's comment again. Find another way to say these phrases. Which word can we use instead of *not a* and *not any* with *there is/there are*?

There aren't any traffic jams.
There isn't a better way to travel.

d Match these positive words to the negative words/phrases in pink on the internet forum.

love *hate*   everyone _____
always _____   all _____
usually _____   both _____

e Check in **GRAMMAR 1.2** p128.

6 a Make these sentences negative. There is sometimes more than one possible answer.

1 I often visit my grandmother.
   I don't often visit my grandmother.
2 Everyone in my family likes tennis.
3 My mum's lost her mobile.
4 I think I'll buy a new phone.
5 There's a doctor in the village.
6 All of my friends have got cars.
7 Both of my brothers like cooking.
8 There's some milk in the fridge.

b Work in pairs. Compare answers.

7 **CD1 ▶ 3** **PRONUNCIATION** Listen and practise.
I don't often visit my grandmother.

Get ready … Get it right!

8 Write four sentences about things you like and four sentences about things you don't like. Use the phrases from **1** and your own ideas.

I really enjoy watching old films.
I can't stand going to the dentist.

9 a Find one student in the class who agrees with each of your sentences. Ask follow-up questions if possible.

> I really enjoy watching old films.

> Yes, me too. What was the last one you watched?

b Tell the class two things you have in common with other students.

> Tamek and I both enjoy watching old films.

VOCABULARY 1C AND SKILLS Join the club!

Vocabulary adjectives (1): feelings; prepositions with adjectives
Skills Listening: an informal conversation; Reading: a magazine article

QUICK REVIEW **Likes and dislikes** Write the names of three people you know. Think of one thing they like doing and one thing they don't like doing. Work in pairs. Take turns to tell each other about the people: *My brother Federico can't stand waiting in queues.*

Vocabulary and Speaking
Adjectives (1): feelings

 a Work in pairs. Which of these adjectives do you know? Do they describe positive or negative feelings? Then check new words in **VOCABULARY 1.3** ▶ **p127**.

> relaxed   nervous   pleased   embarrassed   angry   annoyed
> fed up   disappointed   stressed   calm   upset   scared
> satisfied   confused   shocked   glad   concerned   depressed

b Choose six adjectives from **1a**. Make notes on the last time you felt like this.

c Work in pairs. Tell your partner about the adjectives you chose. Ask follow-up questions if possible.

> I felt quite stressed last week because I had to go for a job interview.

> Did you get the job?

Listening and Speaking

 a Work in new pairs. Answer these questions.
1 Have you (or people you know) ever been a member of a club? If so, tell your partner about it.
2 What kinds of clubs are popular in your school, university or city? What do people do in these clubs?
3 What are the advantages and disadvantages of being in a club?

b **CD1** ▶ **4** Listen to four friends, Sally, Eric, Alice and Peter. Put these clubs in the order they talk about them. What do people do in each club?

- a book club
- a glee club
- an animation club
- a drama club

c Listen again. Tick (✓) the true sentences. Correct the false ones.
1 Sally's new play is a ~~musical~~. *comedy*
2 Her character in the play is an angry old lady.
3 Eric's book club meets once a week.
4 He doesn't always finish reading every book.
5 Peter runs an animation club.
6 Eric might go to an animation club meeting.
7 Alice is better at dancing than singing.
8 She's too embarrassed to sing in the restaurant.

d Work in pairs. Compare answers. Would you like to join any of these clubs? Why?/Why not?

HELP WITH LISTENING
Sentence stress (1)

 a **CD1** ▶ **4** Read and listen to the beginning of the conversation. Notice which words are stressed.

SALLY Sorry I'm late. Did you get my text?
PETER Hi, Sally. Yes, I've ordered you the vegetarian pizza.
SALLY Great, thanks a lot.
ERIC Were you working late?
SALLY No, I go to a drama club on Mondays.
ALICE I didn't know you've joined a drama club.

b Find examples of these parts of speech in the conversation in **3a**. Are these types of words usually stressed (S) or not stressed (N)?

> adjectives S   pronouns
> positive auxiliaries   main verbs
> nouns   articles   prepositions
> negative auxiliaries

c Look at Audio Script **CD1** ▶ **4** p156. Listen again and follow the sentence stress.

Reading and Speaking

 a Look at the photos and the headline of the article on p11. What do you think the article is about?

b Before you read, check these words/phrases with your teacher or in a dictionary.

> reduce   clap your hands
> strengthen your immune system
> fake   chemicals

c Read the article. Match topics a–e to paragraphs 1–5.
a It worked for me – try it yourself
b Why laughter is good for you
c Start the day with a laugh
d My first visit to a Laughter Club
e How Laughter Clubs began

Laughter is the best medicine

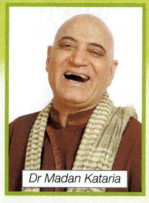

Dr Madan Kataria

1 Do you want to live a happier, less stressful life? Try laughing for no reason at all. That's how thousands of people start their day at Laughter Yoga Clubs around the world – and many doctors now think that having a good laugh might be one of the best ways to stay healthy.

2 The first Laughter Yoga Club was started in Mumbai, India, in 1995 by Dr Madan Kataria. "Young children laugh about 300 times a day. Adults laugh between 7 and 15 times a day," says Dr Kataria. "Everyone's naturally good at laughing – it's the universal language. We want people to feel happy with their lives." There are now more than 6,000 Laughter Clubs in over 65 countries worldwide and there's even a World Laughter Day on the first Sunday in May every year.

3 Many doctors are also interested in the positive effects of laughter on our health. According to a five-year study at the UCLA School of Medicine in California, laughter reduces stress in the body, strengthens your immune system and is very good for the heart. Laughter Yoga is now used in many hospitals for the treatment of serious illnesses and it is also practised in schools, companies, old people's homes and prisons.

4 So, what actually is Laughter Yoga? I went along to my nearest Laughter Club in south London to find out. I was quite nervous about it, to be honest – I wasn't keen on the idea of laughing with a group of strangers, and I was worried about looking stupid. First, our laughter teacher told us to clap our hands and say, "ho ho ho, ha ha ha," while looking at each other. The teacher explained that our bodies can't tell the difference between fake laughter and real laughter, so they still produce the same healthy chemicals.

5 Amazingly, it works. After ten minutes everybody in the room was laughing for real – and some people just couldn't stop! We spent an hour doing different types of laughter exercises and at the end of the class I was surprised by how calm and relaxed I felt. So if you're upset about something at work or just fed up with your daily routine, then just start laughing – you might be very pleased with the results. As Dr Kataria says, "When you laugh, you change, and when you change, the whole world changes around you."

5 a Read the article again. Find the answers to these questions.
1 Where and when did Laughter Yoga Clubs begin?
2 How often do young children and adults laugh?
3 What happens in May every year?
4 How does laughter improve your health?
5 What do people do at a Laughter Club?
6 Why is fake laughter good for your health?
7 How did the writer feel at the end of the class?

b Work in pairs. Compare answers. Would you like to join a Laughter Yoga Club? Why?/ Why not?

HELP WITH VOCABULARY
Prepositions with adjectives

6 a Look at the adjectives in blue in the article. Which preposition comes after them?

good _at_	worried ___
happy ___	surprised ___
interested ___	upset ___
nervous ___	fed up ___
keen ___	pleased ___

b Match these prepositions to the adjectives. Sometimes there is more than one answer.

| of | with | about | by | at |

scared _of, by_
bored ___
frightened ___
annoyed ___
bad ___
satisfied ___
embarrassed ___
depressed ___
angry ___ something
angry ___ someone

c Check in **VOCABULARY 1.4** p127.

7 a Choose six adjectives from **6a** and **6b**. Write the name of one person you know for each adjective.

fed up — Eva

b Work in new pairs. Tell your partner about the people. Ask follow-up questions.

> My sister Eva is fed up with her job.

> Oh, why's that?

8 Work in groups. Look at p112.

1D REAL WORLD — Nice to meet you

Real World question tags

QUICK REVIEW Prepositions with adjectives
Work in pairs. Find one thing that you're both: scared of, interested in, worried about, good at, fed up with, happy about. **A** *I'm scared of spiders.* **B** *Me too!*

1 Work in pairs. Discuss these questions.
1 When did you last meet someone new (apart from students in this class)? Where were you at the time?
2 What did you talk about?
3 Did you get on well with the person? Why?/Why not?

2 a Look at the photo. Where are the people? What are they doing?

b VIDEO 1 CD1 5 Watch or listen to the conversation. Then choose the correct names in these sentences.
1 (Daniel)/Charlie is Lisa's new boyfriend.
2 Lisa/Daniel is Charlie and Rebecca's neighbour.
3 Rebecca's/Lisa's sister shared a flat with Daniel's brother.
4 Daniel/Charlie teaches people how to sail.
5 Charlie/Lisa works for a package tour company.
6 Lisa/Daniel and Rebecca/Charlie both support Manchester United.
7 Rebecca and Charlie have a son called Alex/Harry.

c Work in pairs. Compare answers.

3 a Work in the same pairs. Complete questions 1–6 with these question tags.

| ~~don't you?~~ wasn't it? do you? |
| have you? haven't you? didn't she? |

1 You live next door to Lisa, *don't you?* — a *Yes, I do.*
2 Barbara went to Liverpool university, ___ — b ___
3 You've been diving, ___ — c ___
4 It was a great match yesterday, ___ — d ___
5 You haven't ordered any food yet, ___ — e ___
6 You don't have any kids, ___ — f ___

b Work in the same pairs. Write these short answers in a–f.

| ~~Yes, I do.~~ No, I don't. Yes, she did. Yes, it was. |
| No, I haven't, actually. No, we haven't. |

c VIDEO 1 CD1 5 Watch or listen again. Check your answers to **3a** and **3b**.

Charlie — Daniel — Rebecca — Lisa

REAL WORLD Question tags

4 a Look again at questions 1–6 in **3a**. Then choose the correct words/phrases in these rules.

- We usually use questions with question tags (*don't you?*, etc.) to *check information that we think is correct/find out new information*.
- We usually use the *main verb/auxiliary* in question tags.
- We only use *names/pronouns* in question tags.
- If the main verb is positive, the question tag is usually *positive/negative*.
- If the main verb is negative, the question tag is usually *positive/negative*.

b Look again at short answers a–f in **3a**. Then answer these questions.

1 Which short answers say the information is correct?
2 Which short answer says the information isn't correct?
3 Which word do we use to sound more polite when the information isn't correct?

TIP • We can also use *Yes, that's right.* to say that the information is correct: **A** *You're from London originally, aren't you?* **B** *Yes, that's right. / Yes, I am.*

c Check in **REAL WORLD 1.1** ▶ p128.

5 a **CD1** ▶ 6 Listen to questions 1–6 in **3a** again. Does the intonation on the question tag go up or down?

b **PRONUNCIATION** Listen again and practise. Copy the stress and intonation.

You live next door to Lisa, don't you?

6 a Write question tags to check information about the people in the photo.

1 Lisa and Daniel aren't married, *are they* ?
2 Charlie and Daniel haven't met before, ___ ?
3 Rebecca and Lisa live in the same village, ___ ?
4 Charlie's lived there for about three years, ___ ?
5 Daniel left London last year, ___ ?
6 Daniel and Lisa shared a flat at university, ___ ?
7 Charlie works for a holiday company, ___ ?
8 Rebecca isn't very keen on football, ___ ?
9 Harry is Charlie and Rebecca's son, ___ ?
10 Daniel hasn't got any children, ___ ?

b Work in pairs. Take turns to ask and answer the questions. Then check your partner's answers in Audio Script **CD1** ▶ 5 p156. How many are correct?

Lisa and Daniel aren't married, are they?

No, they aren't.

7 Work in new pairs. Look at p114.

HELP WITH PRONUNCIATION
-ed adjectives

1 a Work in pairs. Look at these *-ed* adjectives. How many syllables does each word have? Write the words in the table and mark the stress.

~~stressed~~   ~~annoyed~~   ~~excited~~   satisfied
worried   confused   frightened   relaxed   scared
concerned   shocked   terrified   embarrassed
exhausted   interested   depressed

1 syllable	*stressed*
● ●	
● ●	*annoyed*
● ● ●	
● ● ●	*excited*

b **7** Listen and check. Listen again and practise.

2 a Work in new pairs. Cover **1a**. Do these words have the same (S) or different (D) stress pattern?

1 stressed annoyed *D*   5 frightened worried
2 concerned exhausted   6 shocked scared
3 depressed confused   7 satisfied relaxed
4 embarrassed interested   8 excited terrified

b **CD1** ▶ 8 Listen and check. Listen again and practise.

continue2learn

■ **Vocabulary, Grammar and Real World**
  ■ **Extra Practice 1 and Progress Portfolio 1** p115
  ■ **Language Summary 1** p127
  ■ **1A–D** Workbook p5

■ **Reading and Writing**
  ■ **Portfolio 1** Describing a holiday Workbook p64
    Reading an email about a holiday
    Writing informal writing; ellipsis of words

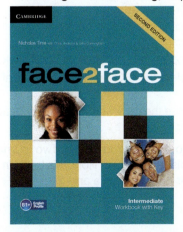

2A Slow down!

Vocabulary collocations (1): work
Grammar be able to, be supposed to, be allowed to, modal verbs (1)

QUICK REVIEW Question tags Choose a partner, but don't talk to him/her yet. Write three things you think you know about your partner. Work in pairs. Ask questions with question tags to check your information is correct: A *You studied here last year, didn't you?* B *Yes, I did.* Ask follow-up questions: A *Where did you study before that?*

Vocabulary and Speaking
Collocations (1): work

1 a Choose the correct verbs in these phrases. Then check in VOCABULARY 2.1 p129.

1 *take/be* work home
2 *be/have* time to relax
3 *get/work* long hours
4 *work/spend* overtime
5 *get/be* a workaholic
6 *meet/take* deadlines
7 *take/be* time off work
8 *have/be* under (a lot of) pressure at work
9 *leave/spend* a lot of time at work
10 *have/be* good working conditions

b Think of three people you know who have jobs. Choose two phrases from **1a** for each person.

c Work in pairs. Tell your partner about the people you chose. Which person works the hardest?

Listening and Speaking

2 a Look at the book cover, the cartoon and the photos. What is the book about, do you think?

b Work in pairs. Guess the correct words or numbers in these sentences.

1 People in *China/Germany* spend 15% less time at work now than in 1980.
2 Some companies in *France/Italy* give their employees three-day weekends.
3 *Europeans/Americans* work 350 hours a year more than *Europeans/Americans*.
4 20% of British people work over *50/60* hours a week.
5 *30%/60%* of people in the UK said they didn't take all their paid holiday.
6 In *German/Japanese* there's a word that means 'death from working too hard'.

c CD1 9 Listen to a radio programme. Two journalists, Kim and Rob, are discussing Carl Honoré's book *In Praise of Slow*. Check your answers to **2a** and **2b**.

3 a CD1 9 Listen to the radio programme again. Fill in the gaps with one or two words.

1 Rob says he **must** take more time off *work* .
2 Honoré says people **should** only work _____ hours a week.
3 Honoré believes that we **ought to** spend more time with _____ .
4 Some French employees **are allowed to** begin their weekend at _____ on Thursday.
5 People **can** get their best _____ when they're doing nothing.
6 In some American companies, employees **can** _____ whenever they want.
7 In the UK people **are supposed to** have a break every _____ .
8 Kim says that lots of people **have to** take _____ .
9 Rob says that these days we**'re able to** continue working when we're _____ .

b Work in pairs. Do you agree with Carl Honoré that we all work too hard and should slow down? Why?/Why not?

Google offices, London

HELP WITH GRAMMAR *be able to, be supposed to, be allowed to,* modal verbs (1)

4 a Look at the sentences in **3a**. Then complete these rules with the verb forms in bold. Use the infinitive form if necessary.

We use …

- _can_ and _____ to talk about ability or possibility.
- _____ to say a person is expected to do something.
- _____ and _____ to say we have permission to do something.
- _must_ and _____ to say something is necessary.
- _____ and _____ to give advice.

b Look again at the verb forms in bold in **3a**. Answer these questions.

1 Do we use the infinitive or verb+*ing* after these verb forms?
2 Which verb forms include *to*?
3 How do we make these verb forms negative?
4 How do we make questions with these verb forms?

c Look at these sentences. Then complete the rules with *mustn't* or *don't have to*.

You **mustn't** send personal emails from the office. You can only send work emails.

You **don't have to** wear a suit to work, but you can if you want to.

- We use _____ to say something isn't necessary.
- We use _____ to say something is not allowed.

d Check in **GRAMMAR 2.1** ▶ p130.

5 a Kim (K) and Rob (R) are talking after the radio programme. Read their conversation and choose the correct verb forms. Who has the best working conditions?

K So, do you think you ¹(should)/are allowed to relax more?
R Absolutely! ²*I'm able to/I must* try to slow down a bit.
K ³*Are you able to/Should you* start work when you want?
R No, not really. ⁴*I'm supposed to/I can* be in the office at eight. What about you?
K I ⁵*don't have to/mustn't* be at work until ten.
R Lucky you. ⁶*Are you allowed to/Should you* work at home?
K Yes, we ⁷*ought to/can* work at home two days a week.
R Oh, we ⁸*have to/are able to* be in the office every day.
K Perhaps you ⁹*ought to/are supposed to* look for another job.
R Yes, maybe. Anyway, I ¹⁰*have to/can* go. I ¹¹*mustn't/don't have to* be late for my next meeting. Bye!

b CD1 ▶ 10 Listen and check.

6 CD1 ▶ 11 **PRONUNCIATION** Listen and practise the sentences in **5a**. Copy the stress.

Do you think you should relax more?

Get ready … Get it right!

7 Write sentences describing the rules at the place where you work, your school or university. Use language from **4a** and these ideas.

- what you can wear
- what time you start and finish
- using mobiles, the internet, etc.
- food and drink
- how to behave
- breaks and holidays
- getting work done on time
- any other ideas

In my company all the managers have to wear a suit and tie.

At my school we're allowed to wear what we want.

8 a Work in groups. If you work or study in the same place, compare sentences. Do you agree with your partners' ideas?

If you work or study in different places, tell other students your sentences. Ask questions to find out more information. Which place has the best rules, do you think?

b Tell the class about two of the rules your group discussed.

2B Street food

Vocabulary food and ways of cooking
Grammar Present Continuous and Present Simple

QUICK REVIEW Modal verbs, *be supposed to*
Think of one thing you: have to do, ought to do, should do, don't have to do, are supposed to do next week. Work in pairs. Tell your partner about these things. Who is going to have the busiest week?

Vocabulary and Speaking
Food and ways of cooking

 a Try to put these words into groups 1–5. Some words can go in more than one group.

a peach	beans	grill	peanuts	lamb
a chilli	an onion	a coconut	barbecue	
flour	a cucumber	a pineapple	beef	boil
herbs	spices	an avocado	fry	a lettuce
sauce	stir fry	a hot dog	cream	
a green/red pepper	noodles	bake	a pie	

1 fruit *a peach*   4 other food words
2 vegetables   5 ways of cooking
3 meat

b Work in pairs. Compare your groups 1–5. Then check new words in **VOCABULARY 2.2** ▶ p129.

c Work with your partner. Answer these questions.
1 Which of the types of food in **1a** do you often eat? Which do you never eat?
2 How do people in your country usually cook the meat and vegetables in **1a**?

Speaking and Reading

2 a Work in new pairs. Look at photos A–C. Have you ever tried these types of street food? If so, did you like them? If not, which would you like to try?

b Read the blog. How do you make the types of food in photos A–C?

3 a Read the blog again. Answer these questions.
1 Why does Steve travel a lot?
2 Why does he like eating street food?
3 When did he start his blog?
4 How often does he visit Bangkok?
5 Where was Steve on May 19th?
6 Does he like spicy food?

b Work in pairs. Discuss these questions.
1 What kinds of street food can you buy in your country? What are the ingredients? How is it cooked?
2 Do you ever eat street food? If so, what do you eat?

A

pad thai

Steve's STREET FOOD BLOG

I live in London, but I travel all over the world for my job (I'm a photographer) and I always try the street food wherever I go. For me there's nothing better than sitting in a square or a park eating cheap, freshly-cooked street food – it's the best way to get to know a country and its people. I started blogging about street food over three years ago and my blog is becoming more popular every year. Now I'm writing a book about street food around the world – when I'm not working, blogging or eating, of course!

APRIL 27TH More and more people are visiting Thailand on holiday these days, but most of them don't stay in Bangkok for very long. Big mistake. I come here every year and I can tell you that the country's capital has got some fantastic street food – take pad thai, for example. It's very quick to make – stir fry some noodles, then add eggs, fish sauce, chillies, chicken, peanuts, herbs and spices – and it's one of the most incredible dishes you've ever tasted.

MAY 19TH I'm blogging from a busy food market in the centre of Jakarta. People still eat a lot of street food in Indonesia, and satay is probably the country's most popular dish. When people make satay, they often grill the lamb or chicken, but it tastes better if it's barbecued over an open fire. Then cover the cooked meat with a spicy peanut sauce and serve with onions, cucumber and rice cakes. Delicious!

JUNE 5TH We're working in Mexico for a few days and at the moment I'm sitting in one of Mexico City's busy parks – and I've just eaten one of the best burritos I've had in my life! If you want to make the perfect burrito, start with a freshly-made flour tortilla – a type of flat bread – then fill it with grilled beef or chicken and serve with beans, rice, sour cream, onions, lettuce and avocado. So why was this one so good? The extra-hot chilli sauce!

B a burrito

C satay

HELP WITH GRAMMAR
Present Continuous and Present Simple

4 **a** Look at the blog again. Match the verb forms in blue to these meanings. There are two verb forms for each meaning.

- We use the **Present Continuous** for things that:
  a are happening at the moment of speaking or writing. *'m blogging*
  b are temporary and happening around now, but maybe not at this exact moment.
  c are changing over a period of time.
- We use the **Present Simple** for:
  a habits and routines with *always, sometimes, never, every day, every year*, etc. *try*
  b things that are permanent, or true for a long time.
  c verbs that describe states (*be, have got, want*, etc.).

b Look at these verbs. Do they usually describe activities (A) or states (S)? Do we usually use state verbs in the Present Continuous?

be S	watch A	talk	seem	spend
agree	eat	taste	prefer	know	learn
own	buy	understand	cook	remember
believe	take	need	happen	love

c How do we make the positive, negative and question forms of the Present Continuous and Present Simple?

d Check in **GRAMMAR 2.2** p131.

5 **CD1** **12** **PRONUNCIATION** Listen and practise. Copy the stress and contractions (*I'm*, etc.).

I'm blogging from a busy street food market.

6 **a** Read Steve's blog entry from Los Angeles. Put the verbs in brackets in the Present Simple or Present Continuous.

www.stevesstreetfoodblog.com/LAfestival

JULY 16TH I¹ _'m staying_ (stay) with my cousin in Los Angeles and I² _____ (blog) from the L.A. Street Food festival, which ³ _____ (happen) here every summer. A lot of people in Los Angeles really ⁴ _____ (love) street food and the festival ⁵ _____ (become) more popular every year. There ⁶ _____ (be) over 60 stalls at this year's festival and 1,500 people ⁷ _____ (enjoy) the food, the drinks and the sunshine. I ⁸ _____ (come) here every year and I ⁹ _____ (not understand) why more cities ¹⁰ _____ (not have) festivals like this one. At the moment I ¹¹ _____ (have) Indian meatballs with fried green peppers in a spicy coconut sauce, and my cousin ¹² _____ (eat) the longest hot dog I've ever seen! After this we ¹³ _____ (want) to try some pineapple and strawberry ice cream!

b Work in pairs. Compare answers.

7 **a** Write four sentences in the Present Continuous about how eating habits in your country are changing. Use these ideas or your own.

- street food
- organic food
- food from other countries
- fast food
- supermarkets
- the amount people eat
- prices
- quality of food

People are eating more street food these days.

b Work in groups. Compare sentences. Are any the same?

Get ready ... Get it right!

8 Make questions with *you*. Put the verbs in brackets in the Present Simple or Present Continuous.

1 _Are you feeling_ (feel) hungry now?
2 _____ (usually eat) a lot of street food?
3 _____ (cook) for yourself every day?
4 _____ (try) to eat more healthily these days?
5 _____ (want) to learn how to cook?
6 _____ (look) for somewhere to live?
7 _____ (often read) blogs?
8 _____ (watch) any good TV series at the moment?

9 **a** Ask other students your questions. Try to find one person who answers *yes* for each question. Then ask two follow-up questions.

b Work in groups. Tell other students three things you found out about the class.

VOCABULARY 2C AND SKILLS > Sleepless nights

Vocabulary sleep; gradable and strong adjectives; adverbs
Skills Listening: a TV interview; Reading: a newspaper article

QUICK REVIEW Food and ways of cooking
Write four ways of cooking (*boil*, etc.) and two types of food you can cook for each verb (*potatoes*, *noodles*, etc.). Work in pairs. Take turns to say two types of food. Your partner guesses the verb: A *Potatoes and noodles.* B *You can boil them.* A *Yes, that's right.*

Vocabulary and Speaking Sleep

1 Work in pairs. Which of these words/phrases do you know? Then check new words/phrases in VOCABULARY 2.3 p129.

> fall asleep   wake up   get (back) to sleep
> be wide awake   be fast asleep   snore
> have trouble sleeping   have insomnia
> take a sleeping pill   have a dream
> have a nightmare   be a light/heavy sleeper
> have a nap

2 a Choose five words/phrases from **1** that are connected to you, or people you know.

b Work in groups. Take turns to talk about the words/phrases you chose. Ask follow-up questions if possible.

Listening

3 Work in pairs. Look at these sentences about sleep. Try to choose the correct words or numbers.

1 Tiredness causes *more/less* than half of all road accidents in the USA.
2 *10%/30%* of people in the UK have problems getting to sleep or staying asleep.
3 Nowadays people are sleeping *30/90* minutes less than they did 100 years ago.
4 Teenagers need *more/less* sleep than adults.
5 Teenagers naturally wake up *two/three* hours later than adults.
6 We use *less/the same amount of* energy when we're asleep compared to when we're resting.

4 a CD1 ▶ 13 Listen to a TV interview with a sleep scientist. Check your answers to **3**.

b Listen again. Answer these questions.
1 How many British people have serious insomnia?
2 How were sleeping habits different 100 years ago?
3 Who needs the least amount of sleep?
4 What happened when a British school started lessons an hour later?
5 What do our brains do when we're asleep?

HELP WITH LISTENING Weak forms (1)

• In sentences we say many small words with a schwa /ə/ sound. These are called weak forms.

5 a CD1 ▶ 14 Listen to the strong and weak forms of these words. Do we usually say these words in their strong or weak forms?

	strong	weak		strong	weak
do	/duː/	/də/	of	/ɒv/	/əv/
you	/juː/	/jə/	and	/ænd/	/ən/
at	/æt/	/ət/	to	/tuː/	/tə/
for	/fɔː/	/fə/	can	/kæn/	/kən/

b Look at these sentences from the beginning of the interview. Which words do we hear as weak forms?

How many people (do) (you) know who have trouble sleeping at night? For many of us insomnia's part of life, and not being able to get to sleep isn't just annoying, it can also be very dangerous.

c CD1 ▶ 13 Listen and check. Are weak forms stressed?

d Look at Audio Script CD1 ▶ 13 p157. Listen to the interview again. Notice the weak forms and sentence stress. Which other words do we often hear as weak forms?

Reading, Vocabulary and Speaking

6 a Work in pairs. Think of at least five things people can do to help them get to sleep.

b Read the article. Why does Kevin have insomnia? What has he tried to do to get a good night's sleep?

c Read the article again. Answer these questions.
1 How much sleep did Kevin get last night?
2 What happens on a typical night?
3 When does he sleep well?
4 What does he find stressful about his job?
5 Which cure for insomnia hasn't he tried? Why not?

d Work in pairs. Compare answers. What advice would you give Kevin?

It's a nightmare!

Kevin Wells talks about how insomnia is making his life impossible.

I've always had trouble sleeping, but these days my insomnia is getting worse. Actually, my problem isn't getting to sleep, it's staying asleep. Take last night, for example. I was exhausted when I went to bed at 11.00 and I was fast asleep by 11.30. But then I woke up at 3.00 after a terrible nightmare. Soon I was wide awake and it was impossible to get back to sleep. Sometimes when I'm awake at that time I get extremely depressed and feel like it's the end of the world. So I read a book, answered some emails, and finally got back to sleep at about 5.30. The alarm went off at seven and I went off to work feeling awful.

That's a typical night for me. I've had insomnia for so long I'm amazed if I ever sleep through the night, and by the end of the week I always feel really shattered. I only get a good night's sleep when I'm on holiday – but when I do I feel absolutely fantastic the next day.

I know that work is part of the problem. I'm a website designer and I have to meet deadlines every week, which is very stressful. It's a brilliant job and I don't want to give it up, but I work really long hours and I'm always under a lot of pressure. I often work at home, so it's incredibly difficult to relax at the end of the day because there's always more work I can do. Money's also a huge worry for me because I've just bought a new flat and I'm getting married soon, which will be very expensive.

I've tried nearly everything to cure my insomnia, but nothing works for long. I started going to the gym, but it didn't help me sleep, it just made me more exhausted. I have a fairly healthy diet and I don't drink coffee after 4 p.m. any more. I've tried relaxation CDs, hypnosis, online support groups – I even bought a new bed. I don't want to start taking sleeping pills because I'm terrified of becoming addicted to them. Perhaps it's time for me to accept that insomnia is part of my life – then maybe I'll stop worrying so much and get some sleep!

HELP WITH VOCABULARY
Gradable and strong adjectives; adverbs

7 a Complete the table with the strong adjectives in pink in the article. What other strong adjectives do you know that mean 'very good'?

gradable adjectives	strong adjectives
good	brilliant , _____
bad	_____ , _____
tired	_____ , _____
big	_____
difficult	_____
frightened	_____
surprised	_____

b Match the gradable adjectives in A to the strong adjectives in B.

A	B
tasty small cold hot beautiful big interested angry happy dirty	filthy furious delicious delighted fascinated gorgeous boiling tiny enormous freezing

c Look at the adverbs in blue in the article. Which of these adverbs do we use with: gradable adjectives (G), strong adjectives (S)? Which adverb do we use with both types of adjective?

| extremely G   really   absolutely |
| incredibly   very   fairly |

d Check in VOCABULARY 2.4 p130.

8 a Fill in the gaps with an adverb from **7c**. Use different adverbs where possible. Complete the sentences for you.

1 I'm usually _____ exhausted after …
2 It's _____ difficult for me to …
3 I was _____ delighted when …
4 I've got a/an _____ beautiful …
5 I think … is _____ delicious.
6 I'm _____ interested in …
7 I was _____ surprised/angry when …
8 I thought … was _____ brilliant/awful.

b Work in pairs. Take turns to say your sentences. Ask follow-up questions if possible.

9 a Work in groups. Write a sleep survey. Write at least five questions. Use words/phrases from **1** or your own ideas.

How long does it take you to get to sleep?

b Ask other students in the class. Write the answers.

c Work in your groups. Compare answers.

d Tell the class two things you found out.

2D REAL WORLD — What's the matter?

Real World showing concern, giving and responding to advice

> **QUICK REVIEW** Gradable and strong adjectives
> Write five strong adjectives (*gorgeous*, etc.). Work in pairs and compare lists. What are the gradable adjectives for each one (*beautiful*, etc.)? Then think of one thing, place or person for each strong adjective: *The dress my sister wore for her wedding was absolutely gorgeous.*

1 Work in pairs. Discuss these questions.
1 What types of problem do people often ask for advice about?
2 Who was the last person you asked for advice? What did you ask them about? Did their advice help you?
3 When did you last give someone advice? What was it about? Did he/she take your advice? Why?/Why not?

2 a Work in new pairs. Look at the photos. What do you remember about Lisa, Rebecca and Charlie?

b 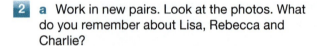 Watch or listen to two conversations. What problems do Rebecca and Charlie talk about?

c Work with your partner. Compare answers.

3 a Work in the same pairs. Do you think these sentences are true (T) or false (F)?

Conversation 1
a The baby wakes up two or three times every night.
b Rebecca and Charlie are arguing more than usual.
c Rebecca thinks Charlie is spending too much money.
d Lisa thinks that Rebecca and Charlie should have two evenings off a week.

Conversation 2
e Andy thinks that Rebecca and Charlie should sleep in separate rooms.
f Charlie thinks Rebecca buys too many things for herself.
g Andy doesn't think Charlie will lose his job.
h Andy thinks Charlie should take Rebecca on holiday.

b  Watch or listen again. Check your answers.

c Work with your partner. Compare answers. Correct the false sentences.

Lisa   Rebecca

REAL WORLD
Showing concern, giving and responding to advice

4 a Write these headings in the correct places 1–3.

| giving advice | responding to advice | showing concern |

1 _____
Oh, dear. What's the matter?   Oh, how awful!
I can see why you're upset.   I'm sorry to hear that.
Oh, dear. What a shame.   Yes, I see what you mean.

2 _____
Have you tried talking to him about it?
Perhaps you **ought to** spend more time together.
Maybe you **should** sleep in separate rooms.
Why don't you talk to her about it?
I'd take her out for a really nice meal.

3 _____
Yes, you could be right.
Well, it's worth a try, I guess.
I've tried that, but (we just start arguing again.)
Yes, that's a good idea.
I might try that.

b Which verb forms come after the phrases in bold?

c Look at these ways to ask for advice. Fill in the gaps with *I should* or *should I*.
1 What _____ do?
2 What do you think _____ do?

d Check in **REAL WORLD 2.1** p131.

Charlie   Andy

HELP WITH LISTENING
Intonation (1): sounding concerned

5 CD1 ▶16 Listen to the same sentences said twice. Which person sounds more concerned, a or b?

1 (a) b   3 a b   5 a b
2 a b   4 a b   6 a b

6 CD1 ▶17 **PRONUNCIATION** Listen and practise the phrases in 4a. Copy the stress and intonation.

Oh, dear. What's the matter?

7 a Use these prompts to write two conversations.

BOB   Hi, Tim. You look terrible. [1]What / matter?
1 *What's the matter?*
TIM   My girlfriend and I have had a big argument.
BOB   [2]Oh dear. / sorry / hear that.
TIM   And now she won't answer my calls. [3]What / I do?
BOB   [4]Perhaps / ought / write her an email to say sorry.
TIM   [5]Well, / worth / try, / guess.
BOB   [6]And I / send her some flowers.
TIM   [7]Yes, / good idea. [8]I / try that. Thanks a lot.

MIA   Look at this plant. It's dying, isn't it?
LIZ   [9]Yes, / see what / mean.
MIA   [10]What / think I / do?
LIZ   [11]Have / try / give / it more water?
MIA   [12]Yes, / try / that, but it didn't work.
LIZ   [13]Well, why / put it in a bigger pot?
MIA   [14]Yes, / could / right. Thanks for the advice.

b Work in pairs. Compare answers.

c Practise the conversations with your partner.

8 Work in groups of three. Student A p102. Student B p107. Student C p113.

HELP WITH PRONUNCIATION
Strong and weak forms

1 CD1 ▶14 Work in pairs. Do you remember how we say the strong and weak forms of these words? Listen and check. Listen again and practise.

| do | you | at | for | of | and | to | can |

2 a CD1 ▶18 Listen to this conversation. Circle the words in pink that you hear in their strong forms.

JO   Which company do you work (for)?
ED   It's called Getaway Holidays. I work for the owner.
JO   Really? I'm thinking of going on holiday soon. Do you think you can get me a cheap flight?
ED   Yes, maybe I can. Where do you want to fly to?
JO   Well, my brother's working at a hotel in the Caribbean and I'd like to go and see him.
ED   Which hotel is he working at?
JO   It's called The Island Palace. Do you know it?
ED   Yes, I do. How long do you want to go for?
JO   About three weeks if I can.
ED   OK, I'll see what I can do for you. Text me!

b Work in pairs. Compare answers. When do we usually use the strong forms of the words in **1**?

c Listen again. Practise each line of the conversation.

d Work in pairs. Practise the conversation. Take turns to be Jo and Ed.

continue2learn

▶ **Vocabulary, Grammar and Real World**
- **Extra Practice 2 and Progress Portfolio 2** p116
- **Language Summary 2** p129
- **2A–D** Workbook p10

▶ **Reading and Writing**
- **Portfolio 2** Notices at work Workbook p66
  Reading notices
  Writing notices; abbreviations

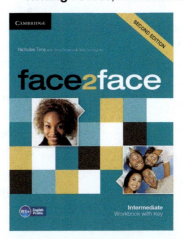

21

3A The tourist trade

Vocabulary phrasal verbs (1): travel
Grammar Present Perfect Simple: experience, unfinished past and recent events

QUICK REVIEW Giving and responding to advice Write three problems that you, or people you know, have at the moment. Work in pairs. Take turns to tell your partner the problems and give advice.

Vocabulary and Speaking
Phrasal verbs (1): travel

1 a Work in pairs. Can you guess the meaning of the phrasal verbs in bold in these sentences? Then check in **VOCABULARY 3.1** p132.

1 Have you ever **set off** very early to go on holiday?
2 What's the best way for tourists to **get around** your country?
3 What problems do people sometimes have to **deal with** on holiday?
4 When people stay in a hotel, what happens when they **check in**?
5 What time do they usually have to **check out**?
6 Did anyone **see** you **off** the last time you went on holiday?
7 Did anyone **pick** you **up** from the airport or the station when you **got back**?
8 Have you ever had to **put up with** noisy people on holiday?
9 Does anyone **look after** your pets or plants when you **go away**?
10 Are you **looking forward to** your next holiday?

b Work in new pairs. Ask and answer the questions in **1a**. Ask follow-up questions if possible.

> Have you ever set off very early to go on holiday?
>
> Yes, I have, actually.
>
> What time did you leave home?
>
> At 3.30 a.m.!

Megan, hiking tour guide, Banff, Canada

Clive, hotel manager, the Lake District, UK

Listening

2 a CD1 ▶19 Look at the photos of Megan and Clive. Listen to them talking about their jobs. Answer these questions.

1 Do they like their jobs?
2 What problems do they have in their jobs?

b Work in pairs. Who said these sentences, Megan or Clive?

a I've worked in the USA and in Europe, and I really enjoyed my time there too.
b We've been away a few times, but each time there was a problem at the hotel.
c My wife and I started working in the hotel industry 19 years ago.
d Three days ago a guy set off on his own into the mountains without telling anyone where he was going.
e I've lived in this country for about three years.
f We've had this place since 2008.
g I've just been to Banff to pick him up from the hospital.
h My wife's gone to see some friends off at Manchester airport.

c Listen again. Check your answers and put the sentences in the order you hear them.

HELP WITH GRAMMAR
Present Perfect Simple

3 a Look at the sentences in **2b** again. Then complete these rules with Present Perfect Simple (PPS) or Past Simple (PS). Which sentences in **2b** match each rule?

- We use the _____ for experiences that happened some time before now, but we don't know or don't say when they happened. To give more information about an experience we use the _____ .
- We use the _____ to say when something happened.
- We use the _____ for something that started in the past and continues in the present.
- We use the _____ for something that happened a short time ago, but we don't say exactly when.

b How do we make positive sentences, negatives and questions in the Present Perfect Simple?

c Look at sentences e–h in **2b** again. What is the difference between: *for* and *since*? *been* and *gone*?

d Which of these words/phrases can we use with the Present Perfect Simple? Which do we use with the Past Simple?

never	ago	ever	recently	lately
before	in 1997	this week		last week
just	at 10 o'clock	yet	already	

e Look at this sentence. Then choose the correct verb form in the rule.

This is the first time we've run a hotel in a touristy place like the Lake District.

- After *this is the first time*, *this is the second time*, etc. we use the *Present Simple*/*Present Perfect Simple*.

f Check in **GRAMMAR 3.1** p133.

4 **CD1 20** **PRONUNCIATION** Listen and practise. Copy the stress and contractions (*I've*, etc.).

I've worked in the USA and in Europe.

HELP WITH LISTENING
Present Perfect Simple or Past Simple

5 a **CD1 21** Listen to how we say these phrases. Notice the difference.

1	I've met	I met	4	they've told	they told
2	you've had	you had	5	he's wanted	he wanted
3	we've won	we won	6	she's lived	she lived

b **CD1 22** Listen to six sentences. Are the verbs in the Present Perfect Simple (PPS) or Past Simple (PS)?

6 a Read about Lewis and Veronica's restaurant in the Canary Islands. Put the verbs in brackets in the Present Perfect Simple or Past Simple.

When we ¹ _were_ (be) younger we ² _____ (come) here on holiday every year. Then we ³ _____ (move) here in 2007 and ⁴ _____ (open) a restaurant. We ⁵ _____ (live) here since then and we ⁶ _____ (just open) a guest house on the other side of the island. Of course, we ⁷ _____ (have) a lot of visitors from home since then. My parents ⁸ _____ (arrive) last week – it's the fourth time they ⁹ _____ (visit) us this year! Veronica's family are arriving today too – she ¹⁰ _____ (just go) to pick them up at the airport. The main problem is holidays. We ¹¹ _____ (go) to Turkey twice, but our last holiday ¹² _____ (be) 18 months ago and we ¹³ _____ (not have) any time off since then.

b Work in pairs. Compare answers. Discuss why you chose each answer.

c **CD1 23** Listen and check.

7 Work in pairs. Student A p102. Student B p107.

Get ready … Get it right!

8 Write these people, things and places on a piece of paper. Don't write them in order.

- a friend you've known for most of your life
- someone you met on your last holiday
- something you've had for ages
- something you got for your last birthday
- a place you went to last year
- a place you've been to this year

9 a Work in pairs. Swap papers. Ask and answer questions about the people, things and places on your partner's paper.

b Tell the class two things you found out about your partner.

3B Lonely Planet

Vocabulary phrases with *travel*, *get* and *go on*
Grammar Present Perfect Continuous and Present Perfect Simple

QUICK REVIEW Present Perfect Simple Work in pairs. Ask questions with *Have you ever … ?* to find out five things you've done in your life that your partner hasn't done.

Vocabulary
Phrases with *travel*, *get* and *go on*

1 Work in pairs. Do we use these words/phrases with: 1 *travel*, 2 *get*, 3 *go on*? Then check in **VOCABULARY 3.2** p132.

> on your own 1 into/out of a car 2 a trip 3
> back from somewhere   a guided tour   independently
> a journey   first/business/economy class   a cruise
> here/there by (10.30)   together/separately   light
> on/off a bus/plane/train   a package holiday   a taxi

2 **a** Complete these sentences with the correct form of *travel*, *get* or *go on*.
  1 I like _____ long car journeys.
  2 I sometimes _____ a taxi home after work.
  3 I _____ a guided tour last year.
  4 I like _____ on my own.
  5 I sometimes _____ taxis when I'm late.
  6 I _____ never _____ a cruise.
  7 When I go away, I usually _____ light.

b Tick the sentences in **2a** that are true for you. Change the other sentences to make them true for you.

c Work in pairs. Compare sentences. How many are the same?

Speaking and Reading

3 **a** Work in groups. Discuss these questions.
  1 Which places do guide books about your country recommend for tourists? Why?
  2 What are the advantages and disadvantages of using a guide book in a new country?
  3 Have you ever taken a guide book on holiday? If so, was it useful? Why?/Why not?

b Look at the photos and read the article. Then match headings 1–5 to paragraphs A–E.
  1 A romantic adventure
  2 Online, on TV and on your phone
  3 Guide books for the planet
  4 How to understand the world
  5 Their first best-seller

the world's greatest travellers

A Nobody has changed the way we travel more than Tony and Maureen Wheeler, the founders of the publishing company Lonely Planet. ¹**The company has been publishing guide books for 40 years** and it sells over 5 million books a year in English. It also publishes books in seven other languages and the Lonely Planet website is one of the most popular travel sites on the internet.

B The story began when Tony and Maureen met on a park bench in London in 1971. They got married a year later and for their honeymoon they travelled across Europe and Asia to Australia in an old van. A few months later they arrived in Sydney with only 27 cents in their pockets. Everyone they met asked them about their incredible journey, so they decided to write a book about it. They wrote a 93-page guide book called *Across Asia on the Cheap* at their kitchen table and it sold 8,000 copies in three months.

C With the money they made from the book, Tony and Maureen spent the next 18 months travelling around southeast Asia. They wrote their second guide book, *Southeast Asia on a Shoestring*, in a Singapore hotel room. ²**The book has been a best-seller since it was published in 1973** and has sold over a million copies.

D ³**Lonely Planet has published over 650 books since the company began** and it employs around 450 people and over 200 authors. The Lonely Planet website is visited by about 5 million people every month and their internet forum, called The Thorn Tree, is one of the most popular places online for advice on travelling independently.

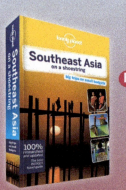

⁴**Their television company, Lonely Planet TV, has been making programmes since 2004** and there's also a monthly Lonely Planet magazine and apps for your phone.

E The company has certainly come a long way since Tony and Maureen's honeymoon adventure. "I think we've done a good thing," says Maureen, "and I still believe that travel is the best way for people to understand the world."

4 Read the article again. Answer these questions.
  1 How long has Lonely Planet been publishing guide books?
  2 What did Tony and Maureen do on their honeymoon?
  3 Where did they write their second guide book?
  4 How many books has Lonely Planet published?
  5 What is The Thorn Tree?
  6 What else do Lonely Planet do?

HELP WITH GRAMMAR Present Perfect Continuous and Present Perfect Simple

5 **a** Look at sentences 1 and 2 in bold in the article. Then fill in the gaps in these rules with Present Perfect Continuous (PPC) or Present Perfect Simple (PPS).

- We usually use the _____ to talk about an **activity** that started in the past and continues in the present.
- We usually use the _____ to talk about a **state** that started in the past and continues in the present.

b Fill in the gaps for the Present Perfect Continuous with *'ve, haven't, 's, hasn't, been* or verb+*ing*.

POSITIVE
I/you/we/they + _____ or have + been + verb+*ing*
he/she/it + _____ or has + been + _____

NEGATIVE
I/you/we/they + _____ + been + verb+*ing*
he/she/it + _____ + _____ + verb+*ing*

c Look at sentences 3 and 4 in bold in the article. Then choose the correct words in these rules.

- We usually use the Present Perfect *Continuous/ Simple* to say **how long** an activity has been happening.
- We usually use the Present Perfect *Continuous/ Simple* to say **how many** things are finished.

d Look at questions 1 and 4 in **4**. How do we make Present Perfect Continuous questions with *How long …* ? How do we make Present Perfect Simple questions with *How many …* ?

e Check in GRAMMAR 3.2 p134.

6 **a** Put the verb in brackets in the Present Perfect Continuous or the Present Perfect Simple. Use the Present Perfect Continuous where possible. Then choose *for* or *since* where necessary.

1 I *'ve been working* (work) here (for)/since six months.
2 How long _____ you _____ (travel)?
3 Scott _____ (write books) for/since 2006.
4 He _____ (write) five books so far.
5 They _____ (not play) golf for/since long.
6 How long _____ he _____ (have) that car?
7 I _____ (know) Zak for/since we were kids.
8 We _____ (wait) for/since two hours.

b Work in pairs. Compare answers. Discuss why you chose each verb form.

c CD1 ▶24 **PRONUNCIATION** Listen and check. Listen again and practise. Copy the stress and weak forms.

I've been /bɪn/ working here for /fə/ six months.
How long have /əv/ you been /bɪn/ travelling?

7 Work in groups. Student A p102. Student B p107.

Get ready … Get it right!

8 **a** Draw a timeline of your life. Write when these things happened on the line.

- you started living in your house/flat
- you first met your oldest friend
- you started learning English
- you started the job/course you're doing now
- you first met your boyfriend/girlfriend/husband/wife
- you got your favourite possession(s)
- you bought the car/mobile/computer you have now
- your own ideas

b Plan what you're going to say about your timeline. Use the Present Perfect Continuous or Present Perfect Simple with *for* and *since*.

9 **a** Work in pairs. Take turns to talk about your timeline. Ask follow-up questions if possible.

> I've been living in my flat since May 2011.

> Where did you live before that?

b Tell the class two things you found out about your partner.

3C VOCABULARY AND SKILLS — Voluntourism

Vocabulary word building (1): suffixes for adjectives and nouns
Skills Listening: a radio interview; Reading: holiday blogs

QUICK REVIEW Present Perfect Continuous
Work in groups. Ask questions with *How long … ?* to find out who has been: coming to this school the longest, learning English the longest, working in the same job the longest, living in the same house or flat the longest.

Speaking and Listening

1 Work in pairs. Discuss these questions.
 1 Which holidays can you remember from your childhood?
 2 What's the best (or worst) holiday you've ever had?
 3 Imagine your perfect holiday. Where would you go? What would you do there?

2 a CD1 25 Listen to an interview with Alison Armstrong, a travel expert. What is 'voluntourism'? Why is it becoming so popular?

 b Listen again. Choose the correct words, phrases or numbers in these sentences.
 1 *17%/25%* of people in the UK take a year off before they are *17/25*.
 2 Voluntourism holidays are *only for young people/for people of all ages*.
 3 Alison thinks it's *easy/hard* to meet local people on a normal holiday.
 4 Tourists *have to/don't have to* pay to go on voluntourism holidays.
 5 The presenter *thinks/doesn't think* these holidays are a good idea.

 c Work in pairs. Compare answers.

HELP WITH LISTENING
Linking (1): consonant–vowel links
• We usually link words that end in a consonant sound with words that start with a vowel sound.

3 a CD1 25 Listen to the beginning of the interview again. Notice the consonant–vowel links.

Good‿afternoon‿and welcome to *Take‿a Break*. Today we're taking‿a look‿at the rise‿in voluntourism‿around the world. I'm here with‿Alison‿Armstrong from the travel website voluntours.net. Alison, first‿of‿all, can you tell‿all‿our listeners what voluntourism‿is?

 b Look at Audio Script CD1 25 p159. Listen again and notice the linking.

Reading, Vocabulary and Speaking

4 a Two tourists have written blogs on the Voluntours website. Work in two groups. Group A, read Shelley's blog. Group B, read William's blog. Find the answers to these questions.
 1 Where is he/she on holiday?
 2 How long has he/she been there?
 3 Where is he/she staying?
 4 What sort of work does he/she do?
 5 What does he/she do on his/her days off?
 6 What's the best thing about the holiday?
 7 What's the most difficult thing?
 8 Would he/she recommend the holiday?

 b Work with a student from the other group. Ask and answer the questions.

 c Read your partner's blog. Check his/her answers.

 d Would you like to go on either of these holidays? Why?/Why not?

---

www.voluntours.net/mediacentre/blogs

VOLUNTOURS
Giving the world a helping hand

Shelley Parker, Australia

I'm on a voluntourism holiday in Nepal and wanted to tell everyone all about it! I've been working at a school in a village near Kathmandu for two weeks and I've enjoyed every minute of it. The best thing about the holiday has been working with the children. I spend six hours a day at the school, mainly helping the teachers in the classroom and organising games for the younger kids. I've also been teaching English to the older children, which is great fun. I'm amazed at the *kindness* and *patience* of the local staff, they've really helped me feel at home. I'm staying with a Nepalese family in the village and I share a room with another volunteer. My bed isn't very *comfortable*, but I'm usually so exhausted it doesn't matter! On our days off we go walking in the mountains and I'm getting very fit and *healthy*. The scenery here is absolutely wonderful and I love being surrounded by *nature*. But it can be a bit *dangerous* so we always take a guide with us. The most *difficult* thing about the holiday is being away from my family – this is the first time I've been out of Australia. I'm glad this type of holiday is becoming more *popular* with young people and I'd recommend this experience to anyone.

Nepal

Grenada

William Boyd, Scotland

I've been staying on Grenada, an island in the Caribbean, for three weeks and I'm having a brilliant time! There are nine volunteers in our group and everyone's very kind and helpful. We're staying at a campsite by the beach and I share a tent with two other volunteers. At first I had a lot of difficulty getting to sleep and I missed the comfort of my own bed, but I'm sleeping OK now and I love living in such a natural environment. We take turns to prepare meals for the group, which is the worst part of the holiday for me because I hate cooking. We have one day off a week, which I spend diving around the coral reefs near here. But of course the main reason we're here is to protect the turtles from other animals and people who want to steal their eggs. We also check each turtle's health and measure how big they are. Turtles have been living on our planet for 230 million years – they're even older than the dinosaurs – but now they're in danger of becoming extinct. You have to be very patient, but it's incredible to watch a turtle walk out of the sea and lay her eggs on the beach. That's definitely been the most amazing part of the holiday for me. I'm not surprised voluntourism is increasing in popularity and I'd definitely recommend coming to Grenada.

HELP WITH VOCABULARY
Word building (1): suffixes for adjectives and nouns

- We sometimes make adjectives from nouns, and nouns from adjectives, by adding a suffix (-ness, -ous, etc.).

5 a Work in pairs. Look at the words in blue and pink in the blogs. Which are adjectives and which are nouns? Underline the suffix in each pair of words.

kind   kind<u>ness</u>

b Write the words in the correct places in these tables.

adjective	noun	suffix
kind	kindness	-ness
		-ce
		-y
		-ity

noun	adjective	suffix
		-ous
		-able
		-al
		-y

c Which words in **5b** only add the suffix? Which words have extra changes in spelling?

d Look at the suffixes of these words. Are they adjectives (A) or nouns (N)?

knowledgeable A   sadness N
traditional   noisy   confidence
adventurous   activity   musical
possibility   honesty   fashionable
famous   touristy   importance
laziness   modesty

e What are the nouns for the adjectives in **5d**? What are the adjectives for the nouns?

knowledgeable → knowledge   sadness → sad

f Check in VOCABULARY 3.3 ▶ p133.

6 Work in pairs. Take turns to test each other on the nouns and adjectives in **5b** and **5d**.

possible   possibility

7 Work in groups of three. Student A p105. Student B p110. Student C p113.

27

REAL 3D WORLD: A trip to India

Real World asking for and making recommendations

QUICK REVIEW Suffixes for adjectives and nouns Work in pairs. Student A: write six adjectives you can remember from lesson 3C. Student B: write six nouns you can remember from lesson 3C. Take turns to say your words. Your partner says the noun or adjective: A *Kind*. B *Kindness*.

1 Work in groups. Look at the photos. What do you know about India? Would you like to go there? Why?/Why not?

2 a VIDEO 3 CD1 26 Look at the photo on p29. Ella and Mike are going on a trip to Delhi. They're asking Rebecca and Charlie for recommendations. Watch or listen to their conversation and tick the topics they talk about. Which two topics don't they talk about?

- the best time to visit
- things (not) to see in the city
- things to see outside Delhi
- dangers and problems
- getting around
- changing money
- places to eat
- places to stay

b Watch or listen again. Tick the true sentences. Correct the false ones.

Rebecca and Charlie think that …
1 … rickshaws are the best way to get around the city.
2 … it's better to travel to other cities by bus.
3 … Ella and Mike should visit the museums in Delhi.
4 … they should go to the Red Fort in Old Delhi.
5 … they can visit the Taj Mahal and come back the same day.
6 … there's only one good restaurant in Connaught Place.

REAL WORLD
Asking for and making recommendations

3 a Fill in the gaps with the words in the boxes.

asking for recommendations

| ~~good~~ | visiting | tips | about | best |

Do you know any ¹ *good* places to stay/eat?
What's the ² _____ way to (get around)?
What else is worth ³ _____ ?
What ⁴ _____ (places outside Delhi)?
Have you got any other ⁵ _____ ?

recommending things

| worth | best | definitely | must | recommend |

It's probably ⁶ _____ to (use rickshaws).
I'd ⁷ _____ (the trains).
You should ⁸ _____ see (the Red Fort).
That's well ⁹ _____ seeing.
You really ¹⁰ _____ go to (Agra) to see (the Taj Mahal).

not recommending things

| bother | Don't | wouldn't | worth |

Don't ¹¹ _____ going to (the museums).
It isn't really ¹² _____ visiting, (I don't think).
¹³ _____ drink anything with ice in it.
I ¹⁴ _____ eat any salads.

responding to recommendations

| useful | heard | know | sounds |

That's good to ¹⁵ _____ .
That ¹⁶ _____ good.
Thanks, that's really ¹⁷ _____ .
Yes, I've ¹⁸ _____ that before.

b Which verb form comes after these phrases?
1 It's (well/not) worth …
2 Don't bother …
3 I'd/I wouldn't …

c Check in REAL WORLD 3.1 ▶ p134.

4 CD1 27 PRONUNCIATION Listen and practise the sentences in **3a**. Copy the stress.

Do you know any good places to stay?
What's the best way to get around?

Ella Mike Rebecca Charlie

5 a Use these prompts to write conversations.

1
A / know / good places to eat in town?
Do you know any good places to eat in town?
B Well, you / definitely go / Nero's in the city centre.
A What / places near where we're staying?
B / recommend the Grove Restaurant. It's opposite the hotel.
A Thanks, that / useful.

2
A Where / best place / stay?
B / probably best / stay in the Madison. It's the nicest hotel in the city.
A OK, thanks. / got / other tips?
B I / carry too much money at night.
A / good / know. Thanks.

3
A What / best places / visit in the city centre?
B / must go to the National Art Gallery. It's amazing.
A What else / worth / see ? Are there any good museums?
B Well, I / bother / go / the City Museum. It / not worth / visit, / I / think.
A Yes / hear / before.

b Work in pairs. Compare answers.

c Practise the conversations with your partner.

6 a Choose a town, city or country you know well. Make a list of at least four recommendations you can give about the place you have chosen. Use the topics in **2a** or your own ideas.

b Work in pairs. If you have chosen different places, take turns to ask for and give recommendations. If you have chosen the same place, take turns to be a tourist and ask your partner for recommendations. Use language in **3a** and your own ideas.

HELP WITH PRONUNCIATION
The schwa /ə/ in suffixes

1 a 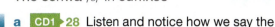 **28** Listen and notice how we say the suffixes in blue. We say each suffix with a schwa /ə/.

kind**ness**	lazi**ness**	assist**ant**	account**ant**
danger**ous**	fam**ous**	comfort**able**	fashion**able**
music**al**	natur**al**	improve**ment**	argu**ment**
auth**or**	direct**or**	collec**tion**	deci**sion**

b Listen again and practise. Are the suffixes stressed?

2 a Underline the suffixes from **1a** in these sentences.

1 It's dangerous to be ambitious and adventurous.
2 The accountant's assistant is very important.
3 She's knowledgeable, reliable and fashionable.
4 He felt both happiness and sadness after his illness.
5 The director had three visitors – an author, a doctor and an actor.
6 We had a discussion and made a decision to do some revision.
7 It's a traditional medical centre that uses natural herbal medicine.
8 There's disappointment in the government because there's no improvement in unemployment.

b CD1 **29** Listen and practise the sentences.

c Work in pairs. Take turns to say the sentences.

continue2learn

▶ **Vocabulary, Grammar and Real World**
  ■ **Extra Practice 3 and Progress Portfolio 3** p117
  ■ **Language Summary 3** p132
  ■ **3A–D** Workbook p15

▶ **Reading and Writing**
  ■ **Portfolio 3** Holiday arrangements Workbook p68
    Reading a formal letter
    Writing formal writing; American and British English

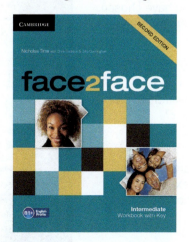

4A Musical experiences

Vocabulary collocations (2): music
Grammar Past Simple and Past Continuous; *used to*

QUICK REVIEW Asking for and making recommendations Work in pairs. Student A, imagine you are a tourist in the town/city you are in now. Ask your partner for recommendations for places to stay, eat and visit. Student B, answer your partner's questions and make recommendations.

Vocabulary and Speaking
Collocations (2): music

1 Work in pairs. Match the verbs in A to words/phrases in B. Then check in **VOCABULARY 4.1** p135.

A	B
do/play be release	a new single/album/CD a concert/a gig a big fan of a singer/band
do download be/go	on tour an encore a track onto my phone
have see be/go	onstage someone play live an album/a CD in the charts

2 a Write the names of three bands, musicians, composers or singers you like. Choose phrases from **1** that you can use to talk about them.

b Work in pairs. Talk about the bands or people you have chosen. Ask questions to find out more information.

> I'm a big fan of Coldplay.

> Yes, me too. Have you ever seen them play live?

Reading

3 Read about Nikki and Danny's best ever musical experiences. What was special about each one?

NIKKI WILLIAMS, USA

Five years ago I **was living** in New York with my cousin and I used to go to a lot of gigs. Back then I was one of Lady Gaga's biggest fans and I **listened** to her second album all the time. For my 21st birthday my boyfriend **bought** tickets to see her play live – I've never been so excited in my life! We had really good seats near the front and when Lady Gaga came onstage the whole crowd went absolutely crazy. **It was a fantastic atmosphere and all the fans were singing along.** That night she sang for over two hours and changed her costume about 20 times! **While she was doing** an encore, she threw her shoes into the crowd – and I caught one of them! **My boyfriend wanted** to sell it on eBay, but I wouldn't let him. Now it's my most valuable possession – and a great souvenir of a fantastic gig.

DANNY BREEN, IRELAND

When I was a teenager in Dublin I **loved** dance music and wanted to become a famous DJ. I **practised** for hours every day in my bedroom and I used to DJ at friends' parties. **Then I moved** to London and got a job working behind the bar at a club called Dreamworld. One Saturday night the main DJ didn't turn up and the manager asked me to play instead. **Twenty minutes later I was standing** in front of 1,000 people! I was incredibly nervous, but as soon as I started playing the first track I began to relax. **All the clubbers were dancing** and having a good time – it was the best feeling in the world. **While I was playing** my last track, the manager came over and congratulated me. I gave up DJing later that year because I broke my arm, but I'll never forget that amazing night!

4 a Read about Nikki and Danny again. Answer these questions.

1. When did Nikki see Lady Gaga live?
2. Where did Nikki and her boyfriend sit?
3. How long was Lady Gaga onstage?
4. What did her boyfriend want to do with the shoe?
5. Where did Danny first start DJing?
6. Where did he work when he moved to London?
7. Why did his manager ask him to DJ in the club?
8. Why did Danny give up DJing?

b Work in pairs. Compare answers.

HELP WITH GRAMMAR Past Simple and Past Continuous, *used to*

5 a Look at the phrases in bold in the texts. Match the verb forms in blue to these meanings. There are two verb forms for each meaning.

- We use the **Past Simple** for:
  a a single completed action in the past. *bought*
  b a repeated action or habit in the past.
  c a state in the past.
- We use the **Past Continuous** for:
  a an action in progress at a point of time in the past. *was living*
  b the background events of a story.
  c an action in progress when another (shorter) action happened.

b How do we make the positive, negative and question forms of the Past Simple and Past Continuous?

c Check in **GRAMMAR 4.1** p136.

6 a Look at sentences a–d. Then answer questions 1–3.

a I used to go to a lot of gigs.
b I listened to her second album all the time.
c I was one of Lady Gaga's biggest fans.
d That night she sang for over two hours.

1. Which sentences talk about repeated actions, habits or states in the past?
2. Can we use *used to* in sentences b, c or d? Why?/Why not?
3. Which verb form comes after *used to*?

b How do we make the positive, negative and question forms of *used to*?

c Check in **GRAMMAR 4.2** p137.

7 CD1 30 PRONUNCIATION Listen and practise. Copy the stress and weak forms.

she threw her shoes into the crowd → While she was /wəz/ doing an encore, she threw her shoes into the crowd.

8 a Read about Sophie. What was her best ever musical experience?

SOPHIE TAYLOR, UK When I ¹was/was being younger I ²played/was playing the guitar, but I ³didn't use to like/didn't like it very much. Then my aunt ⁴gave/was giving me a violin for my 14th birthday. I ⁵had/used to have violin lessons every week and I ⁶was loving/loved learning how to play a new instrument. Last year I ⁷joined/was joining the school orchestra and in March we ⁸won/used to win a music competition in our city. The prize ⁹was/used to be the opportunity to play at the Schools Prom at the Albert Hall in London! The big night finally ¹⁰used to arrive/arrived, and while we ¹¹waited/were waiting to go onstage I ¹²started/used to start shaking because I was so nervous! But as soon as we ¹³got/were getting onstage I ¹⁴used to begin/began to relax and enjoy myself. When we ¹⁵played/were playing the last piece of music I ¹⁶noticed/was noticing my mum and dad in the audience. They both ¹⁷looked/used to look very proud!

b Read about Sophie again. Choose the correct verb forms. Sometimes both verb forms are possible.

c Work in pairs. Compare answers.

9 a Make questions with *you* and these words. Use a form of *used to* if possible.

1. Who / be / your best friend when you were 12?
2. Where / first meet him or her?
3. / like the same music?
4. / go to gigs together?
5. / buy the same singles or albums?
6. / like the same TV programmes?
7. When / last see him or her?

b Work in new pairs. Ask and answer the questions in **9a**.

Get ready … Get it right!

10 Work in groups. Look at p113.

4B Modern adventurers

Vocabulary adjectives (2): character
Grammar Past Perfect

QUICK REVIEW Past Continuous Write two true and two false sentences about what you were doing at different times of the day yesterday: *At 3 p.m. yesterday I was playing tennis.* Work in pairs. Swap sentences. Ask questions to find out which sentences are false: *Who were you playing tennis with?*

Ed Stafford

Vocabulary and Speaking
Adjectives (2): character

1 a Work in pairs. Which of these character adjectives do you know? Then check new words in **VOCABULARY 4.2** p135.

> adventurous   talented   sensible   sensitive
> brave   determined   reliable   independent
> organised   stubborn   ambitious   confident
> practical   generous   mean   responsible
> aggressive   optimistic   pessimistic

b Think of four people you know. Choose adjectives from **1a** to describe them. Think of reasons why you chose those adjectives.

c Work in pairs. Take turns to tell your partner about the people you know. Who do you think is the most interesting?

> My friend Gregory is very talented.
> He's a designer and he works …

Listening and Speaking

2 Work in new pairs. Discuss these questions.
1 What's the most adventurous thing you've ever done?
2 Are there any famous adventurers from your country? If so, what do you know about them?
3 Look at the photos and the map. Why do you think the two men look so happy?

3 a Before you listen, check these words/phrases with your teacher or in a dictionary.

> a jungle   an expedition   insect repellent   an ant
> a wasp   a scorpion   a sting   a marathon

b **CD1 31** Listen to a conversation between two TV producers, Paul and Josie. Answer these questions.
1 What is the first episode of Josie's new TV series about?
2 What problems did Ed Stafford have on the journey?
3 How did his friends and family know where he was?
4 What did he do when he got home?

4 a Work in pairs. Can you remember what Paul and Josie said about these numbers and people?

a 2010   d 68 days   g 200,000
b 2½ years   e Cho   h 600, 12
c Luke Collyer f 6,000 miles   i 27 hours

b **CD1 31** Listen again. Check your answers.

c Work in new pairs. Compare answers. Which adjectives in **1a** describe Ed Stafford, do you think?

HELP WITH GRAMMAR Past Perfect

5 a Look at the verb forms in bold in these sentences. Then answer the questions.

Cho **joined** the expedition after Luke **had gone** back to the UK.
He also **read** messages that people **had sent** him.
Ed **calculated** that he**'d walked** about 6,000 miles.

1 Which action happened first in each sentence?
2 Which action happened second?
3 Which verbs are in the Past Simple?
4 Which verbs are in the Past Perfect?

b Choose the correct word in the rule.
• When there is more than one action in the past, we often use the Past Perfect for the action that happened *first/second*.

c Look at these two sentences. What is the difference in meaning?
1 *When I turned on the TV, the programme started.*
2 *When I turned on the TV, the programme had started.*

d Fill in the gaps for the Past Perfect with *hadn't*, *had* or *past participle*.

POSITIVE subject + _____ or 'd + past participle

NEGATIVE subject + _____ + _____

e Check in **GRAMMAR 4.3** p137.

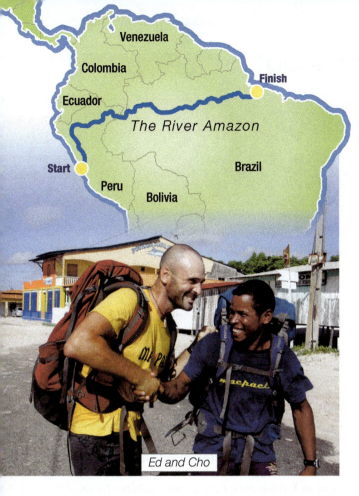

Ed and Cho

6 CD1 32 PRONUNCIATION Listen and practise. Copy the stress, weak forms and contractions.

Luke had /əd/ gone back to /tə/ the UK → Cho joined the expedition after Luke had /əd/ gone back to /tə/ the UK.

7 a Put the verbs in brackets in the Past Perfect or Past Simple.

1 Nobody _had walked_ (walk) the Amazon before Ed Stafford.
2 We _____ (not think) of going to Brazil until we _____ (hear) about Ed Stafford's adventure.
3 I _____ (go) to the shop to get some bread, but they _____ (sell out).
4 The meeting _____ (finish) by the time I _____ (get) there.
5 I _____ (invite) Florence to dinner, but she _____ (already arrange) to do something else.
6 When I _____ (get) to the airport, I realised that I _____ (forget) my passport.
7 Erica _____ (ask) me to go to Spain with her, but I _____ (already book) a holiday in Italy.
8 I _____ (see) Trevor Robertson when I _____ (be) in town yesterday. I _____ (not see) him for ten years!

b Work in pairs. Compare answers.

HELP WITH LISTENING
Past Simple or Past Perfect

8 a CD1 33 Listen to these sentences. Notice the difference between the Past Simple and the Past Perfect.

1 I finished work.   I'd finished work.
2 He left home.   He'd left home.
3 My parents bought it. My parents had bought it.
4 Nick worked there.   Nick had worked there.

b CD1 34 Listen to six pairs of sentences. Which do you hear first: the Past Simple (PS) or the Past Perfect (PP)?

9 a Read about the swimmer Martin Strel. What is his connection to Ed Stafford?

b Read about Martin Strel again. Put the verbs in brackets in the Past Simple or Past Perfect.

c CD1 35 Listen and check your answers.

BIG RIVER MAN

Martin Strel – or Big River Man, as he is often called – is a long-distance swimmer from Slovenia. Martin ¹ _taught_ (teach) himself to swim when he was six, and in 1997 he ² _____ (become) the first man to swim from Africa to Europe by crossing the Mediterranean Sea. Seven people ³ _____ (already try) to complete this swim without success. In 2002 Strel ⁴ _____ (swim) the length of the Mississippi, which ⁵ _____ (take) him 68 days. The year before that he ⁶ _____ (break) the world non-stop record by swimming for 84 hours and 10 minutes without stopping. But he's probably best known as the man who ⁷ _____ (swim) the length of the Amazon in 2007, something nobody ⁸ _____ (ever do) before. He ⁹ _____ (travel) 5,268 km and ¹⁰ _____ (swim) for over 10 hours a day. By the time he ¹¹ _____ (arrive) at Belém, in Brazil, he ¹² _____ (be) in the water for 66 days. He now runs an adventure swimming holiday company with his son in Slovenia.

Get ready … Get it right!

10 Work in groups. Look at p114.

VOCABULARY 4C AND SKILLS ▶ Unusual days out

Vocabulary guessing meaning from context
Skills Reading: a magazine article; Listening: a radio discussion

QUICK REVIEW Past Perfect Write two things you had done, or had learned to do, by the time you were 5, 10 and 15 years old. Work in pairs. Talk about the things on your list. *By the time I was five, I'd learned how to ride a bike.* Did you talk about any of the same things?

Speaking and Reading

1 a Make a list of the five best museums, art galleries or famous buildings for tourists to visit in your country.

b Work in pairs. If you're from the same country, decide on the top five places from both lists. If you're from different countries, take turns to tell your partner about the places on your list.

2 a Work in new pairs. Look at photos A–E. What can you see in each photo?

b Read the article. Match photos A–E to the museums in the article.

c Read the article again. Answer these questions.
1 In which two places can you see the Museum of Bad Art?
2 Who was Imelda Marcos and how many shoes did she have?
3 How can you explore the Cancún Underwater Museum?
4 Why is the Miniatur Wunderland 'huge and tiny at the same time'?
5 What can you see at the Hamburger Museum?

d Work in pairs. Compare answers. Which museum would you most like to visit? Why?

The world's weirdest museums

*If you're bored of traditional museums, then perhaps it's time to try something new. **Matthew Clifford** visits some of the strangest museums on the planet.*

Have you ever wandered around a famous art gallery looking at paintings by well-known artists and secretly thought they were dreadful? Well, perhaps you should check out the Museum of Bad Art in Massachusetts, USA. It's the only museum in the world that celebrates bad art in all its forms. From blue-faced people to surreal landscapes, nothing is too bizarre for this museum (which you can also visit online).

If fashion is more your thing, then you might want to visit the Marikina Shoe Museum in the Philippines. The highlight of this museum is Imelda Marcos's massive shoe collection. When her husband was President she famously owned over 3,000 pairs of shoes, and 749 pairs are now displayed in the museum. Oh, and there's also a giant high-heeled shoe you can drive around like a car.

Another unusual day out is the Cancún Underwater Museum off the coast of Mexico. It was created by an English artist named Jason deCaires Taylor, who placed about 300 life-size concrete sculptures of real people on the seabed. You need to be able to dive or snorkel to explore the museum, or you can hire a glass-bottomed boat. The sight of brightly-coloured tropical fish swimming between the sculptures, which appear to be frozen in time, is absolutely breathtaking.

In the days before video games, boys used to spend their free time playing with toy trains. Ask your grandad – or better still, take him to visit the largest miniature railway museum in the world. The Miniatur Wunderland in Hamburg, Germany, is huge and tiny at the same time. It has 13,000 metres of track, 930 trains with over 14,000 carriages, 300,000 lights, 228,000 trees and 215,000 human figures. It's an impressive sight – and they haven't finished building it yet!

Are you feeling a bit peckish? If so, perhaps the Hamburger Museum at Daytona Beach, Florida, is the place for you. There are burger-shaped biscuit jars, clocks, hats, music boxes, pencil holders, children's toys, and much more. The museum was set up by a man called Hamburger Harry, who has collected over 1,000 burger-related items. The best exhibit is probably the bed that's shaped like a giant cheeseburger – or perhaps it's the hamburger-shaped Harley-Davidson motorbike!

HELP WITH VOCABULARY
Guessing meaning from context

3 a Look at the words in blue in the article. What parts of speech are they? Do you know a similar word in your language or another language you know?

b Choose the correct meanings, a or b. What information in the article helped you decide?

1	wandered	a walked around slowly	b walked around quickly
2	well-known	a common	b famous
3	bizarre	a expensive	b strange
4	highlight	a most interesting part	b biggest part
5	appear	a want	b seem
6	carriages	a parts of a train that people travel in	b the people who drive trains
7	peckish	a a bit thirsty	b a bit hungry
8	set up	a started	b bought

c Work in pairs. Look at the words in pink in the article. What part of speech are they? Can you guess what they mean?

d Check in VOCABULARY 4.3 p136.

Listening and Speaking

4 a Work in groups. Where can you go for a free day out in the town or city you're in now?

b CD1 36 Listen to a radio programme about free days out in London. Put these things in the order they are discussed.
- radio and TV programmes
- city farms
- the Houses of Parliament
- free music
- a trial at the Old Bailey
- downloadable walking tours
- museums and art galleries

c Listen again. Tick the true sentences. Correct the false ones.
1 It's free to visit the British Museum.
2 You need to take a map when you follow a downloadable walking tour.
3 You can see free opera at lunchtime on Sundays.
4 You can get tickets online to see a TV programme being recorded.
5 You can go on a tour of the Houses of Parliament for free.
6 You need some ID to get into the Old Bailey.
7 You can't feed the animals at city farms.

d Work in pairs. Compare answers. Which of the free activities discussed on the programme would you like to do? Why?

D

E

HELP WITH LISTENING
Linking (2): /w/, /j/ and /r/ sounds

- When a word ends in a vowel sound and the next word also starts with a vowel sound, we often link these words with a /w/, /j/ or /r/ sound.

word ends in	linking sound
/uː/ /əʊ/ /aʊ/	/w/
/ɪ/ /iː/ /aɪ/	/j/
/ə/ /ɜː/ /ɔː/ /eə/	/r/

5 a CD1 37 Listen to these sentences from the radio programme. Notice the linking sounds.

To /w/ a lot of people, London appears to be /j/ a very /j/ expensive city to visit.

There /r/ are /r/ actually /j/ a lot of things you can do /w/ in the city for free.

My favourite is the tour /r/ of the /j/ area /r/ around London Bridge.

And you can also go /w/ and see /j/ a radio /w/ or TV programme being recorded.

b Look at Audio Script CD1 36 p160. Listen to the programme again and notice the linking sounds.

6 a Think of a free time activity you've done recently. Choose one of these ideas or your own. Then make notes on what happened that day.

a museum	an art gallery	
the cinema	the theatre	the zoo
the countryside	the beach	a party
a sports event	visiting friends	

b Work in groups. Take turns to tell each other about your free time activity. Try to talk for at least one minute. Which was the most interesting story, do you think?

35

4D REAL WORLD — It's only a game!

Real World softening opinions and making generalisations

QUICK REVIEW Character adjectives Write eight character adjectives. Then work in pairs and compare lists. Use adjectives from both lists to describe people you know.

1 Work in groups. Discuss these questions.
1 Do you, or people you know, support a football team? If so, why did you/they choose that team?
2 Do football fans ever get into fights in your country? If so, why?
3 Do you think footballers earn too much?

2 a VIDEO 4 CD1 38 Look at the photo. Then watch or listen to the conversation. Why don't Rebecca and Lisa like football very much?

b Work in pairs. Try to write the correct names in these sentences.
1 _Rebecca_ isn't very keen on football.
2 _____ says there was more football violence when he was younger.
3 _____ thinks footballers are paid too much.
4 _____ says that football is part of the entertainment industry.
5 _____ thinks footballers are badly behaved.
6 _____ says football isn't a matter of life and death – it's much more important than that.
7 _____ gives Harry a Manchester United shirt.

c Watch or listen again. Check your answers.

REAL WORLD
Softening opinions and making generalisations

- Sometimes English speakers soften their opinions so that they don't sound rude or offensive.

3 a Match 1–6 to a–f.
1 **Some of them can** be
2 **On the whole, most**
3 Footballers **tend to** earn
4 That's **not very**
5 **Generally speaking,**
6 **Perhaps some** people **can**

a sensible behaviour, is it?
b **rather** a lot of money.
c **quite** aggressive **at times**.
d fans just want to see a good game.
e take it **a bit** too seriously.
f **most** footballers are just normal people.

b Look at the sentences in **3a** again. Choose the correct words/phrases in these rules.
- After *tend to* we use *the infinitive*/*verb+ing*.
- *Rather, quite, not very* and *a bit* usually come *before*/*after* an adjective.
- We often put *generally speaking* and *on the whole* at the *beginning*/*end* of a sentence.

c Look at these sentences. Then answer the questions.
A *That's stupid behaviour.*
B *That's not very sensible behaviour.*
1 Which sentence is softer and more polite?
2 Do we use *not very* with positive or negative adjectives?

d Check in REAL WORLD 4.1 p137.

Charlie   Daniel   Rebecca   Lisa

4 CD1 ▶39 **PRONUNCIATION** Listen and practise the sentences in **3a**. Copy the stress.

Some of them can be quite aggressive at times.

5 a Use the words/phrases in brackets to soften these opinions about children.

1 Children don't do enough sport. (On the whole; most)
On the whole, most children don't do enough sport.
2 They're very stubborn. (Perhaps; tend to; a bit)
3 They're rude to their teachers. (can; quite; at times)
4 They're very unhealthy. (some of them; not very)
5 They watch a lot of TV. (On the whole; tend to; quite)
6 They're impatient. (Generally speaking; not very)
7 They're selfish. (Some of them; can; rather; at times)
8 They spend too much time playing video games. (Perhaps; some of them; a bit)

b Work in pairs. Compare sentences. Do you agree with the sentences you have written? Why?/Why not?

6 a Work on your own. Think of reasons why you tend to agree or disagree with these sentences. Decide how you can use language in **3a** to soften your opinions.

1 Men watch too much sport.
2 Men are better at sport than women.
3 Teenagers are lazy and sleep too much.
4 Fast food is very bad for your health.
5 People don't care enough about the environment.
6 Students always cheat in exams.

b Work in groups. Discuss the sentences in **6a**.

c Tell the class which sentences everyone in your group agreed or disagreed with.

HELP WITH PRONUNCIATION The letters *or*

1 a CD1 ▶40 Listen and notice three ways we say the letters *or*. Listen again and practise.

1 /ɔː/   org̱anised   morning   divorced
2 /ə/   forget   opportunity   stubborn
3 /ɜː/   worse   world   workaholic

b Look at the words in **1a** again. How do we say the letters *or*: when this syllable is stressed? when this syllable is not stressed? after the letter *w*?

2 a Work in pairs. Match the letters *or* in these words to sounds 1, 2 or 3 in **1a**.

correct 2   worst   enormous   information   snoring
worth   gorilla   gorgeous   boring   motorbike
homework   unfortunately   uniform   mirror

b CD1 ▶41 Listen and check. Listen again and practise.

3 Work in pairs. Take turns to say these sentences.

1 Unfortunately it wasn't the correct information.
2 The enormous stubborn gorilla is still snoring.
3 He's a boring workaholic, but he's very organised.
4 After he got divorced, things got worse and worse.
5 Don't forget to wear a uniform in the morning.
6 How much is that gorgeous motorbike worth?
7 This is the worst homework in the world!

continue2learn

■ **Vocabulary, Grammar and Real World**
  ■ **Extra Practice 4 and Progress Portfolio 4** p118
  ■ **Language Summary 4** p135
  ■ **4A–D** Workbook p20

■ **Reading and Writing**
  ■ **Portfolio 4** Reviewing a novel Workbook p70
     Reading book reviews
     Writing book reviews: organisation, useful phrases

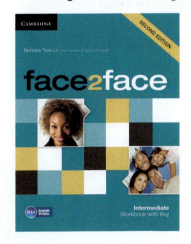

5A Our new home

Vocabulary homes
Grammar making comparisons: comparatives, superlatives, (*not*) *as … as*, etc.

QUICK REVIEW Making generalisations
Write three sentences to describe typical characteristics of your nationality: *We tend to …* , *We can be rather/a bit/quite …* , *Most people aren't very …* , *Generally speaking, …* , *On the whole, …* . Work in groups. Tell the group your sentences. Do you agree with your partners' sentences? Why?/Why not?

Vocabulary and Speaking
Homes

1 Work in pairs. Put these words/phrases into groups 1–3. Then check in **VOCABULARY 5.1** p138.

> in the city centre   an apartment block
> a balcony   in the country   a loft
> in the suburbs   a study
> in a quiet/lively/friendly neighbourhood
> a cottage   in a residential area
> a garage   a detached house   a roof
> on the ground/first/top floor
> a terraced house   stairs

1 homes and buildings *an apartment block*
2 parts of a home *a balcony*
3 location *in the city centre*

2 a What are the five most important things to look for in a new home? Use words/phrases in **1** and your own ideas.

a garden or a balcony
in a quiet neighbourhood

b Work in new pairs. Compare ideas and give reasons for your choices. Did you choose any of the same things?

Reading and Listening

3 a Read about three places to rent in Bristol, England. Which do you like best? Why?

b CD1 42 Tim and Jo are looking for a new place to live. Listen to their conversation. Which place do they want to see again? Why?

---

  www.brownandwood.co.uk/bristol

PROPERTIES TO RENT ▶ Bristol

 B&W

BISHOPSTON
Spacious terraced house in friendly neighbourhood

Three bedrooms (two double and one single), bathroom, large living room, new kitchen, loft, gas central heating, attractive front and back gardens.

Unfurnished
£1,100 pcm

REDLAND
Large detached house in quiet residential area

Large kitchen/breakfast room, three double bedrooms, new bathroom, living room, electric central heating, garage, front and back garden.

Unfurnished
£1,350 pcm

HOTWELLS
Spacious flat on top floor of new apartment block

Two double bedrooms, bathroom, kitchen, living room, electric central heating, air conditioning, balcony with river views, parking space.

Unfurnished
£1,200 pcm

4 a Work in pairs. Look at these sentences. Do you think they describe the house in Bishopston (B), the house in Redland (R) or the flat in Hotwells (H)?

1 It seemed slightly bigger than where we live now. *B*
2 It's the least expensive place we've seen so far.
3 It's one of the oldest houses we've looked at.
4 It's a little further away from the city centre.
5 It was a lot more spacious than I'd expected.
6 It had the most amazing view.
7 It's got the worst kitchen I've ever seen.
8 The back garden was far smaller than I'd expected.
9 It was much noisier than the other two.
10 The first place we saw was better.
11 It's a bit less expensive than the Redland house.

b CD1 42 Listen again and check.

HELP WITH GRAMMAR
Making comparisons

5 a Look at the words/phrases in blue in the sentences in **4a**. Then answer these questions.

1 Which are comparatives?
2 Which are superlatives?
3 When do we use *-er* or *-est*?
4 When do we use *more* or *most*?
5 Which comparatives and superlatives are irregular?
6 What are the opposites of *more* and *most*?

TIP • We can also use *more* or *most* with nouns: *It's got more space. It's got the most rooms.*

b Look at the words in pink in the sentences in **4a**. Which mean: a big difference? a small difference?

c Look at the phrases in bold in these sentences. Then answer the questions.

It's **the same** size **as** our house.
It's **not as** big **as** the other two places.
It was **different from** anything else we've seen.
It's **as** small **as** the one we've got now.
It's very **similar to** where we live now.

1 Which phrases mean the things we are comparing are: the same? nearly the same? not the same?
2 Do we use the adjective or its comparative form with (*not*) *as … as*?

d Check in GRAMMAR 5.1 p139.

6 CD1 43 PRONUNCIATION Listen and practise. Copy the stress and weak forms.

It seemed slightly bigger than /ðən/ where we live now.

It's not as /əz/ big as /əz/ the other two places.

7 Fill in the gaps with the comparative or superlative forms of the adjectives in brackets. Use *the* where necessary.

The terraced house in Bishopston is:
1 *the smallest* (small) of the three properties.
2 _____ (near) to the shops than the flat.
3 _____ (expensive) of the three properties.

The detached house in Redland is:
4 in a _____ (busy) street than the terraced house.
5 much _____ (attractive) than the flat.
6 _____ (far) from the city centre.

The top-floor flat in Hotwells is:
7 a lot _____ (bright) inside than the two houses.
8 _____ (modern) of the three properties.
9 in _____ (friendly) neighbourhood in the city.

8 a Rewrite these sentences with the words in brackets.

1 Her flat is more spacious than mine. (not as … as)
   My flat isn't as spacious as hers.
2 I'm not as organised as her. (more)
3 I don't look the same as her. (different)
4 Her taste in music is almost the same as mine. (similar)
5 I'm a bit more confident than her. (less)
6 I'm more ambitious than her. (not as … as)
7 I'm much less stubborn than her. (more)
8 We're the same age. (as … as)

b Choose a woman or girl you know well. Tick sentences in **8a** that are true for you and her.

c Work in pairs. Tell your partner about the woman or girl you chose. Use sentences from **8a**.

Get ready … Get it right!

9 Choose three houses or flats that you know well. Write six sentences to compare these homes. Use the language in **5** and these ideas.

- location and size of house/flat
- size of rooms/balcony/garden
- age and condition of house/flat
- distance from shops/centre/station
- type of neighbourhood
- your own ideas

My friend Julia's house is a bit larger than mine.
My sister's flat is a lot closer to the city centre.
My grandparents' flat is probably the oldest.

10 a Work in pairs. Tell your partner about the houses or flats you chose. Ask follow-up questions.

b Tell the class two interesting things about the homes you talked about.

5B A load of old junk

Vocabulary phrasal verbs (2)
Grammar the future: *will*, *be going to*, Present Continuous

QUICK REVIEW Making comparisons Write the names of five people in your family. Think of how you can compare these people to yourself and other people in your family. Work in pairs. Take turns to tell your partner about the people.

Reading, Vocabulary and Speaking
Phrasal verbs (2)

1 a Work in pairs. Which of these words do you know? Check new words with your teacher or in a dictionary.

| get rid of | keep | stuff | junk |
| a drawer | a cupboard | a pile | |

b Read the article. Tick the true sentences. Correct the false ones.

1 The article tells you how to get rid of junk.
2 You need about an hour for each room.
3 You should put things in three piles.
4 Put things you don't want in a junk drawer.
5 Don't buy things if you've got something similar.

c What do you think of the advice in the article? Do you need to do this in your home?

2 Work in pairs. Guess the meaning of the phrasal verbs in bold in the article. Check in VOCABULARY 5.2 p138.

Just get rid of it!

Is your home full of stuff that you never use? If so, the time has come to get rid of all your junk and create a peaceful, relaxed atmosphere in your home.

- Give yourself at least two hours to **clear out** a room.
- Make a space on the floor and empty all the cupboards and drawers.
- **Sort out** the things you haven't used for six months and make three piles: things to **give away**, things to **throw away**, things to keep.
- Put the first and second piles into separate rubbish bags and **take** them **out** of the room.
- Allow yourself one junk drawer in each room for the stuff you can't decide about.
- **Tidy up** the room and **put** everything **away**, then sit down and enjoy the calm space you have created.

And here's how to stop all your junk **coming back**.

- Before you buy anything, ask yourself: Have I got something similar? Do I need it? Where will I put it?
- When you buy something new, always **throw out** something else.
- **Go through** the cupboards and drawers in a different room every month and throw away anything you don't need.

3 Work in pairs. Student A p103. Student B p108.

Listening and Speaking

4 a Work in pairs. Look at the picture. Tim and Jo are moving house. What is in piles 1–3?

b Work in the same pairs. Which pile do you think Tim and Jo are going to: give away? throw away? keep?

c CD1 44 Listen and check your answers to **4b**.

5 a Work in pairs. Match these sentences to things A–E in the picture.

1 He's picking it up tomorrow evening after work.
2 Yes, you're probably right. OK, I'll throw those away.
3 I'm going to sort out the rest of them at the weekend.
4 But you'll never listen to them again.
5 It's twenty years old! It's going to break the first time she uses it.

b CD1 44 Listen again and check.

HELP WITH GRAMMAR
The future

6 a Look at sentences 1–3 in **5a**. Then fill in the gaps in these rules with *will*, *be going to* or the Present Continuous.

a We use _____ when we decide to do something at the time of speaking.
b We use _____ when we already have a plan or an intention to do something.
c We use _____ when we have an arrangement with another person.

b Look at sentences 4 and 5 in **5a**. Then choose the correct verb forms in these rules.

d We use *will*/*be going to* for a prediction that is based on present evidence (something we can see now).
e We use *will*/*be going to* for a prediction that is a personal opinion and is not based on present evidence.

c How do we make the positive, negative and question forms of *will* and *be going to*?

d Check in GRAMMAR 5.2 p140.

HELP WITH LISTENING Future verb forms

7 a CD1 45 Listen and write the sentences you hear. You will hear each sentence twice.

b Listen again to sentences 1 and 2. What are the two ways we can say *going to*?

c Work in pairs. Match the sentences you wrote in **7a** to rules a–e in **6a** and **6b**.

8 CD1 46 PRONUNCIATION Listen again and practise. Copy the stress.

9 a Read the rest of Tim and Jo's conversation. What are they going to: give away? throw away? keep?

JO What about these curtains? Shall we give them to your brother?
TIM Sorry, but I don't think ¹*he'll use*/*he's using* them.
JO OK, ²*I'm throwing*/*I'll throw* them away. They're really old anyway.
TIM And what about your guitar?
JO Barry wants that. ³*He's coming*/*He'll come* to pick it up on Friday.
TIM Right, ⁴*I'll put*/*I'm going to put* it in the 'give away' pile.
JO Do you want to keep your old trainers?
TIM Yes, definitely. ⁵*I'm starting*/*I'm going to start* running again soon.
JO Yeah, right. Shall we keep this mirror? ⁶*It's looking*/*It'll look* nice in the new house.
TIM Yes, why not? Oh, is it half past three already? Don't forget ⁷*we're meeting*/*we'll meet* the estate agent at four.
JO You go. ⁸*I'm finishing*/*I'll finish* sorting out this stuff.

b Read the conversation again. Choose the correct verb forms.

c CD1 47 Listen and check. What does Jo do when Tim leaves?

10 a Write two things you have arranged to do, two things you have planned to do and two things you will probably do in the next four weeks.

b Work in groups. Tell each other your ideas. Who's going to have the busiest or the most interesting four weeks?

Get ready ... Get it right!

11 Make a list of six things in your home that you want to get rid of. Use these ideas or your own.

CDs	video games	electrical equipment
DVDs	toys	books	computer equipment
clothes	furniture	sports equipment

12 a Try to sell or give away your things to other students. Each person has £50 to spend. Write who agrees to buy or take each thing.

> Do you want to buy my MP3 player?

> Maybe. I'll give you £10 for it.

b Work in groups. Tell other students about the things on your list. Who made the most money?

5C VOCABULARY AND SKILLS > Birthdays

Vocabulary verb patterns (1)
Skills Reading: a magazine article; Listening: Personal stories

QUICK REVIEW *be going to* Work in pairs. Find five things you're going to do next weekend that your partner isn't going to do: **A** *Are you going to have a lie-in on Sunday?* **B** *No, probably not.*

Speaking, Reading and Vocabulary

1 Work in groups. Discuss these questions.
   1 How do people celebrate birthdays in your country?
   2 When's your birthday? What are the advantages and disadvantages of having a birthday at that time of the year?
   3 Where were you on your last birthday? What did you do?

2 **a** Before you read, check these words with your teacher or in a dictionary.

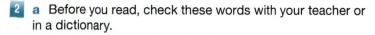

a candle   shine   seaweed   blindfold   a donkey   a stick

b Work in pairs. Look at photos A–E. What do you know about these birthday traditions?

c Read the article. Put the photos in the order they are discussed.

3 **a** Read the article again. Answer these questions.
   1 Why are birthday cakes round and why do we put candles on them?
   2 How much does Time-Warner earn from *Happy Birthday to You* every year?
   3 What do people eat on their birthdays in China and Korea?
   4 Why did people send birthday cards a hundred years ago?
   5 What does a piñata usually look like and how do you get the sweets out of it?
   6 What happens on Tet in Vietnam?

b Work in pairs. Compare answers. Which things in the article did you find the most interesting or surprising?

Happy birthday to you!

Margaret Robson investigates the origins of birthday traditions around the world.

For many people, you **can't** celebrate your birthday without a birthday cake. These have been common in Western countries since the 15th century, but people have been making them for over 2,000 years. It was the Ancient Greeks who **decided** to make the cakes round so that they look like the full moon. They also put candles on the cakes to **make** them shine like the moon. Nowadays parents tell their children to make a wish before they blow out the candles (one candle for each year, of course). In China they have small birthday cakes called sou bao, which are the same shape and colour as a peach, while in Korea, the traditional birthday food isn't cake, but seaweed soup.

In most English-speaking countries, people **start** singing *Happy Birthday to You* before the cake is cut. This is the most recognised song in the English language, but it isn't as old as you **might** think. It first appeared in print in 1912 and was bought by The Time-Warner Company for $5 million in 1998. The company earns over $2 million from public performances of the song every year.

Everyone **likes** getting birthday cards, of course, but this is also a fairly new tradition. People only **began** sending birthday cards about 100 years ago if they **couldn't** come to a person's birthday party or if they didn't **remember** to send a present. The British love sending birthday cards – they send about 800 million every year – but in places like Spain, sending cards still isn't very common.

For a lot of people who live in Latin America, the piñata is central to birthday celebrations. A piñata is a container, usually in the shape of a donkey, filled with sweets and hung from a tree. The birthday person is blindfolded and then tries to hit the piñata with a stick. The person **keeps** hitting the piñata until it breaks open and the sweets fall to the ground.

Interestingly, not everyone celebrates their birthday on the day they were born. In Vietnam, everyone celebrates their birthday on New Year's Day – or Tet, as it's called in Vietnamese. On the first morning of Tet, adults give children a red envelope containing 'lucky money' to **help** them celebrate becoming one year older.

Whatever your country's traditions, a birthday **should** always be a special day. So I hope you enjoy yourself next time someone **asks** you to go to a birthday party – and don't **forget** to buy them a present!

HELP WITH VOCABULARY
Verb patterns (1)

4 a Look at the verbs in bold in the article. Underline the verb form that follows them. Then write the infinitive form of the verbs in bold in the table.

start	+ verb+*ing*
decide	+ infinitive with *to*
can	+ infinitive
tell	+ object + infinitive with *to*
make	+ object + infinitive

b Write these verbs in the table in **4a**. Some verbs can go in more than one place.

enjoy	need	allow	would	finish	teach
let	would like	will	want	mind	plan
prefer	must	hate	continue	learn	
pay	seem	would rather			

c Check in VOCABULARY 5.3 p139.

5 Work in pairs. Student A p103. Student B p108.

 Ashley  Jean  Ruby  Stuart

Listening and Speaking

6 a CD1 48 Listen to four people talking about their most memorable birthdays. Which person:
1 got a very unusual card on his/her birthday?
2 was very happy to have his/her own birthday cake?
3 met someone special at his/her birthday party?
4 had three million people at his/her birthday party?

b Work in pairs. Compare answers. Explain why each person's birthday was so memorable.

HELP WITH LISTENING Fillers and false starts

- In spoken English we often use fillers (*well*, *you know*, *um*, etc.) and false starts (*I've … I've been*, etc.) to give us time to think.

7 a Underline the fillers and false starts in these sentences.
1 <u>So it's</u> … I mean, it's always a bit strange because people kind of forget about my birthday.
2 You see, my husband died um thirteen years ago, but er you know life goes on, doesn't it?
3 I never … um I didn't enjoy birthdays very much when I was a kid because you know I always had to like share it with my sister.
4 Well, I don't like … er I hate getting older, so I just sort of pretend that it's a normal day.

b Look at Audio Script CD1 48 p162. Listen to Ashley and Jean and notice all the fillers and false starts. Then listen to Ruby and Stuart and underline all the fillers and false starts.

8 a Think about your most memorable birthday. Make notes on these things.
- where you were that day
- who you spent your birthday with
- what you did during the day and in the evening
- what you had to eat and drink
- what presents you got
- why your birthday was so memorable
- any other things that made the birthday special

b Work in groups. Tell each other about your memorable birthdays. Which do you think is the most interesting?

c Tell the class about one of your group's memorable birthdays.

43

5D REAL WORLD — Things I need

Real World explaining what you need
Vocabulary materials

QUICK REVIEW Verb patterns (1) Choose four of these phrases and write sentences about you: *I'd like, I keep, I forgot, I might, I started, I'm planning, I've decided, I often help, I usually let.* Work in pairs. Take turns to say your sentences. Ask follow-up questions.

1 a Work in pairs. Which of these materials do you know? Then check new words in VOCABULARY 5.4 ▶ p139.

> wool   rubber   metal   cardboard   plastic   leather
> paper   cotton   wood   tin   glass   steel

b Work in the same pairs. Write one thing that is made of each material in 1a. Don't write them in order.

c Swap papers with another pair. Write the correct materials next to the things on their paper.

d Check your answers with the pair who wrote the list.

2 a VIDEO▶5 CD2▶1 Katharina is from Holland, but now she lives in the UK. Watch or listen to two conversations in a department store. Tick the things in photos A–H that she wants to buy.

b Work in pairs. Match these words for the things Katharina wants to buy to four of the photos A–H.

> ear muffs   stain remover   a blender   needles

c Watch or listen again. Check your answers and match the things in 2b to places 1–4 in the department store.

1 on the ground floor   3 near the escalator
2 on the second floor   4 on the top shelf

REAL WORLD Explaining what you need

3 a Write these headings in the correct places a–d.

> describing what something looks like
> describing what something is used for
> checking something is the right thing
> saying you don't know the name of something

a _____
I'm sorry, I've forgotten what it's called.
I don't know what it's called in English.
I can't remember what they're called.
I'm sorry, I don't know the word for them.

b _____
It's a thing for (making soup).
It's stuff for (getting marks off your clothes).
You use it when (you get coffee on your shirt).
You use them to (mend your clothes).

c _____
It's a type of (liquid).
They're made of (metal).
They've got (a hole in the end).
They look like (headphones).

d _____
Is this what you're looking for?
Do you mean (a blender)?
Oh, you mean (stain remover).

b Look again at the phrases in 3a. Then choose the correct words in these rules.

- We often use *stuff* to talk about **countable/uncountable** nouns we don't know the name of.
- After *It's a thing for …* and *It's stuff for …* we use **the infinitive/verb+ing**.
- After *You use it/them …* we use **verb+ing/the infinitive with to**.

c Check in REAL WORLD 5.1 ▶ p140.

Lisa   Katharina

4 CD2 2 PRONUNCIATION Listen and practise the sentences in **3a**. Copy the stress.

I'm sorry, I've forgotten what it's called.

5 a Write conversations between Katharina (K) and a sales assistant (S) from these prompts.

K ¹It's / thing / boil / water.
1 It's a thing for boiling water.
²I / sorry, I / forget / what / called.
S ³Is this / you / look / for?
K Yes, that's right. ⁴What / called / English?
S A kettle.

K ⁵It's stuff for / make / things smell nice.
⁶I / sorry, I / not know / word / it.
S ⁷Do / mean perfume?
K ⁸No, you use / when / want / make a room smell nicer.
S ⁹Oh, / mean air freshener.

K ¹⁰I / not know / what they / call / English.
¹¹They / make / metal and they / got / round top.
S ¹²I / not sure what / mean.
K ¹³You use them / put posters / the wall.
S ¹⁴Oh, / mean drawing pins.

K ¹⁵I / sorry, / can't remember / it's called.
¹⁶You use it / cut up paper.
S ¹⁷Do / mean / pair / scissors?
K ¹⁸No, / type / machine. ¹⁹It / look / a rubbish bin.
S ²⁰Oh, / mean a shredder.

b Work in pairs. Compare answers. Match the things Katharina wants to buy to four of the photos A–H.

c Practise the conversations in **5a** with your partner. Take turns to be the sales assistant.

6 Work in new pairs. Student A p104. Student B p109.

HELP WITH PRONUNCIATION
/dʒ/, /j/ and /juː/

1 CD2 3 Listen to these sounds and words. Listen again and practise.
1 /dʒ/ **j**ungle **j**acket gor**ge**ous lar**ge**
2 /j/ **y**ellow **y**oga **y**esterday **y**oung
3 /juː/ **u**niversity st**u**dent T**u**esday f**ew**

2 a Work in pairs. Look at the letters in bold in these words. Match the words to sounds 1–3 in **1**.

your 2	**j**ourney	**u**sually	**y**ear
h**u**ge	ve**g**etable	barbec**ue**	J**u**ly
yet	dan**g**erous	m**u**sic	**o**nions

b CD2 4 Listen and check. Listen again and practise.

3 a Cover **1** and **2a**. Underline four of these sounds in each sentence.
1 /j/ Your younger sister went to yoga yesterday.
2 /dʒ/ She grows gorgeous large vegetables in July.
3 /juː/ I usually have huge barbecues with great music.
4 /j/ There aren't any yellow onions yet this year.
5 /dʒ/ Wear a jacket on your dangerous jungle journey.
6 /juː/ A few students went to university on Tuesday.

b Work in pairs. Compare answers. Then take turns to say the sentences. Check your partner's pronunciation.

continue2learn

■ **Vocabulary, Grammar and Real World**
  ■ **Extra Practice 5 and Progress Portfolio 5** p119
  ■ **Language Summary 5** p138
  ■ **5A–D** Workbook p25

■ **Reading and Writing**
  ■ **Portfolio 5** Emails with news Workbook p72
    Reading an informal email
    Writing short emails and notes; useful phrases

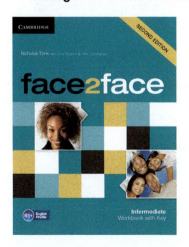

6A Make up your mind

Vocabulary *make* and *do*
Grammar first conditional and future time clauses

QUICK REVIEW Explaining what you need Write a list of four things in your house. Work in pairs. Take turns to describe the things to your partner. Don't say the thing: *It's made of metal and you use it to mend clothes.* Your partner guesses what the things are: *A needle?*

Vocabulary and Speaking
make and *do*

1 a Work in pairs. Do we use *make* or *do* with these words/phrases? Then check in **VOCABULARY 6.1** p141.

> the cleaning   a decision   a course   a mistake
> homework   money   friends   nothing   exercise
> the washing-up   a noise   the shopping   dinner
> some work   the washing   a degree   an excuse
> someone laugh/cry   an exam   up your mind
> the housework   progress   a cake   an appointment
> someone a favour   a mess of something

do the cleaning   *make a decision*

b Work in pairs. Take turns to test each other.

a decision   *make a decision*

2 a Fill in the gaps in these questions with the correct form of *make* or *do*.

1 Are you going to **do** some shopping after class?
2 Did you _____ someone a favour last weekend?
3 Are you good at _____ people laugh?
4 Do you usually _____ the washing-up?
5 Have you _____ any exercise this week?
6 Do you ever have to _____ excuses for being late?
7 Are you _____ another course at the moment?
8 Have you _____ any new friends this year?
9 Do you like _____ nothing at the weekend?
10 Do you usually have to _____ dinner for other people?

b Ask other students your questions from **2a**. Try to find one person who answers *yes* to each question. Ask follow-up questions if possible.

Are you going to do some shopping after class?   *Yes, I am.*

What are you going to buy?

Lily

Speaking and Listening

3 a Work in pairs. Discuss these questions.
1 Do you find it easy to make decisions? Why?/Why not?
2 What was the last big decision you made? How did you decide what to do?

b CD2 5 Listen to Lily talking to her brother, Adam. Work in pairs. Student A, answer these questions about Lily. Student B, answer these questions about Adam.
1 Does she/he have a job at the moment? If so, what does she/he do?
2 What decision does she/he have to make?
3 What advice does she/he give to the other person?

c Work with your partner. Compare answers. What do you think Lily and Adam should do?

4 a Work in the same pairs. Who said these sentences, Lily or Adam?
1 If I start teaching again, I'll be exhausted after a year.
2 What will you study if you do another degree?
3 You might not get in this year if you don't apply soon.
4 But unless I do it soon, I'll be too old.
5 I'll ask them before they go on holiday.
6 As soon as I make up my mind, I'll let you know.
7 I'll make a decision after I talk to him.
8 I won't say anything until you decide what to do.
9 I'll call you when I know what I'm doing.

b CD2 5 Listen again and check.

Adam

HELP WITH GRAMMAR
First conditional and future time clauses

FIRST CONDITIONAL

5 a Look at this first conditional. Answer questions a–c.

If I start teaching again, I'll be exhausted after a year.

a Which is the *if* clause?
b Which is the main clause?
c Which verb form do we use in each clause?

b Look at sentences 1–3 in **4a**. Answer questions a–e.

a Do these sentences talk about the present or the future?
b Does the *if* clause talk about things that are possible or certain?
c Is the *if* clause always first in the sentence?
d How do we make questions in the first conditional?
e Which word in sentence 3 means 'will perhaps'?

c Look at sentence 4 in **4a**. Answer questions a–b.

a Which word means 'if not'?
b How can you say this sentence with *if*?

d Check in **GRAMMAR 6.1 ▶ p142**.

FUTURE TIME CLAUSES

6 a Look at sentences 5–9 in **4a**. Answer questions a–c.

a Do these sentences talk about the present or the future?
b Which verb form do we use in the main clause?
c Which verb form do we use in clauses beginning with *before*, *as soon as*, *after*, *until* and *when*?

b Check in **GRAMMAR 6.2 ▶ p142**.

7 CD2 ▶ 6 PRONUNCIATION Listen and practise. Copy the stress.

I'll be exhausted after a year. →
If I start teaching again, I'll be exhausted after a year.

8 Rewrite these sentences. Use the words in brackets. Change the verb forms if necessary.

1 He won't do it unless we pay him. (if)
   He won't do it if we don't pay him.
2 I'll come out tonight if I don't have to work. (unless)
3 Perhaps he'll call you if he has time. (might)
4 I'll have to sell the car unless I find a job soon. (if)
5 If Tony doesn't get here in the next ten minutes, we'll go without him. (unless)
6 Maybe I'll go away this weekend unless my friends come to visit. (might; if)

9 Look at these sentences about the future. Fill in the gaps with the correct form of *make* or *do*.

1 She *'ll make* a decision when her boss gets back.
2 I _____ dinner after I _____ the washing-up.
3 I _____ some work before they arrive.
4 If you _____ the cleaning, I _____ the shopping.
5 As soon as I _____ some progress, I'll let you know.
6 I _____ my homework after this programme finishes.
7 You won't _____ any money until you _____ a business course.
8 I _____ an appointment with the doctor when I have time.
9 I _____ the washing if you _____ Jamie's birthday cake.

10 a Complete these sentences for you.

1 As soon as I get home today, I …
2 Before I go to bed tonight, I …
3 If I'm bored this weekend, I …
4 I'll be at the next class unless …
5 After I finish this course, I …
6 I want to study English until …
7 I'm going to … this weekend unless …
8 When I retire, I think I …
9 I'll be very happy if …
10 I might move house when …

b Work in pairs. Take turns to say your sentences. Are any the same?

Get ready … Get it right!

11 Work in groups of three. Student A p103. Student B p108. Student C p113.

6B Fear of failure

Vocabulary reflexive pronouns
Grammar zero conditional; conditionals with imperatives and modal verbs; *in case*

QUICK REVIEW *make* and *do* Write four phrases with *make* or *do* that are connected to you, or people you know. Work in pairs. Tell your partner why you chose these phrases. Ask follow-up questions: **A** *I chose 'do exercise' because I go running quite a lot.* **B** *How far do you run?*

Speaking and Reading

1 Work in groups. Discuss these questions.

1 When you were a child, what did your parents make you do? What did they let you do? Talk about these things and your own ideas: helping in the home, going out on your own, free time activities, toys and games, birthdays, homework, etc.
2 Do you think parents worry too much about how well their children do at school? Why?/Why not?

2 a Before you read, check these words/phrases with your teacher or in a dictionary.

> success   failure   develop
> praise   make an effort   good grades

b Read the article. Which sentence describes the article best?

1 Children's results at school are the most important thing.
2 Praise the effort that children make, not the grades they get.
3 Only clever children will be successful in life.

c Read the article again. Answer these questions.

1 What do pushy parents want their children to do?
2 What does Graeme Atkins think children also learn at school?
3 Why does Sarah Vine think parents shouldn't criticise children for not getting good grades?
4 What problems can children who are frightened of failure have in the future?

d Work in pairs. Compare answers.

How to Measure Success

As everybody knows, [1]**if you have children, you want them to be happy and successful.** These days children are under more pressure than ever to do well at school, but is this helping or damaging our kids? We read a lot of stories these days about pushy parents who make their children study all the time so that they can get into the best universities. This means children spend most of their free time studying by themselves to please their parents. However, the latest research suggests that this approach can do more harm than good.

"[2]**If children study all the time, they don't develop in other ways,**" says Graeme Atkins, a child psychologist. "School isn't only about learning in class – it's also about learning how to get on with other children and how to become part of society. [3]**If parents want their children to be happy, they shouldn't put too much pressure on them.** It's important that they are allowed to enjoy themselves."

It's also important how parents deal with success and failure. "One of the worst things that a parent could do is to praise their child for getting an A," says Sarah Vine, a child education counsellor. "[4]**If you want to help your children, praise the effort they make** – not the grades they get. Not every child can be top of the class, but [5]**if you criticise children for not getting good grades, they can feel like they're failures** – and that can lead to psychological problems when they become adults. We should also encourage children to work things out themselves, but in many classrooms a lot of students are scared of answering questions in case they get them wrong."

So perhaps parents should worry less about their children's grades and instead just encourage them to try hard at everything they do. As we all know, making mistakes is part of the learning process, but it seems that children who are frightened of failure will find it harder to be happy and successful in life.

HELP WITH GRAMMAR Zero conditional; conditionals with imperatives and modal verbs; *in case*

3 a Look at sentences 1 and 2 in bold in the article. These are called zero conditionals. Choose the correct words in these rules.

- Zero conditionals talk about things that are *possible in the future/always true*.
- In zero conditionals both verbs are in *the Present Simple/a future verb form*.

b Look at sentences 3–5 in the article. Answer these questions.

a Which sentences have a modal verb in the main clause?
b Which sentence has an imperative in the main clause?
c Which verb form is in the *if* clause in each sentence?

c Look at this sentence from the article. Then choose the correct words/phrases in the rules.

*Students are scared of answering questions **in case** they get them wrong.*

- We use *in case* to talk about something that *might/is definitely going to* happen.
- *In case* and *if* have *the same/different* meanings.

d Check in **GRAMMAR 6.3** p142.

48

HELP WITH LISTENING
Zero or first conditional

6 a 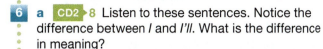 Listen to these sentences. Notice the difference between *I* and *I'll*. What is the difference in meaning?

If my children make a lot of effort, I praise them.
If my children make a lot of effort, I'll praise them.

b CD2 9 Listen and write the sentences you hear. You will hear each sentence twice. Which are zero conditionals? Which are first conditionals?

HELP WITH VOCABULARY
Reflexive pronouns

7 a Look at sentences a–c from the article. Notice the reflexive pronouns in bold. Then choose the correct words/phrases in the rules.

  a It's important that they are allowed to enjoy **themselves**.
  b This means children spend most of their free time studying by **themselves**.
  c We should also encourage children to work things out **themselves**.

  • In sentence a, *They* and *themselves* are **the same/different** people.
  • In sentence b, *by themselves* means **with other people/alone**.
  • In sentence c, *themselves* emphasises that children do this **with/instead of** someone else.

b What are the reflexive pronouns for *I*, *you* (singular), *he*, *she*, *it*, *we*, *you* (plural) and *they*?

c Check in VOCABULARY 6.2 p141.

8 Fill in the gaps with the correct reflexive pronoun.
  1 I made my daughter's jumper *myself*.
  2 My son likes playing by _____ .
  3 We want to educate our children _____ .
  4 Deborah looks after three children by _____ .
  5 I usually cut the kids' hair _____ .
  6 The party was great. All the kids enjoyed _____ .

4 CD2 7 **PRONUNCIATION** Listen and practise. Copy the stress.

you want them to be happy and successful → If you have children, you want them to be happy and successful.

5 a Fill in the gaps with these verb forms. Then choose *if* or *in case*.

| ~~feel~~ | should start | don't want | give | is playing |
| have | don't get | can't work | get | lose |

  1 I *feel* terrible *if/in case* I _____ enough sleep.
  2 I usually _____ a glass of water by the bed *if/in case* I _____ thirsty in the night.
  3 I _____ saving money *if/in case* I _____ my job.
  4 I _____ *if/in case* someone _____ music.
  5 *If/In case* you _____ those clothes, _____ them to charity.

b Work in pairs. Compare answers. Are any of sentences 1–4 true for you?

Get ready ... Get it right!

9 Work in pairs. Write your top five tips on how to be successful at learning languages.

If you don't understand something, ask the teacher. Always have a dictionary with you in case you need to look something up.

10 a Work with another pair. Tell each other your tips. Then choose the best five tips.

b Compare tips with another pair or with the whole class. What are the best five tips?

VOCABULARY AND SKILLS 6C > Touch wood

Vocabulary synonyms
Skills Listening: an informal conversation; Reading: a magazine article

> **QUICK REVIEW Zero conditional** Think about what you usually do if you: feel a bit depressed, get a cold, can't get to sleep, feel stressed, have too much work to do. Work in groups. Tell the group your ideas: *If I feel a bit depressed, I eat chocolate and watch TV!* Do any people in your group do the same things?

Vocabulary and Speaking

1 a Work in pairs. Match these words/phrases to photos A–H.

> a black cat   a shooting star   a mirror   salt
> a ladder   wood   a lucky charm   an umbrella

b Read about some British superstitions. Fill in the gaps with words/phrases from **1a**.

British superstitions

If ¹_____ walks in front of you, you'll have good luck.
If you break ²_____ , you'll have seven years' bad luck.
If you carry ³_____ like a rabbit's foot, it'll bring you good luck.
If you see ⁴_____ in the sky, you can make a wish.
If you want a good thing to continue, you should touch ⁵_____ .
If you spill ⁶_____ on the table, you should throw it over your shoulder.
If you walk under ⁷_____ or open ⁸_____ in the house, you'll have bad luck.

2 Work in groups. Discuss these questions.
1 Which of the British superstitions are true in your country?
2 What other superstitions do people have in your country?
3 Do you believe in any superstitions? If so, which ones?

Listening

3 a Before you listen, check these words with your teacher or in a dictionary.

> the Romans   crops   fertility   good/evil spirits

b CD2 ▶10 Listen to Edward and Charlotte talking about superstitions. Tick the British superstitions in **1b** they talk about.

c Listen again. Complete these sentences.
1 The idea of seven years' bad luck was started by _____ .
2 Rabbits were good luck because they had a lot of _____ .
3 People used to believe that good spirits lived in _____ .
4 Many years ago salt was used as a _____ .
5 In the UK you throw salt over your _____ shoulder.

HELP WITH LISTENING
Sentence stress (2)

4 a Choose the correct words/phrases in these rules.
- We *usually/don't usually* stress names, nouns, main verbs, adjectives and negative auxiliaries.
- We *usually/don't usually* stress pronouns, prepositions, articles and positive auxiliaries.

b Work in pairs. Look at the beginning of the conversation. Which words do you think are stressed?

EDWARD Charlotte, are you very superstitious?
CHARLOTTE No, not really. Why do you ask?
EDWARD I'm reading a fascinating book called *The History of Superstitions*. Did you know that in Britain, people think that seeing a black cat is good luck, but in nearly every other country in the world it's bad luck?

c CD2 ▶10 Listen to the beginning of the conversation again. Check your answers.

d Look at Audio Script CD2 ▶10 p163. Listen to the conversation again. Follow the sentence stress. Are question words (*Why*, etc.), adverbs (*very*, etc.) and connecting words (*and*, etc.) usually stressed or unstressed?

Speaking, Reading and Vocabulary

5 a Work in pairs. Do you agree or disagree with these sentences? Give reasons for your answers.
1 Some people are born lucky.
2 Some people make their own luck.
3 People can learn to be lucky.

b Read the article about luck. Does Dr Wiseman agree or disagree with the sentences in **5a**?

c Read the article again. Which of these sentences is correct? Correct the mistakes in the other sentences.
1 Maureen Wilcox won the lottery in June 1980.
2 Dr Wiseman has spent nearly ten years studying luck.
3 Lucky people behave in the same way as unlucky people.
4 Unlucky people meet more new people than lucky people.
5 The volunteers at luck school were all unlucky people.
6 All the volunteers who went to luck school became luckier.

d Work in pairs. Compare answers. What do you think of Dr Wiseman's ideas about luck?

HELP WITH VOCABULARY Synonyms

6 a Look at the words/phrases in pink in the article. Check any words/phrases you don't know with your teacher.

b The words in blue in the article are synonyms of the words in pink. Write them in the correct place in the tables. Write the infinitive form of the verbs.

choose	pick
satisfied	
lucky	
behave	
notice	

by chance	
attitude	
sure	
deal with	
show	

c Match a word/phrase in A to a synonym in B.

A	B
concerned	chat to someone
frightened	glad
make a decision	have a go at doing
try to do	huge
talk to someone	scared
nice	make up your mind
enormous	worried
pleased	brilliant
wonderful	awful
terrible	pleasant

d Check in VOCABULARY 6.3 ▶ p141.

7 Work in pairs. Test each other on the synonyms in **6b** and **6c**.

| by chance | accidentally |

8 Work in two groups. Group A p103. Group B p108.

The secrets of luck

In June 1980, Maureen Wilcox became one of the US lottery's biggest losers. She chose the winning numbers for both the Rhode Island and Massachusetts lotteries. But unfortunately for her, the numbers she picked for the Rhode Island lottery were the correct ones for the Massachusetts lottery, and vice versa.

We all know lucky people – they have good relationships, successful careers and are very satisfied with their lives. But what makes them so lucky? Dr Richard Wiseman has been studying luck for over ten years and has found that lucky people have a completely different approach to the world.

Dr Richard Wiseman

FOUR WAYS TO BE LUCKY

The results of his work revealed that people aren't born lucky. Instead, fortunate people behave in a way that creates good luck in their lives.

- They notice opportunities that happen by chance more often than unlucky people. They also meet more new people and have more new experiences.
- They tend to make good decisions by listening to their intuition.
- They're optimistic and are certain that the future is going to be full of good luck. This positive attitude often makes good things happen.
- They're also good at coping with bad luck and often cheer themselves up by imagining things could be worse than they are.

LUCK SCHOOL

Dr Wiseman tested his ideas by starting a luck school, where he hoped that unlucky people could learn to be lucky. 400 volunteers spent a month doing exercises to help them think and act like a lucky person. These exercises helped the volunteers spot opportunities that happen accidentally, trust their intuition more, feel sure they're going to be lucky and become better at dealing with bad luck. The results were dramatic and showed that 80% of the volunteers were now happier and more content with their lives – and most important of all, luckier.

Dr Wiseman's ideas won't help you win the lottery, but they might help you in your day-to-day life – fingers crossed!

6D REAL WORLD > The village festival

Real World discussion language

QUICK REVIEW Synonyms Write six pairs of synonyms (*sure*, *certain*, etc.). Work in pairs. Take turns to say one of your words/phrases. Your partner guesses the synonym.

1 Work in groups. Discuss these questions.
1 Have you ever been to a festival or street party in your town or city? If so, tell the group about it.
2 What sort of entertainment is there at traditional festivals in your country?
3 What are the best and worst things about going to a festival?

2 a Check these words/phrases with your teacher or in a dictionary.

a stage	charge someone £5
a raffle	donate	a stall
involve people in something		

b VIDEO 6 CD2 11 Look at the photo. The people are discussing their village festival. Watch or listen to their conversation. What sort of entertainment are they planning to have at the festival?

3 a Work in pairs. Do you think these sentences are true or false? If you think they're false, explain why.
1 The festival is to celebrate the 300th anniversary of the village.
2 They're going to charge people £5 to get into the festival.
3 They're going to advertise for local bands to play for free.
4 They want people in the village to donate prizes for the raffle.
5 Ian's going to ask the head teacher of the school to put on a musical.
6 Lisa thinks the people in the village should make the food.
7 Rebecca suggests having some competitions for people in the village.

b VIDEO 6 CD2 11 Watch or listen again. Check your answers.

Lisa Duncan Ian Rebecca

REAL WORLD Discussion language

4 a Fill in the gaps with the words in the boxes.

~~make~~	How	say
point	could	thought
suggest	about	

That's	idea	bad
Sorry	sure	could
sounds	worth	

asking to speak

May I ¹ *make* a suggestion?
Can I make a ² _____ here?
Can I just ³ _____ something here?

making suggestions

⁴ _____ about (having some live music)?
We ⁵ _____ (hire some professional musicians).
What ⁶ _____ (charging people £5 each)?
Have you ⁷ _____ of (asking the school to put on a musical)?
I ⁸ _____ we (have some competitions).

b Check in REAL WORLD 6.1 p142.

ways of agreeing

Yes, that ⁹ _____ like a good idea.
Well, it's (definitely) ¹⁰ _____ a try.
Yes, that's not a ¹¹ _____ idea.
Yes, that ¹² _____ work.
¹³ _____ a great/brilliant idea!

ways of disagreeing

I'm not ¹⁴ _____ about that. For one thing, …
¹⁵ _____ , I don't think we should do that.
I'm not sure that's a good ¹⁶ _____ .

5 CD2 12 PRONUNCIATION Listen and practise the sentences in **4a**. Copy the stress and polite intonation.

May I make a suggestion?

6 a Ian (I), Rebecca (R), Lisa (L) and Duncan (D) continue their discussion about the festival. Put the words in sentences 1–13 in order.

I   OK, next we need to decide a date for the festival.
R   ¹make / a / I / suggestion / May ?
1   *May I make a suggestion?*
I   Of course.
R   ²having / August / about / What / the / in / festival ?
L   ³like / Yes, / idea / good / sounds / that / a .
     The weather's usually good in August.
D   ⁴festival / three-day / have / we / Perhaps / a / could .
I   ⁵do / don't / should / that / I / think / Sorry, / we .
     I think two days is enough.
D   Yes, you're probably right.
I   OK, what other entertainment can we have?
L   ⁶match / How / organising / about / a / football ?
I   ⁷idea / bad / Yes, / a / not / that's .
D   ⁸we / club / suggest / football / to / talk / the / I / local .
R   ⁹here / say / I / something / just / Can ?
I   Yes, of course.
R   ¹⁰thought / the festival / Have / a celebrity / of / asking / you / to open ?
L   ¹¹that's / idea / a / Yes, / brilliant !
I   ¹²it's / try / Well, / worth / a / definitely .
D   ¹³sure / good / I'm / Sorry, / a / that's / idea / not .
     For one thing, celebrities are expensive. And also …

b Work in pairs. Compare answers.

7 a Your class is going to organise a festival at your school, college or university. Work in pairs. Think of ideas for these topics. Use language from **4a** in your discussion.

- when and where to have the festival
- music
- competitions
- other types of entertainment
- food and drink
- how to pay for the festival
- how to advertise the festival
- any other ideas

b Work in groups of four. Discuss the festival with your partners and decide on the things in **7a**. Make notes of any decisions your group makes.

> May I make a suggestion?
> Yes, of course.
> How about having the festival at the end of term?
> Yes, that's not a bad idea.

c Tell the class about your group's plans for your festival. Which festival will be the best, do you think?

HELP WITH PRONUNCIATION
Words ending in *-ate*

1 a CD2 13 Listen and notice the two ways we say *-ate* at the end of words. How do we usually say *-ate* at the end of: verbs? nouns and adjectives?

1   /eɪt/   educ**ate**   oper**ate**   investig**ate**   demonstr**ate**
2   /ət/   fortun**ate**   intermedi**ate**   certific**ate**   priv**ate**

b Listen again and practise.

2 a Work in pairs. Match the way we say *-ate* at the end of these words to sounds 1 or 2 in **1a**.

decorate 1   considerate   donate
immediate   create   climate   meditate
pirate   appreciate   chocolate

TIP • A few words ending in *-ate* can be verbs and nouns or adjectives: *graduate* /eɪt/ (verb); *a graduate* /ət/ (noun); *separate* /eɪt/ (verb); *separate* /ət/ (adjective).

b CD2 14 Listen and check. Listen again and practise.

3 Work in pairs. Take turns to say these sentences. Check your partner's pronunciation.

1   I get a certificate from my intermediate English class.
2   We're fortunate that people donate money to charity.
3   Some of our graduates investigate climate change.
4   She's going to graduate from a private university.
5   They educate and meditate in separate rooms.
6   Considerate people appreciate good chocolate!

continue2learn

■ **Vocabulary, Grammar and Real World**
  ■ **Extra Practice 6 and Progress Portfolio 6** p120
  ■ **Language Summary 6** p141
  ■ **6A–D** Workbook p30

■ **Reading and Writing**
  ■ **Portfolio 6** Letters to a newspaper Workbook p74
    Reading an article and two comments
    Writing giving an opinion

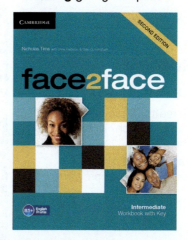

7A Have a go!

Vocabulary goals and achievements
Grammar ability: *be able to*, *manage*, *be useless at*, etc.

QUICK REVIEW Discussion language
Decide if you agree or disagree with these sentences: 1 Video games are bad for children. 2 People depend on computers too much. 3 Twenty is too young to get married. Then work in groups and discuss the sentences.

Vocabulary and Speaking
Goals and achievements

1 a Look at these questions. Which of the words/phrases in bold do you know? Check new words/phrases in **VOCABULARY 7.1** p143.

1 Would you like to **have the opportunity** to travel more than you do now?
2 Do you know any people who have **achieved their goals** in life?
3 What do you **put a lot of effort into**?
4 Have you ever **messed up** an exam or an interview?
5 Do you ever **dream of** becoming rich or famous?
6 Do you think you've **made the most of** the opportunities you've had in life?
7 Do you always try to **do your best** at everything you do?
8 Think of a time when you weren't successful at something. What **went wrong**?
9 Do you enjoy **taking part in** competitive sports?
10 Do you think that parents should always **encourage** their children to do what they want in life?

b Work in pairs. Ask and answer the questions. Ask follow-up questions if possible.

> Would you like to have the opportunity to travel more than you do now?
>> Yes, definitely.
> Where would you like to go?

Speaking and Reading

2 Work in new pairs. Discuss these questions.
1 Do you ever watch reality TV programmes? If so, which ones do you watch? If not, why don't you watch them?
2 Would you like to appear on a reality TV programme yourself? If so, which programme? If not, why not?

3 a Read the web page about a new reality TV programme called *Have a go!*. Complete these sentences.

1 Contestants on *Have a go!* have to … *learn a new skill.*
2 Vicky's teacher has been an opera singer for …
3 Vicky thought that the most difficult thing was …
4 She was surprised at the end of the programme because …
5 Ben thinks the most important part of being a magician is …
6 He says that he can't do …
7 He's planning to …

b Read about the contestants again. Find all the words/phrases in bold in **1a**.

Have a go!
is a new reality TV show where members of the public have just four weeks to learn a new skill before they perform live in front of a studio audience. Here's how last week's contestants felt about the experience.

Vicky, opera singer
Four weeks ago I didn't have a clue how to sing opera. I'd never sung in public in my life, apart from karaoke, and I'd never dreamed of singing onstage. Luckily I had a fabulous teacher, Irene, who's been an opera singer for over twenty years. She's very good at encouraging people and I was determined to make the most of the opportunity. At first I found it impossible to breathe and sing at the same time, but the more I practised, the better I got. The hardest part was learning the words, which were in Italian! I was useless at learning languages at school and I was terrified of forgetting the words. Fortunately I was able to give a good performance – and I couldn't believe it when they told me I'd won! It shows that if you put a lot of effort into something, you can achieve your goals.

Ben, magician
I used to love magic when I was a kid, but I had no idea how to do any magic tricks. So when I had the opportunity to become a magician I jumped at the chance. My teacher, Silvio, is a very talented magician and he knows how to do some really amazing tricks. The most important part of being a magician is misdirection – making people look where you want them to. I found some of the tricks quite easy to learn, but I'm no good at doing card tricks – they always seem to go wrong! Before I went onstage yesterday I was incredibly nervous, but I managed to do all the tricks without messing them up. I was disappointed that I wasn't able to win, but I did my best and really enjoyed taking part in the programme. I'm going to continue doing magic – and I'll always be popular at kids' parties!

Ben

HELP WITH GRAMMAR Ability

4 a Look at the words/phrases in blue on the web page. Match them to these meanings.
- things you can or could do
- things you can't or couldn't do

b Look at this sentence. Then answer the questions.

I managed to do all the tricks without messing them up.

1 Did Ben do all the magic tricks successfully?
2 Was this easy or difficult for him?

c Look at the web page again. Then complete these phrases with *infinitive*, *infinitive with to* or *verb+ing*.

1 not have a clue how + *infinitive with to*
2 be quite/very/really good at + …
3 find something impossible/quite easy + …
4 be useless at + …
5 (not) be able to + …
6 have no idea how + …
7 know how + …
8 be no good at + …
9 manage + …

d Which other adjectives can we use with: *be* + adjective + *at*?

be brilliant at   be hopeless at

e Check in GRAMMAR 7.1 p144.

5 CD2 16 PRONUNCIATION Listen and practise. Copy the stress and weak forms.

I didn't have a clue how to /tə/ sing opera.
She's very good at /ət/ encouraging people.

6 a Read about Zoe and Vince. Did Zoe enjoy appearing on *Have a go!*? If not, why not?

b Read about Zoe and Vince again. Put the verbs in brackets in the correct form.

Zoe and Vince, ballroom dancers

ZOE I was quite good at ¹ *dancing* (dance) at school and Vince knows how ² _____ (salsa), but neither of us had a clue how ³ _____ (do) ballroom dancing. Our teacher, Evelyn, spent four weeks trying to teach us a three-minute dance sequence. I was able to ⁴ _____ (learn) the dance quite quickly, but Vince found it difficult ⁵ _____ (remember) all the steps and he had no idea how ⁶ _____ (catch) me correctly. We practised and practised, but unfortunately it all went wrong on the night. Halfway through the dance Vince missed a catch and I fell onto the floor. We managed ⁷ _____ (carry on) and finish the dance, but I was really upset that Vince had messed up our big opportunity to become famous. I didn't think he'd be so hopeless at ⁸ _____ (dance) in public. My friends had a good laugh about it, though!

7 a Rewrite these sentences using the words in brackets.

1 I can play tennis quite well. (good)
  I'm quite good at playing tennis.
2 I can't remember people's names. (useless)
3 I don't know how to cook. (idea)
4 I can understand songs in English. (find / easy)
5 I was able to run 15 km last weekend. (manage)
6 I have no idea how to change a wheel on a car. (clue)
7 I can't type without looking at the keyboard. (find / impossible)
8 I find it hard to make decisions. (no good)
9 I know someone who can play the guitar very well. (brilliant)

b Work in pairs. Compare sentences. Are any true for you?

Get ready … Get it right!

8 Write three true sentences and three false sentences about things you can and can't do. Use a different phrase from **4c** in each sentence.

I'm quite good at doing crosswords.
I have no idea how to ride a motorbike.

9 a Work in pairs. Take turns to say your sentences. Your partner can ask two questions about each sentence. Then guess if your partner's sentences are true or false.

b Tell the class two things your partner can or can't do. Which student has the most interesting or unusual ability?

Vicky

7B What would you do?

Vocabulary computers (1)
Grammar second conditional

QUICK REVIEW **Ability** Write one thing: you're quite good at; you haven't got a clue how to do; you were able to do when you were a child; you know how to do; you never managed to do. Work in pairs. Tell each other about the things on your list.

Vocabulary and Speaking
Computers (1)

 a Work in pairs. Which of these words/phrases connected to computers do you know? Check new words/phrases in **VOCABULARY 7.2** p143.

> a password   install software   back up
> store   a hard drive   a memory stick   spam
> an attachment   a virus   crash   copy in
> forward   delete   print   scan   WiFi

b Work on your own. Write five questions about computers to ask your partner. Use vocabulary in **1a**.

Do you store all your photos on your hard drive?

When did you last install some software onto your computer?

c Work with your partner. Ask and answer your questions. Ask follow-up questions if possible.

> Do you store all your photos on your hard drive?

> No, I store them online.

Speaking and Listening

 a Work in pairs. Look at the photos. Why do you think the internet is important to each person's company?

b **CD2** 17 Listen and check your answers. What disadvantage of the internet does each person talk about?

c Work with your partner. Match these sentences to the people in the photos.
1 If I lost my laptop, I'd probably lose my job!
2 If the internet didn't exist, I wouldn't have a business.
3 If we didn't have WiFi, this place would be empty.
4 We'd lose a lot of customers if our website crashed.
5 If they turned off their computers, they might make some new friends.
6 If we didn't have so many online meetings, I could get out of the office more often.

d Listen again and check.

Judy, company director

HELP WITH GRAMMAR Second conditional

 a Look at sentences 1–4 in **2c**. Choose the correct words/phrases in these rules.
- We use the second conditional to talk about *real/imaginary* situations.
- The second conditional talks about *the present or future/ the past*.
- In the *if clause/main clause* we use the Past Simple.
- In the *if clause/main clause* we use 'd, would or wouldn't + infinitive.

b Look at these sentences. Then answer the questions.
A *If I have enough money, I'll buy a new laptop.*
B *If I had enough money, I'd buy a new laptop.*
1 Which sentence is a real possibility (the person might buy a new laptop)?
2 Which sentence is an imaginary situation (the person can't buy a new laptop)?

TIP • We can say *If I/he/she/it was* … or *If I/he/she/it were* … in the second conditional.

c Look at sentences 5 and 6 in **2c**. Which modal verb can we use in the main clause to mean: would perhaps? would be able to?

d Fill in the gaps in these questions with *if, do* or *would*. What are the short answers for question 2?
1 What _____ you _____ _____ you lost your laptop?
2 _____ someone asked you to lend them your computer, _____ you _____ it?

e Check in **GRAMMAR 7.2** p144.

4 **CD2** 18 **PRONUNCIATION** Listen and practise. Copy the stress and contractions (*I'd*, etc.).

I'd probably lose my job →
If I lost my laptop, I'd probably lose my job!

Wesley, café owner

Frank, sales manager

5
a Fill in the gaps with the correct form of the verbs in brackets. Then complete the sentences for you.

1 If I _____ (win) a holiday anywhere in the world, I _____ (go) to …
2 If I _____ (not live) where I do, I _____ (like) to live in …
3 If I _____ (can) change places with one person in the world, I _____ (choose) …
4 If I _____ (be) a film star, I _____ (like) to make a film with …
5 If I _____ (live) in a different country, I _____ (miss) …
6 If I _____ (can) talk to a famous person from history, I _____ (talk) to … about …

b Work in pairs and compare sentences. Continue the conversations if possible.

> If I won a holiday, I'd go to Africa.
>
> What would you do there?
>
> I'd go on a safari.

6 Work in new pairs. Student A p105. Student B p110.

HELP WITH LISTENING
First or second conditional

7 a CD2 19 Listen to these sentences. Notice the difference between the verb forms. What is the difference in meaning?

If I have time, I'll help you.
If I had time, I'd help you.

b CD2 20 Listen to six pairs of sentences. Which do you hear first: the first conditional or the second conditional?

8 a Choose the correct words in these conversations.

1
PETE Oh, dear. I'll never finish these T-shirts by 5 o'clock.
JUDY Sorry, ¹*I'll/I'd* help you if I ²*don't/didn't* have all these calendars to do.
PETE If Megan ³*is/was* here, she ⁴*can/could* do some of them, but she's still on holiday.
JUDY Well, don't worry. If you ⁵*don't/didn't* finish them, ⁶*I'll/I'd* email the customer and explain.

2
FRANK What time's my online meeting with the sales reps?
RUTH It's at 3.30. But Brian emailed to say that he might not be able to do it. If he ⁷*misses/missed* the meeting, ⁸*I'll/I'd* ask him to call you tomorrow.
FRANK Great, thanks. And can you help me back up these documents online? I ⁹*won't/wouldn't* ask if I ¹⁰*know/knew* how to do it, but I'm useless at this kind of thing.
RUTH Yes, of course. If you ¹¹*give/gave* me your laptop, ¹²*I'll/I'd* do it now.

b CD2 21 Listen and check.

Get ready … Get it right!

9 a Write these things on a piece of paper. Don't write them in order.

- three of your possessions that you couldn't live without
- three things you don't have, but would like to have

a laptop   a car

b Write second conditionals about how your life would be different with or without these things.

If I didn't have a laptop, I couldn't work on the train.
If I had a car, I'd go away for the weekend more often.

10 a Work in pairs. Swap papers. Take turns to ask and answer questions about the things on your partner's paper.

> Have you got a laptop?
>
> Yes, I have.
>
> Why is it important to you?
>
> Because I travel a lot for work. If I didn't have a laptop, …

b Tell the class two things about your partner.

VOCABULARY AND SKILLS 7C — Social networking

Vocabulary computers (2); articles: *a*, *an*, *the*, no article
Skills Reading: a magazine article; Listening: an informal conversation

QUICK REVIEW Second conditional
Decide what you would do if you: won the lottery, were the leader of your country, spoke English fluently, were ten years younger. Work in groups and compare ideas. Which students have the same ideas as you?

Vocabulary and Speaking
Computers (2)

1 a Look at these sentences. Which of the words/phrases in bold do you know? Check new words/phrases in VOCABULARY 7.3 p143.
1 I'm on a **social networking site** such as Facebook, Google+ or Twitter.
2 I **update** my **status** every day.
3 I change my **profile** quite often.
4 I've **downloaded** one or two new apps recently.
5 I sometimes **upload** videos to websites like YouTube.
6 I sometimes **post comments** on news sites and **forums**.
7 I'm on Twitter and I **tweet** quite often.
8 I also **follow** some famous people on Twitter.
9 I often share **links** to interesting websites, blogs or videos with my friends.

b Work on your own. Tick the sentences that are true for you.

c Work in pairs. Compare sentences. Ask follow-up questions if possible.

Speaking and Reading

2 a Work in groups. Discuss these questions.
1 In what ways do social networking sites help people's social lives?
2 What problems can social networking sites cause?
3 How is social networking affecting teenagers and children, do you think?

b Before you read, check these words/phrases with your teacher or in a dictionary.

> a collection   lonely   loneliness
> bullying   be addicted to

c Read the article. Which of the ideas that you discussed in **2a** are mentioned in the article?

3 a Read the article again. Answer these questions.
1 Why doesn't Robin Dunbar think we can have 1,000 friends?
2 Why does the writer think some people collect friends?
3 How did people get a free burger from Burger King?
4 What does the British children's charity say about loneliness and online bullying?
5 What do some young people find difficult to cope with?
6 Why do professional people use sites like Linkedin?

b Work in pairs. Compare answers. Do you agree with the points discussed in the article? Why?/Why not?

The lonely generation?

These days, millions of people organise their lives on social networking sites like Facebook, Google+ or Twitter, and many of them can't go a day – or even an hour – without checking for status updates. But what effect is this having on society and how is it changing the way we see our friends?

The scientist Robin Dunbar suggests that the largest number of active social relationships a person's brain can deal with is 150. However, most people have hundreds, sometimes even thousands, of Facebook friends, partly because making friends online is so easy. When you receive a friend request, you just click 'Confirm' and you have a new person to add to your collection of online friends. But do you really want to be friends with the person, or are you just trying to appear more popular? To illustrate the point, the Burger King chain of restaurants in the USA offered to give people a free burger if they deleted 10 friends from their Facebook page. Amazingly, over 530,000 people did just that, which shows how little some people value many of these online friendships.

Experts are also concerned that spending so much time online is making children feel lonelier than ever before. According to a children's charity in the UK, the number of calls they receive about loneliness from teenage boys has gone up by 500% compared to five years ago. The charity also reports that online bullying is also increasing. In another report, a third of people at university said they spent too much time communicating online and not enough in person. So it's not surprising that young people who are addicted to social networking sites find it harder to form strong, long-lasting relationships. For them, to be offline is to be disconnected from their network of friends, which can be very hard to cope with.

Of course, you don't have to be at school or university to use social networking sites. Many professional people use networking sites like Linkedin to make work contacts. And of course being part of a global professional network means that people can make the most of opportunities anywhere in the world. So if you're a designer working in Dublin or an engineer who's moving to Egypt, the online community is one of the most effective ways to help your career.

Social networking sites are one of the most amazing success stories of the internet and Facebook now has over a billion users all over the world. However, the effect these sites are having on our friendships is changing our society forever.

Sorry – I'd love to come out, but I'm busy updating my Facebook status.

HELP WITH VOCABULARY
Articles: *a*, *an*, *the*, no article

4 **a** Look at the words/phrases in blue in the article. Match one word/phrase to each of these rules.

- **We use *a* or *an*:**
- a when we don't know, or it isn't important, which one. *a day*
- b with jobs.
- c to talk about a person or thing for the first time.
- **We use *the*:**
- d to talk about the same person or thing for the second/third/fourth, etc. time.
- e when there is only one (or only one in a particular place).
- f with countries that are groups of islands or states.
- g with superlatives.
- **We don't use an article:**
- h for most towns, cities, countries and continents.
- i to talk about people or things in general.
- j for some public places (school, hospital, etc.) when we talk about what they are used for in general.

b Check in VOCABULARY 7.4 p143.

5 **a** Look at the words/phrases in pink in the article. Match them to rules a–j in **4a**. There is one word/phrase for each rule.

b Work in pairs. Compare answers.

6 Work in new pairs. Student A p104. Student B p109.

Listening and Speaking

7 **a** CD2 22 Look at the photo of three work colleagues, Jenny, Simon and Gary. Then listen to them talking about how they use social networking sites. Put these topics in the order they talk about them.

- videos and YouTube
- how Jenny uses Facebook
- today's office meeting
- Twitter and tweeting
- number of Facebook friends
- how often Simon goes on Facebook

b Listen again. Are these sentences true or false?
1 All three people went to the meeting.
2 Simon goes on Facebook five times a day.
3 Jenny doesn't use Facebook as much as she used to.
4 She saw her friends more often because of Facebook.
5 Simon says that his sister has more Facebook friends than Jenny.
6 Gary likes following famous people on Twitter.
7 Simon watches videos of baby animals on YouTube.

c Work in pairs. Compare answers. If a sentence is false, explain why.

Jenny Gary Simon

HELP WITH LISTENING Weak forms (2)

- Remember: in sentences we say many small words with a schwa /ə/ sound. These are called weak forms.

8 **a** Work in pairs. How do we say the strong and weak forms of these words?

| do | you | at | for | of | and | to | can |

b CD2 23 Listen and notice the difference between the strong and weak forms of these words.

	strong	weak		strong	weak
are	/ɑː/	/ə/	but	/bʌt/	/bət/
was	/wɒz/	/wəz/	as	/æz/	/əz/
were	/wɜː/	/wə/	from	/frɒm/	/frəm/
your	/jɔː/	/jə/	them	/ðem/	/ðəm/

c Look at these sentences from the conversation. Which words do we hear as weak forms?
1 Here are your drinks. We were lucky to get a table, weren't we?
2 But I was spending hours and hours on it and it wasn't as much fun as it used to be.
3 No, but I like reading tweets from film stars and footballers and people like that.
4 Well, my wife posts videos of the children so our relatives can watch them.

d CD2 24 Listen and check.

e Look at Audio Script CD2 22 p165. Listen to the conversation again. Follow the sentence stress and notice the weak forms.

9 **a** Work in groups. Write a survey about the internet and social networking. Write at least five questions. Use words/phrases from **1a** or your own ideas.
1 *Which social networking sites are you on?*

b Ask other students in the class. Write the answers.

c Work in your groups. Compare answers.

d Tell the class what you found out about other students' social networking and internet habits.

59

7D REAL WORLD — Can you tell me ...?

Real World indirect and direct questions

QUICK REVIEW Computers Write eight words/phrases connected to computers (*update your status*, *blog*, etc.). Work in pairs. Compare lists. Then say when you last did some of the things on both lists: *I updated my Facebook status last night.*

Tanya   *Charlie*

Rebecca   *Charlie*

1 a Look at the photos. Where is Charlie in each photo? What do you think the people are talking about?

b VIDEO 7 CD2 25 Watch or listen to Charlie's conversations with a colleague, Tanya, and his wife, Rebecca. Then choose the correct words/phrases in these sentences.

Conversation 1
a Charlie and Tanya are discussing a *meeting/conference* next week.
b Their clients are arriving on *Monday/Tuesday* from *London/New York*.
c Charlie and Tanya are going to take the clients for lunch in a *hotel/pub*.
d Barry Mackenzie *is definitely/might be* coming to the meeting.

Conversation 2
e Harry's first birthday party is at *one/three* o'clock on *Friday/Saturday*.
f Rebecca's parents *are/aren't* staying with Charlie and Rebecca.
g They *know/don't know* how many people are coming to the party.
h Charlie *gets on/doesn't get on* well with Rebecca's uncle.

2 a VIDEO 7 CD2 25 Watch or listen again. Put these questions in the order you hear them.

Conversation 1
a Could you tell me what time it starts?
b Have you any idea if he's been invited?
c Can you tell me when they're arriving?
d Do you know whether we've booked them a hotel room?
e Do you think we should email everyone again?

Conversation 2
f When are they arriving?
g What time does it start?
h Should we email everyone again?
i Has he been invited?
j Have we booked them a hotel room?

b Work in pairs. Compare answers. Then match questions a–e to questions f–j.

REAL WORLD
Indirect and direct questions

3 a Look at indirect questions a–e and direct questions f–j in **2a**. Then choose the correct word in this rule.

- In more formal situations we often use *indirect/direct* questions because they sound more polite.

b Look again at questions a–e in **2a**. Notice the phrases in blue that we use to introduce indirect questions. Then choose the correct word/phrase in these rules.

- We use *if* or *whether* in indirect questions when there *is/isn't* a question word.
- In indirect questions, *if* and *whether* are *the same/different*.
- We *use/don't use* *if* or *whether* with *Do you think … ?*

c Look at the phrases in pink in questions a–e in **2a**. Then choose the correct word in the rule.

- In indirect questions, the main verb is in the *positive/question* form.

d Check in REAL WORLD 7.1 p144.

HELP WITH LISTENING
Intonation (2): being polite

- We know if people are being polite by how much their voices move up and down. If their voices are flat, they often sound rude or impatient.

4 CD2 26 Listen to the same questions said twice. Which sounds more polite, a or b?

1 (a) b   3 a b   5 a b
2 a b   4 a b

5 CD2 27 **PRONUNCIATION** Listen and practise the questions in **2a**. Copy the polite intonation.

Could you tell me what time it starts?

6 Put these words in order to make indirect questions.

1 whether / you / this / office / is / me / Can / tell / Mr Maxwell's ?

Can you tell me whether this is Mr Maxwell's office?

2 think / the meeting / be / will / you / Do / Elizabeth / at / tomorrow ?

3 Could / been / 's / me / how long / you / he / here / tell / working ?

4 Ismay and Ali / holiday / you / Do / going / are / on / know / when ?

5 idea / Have / if / went / Wayne / you / any / away / weekend / last ?

6 whether / you / Manchester / me / to / Can / goes / train / this / tell ?

b Work in pairs. Compare answers.

7 a Look at these direct questions that tourists often ask. Rewrite the questions as indirect questions. Use these phrases.

1 Is there a bookshop near here?
   Do you know …
2 How do I get to the station?
   Could you tell me …
3 Should I give taxi drivers a tip?
   Do you think …
4 What time do the banks close?
   Have you any idea …
5 Where's the nearest post office?
   Can you tell me …

b Imagine you're a tourist in the town/city you're in now. Write three more indirect questions to ask someone who lives here.

c Work in pairs. Take turns to be the tourist. Ask and answer the questions from **7a** and **7b**.

> Excuse me. Do you know if there's a bookshop near here?

> Yes, there is. Go along this road …

HELP WITH PRONUNCIATION
Natural rhythm

1 a CD2 28 Listen to these sentences. Notice the sentence stress, linking and weak forms in pink. These help to give English its natural rhythm.

1 Where would you live_if you had_a lot_of money?
2 I've been living_in_England for one_and_a half years.
3 While_I was_on my way home, I met_an_old friend.
4 Who do you think_I should invite to the wedding?

b Listen again and practise.

2 a Work in pairs. Mark the stress and linking in this conversation. Then circle the weak forms.

ANN Hi, Tom. What are you doing at the moment?
TOM I'm trying to download an attachment, but my laptop keeps crashing. Do you think it's got a virus?
ANN Maybe. Perhaps the software's a bit out of date. When did you last update it?
TOM I can't remember. And it slows down every time I try to send an email.
ANN I think it's time to get yourself a new computer.
TOM I was thinking exactly the same thing!

b Look at Audio Script CD2 29 p166. Then listen and check. Listen again and practise each line of the conversation.

c Work in pairs. Practise the conversation in **2a**. Check your partner's pronunciation. Take turns to be Tom.

continue2learn

■ **Vocabulary, Grammar and Real World**
   ■ **Extra Practice 7 and Progress Portfolio 7** p121
   ■ **Language Summary 7** p143
   ■ **7A–D** Workbook p35

■ **Reading and Writing**
   ■ **Portfolio 7** Giving instructions Workbook p76
     Reading instructions
     Writing connecting words (1): useful phrases

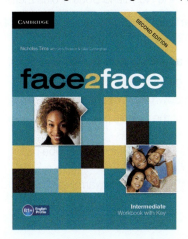

8A Angry planet

Vocabulary bad weather and natural disasters
Grammar the passive

QUICK REVIEW Indirect questions Imagine you are new to this town or city. Write three indirect questions you want to ask: *Can you tell me how to get to the nearest station?* Work in pairs. Ask and answer the questions.

Vocabulary and Speaking
Bad weather and natural disasters

1 Work in pairs. Which of these words do you know? Check new words in **VOCABULARY 8.1** p145.

a storm   thunder   lightning   a gale   a hurricane
a tornado   a heat wave   a blizzard   a flood
a tsunami   an earthquake   a drought   a landslide

2 Work in groups. Discuss these questions.
1 Have there been any stories about bad weather or natural disasters in the news recently? If so, where? What happened?
2 Have you ever experienced very bad weather? If so, tell the group what happened.
3 Do you think the weather where you live has changed since you were a child? If so, how?

Reading

3 a Before you read, check these words with your teacher or in a dictionary.

prevent   melt   deep   erupt   evaporate

b Work in pairs. Look at questions 1–5. What do you think the answers are? Give reasons if possible.
1 Can people predict where and when earthquakes will happen?
2 What can we do to help prevent droughts?
3 What causes a tsunami?
4 Is the Earth really getting warmer?
5 What will happen if the North and South Poles melt?

c Read the Q&A article. Match questions 1–5 in **3b** to paragraphs A–E. Were your answers correct?

d Read the article again. Answer these questions.
1 Why do tsunamis get stronger near the coast?
2 Why does cutting down trees cause droughts?
3 What percentage of the world's population live on or near the coast?
4 Which parts of the world are more likely to be hit by earthquakes?
5 What evidence is there for global warming?

Q&A Natural disasters

A
Tsunamis **are caused** by earthquakes under the ocean, or they **can** also **be caused** by a landslide or a volcano erupting. A large quantity of water is pushed to the surface of the ocean, creating waves. In the deep ocean these waves are small, but they get bigger and more dangerous as they get closer to the coast because the ocean is less deep there. The tsunami in South Asia in 2004 destroyed a large number of coastal towns and villages and about a quarter of a million people **were killed**.

B
A drought is caused by not enough rainfall, and of course we can't control the weather – not yet, anyway. Droughts often happen because all the trees **have been cut down** in a particular area. This means the rainwater evaporates because it isn't held in the ground by the trees. So part of the solution is to plant more trees. In north Africa, tens of millions of trees are going to be planted in the next decade, which may help to reduce the number of droughts in the region.

C
If this happens, the sea level will rise around the world and a lot of towns and cities on the coast **will be flooded**. This is a frightening thought because over half the world's population live near the coast and many of these places will be destroyed.

D
It's still not possible to make an accurate prediction of the place, time and strength of an earthquake. However, it is possible to predict which places **are going to be hit** by an earthquake sometime in the future. A recent report identified the five most likely places for future earthquakes as the Caribbean, Chile, Indonesia, Japan and North America.

E
Yes, it is. The world's temperature has been measured accurately for about 150 years and it shows that on average it has increased by about 1.5°C. Also, eight of the ten hottest years have been recorded in the last two decades, which is very good evidence that this increase in temperature **is being caused** by man-made climate change.

5 a Look again at the Q&A article. Underline other examples of the passive.

b Work in pairs. Compare answers.

6 CD2 30 **PRONUNCIATION** Listen and practise. Copy the stress and weak forms.

Tsunamis are /ə/ caused by earthquakes under the ocean.

7 a Read about Roy Sullivan. What happened to him?

The Earth ¹*hits/is hit* by lightning 8.6 million times a day. Scientists say there's a 1 in 3 million chance you ²*will hit/will be hit* by lightning, but that depends on how much time you ³*are spent/spend* outdoors. Roy Sullivan, a park ranger from Virginia, USA, ⁴*hit/was hit* by lightning seven times in his lifetime. On different occasions he ⁵*lost/was lost* his toenails, hair and eyebrows. The final lightning strike ⁶*happened/was happened* while he was fishing and he ⁷*took/was taken* to hospital with chest and stomach burns.

b Read the text again. Choose the correct verb forms.

8 a Look at the photo. Which city is it? What problems does this city have?

HELP WITH GRAMMAR The passive

4 a Look at these sentences. Then answer questions 1–4.

ACTIVE	Earthquakes under the ocean **cause** tsunamis.
PASSIVE	Tsunamis **are caused** by earthquakes under the ocean.

1 What is the subject of each sentence?
2 What is the object of the active sentence?
3 In which sentence is the focus on: tsunamis? earthquakes under the ocean?
4 In which sentence do we use *by* to say what does the action (the agent)?

b Look at this sentence. Then choose the correct phrase in the rule.

Droughts often happen because all the trees have been cut down.

- We often use the passive when *we know/we don't know* who or what did the action.

c Look at the passive forms in bold in the article. Write them in the table.

verb form	be	past participle
Present Simple	are	caused
Present Continuous		
Present Perfect Simple		
Past Simple		
be going to		
will		
can		

d How do we make negatives in the passive?

e Check in GRAMMAR 8.1 ▶ p146.

b Put the verbs in the correct form of the passive. There is sometimes more than one possible answer.

These days parts of Venice ¹_____ (flood) one day in three. People believe the water will rise another 20 cm in the next 50 years. This means that Venice ²_____ (flood) much more often. A lot of money ³_____ (already collect) for the Save Venice Fund and now many old buildings ⁴_____ (repair). However, more money must ⁵_____ (find) quickly and some people don't think the city can ⁶_____ (save). Most experts agree that if important work ⁷_____ (not do) soon, some of the world's most beautiful buildings ⁸_____ (lose) forever.

Get ready ... Get it right!

9 Work in groups. Group A p106. Group B p111.

8B Recycle!

Vocabulary containers
Grammar quantifiers: *a bit of, too much/many, (not) enough, plenty of,* etc.

QUICK REVIEW Weather Write five weather words that are connected to you, or to people you know. Work in pairs and compare words. Tell your partner why you have chosen your five words: *I chose 'a storm' because I saw an amazing storm last month.*

Vocabulary Containers

1 a Work in pairs. Match the containers in A to the things in B. Find at least two things for each container. Then check in **VOCABULARY 8.2** ▶ p145.

A
a bottle of   a bag of   a tin of   a box of
a can of   a carton of   a jar of   a packet of

B
milk   honey   tuna   biscuits   sweets   cat food   orange juice
beer   jam   marmalade   ketchup   soup   chocolates
potatoes   beans   olive oil   tissues   lemonade   crisps

b Work with your partner. What other words can you use with the containers in **1a**?

a packet of cigarettes   a tin of dog food

2 a Work in new pairs. Test your partner on the phrases in **1a** and **1b**.

milk   a bottle of milk or a carton of milk

b Tell your partner which things in **1a** are in your kitchen.

Speaking and Listening

3 Work in groups. Discuss these questions.
1 Are there any recycling laws in your country? If so, what are they?
2 Can you recycle things where you live? If so, what do you recycle?
3 What do you throw away that could be recycled?

4 a Look at the picture. Which things from **1a** can you see in the kitchen?

b **CD2 ▶ 31** Listen to James, Val and Pete. Choose the correct answers.
1 Val and Pete *don't have anything/have something* to eat.
2 James *recycles some/doesn't recycle any* of his rubbish.
3 The UK recycles *70%/40%* of its rubbish.
4 British people throw away *3/7* times their own body weight in rubbish every year.
5 Parts for fridges can be made from *tins/plastic bottles*.
6 James *is/isn't* going to recycle in the future.

64

5 a Work in pairs. Who says these sentences, Val, Pete or James?

1 Oh, there's a bit of pasta left if you're hungry. *James*
2 Well, I've found some coffee, but there's no sugar.
3 There's enough milk for two cups, but not enough for three.
4 There are plenty of tins of cat food in the cupboard.
5 Too much rubbish is just thrown away.
6 Hardly any people in our building recycle stuff.
7 And there aren't enough places to recycle in this city.
8 Look, there's loads of paper and several plastic bottles.
9 Well, there's plenty of information on the internet.
10 Yes, too many people just don't make the effort.
11 I've got a few friends who recycle things.
12 We made a little progress there, I think.

b CD2 31 Listen again and check.

HELP WITH GRAMMAR
Quantifiers

6 a Look at the words in pink in **5a**. Are they countable nouns (C) or uncountable nouns (U)?

b Look at the words/phrases in blue in **5a**. Write them in the table.

quantity	plural countable nouns (*bottles*, *tins*, etc.)	uncountable nouns (*rubbish*, *stuff*, etc.)
nothing	not any / no	not any
a small quantity	not many / hardly any	not much
a large quantity	a lot of/lots of / loads of	a lot of/lots of
more than we want		
less than we want		
the correct quantity	enough	

c Look at these sentences. Then choose the correct words in the rules.

I've found some coffee.   *There isn't any sugar.*
Is there any milk?   *There's a lot of stuff here.*
I haven't got many cups.   *Is there much rubbish?*

- We usually use *some/any* in positive sentences.
- We usually use *some/any* in negative sentences and questions.
- We don't usually use *a lot of/much* or *many* in positive sentences.

d Check in GRAMMAR 8.2 p146.

HELP WITH LISTENING
Quantifiers

7 a CD2 32 Listen and write the sentences you hear. You will hear each sentence twice.

b How many words are there in each sentence? Contractions (*there's*, etc.) count as two words.

c Work in pairs. Compare sentences. Underline the quantifiers in each sentence.

8 CD2 33 PRONUNCIATION Listen again and practise. Copy the linking.

I think there's‿a bit‿of milk‿in the fridge.

9 a Choose the correct words/phrases.

1 There are *no/any* recycling bins in my street.
2 I probably drink *too much/too many* coffee.
3 I got *too many/hardly any* sleep last night.
4 I know *a few/a little* words in other languages.
5 I know *a bit of/several* people from the UK.
6 I always have *many/plenty of* time to do my homework.
7 I haven't got *enough/several* money to go on holiday.
8 I've been to *some/any* interesting places.
9 I probably eat *too much/too many* sweets.
10 I usually have *several/a little* milk in my tea.

b Tick the sentences in **9a** that are true for you.

c Work in pairs. Take turns to say your true sentences. Ask follow-up questions if possible.

Get ready ... Get it right!

10 Write four good things and four bad things about the town or city you are in now. Use these ideas and your own. Use the quantifiers from **6b** in your sentences.

rubbish	recycling bins	traffic	cycle lanes
parks	public transport	places to park
pollution	shops	places to go at night
cinemas	art galleries	noise at night

There's too much rubbish in the streets.
There aren't enough recycling bins.

11 a Work in groups. Tell the other students your sentences. Discuss your ideas. Do you agree? Then choose the two best and two worst things about this town or city.

b Tell the class the two best and two worst things about this town or city.

VOCABULARY AND SKILLS 8C — Dangers at sea

Vocabulary word building (2): prefixes and opposites, other prefixes and suffixes
Skills Listening: a TV news report; Reading: a newspaper article

QUICK REVIEW Containers Work in pairs. Take turns to say a container. Your partner says as many things as possible that can come in that container: **A** *A tin.* **B** *Soup, beans, … .*

Speaking and Listening

1 Work in groups. Discuss these questions.
1 When did you last go to the beach? Where was it? What did you do there?
2 Do you have a favourite beach? If so, where is it?
3 What kind of problems can people have at the beach?

2 a Before you listen, check these words with your teacher or in a dictionary.

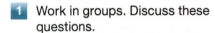
a shark   attack
bite (bit, bitten)   oxygen

b CD2 34 Listen to a TV news report. Answer these questions.
1 What has happened in the USA?
2 What are dead zones?
3 What causes dead zones?
4 How many dead zones are there in the world?

c Listen again. Choose the correct answers.
1 There have been *six/eight* shark attacks in the USA this year.
2 The tourist was attacked *a long way from/quite near* the beach.
3 He was bitten on the *arm/leg*.
4 The dead zone off the coast of Texas is *quite small/very big*.
5 There are *a lot/a few* more dead zones than there were five years ago.
6 The evening is a *good/bad* time to go swimming near a dead zone.
7 The Texas Wildlife Department *are/aren't* telling people to stop swimming in the sea.

HELP WITH LISTENING Linking (3): review

3 a Look at this sentence from the news report. Notice the links. Then choose the correct words in the rules.

So what turns an area /r/ of the /j/ ocean into /w/ a dead zone?

- We usually link words that end in a consonant sound with words that start with a *consonant/vowel* sound.
- When a word ends in a *consonant/vowel* sound and the next word also starts with a *consonant/vowel* sound, we often link these words with a /w/, /j/ or /r/ sound.

b Work in pairs. Look at these sentences from the beginning of the news report. Draw the consonant–vowel links and complete the extra linking sounds.

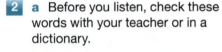
A British tourist has been attacked by /j/ a shark off the coast of Texas, making it the __/__ eighth shark attack in America this year. We now go __/__ over live to __/__ Andrew __/__ Evans for __/__ a special report. Andrew, I __/__ understand that the man didn't do __/__ anything unusual to cause this attack.

c Look at Audio Script CD2 34 p166. Check your answers. Then listen to the news report again and notice the different types of linking.

Reading, Vocabulary and Speaking

4 a Before you read, check these words with your teacher or in a dictionary.

conscious   estimate   a park ranger   harm   a lifeguard   attach

b Look at the title of the article. What do you think happened to Jesse?

c Read the article. Were you correct?

Saving Jesse's Arm

Lucy Atkins describes the battle to save the life of a young boy.

At about 8 p.m. on July 6th, eight-year-old Jesse Arbogast was playing in the sea in a National Park near Pensacola, Florida. It was the end of a perfect day at the beach with his uncle and aunt. Then disaster struck. Jesse was attacked by a two-metre-long male shark, which bit off his right arm from the shoulder and also took a bite out of his leg. By the time his uncle and aunt pulled Jesse out of the water, he was unconscious and had already lost a lot of blood.

While Jesse's aunt was giving the boy the kiss of life, his uncle, Vance Flosenzier, ran into the sea and disappeared under the water. Amazingly, he managed to catch the 90-kilo shark and pull it out of the water onto the beach. Although this might sound impossible, never underestimate a man's strength when a family member's life is in danger.

At that moment two park rangers arrived to help the family and one of them shot and killed the shark. Then he held open the shark's mouth while a volunteer firefighter reached down its throat and pulled out Jesse's arm.

A few minutes later, a helicopter took the boy and his arm to nearby Baptist Hospital, Pensacola, where Dr Ian Rogers and his medical team managed to reattach Jesse's arm in an eleven-hour operation. The doctors knew the operation had been a success when Jesse's fingers turned pink. Of course, after such a terrible accident nobody wants to be over-optimistic, but the medical team are hopeful Jesse will have full use of his arm in the future.

Although Jesse's story is terrifying, it would be incorrect to think that sharks are always so dangerous. Apparently this type of attack was very unusual and sharks are usually harmless to humans. "Shark attacks are very uncommon," agrees JR Tomasovic, chief ranger at the Pensacola park. "You could go ten years without seeing another." However, he says that people shouldn't be irresponsible and should only swim on beaches where there are lifeguards.

5 Read the article again. Tick the true sentences. Correct the false ones.

1 The shark bit off part of Jesse's arm.
2 Jesse's uncle pulled the shark out of the water by himself.
3 Jesse's uncle shot the shark and then got Jesse's arm from inside it.
4 Jesse might be able to use his arm normally in the future.
5 The park ranger said shark attacks are very common.

HELP WITH VOCABULARY
Word building (2): prefixes and opposites, other prefixes and suffixes

6 a Look at the words in blue in the article. Underline the prefixes. Then fill in the gaps in this rule.

- We often use the prefixes *un-*, *dis-*, _____, _____ and _____ to make opposites of words.

b Work in pairs. What are the opposites of these adjectives?

believable	patient	selfish	honest
considerate	polite	organised	regular
reliable	loyal	mature	ambitious
formal	similar	sensitive	helpful

c Check in **VOCABULARY 8.3** p145.

7 a Look at the words in pink in the article. Underline the prefixes and suffixes. Then complete the table with these meanings and the words in pink.

| ~~not enough~~ | too much | without |
| with | do something again | |

prefix/suffix	meaning	examples
under-	not enough	underestimate
re-		
over-		
-ful		
-less		

b Work in pairs. Which prefixes and suffixes can you use with these words? There is sometimes more than one possible answer.

| paid | write | pain | sleep | charge |
| care | marry | success | play | use |

c Check in **VOCABULARY 8.4** p145.

8 a Think of an exciting or frightening experience that has happened to you, or someone you know. Make notes on these things.

- who the story is about
- when and where it happened
- how the story started
- the main events of the story
- what happened in the end

b Work in groups. Take turns to tell your story. Which story do you think is the most exciting or frightening?

c Tell the class about the best story from your group.

REAL WORLD
8D A hiking trip

Real World warnings and advice

QUICK REVIEW Word building Write six words with prefixes or suffixes: *impatient, useless,* etc. Work in pairs. Take turns to say sentences with your partner's words: *My brother's usually quite impatient.*

1 Work in groups. Discuss these questions.
1. Have you ever been hiking or camping? If so, where did you go? If not, would you like to?
2. What problems do you think people can have if they're hiking or camping in the mountains?

Lisa   Rebecca

2 a Look at the photo. Which of these things can you see? Check new words/phrases with your teacher or in a dictionary.

a tent	a camping stove	waterproof clothing
a rucksack	a compass	a sleeping bag
walking boots	spare batteries	a torch

b VIDEO 8 CD2 35 Watch or listen to Lisa and Rebecca's conversation. Put these things in the order they talk about them. There are two things they don't talk about.

- what to wear
- Daniel's tent
- getting lost
- hotels and pubs
- food to take
- dangerous animals
- the best mountains
- crossing rivers

c Watch or listen again. Make a list of all the things that Rebecca advises Lisa to take with her on her hiking trip.

a new tent

d Work in pairs. Compare lists. Why does Rebecca think Lisa should take each thing?

REAL WORLD Warnings and advice
- We give warnings when we think something might be dangerous.

3 a Write these headings in the correct places a–d.

giving advice   responding to advice or warnings
asking for advice   giving warnings

a _____

Could you give me some advice?
What (else) do you think we should take with us?
What should we do if we get lost?
Do you think it's a good idea to tell someone where we're going?

b _____

If I were you, I'd <u>buy</u> a new tent.
Make sure you take plenty of warm clothes.
It's a good idea <u>to take</u> some waterproof clothing **in case** it rains.
Don't forget <u>to take</u> a map.
It's worth <u>taking</u> a compass, **just in case**.
You'd better <u>take</u> a torch **in case** you have to walk in the dark.

c _____

Don't wear new boots **or else** you'll get blisters.
Whatever you do, <u>don't lose</u> sight of each other.
Be careful when you're crossing rivers.
Watch out for wolves.

d _____

That's really useful, thanks.
That's a good idea. I hadn't thought of that.
Right, thanks. That's really helpful.
That sounds like good advice.

b Look at the underlined verb forms in **3a**. Then complete these phrases with *imperative, infinitive, verb+ing* or *infinitive with to*.

1. If I were you, I'd + …
2. You'd better + …
3. It's a good idea + …
4. Don't forget + …
5. It's worth + …
6. Whatever you do, + …

c Check in REAL WORLD 8.1 p146.

4 CD2 36 PRONUNCIATION Listen and practise the sentences in **3a**. Copy the stress.

Could you give me some advice?

5 a Choose the correct words/phrases in these sentences.

MIA I'm going sailing with some friends next weekend. ¹*Should*/*Could* you give me ²*an*/*some* advice?

ZAK Well, ³*make*/*making* sure you always hold onto something. And ⁴*you'll*/*you'd* better ⁵*wear*/*wearing* a lifejacket ⁶*in*/*on* case you fall in.

MIA Yes, that sounds ⁷*like*/*as* good advice. What do you think ⁸*I should*/*should I* take with me?

ZAK Well, it's worth ⁹*take*/*taking* some suncream, ¹⁰*just*/*only* in case. You can get very burnt on boats without realising it.

MIA ¹¹*That's*/*This is* a good idea. I ¹²*haven't*/*hadn't* thought of that. And what should we do ¹³*if*/*in case* the weather changes?

ZAK If I ¹⁴*am*/*were* you, ¹⁵*I'll*/*I'd* come back in immediately. Better safe than sorry. Oh, and watch out ¹⁶*from*/*for* other boats or ferries.

MIA Right, thanks. That's really ¹⁷*help*/*helpful*.

b Work in pairs. Compare answers. Then practise the conversation. Take turns to be Mia.

6 a Look at this advice for people visiting the UK. Fill in the gaps with these words/phrases.

| ~~Don't forget~~ Make sure   It's a good idea   Be careful |
| It's worth   Whatever you do,   Don't   If I were you, |

1 *Don't forget* to book hotels before you travel.
2 _____ you take some warm clothes.
3 _____ don't drive when you're in London. Use the tube instead.
4 _____ to book theatre tickets in advance.
5 _____ spend all your time in London. There's so much to see in the rest of the UK.
6 _____ when crossing the road because they drive on the left.
7 _____ I'd visit the UK in May. It's really beautiful at that time of year.
8 _____ taking an umbrella, just in case!

b Work in pairs. Compare answers.

7 a Write five warnings or pieces of advice for people visiting your country or city. Use phrases from **3a**.

b Work in groups. Take turns to say your sentences. If you're from the same country or city, do you agree with your partners' sentences? Which warning or piece of advice do you think is the most useful?

HELP WITH PRONUNCIATION
/ɪə/, /eə/ and /ɜː/

1 a CD2 ▶ 37 Listen and notice three ways we say the letters *ear*.

1 /ɪə/   **ear**   b**ear**d   disapp**ear**
2 /eə/   w**ear**   b**ear**   p**ear**
3 /ɜː/   **ear**thquake   l**ear**n   s**ear**ch

b Listen again and practise. Do we usually say the letter *r* in the words in **1a**?

2 a Work in pairs. Look at the letters in bold in these words. Match the words to sounds 1–3 in **1a**.

h**ear** 1	**ear**ly	sc**ar**ed	nightm**ar**e	**ear**n
n**ear**	softw**ar**e	f**ear**	sp**ar**e	h**ear**d	b**ee**r
st**air**s	m**ur**der	volunt**eer**	t**ur**n	engin**eer**
f**air**	f**ur**ther	ch**eer**	h**air**	b**ur**glar

b CD2 ▶ 38 Listen and check. Listen again and practise. What other ways can we spell sounds 1–3 in **1a**?

3 Work in pairs. Look at the letters in bold. Circle the word with a different sound.

1 b**ur**glar   (n**ear**)   l**ear**n   5 disapp**ear**   f**ear**   b**ear**
2 b**ear**d   m**ur**der   b**eer**   6 w**ear**   **ear**thquake   t**ur**n
3 s**ear**ch   p**ear**   st**air**s   7 nightm**ar**e   sc**ar**ed   **ear**
4 h**ear**   h**ear**d   f**ur**ther   8 engin**eer**   **ear**ly   ch**eer**

continue2learn

■ **Vocabulary, Grammar and Real World**
  ■ **Extra Practice 8 and Progress Portfolio 8** p122
  ■ **Language Summary 8** p145
  ■ **8A–D** Workbook p40

■ **Reading and Writing**
  ■ **Portfolio 8** Problems and solutions Workbook p78
     Reading letters to an online newspaper
     Writing organising a letter/email: connecting words (2), the passive

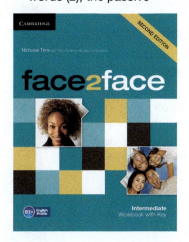

69

9A Get healthy!

Vocabulary health
Grammar relative clauses with *who*, *that*, *which*, *whose*, *where* and *when*

QUICK REVIEW Warnings and advice
Imagine a friend from the UK is coming to live and work in your town/city. Think of five warnings or pieces of advice to give your friend. Work in pairs. Compare sentences. What's the most important warning or piece of advice?

Reading and Listening

1 Work in groups. Discuss these questions.

1. Do you think you have a healthy diet? Why?/Why not?
2. How often do you eat things that you know are bad for you?
3. Has your diet changed since you were a child? If so, how?

2 a Before you read, check these words with your teacher or in a dictionary.

| a fast | go on a retreat | toxins | digest |

b Read the article. Did the journalist feel healthier after doing the retreat? Why?/Why not?

3 a Read the article again. Tick the true sentences. Correct the false ones.

1. You only drink vegetable juice on the retreat.
2. Joanne wasn't looking forward to the experience.
3. Louise worked at the retreat centre.
4. Fasting helps your body get rid of toxins.
5. Joanne felt fine on day two of the retreat.
6. The fifth day was easier than the third day.
7. Joanne has changed her diet since the retreat.

b Work in pairs. Discuss these questions.

1. Would you like to go on a retreat like the one in the article? Why?/Why not?
2. Do you know anyone who has been on a retreat like this? If so, did they enjoy it? Why?/Why not?

Just Juice

Can giving up food really improve your health?
Joanne Fullerton spent a week at a retreat centre to find out.

When I arrived at the Just Juice Retreat Centre, I was feeling a bit nervous. I was going to do a seven-day fast, drinking only fresh organic fruit and vegetable juices. I'm the type of person ¹**that eats three meals a day** and can't wake up without a cappuccino, so the idea of living on juice for a week was rather terrifying.

After checking in, I was taken to the guest house ²**where everyone was staying**. Louise, the woman ³**who I was sharing a room with**, had been on the retreat four times and she looked healthier than anyone I'd ever met. According to Rachel Carr-Hill, the woman ⁴**whose fasting programme we were following**, going without food is one of the best things we can do for our health. The food ⁵**that we usually eat** contains toxins ⁶**which stay in our bodies** and stop our digestive system working properly. When we fast, our body doesn't have to digest food, so it has time to get rid of these toxins.

The first day started with yoga at seven o'clock and then we had 'breakfast' – a big glass of carrot juice. We spent the day listening to talks about health, having massages and relaxing, with a different juice meal every three hours. On the second day I had an awful headache and felt as if I was getting a cold. Apparently this was a normal reaction because my body was starting to get rid of the toxins. On day three my headache was much worse and this was also ⁷**when I started getting *really* hungry**. I began daydreaming about cheeseburgers, pasta, chocolate – anything but more juice. However, by day five the hunger had gone and I felt more relaxed than I'd been for years. At the end of the retreat I'd lost three kilos and felt like a new woman. Now I'm much more careful about what I eat – but I still can't live without my morning cappuccinos!

HELP WITH GRAMMAR
Relative clauses with *who*, *that*, *which*, *whose*, *where* and *when*

- We often use relative clauses to say which person, thing, place, etc. we are talking about.

4 a Look at the relative clauses in bold in the article. Then fill in the gaps with *who*, *that*, *which*, *whose*, *where* and *when*.

- In relative clauses we use:
1 _____ or _____ for people.
2 _____ or _____ for things.
3 _____ for places.
4 _____ for possessives.
5 _____ for times.

b Look at the underlined relative clauses in sentences A and B. Answer the questions and choose the correct word in the rule.

A I'm the type of person <u>that eats three meals a day</u>.
B The food <u>(that) we usually eat contains toxins</u>.

1 What is the subject of *eats* in sentence A?
2 What is the subject of *eat* in sentence B?

- We can leave out *who*, *that* or *which* when it **is/isn't** the subject of the relative clause.

c Check in GRAMMAR 9.1 ▶ p148.

5 a Fill in the gaps with *who*, *that*, *which*, *whose*, *where* or *when*. There can sometimes be more than one possible answer.

1 Most of the food _that_ I buy is organic.
2 I have some friends _____ are vegetarians.
3 I don't know anyone _____ has been on a fast.
4 The food _____ I had last night wasn't very healthy.
5 There's at least one person in my family _____ eats meat every day.
6 In my family, we usually eat vegetables _____ we buy in the market.
7 I don't know anyone _____ lifestyle is really healthy.
8 I tend to go to restaurants _____ they serve healthy food.
9 New Year is a time _____ I always eat too much.
10 I know a shop _____ you can buy really good fruit and vegetables.

b Look again at sentences 1–6 in **5a**. In which of these sentences can you leave out *who*, *that* or *which*?

c Tick the sentences in **5a** that are true for you.

d Work in groups. Compare your sentences. How many are the same?

Vocabulary and Speaking Health

6 a Work in pairs. Choose the correct words/phrases.

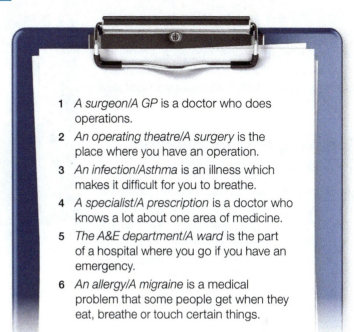

1 *A surgeon/A GP* is a doctor who does operations.
2 *An operating theatre/A surgery* is the place where you have an operation.
3 *An infection/Asthma* is an illness which makes it difficult for you to breathe.
4 *A specialist/A prescription* is a doctor who knows a lot about one area of medicine.
5 *The A&E department/A ward* is the part of a hospital where you go if you have an emergency.
6 *An allergy/A migraine* is a medical problem that some people get when they eat, breathe or touch certain things.

b CD2 ▶ 39 Listen and check. How many did you get right?

7 a Fill in the gaps in these sentences with the other words/phrases from **6a** and *who*, *that*, *which* or *where* if necessary.

1 _____ is an extremely painful headache _____ can also make you feel sick.
2 _____ is a big room with beds in a hospital _____ patients receive medical treatment.
3 _____ is a doctor _____ gives medical treatment to people _____ live in a particular area.
4 _____ is a building or an office _____ you can go and ask a GP or a dentist for medical advice.
5 _____ is a piece of paper _____ the doctor gives you so that you can get the medicine you need.
6 _____ is a disease in part of your body _____ is caused by bacteria or a virus.

b Check in VOCABULARY 9.1 ▶ p147.

8 Work in pairs. Test each other on the words in **6a** and **7a**.

What's a surgeon? — It's a doctor who does operations.

Get ready ... Get it right!

9 Work in groups. Group A p105. Group B p110.

9B Good news, bad news

Vocabulary collocations (3): the news
Grammar Present Perfect Simple active and passive for recent events

QUICK REVIEW Health Write four words/phrases connected to health. Work in pairs. Ask your partner to describe your words/phrases: **A** *What's a migraine?* **B** *It's a really bad headache which can make you feel sick.*

Speaking and Vocabulary
Collocations (3): the news

1 Work in groups. Discuss these questions.
1. Where do you get your news from: the TV, newspapers, the radio or the internet? Which do you prefer? Why?
2. Do you ever read, watch or listen to the news in English? If so, where?
3. What stories are in the news at the moment?

2 a Match the verbs in A to the words/phrases in B. Check in VOCABULARY 9.2 ▶ p147.

A	B
pay off	against something
take part	a debt
protest	a report
take	in a demonstration
publish	somebody to hospital
meet	an offer
discover	a target
accept/reject	a strike
go	something new
call off	on strike

b Work in pairs. Test each other on the phrases in **2a**.

 a strike   call off a strike

Listening

3 a Work in pairs. Look at photos A–D of today's main news stories. What do you think the stories are about?

b CD2 40 Listen to today's news. Put photos A–D in the same order as the news stories.

c Listen again and fill in the gaps in the speech bubbles.

A

B

C

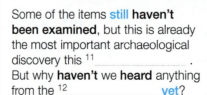

1 *World leaders* **have met** to discuss the global 2 _____ at the World Trade Summit in Hamburg.

At least 3 _____ people **have been arrested** and 4 _____ police officers **have been taken** to hospital.

A new report on the 5 _____ **has just been published**. The report shows that the UK **has failed** to meet its 6 _____ to reduce CO_2 emissions.

We **haven't met** our targets **yet**, that's true, but **we've made** good 7 _____ . The amount of CO_2 produced by the UK **has already been reduced** by 8 _____ in the last three years.

Over 9 _____ ancient gold and silver objects **have been discovered** by a retired 10 _____ in Wales.

Some of the items **still haven't been examined**, but this is already the most important archaeological discovery this 11 _____ . But why **haven't** we **heard** anything from the 12 _____ **yet**?

HELP WITH GRAMMAR
Present Perfect Simple active and passive for recent events

- **Remember**: we use the Present Perfect Simple for giving news about something that happened a short time ago, but we don't say exactly when.

4 **a** Look at these sentences from the news stories. Then answer the questions.

At least forty people **have been arrested**.
The UK **has failed** *to meet its targets.*

1 Which verb form in bold is in the Present Perfect Simple active? Which is in the Present Perfect Simple passive?
2 How do we make the Present Perfect Simple active and Present Perfect Simple passive?

b Look at the words in blue in the speech bubbles. What is the difference in meaning between these words? Where do they usually go in sentences?

TIP • We only use *still* in negative sentences with the Present Perfect Simple: *Some of the items still haven't been examined.*

c Check in **GRAMMAR 9.2** ▶ **p149**.

5 **a** Look again at the verb forms in bold in the speech bubbles. Which are in the Present Perfect Simple active? Which are in the Present Perfect Simple passive?

b Work in pairs. Compare answers.

Listening and Speaking

HELP WITH LISTENING
Present Perfect Simple active or passive

6 **a** **CD2 ▶ 41** Listen to these sentences. Notice the weak forms of *have*, *has* and *been*.

World leaders have /həv/ met to discuss the global economy.
A new report on the environment has /həz/ just been /bɪn/ published.

b **CD2 ▶ 42** Listen to eight sentences. Are the verbs in the Present Perfect Simple active (A) or passive (P)?

7 **CD2 ▶ 42** **PRONUNCIATION** Listen again and practise. Copy the stress and weak forms.

A new survey has /həz/ just been /bɪn/ published.

8 **a** Read these news stories. Put the verbs in brackets in the Present Perfect Simple active or passive.

The government's pay offer ¹_____ (reject) by the Transport Union. The union leader, Alan Stone, ²_____ (just confirm) that train drivers will go on strike at midnight. However, next week's postal strike ³_____ (call off) after the union accepted a pay offer of 3.4%.

Scientists in Cambridge ⁴_____ (find) the gene that causes asthma. The gene is one of many allergy genes that ⁵_____ (discover) in the last few years.

Rock singer Heidi Gee ⁶_____ (just arrive) in the UK for her sell-out tour. Her second album, *Serenity*, ⁷_____ (already sell) over five million copies.

And we ⁸_____ (just hear) that the actor Henry Robson ⁹_____ (take) to hospital after a car accident. His condition ¹⁰_____ (describe) as serious.

b **CD2 ▶ 43** Listen and check.

9 Put the words in brackets in the correct places in these sentences.

1 The strike has lasted three weeks. (already)
2 The Prime Minister has arrived. (just)
3 The relatives haven't been told. (yet)
4 He's been questioned by the police. (already)
5 Two men have been arrested. (just)
6 Has the match finished? (yet)
7 The results haven't been published. (still)

Get ready … Get it right!

10 Work in groups. Group A p104. Group B p109.

VOCABULARY AND SKILLS 9C

Human behaviour

Vocabulary body movements and responses; connecting words
Skills Reading: a magazine article; Listening: a TV interview

QUICK REVIEW **Present Perfect Simple active and passive** Think of three pieces of news about yourself, your family or friends: *I've just booked a holiday. My brother has just been promoted.* Work in groups. Tell the other students your news. Ask follow-up questions if possible.

Vocabulary and Speaking
Body movements and responses

1 a Work in pairs. Which of these verbs do you know? Check in **VOCABULARY 9.3** p147.

> cry laugh smile yawn wave
> shiver blush stretch scratch
> crawl frown sweat

b Take turns to ask your partner when people do the things in **1a**.

> When do people cry?

> When they're upset, in pain or very happy.

Reading

2 a Before you read, check these words with your teacher or in a dictionary.

> evolve bond with someone
> tears an itch forgive

b Work in pairs. Match pictures A–E to these reasons why people do these things.

1 to bond with other people in a group
2 to turn off parts of the brain connected with bad feelings and memories
3 to show that we have broken a social rule
4 to increase the amount of oxygen in the brain
5 to release stress-related chemicals from our bodies

c Read the article. Check your answers.

3 a Read the article again. What other reasons does the article give for each body movement or response?

b Work in pairs. Compare answers. Which piece of information do you think is the most interesting or surprising?

WHY DO WE CRY?
Although we don't enjoy crying, it's actually very good for us. The tears that are produced when we're upset contain large amounts of different chemicals that are related to stress, and crying reduces the amounts of these chemicals we have in our body. This is why we always feel better after a good cry. It's also thought that crying evolved to show other humans that we are unhappy or in pain and we need help from other people in our group.

WHY DO WE YAWN?
When we're tired or bored, we don't breathe very deeply and not enough oxygen is carried to the brain. A yawn takes in more oxygen and increases your heart rate by 30%, making us feel more awake. So if people yawn when you're talking to them, don't get too upset. Despite appearing rude, they could be yawning so they can listen more closely to what you're saying. It is also thought that yawning evolved to help groups of early humans stay awake and notice danger, which may also be why we often yawn when someone else does.

WHY DO WE LAUGH?
Even though most people think we laugh because something is funny, that's usually not true. In fact, laughing at something funny accounts for only 15% of all laughter. More frequently, laughter is a way of bonding with another person or a group, and it's 30 times more common to laugh in social situations than when we're alone. It is believed that humans developed the ability to laugh so that we could signal to other humans that we're playing, or that danger has passed.

WHY DO WE SCRATCH?
The obvious answer is that we have an itch and so we automatically scratch it. Of course, we know the itch will come back in a few minutes and scratching will probably make it worse. In spite of this knowledge, we still can't stop ourselves from scratching. It seems that scratching turns off parts of the brain that are connected to unpleasant feelings and memories, and it also stimulates the parts of the brain that make us happy – which is why it feels so good!

WHY DO WE BLUSH?
People usually blush because they're embarrassed, particularly if they have broken a social rule, for example, getting someone's name wrong. Blushing has evolved to show the other person that we know we have done something wrong, and that we're sorry about this. Interestingly, scientists have shown that people are more likely to forgive you if you blush. However, people might not forgive you so easily if you don't blush at all!

HELP WITH VOCABULARY
Connecting words

4 a Look at the words in blue in the article. Then choose the correct words/phrases in these rules.

- *Although*, *even though*, *despite*, *in spite of* and *however* are similar in meaning to *and/but*.
- We use *although*, *even though*, *despite* and *in spite of* to contrast *two sentences/two clauses in the same sentence*.
- We use *however* to contrast *two sentences/two clauses in the same sentence*.
- We *put/don't put* a comma (,) after *however*.

b Fill in the gaps in these rules with *although*, *even though*, *despite* or *in spite of*.

- After _____ and _____ we usually use a noun or verb+*ing*.
- After _____ and _____ we usually use a clause.

c Check in **VOCABULARY 9.4** p147.

5 a Rewrite these sentences using the words in brackets. Change other words in the sentence if necessary.

1 I went out last night. I felt really tired. (despite)
I went out last night, despite feeling really tired.
2 Robin slept really well. There was a lot of noise. (in spite of)
3 I don't get paid very much. I enjoy my job. (even though)
4 Erica was well-qualified. She didn't get the job. (however)
5 We enjoyed the concert. There weren't many people there. (even though)
6 They watched TV all night. They had to work the next day. (despite)
7 The teacher explained it twice. I still didn't understand it. (even though)

b Work in pairs. Compare answers.

Speaking and Listening

6 a Work in pairs. Discuss these questions.

1 Why do people lie?
2 When do you think it's OK to lie?
3 What makes some people better liars than others?
4 How can you tell if people are lying?

b Look at photos 1–4. Do you think this person is lying or telling the truth in each photo?

c CD2 44 Listen to an interview with Dr Miriam Richards, an expert in body language. Check your answers to **6b**.

7 a Work in pairs. Try to choose the correct words/phrases in these sentences.

1 Good liars often make *more/less* eye contact than usual.
2 People who are lying *often smile a lot/never smile*.
3 Real smiles use the muscles around the *mouth/eyes*.
4 The *left/right* side of the brain controls the right side of the body.
5 The *left/right* side of the brain controls imagination.
6 People often cover their *mouth/nose* when they're lying.

b CD2 44 Listen again. Check your answers.

HELP WITH LISTENING
British and American accents

8 a CD2 45 Listen to these words. Notice how British and American people say the letters in bold differently. You will hear the British accent first.

1 h**o**t, l**o**t, b**o**dy
2 s**aw**, t**a**lk, th**ou**ght
3 **au**nt, **a**sk, c**a**n't
4 g**ir**l, f**or**ty, m**o**ther
5 par**t**y, be**tt**er, wa**t**er

b CD2 46 Listen to six sentences. Which do you hear first: a British accent or an American accent?

c Look at Audio Script CD2 44 p168. Listen again and notice the difference between the interviewer's British accent and Dr Richards's American accent.

9 Are you a good liar? Work in groups. Look at p114.

9D REAL WORLD

At the doctor's

Real World what doctors say; what patients say
Vocabulary health problems, symptoms and treatment

QUICK REVIEW **Body movements and responses** Write four verbs that describe body movements and responses (*blush*, etc.). Work in pairs. Take turns to mime or describe the verbs. Your partner says the verb.

1 Work in pairs. Put these words/phrases into groups 1–3. Then check in **VOCABULARY 9.5** p148.

> asthma   antibiotics   a runny nose
> a blocked-up nose   an allergy   wheezy
> penicillin   hay fever   flu   sneeze
> a migraine   be sick   throw up   an infection
> a sore throat   painkillers   a virus
> paracetamol   a temperature   food poisoning
> a cough   a cold   a rash   diarrhoea
> a stomach ache   cough medicine

1 health problems *asthma*
2 symptoms *a runny nose*
3 treatment *antibiotics*

REAL WORLD What doctors say

2 a Look at these sentences that doctors often say to patients. Fill in the gaps with these words.

> ~~problem~~   back   feeling   taking
> look   eaten   allergic   temperature
> prescription   symptoms

1 Now, what seems to be the _problem_ ?
2 How long have you been _____ like this?
3 Do you know if you're _____ to anything?
4 What have you _____ recently?
5 Come _____ if you're not feeling better in two days.
6 Have you been _____ anything for them?
7 Have you got any other _____ ?
8 Right, let me have a _____ at you.
9 I'm just going to take your _____ .
10 Here's a _____ for some painkillers.

b **CD2 47** Listen and check your answers.

3 **VIDEO 9** **CD2 48** Look at the photos. Then watch or listen to two conversations in a GP's surgery. Answer these questions.

1 What are each patient's symptoms?
2 What does the doctor think is wrong with each patient?

4 **VIDEO 9** **CD2 48** Watch or listen again. Tick the true sentences. Correct the false ones.

Conversation 1
a Mr Philips isn't allergic to anything.
b His children cooked him a meal for his birthday.
c The doctor says he shouldn't eat for a day.
d Mr Philips has to come back and see the doctor again.

Conversation 2
e Mr Green has been taking paracetamol.
f He started feeling ill two days ago.
g The doctor tells him go to bed and rest.
h The doctor gives him a prescription for some antibiotics.

REAL WORLD What patients say

5 a Match the beginnings and the ends of these sentences.

1 I'm not feeling   a feeling very well recently.
2 I haven't been   b getting really bad headaches.
3 I've got   c very well.
4 My chest   d a terrible stomach ache.
5 I keep   e hurts.
6 I can't stop   f to penicillin.
7 Do I need   g sneezing.
8 I'm allergic   h should I take them?
9 How often   i make another appointment?
10 Do I need to   j some antibiotics?

b Look again at sentences 5 and 6 in **5a**. Then choose the correct words/phrases in these rules.

- We use *I keep …* and *I can't stop …* for things that happen *once/lots of times*. We *want/don't want* these things to happen.
- After *I keep …* and *I can't stop …* we use *the infinitive/verb+ing*.

c Check in **REAL WORLD 9.2** p149.

6 CD2 49 PRONUNCIATION Listen and practise the sentences in **5a**. Copy the stress.

I'm not feeling very well.

7 Cross out the incorrect words/phrases in these sentences.
1 I've been feeling *terrible/great/virus* lately.
2 I've got *asthma/a rash/throw up*.
3 I'm allergic to *cats/antibiotics/hay fever*.
4 I keep *waking up at night/a temperature/getting colds*.
5 I can't stop *coughing/being sick/food poisoning*.
6 I feel a bit *wheezy/run down/headache*.
7 You need some *painkillers/migraine/penicillin*.
8 I've got a *sneeze/runny nose/blocked-up nose*.

8 a Work in pairs. Cover p76. Then use these prompts to write a conversation at the doctor's.

DOCTOR   Hello, Mrs Wells. ¹Now, what / seem / be / problem?

1 Now, what seems to be the problem?

MRS WELLS   ²I / not feel / very well recently. ³My chest / hurt / and / can't stop / cough .

DR   ⁴Do / know if you / be / allergic / anything?

MRS W   No, I don't think so.

DR   OK. ⁵Have / got / other symptoms?

MRS W   ⁶Yes, / keep / wake up / night with / blocked-up nose.

DR   ⁷Right, let / have / look / you. ⁸How long / you / feel / like this?

MRS W   For about three days now.

DR   Right. ⁹I / just / go / take / temperature. Yes, it's a bit high. I think you've got a chest infection. ¹⁰Here / prescription / some antibiotics.

MRS W   ¹¹How often / take / ?

DR   ¹²Four times / day for / week. ¹³Come back / you / not feel / better / three days.

MRS W   Thank you, doctor. Goodbye.

b Practise the conversation with your partner. Take turns to be the doctor.

9 Work in new pairs. Student A p106. Student B p111.

HELP WITH PRONUNCIATION
The letters *ough*

1 a Work in pairs. Check you know how to say the sounds and words in the table.

/ɔː/ s**or**t	
/ʌ/ st**u**ff	
/əʊ/ gr**ow**	
/aʊ/ sh**ou**t	
/uː/ t**oo**	
/ɒ/ **o**ff	

b Work in pairs. Write these words in the table.

ought	drought	enough	rough	through
bought	though	brought	cough	
fought	tough	although	thought	

c CD2 50 Listen and check. Listen again and practise.

2 Work in new pairs. Practise saying these sentences.
1 We ought to look through those books we bought.
2 I thought we had brought enough stuff.
3 Even though he was tough, he had a cough.
4 He bought a house in a rough neighbourhood.
5 I think there ought to be a drought.
6 Although they weren't very tough, they fought a lot.

continue2learn

- **Vocabulary, Grammar and Real World**
  - **Extra Practice 9 and Progress Portfolio 9** p123
  - **Language Summary 9** p147
  - **9A–D** Workbook p45
- **Reading and Writing**
  - **Portfolio 9** Applying for a job Workbook p80
    Reading a job advertisement; an application email
    Writing application letters/emails; organisation; useful phrases

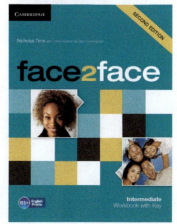

10A The anniversary

Vocabulary contacting people
Grammar *was/were going to, was/were supposed to*

QUICK REVIEW Health problems Write six words/phrases for health problems. Work in pairs. Take turns to mime a word/phrase. Your partner guesses what the problem is.

Vocabulary and Speaking Contacting people

1 Fill in the gaps with the correct form of these verbs. Then check new phrases in bold in VOCABULARY 10.1 p150.

| ~~get~~ | be | give | hear | let | call | keep | leave | lose | get |

1 Who in your family is usually difficult to _get_ **hold of**?
2 Do you usually _____ **your friends a call** on their birthdays?
3 When people _____ **you messages**, do you generally _____ **them back** immediately?
4 How do you usually _____ **someone know** you're going to be late?
5 Have you got friends from ten years ago that you _____ still **in touch with**?
6 Have you _____ **touch with** all your friends from your first school?
7 How do you _____ **in touch with** friends who live far away?
8 Is there a person you haven't _____ from for years that you'd like to _____ **in touch with** again?

2 Work in pairs. Ask and answer the questions in **1**. Ask follow-up questions if possible.

Speaking and Listening

3 a Make a list of five things people need for a successful marriage.

the same interests

b Work in pairs. Explain why you have chosen the things on your list. Then choose the five most important things from both lists.

c Tell the class the five things you chose. Do other students have any of the same things? What's the most important thing?

4 a Look at the picture of a wedding. Which person is: the bride? the groom? the bridesmaid? the best man?

b CD3 ▶ 1 Listen to Peggy talking to her son, Leo, about her wedding anniversary. Then answer these questions.

1 Are Peggy and her husband going away for their anniversary?
2 What do Leo and his sister, Karen, want to do for their parents?
3 Why did they borrow some of their parents' old photos?

c Work in pairs. Try to correct the five mistakes in this summary.

Peggy and her husband, Tom, have been married for thirty years. Their children, Leo and Karen, want to invite everyone who was at their parents' wedding to a party. The best man at the wedding, Derek Bradley, and his sister, Brenda, moved to Australia many years ago. Peggy knows how to get in touch with them. She's lost touch with Trevor Jones and his wife, Sheila.

d Listen again and check.

HELP WITH GRAMMAR
was/were going to, was/were supposed to

5 a Look at these sentences that Peggy said in the conversation. Then answer the questions.

*We **were going to visit** the Bradleys later that year, but we didn't go for some reason.*

*We **were going to spend** our anniversary in the cottage in Wales where we had our honeymoon, but it was already booked.*

1 Did Peggy and Tom plan to visit the Bradleys?
2 Did they visit them?
3 Did they plan to spend their anniversary in the cottage in Wales?
4 Are they going to spend their anniversary there?

*Tom **was supposed to book** the cottage months ago, but he forgot.*

*I **was supposed to call** you back, wasn't I? Sorry, Leo, I was out all day.*

5 Did Tom agree to book the cottage?
6 Did he book it?
7 Did Leo expect his mother to call him back?
8 Did she call him back?

b Fill in the gaps in these rules with *was/were going to* or *was/were supposed to*.

- We use _____ to talk about plans we made in the past which didn't happen, or won't happen in the future.
- We use _____ to talk about things we agreed to do, or other people expected us to do, but we didn't do.

c Which verb form follows *was/were going to* and *was/were supposed to*?

d Check in GRAMMAR 10.1 ▶ p151.

6 CD3 ▶ 2 PRONUNCIATION Listen and practise. Copy the stress and weak forms.

We were /wə/ going to /tə/ spend our anniversary in Wales.

It was /wəz/ going to /tə/ be a surprise party.

7 a Match beginnings of sentences 1–7 to ends of sentences a–g.

1 Karen had agreed to make a list of possible guests, … *b*
2 Peggy and Tom had planned to call Trevor and Sheila, …
3 Leo had agreed to try and find the Bradleys' address on the internet, …
4 Karen had planned to get her parents a present on Monday, …
5 Leo had decided to buy himself a new suit last week, …
6 Karen had expected Leo to get in touch with Jane Lewis, …
7 Leo had expected his parents to go through their old address books, …

a but his computer wasn't working.
b but she didn't know who to invite.
c but he lost her phone number.
d but they couldn't find them.
e but he didn't have enough money.
f but they lost their phone number.
g but she couldn't find her credit card.

b Rewrite the sentences in **7a**. Use *was/were going to* or *was/were supposed to*.

Karen was supposed to make a list of possible guests, but she didn't know who to invite.

Get ready … Get it right!

8 Write three things that you were going to do and three things you were supposed to do in the last four weeks. Make notes on why you didn't do these things.

visit my aunt → had to work instead

9 a Work in pairs. Take turns to tell each other about the things on your list. Ask follow-up questions if possible.

> I was going to visit my aunt last weekend, but I had to work instead.

> Are you going to see her this weekend?

b Tell the class your partner's best reason for not doing one of the things on his/her list.

10B Who's that?

Vocabulary describing people
Grammar modal verbs (2): making deductions

QUICK REVIEW Contacting people Write the names of people you know who: you haven't heard from this month, always call you back, are difficult to get hold of, you've lost touch with, left you a message. Work in pairs. Tell your partner about these people. Ask follow-up questions if possible.

Vocabulary and Speaking
Describing people

 a Tick the words/phrases you know. Then check new words/phrases in VOCABULARY 10.2 p150.

> fair/dark/red/blonde/grey/dyed hair
> long/short/shoulder-length hair
> straight/curly/wavy hair
> her hair up/in a ponytail   going bald
> a moustache/a beard   a dark/light blue suit/jacket
> a striped/flowery/plain tie/dress/shirt
> glasses/lots of jewellery
> in his/her teens/early twenties/mid-thirties/late forties

b Work in pairs. Look at the picture of Tom and Peggy's 25th wedding anniversary party. Take turns to describe the people. Use the words/phrases in **1a** and your own ideas. Your partner guesses who it is.

> She's got her hair up and she's wearing a red dress.

> You mean her?

Listening

 a CD3 3 Listen and match these names to people 1–7 in the picture. Where's Peggy's husband, Tom?

> Peggy 2   Brenda   Jane
> Derek   Nick   Trevor   Sheila

b Listen again. Who said these sentences: Peggy, Karen or Leo?

1 He **could be picking** people **up** from the station. *Karen*
2 That **can't be** her real hair colour.
3 He **must be talking** to some guests in the other room.
4 He **may want** to be on his own for a bit.
5 It **could be** the guy that moved to New York.
6 No, that isn't Derek Bradley.
7 He **can't be having** a cigarette.
8 He **might be** in the bathroom.
9 He's practising his speech in front of the mirror.
10 He **must know** that speech by now.

c Work in pairs. Compare answers.

HELP WITH GRAMMAR
Modal verbs (2): making deductions

3 a Look at the sentences 1–10 in **2b**. Are they talking about the past, the present or the future?

b Match sentences 1–10 in **2b** to meanings a–e.
The speaker …
a knows this is definitely true. 9
b believes this is true.
c thinks this is possibly true.
d believes this isn't true.
e knows this definitely isn't true.

c Look at the verb forms in bold in **2b**. Then fill in the gaps with the correct modal verbs.
- We use _____ to talk about something that we believe is true.
- We use _____ , _____ or _____ to talk about something that we think is possibly true.
- We use _____ to talk about something that we believe isn't true.

d Which sentences in **2b** are talking about: a state? something happening now?

e Complete these rules with verb+*ing* or infinitive.
- To make deductions about states we use: modal verb + _____ .
- To make deductions about something happening now we use: modal verb + be + _____ .

TIP • We don't use *can* or *mustn't* to make deductions: *It could be him.* not *It can be him*. *He can't be a millionaire.* not *He mustn't be a millionaire.*

f Check in GRAMMAR 10.2 ▶ p151.

4 CD3 ▶ 4 PRONUNCIATION Listen and practise the sentences in **2b**. Copy the stress.
He could be picking people up from the station.

5 Look at these sentences Karen said at the party. Choose the correct modal verbs.
1 That woman *could/must* be Mum's cousin, but I'm not sure.
2 Uncle Ian isn't here yet. He *may/can't* be working late.
3 Nick *can't/must* be married yet. He's only seventeen.
4 Jane *must/can't* have dyed hair. In the wedding photo she had dark hair.
5 Sheila *can't/might* want to leave soon, she looks a bit bored.
6 Derek's just arrived from New York. He *must/can't* be feeling very tired.
7 You *must/can't* be hungry, Dad. You've just finished eating!
8 Trevor *could/must* be in the restaurant, or he *may/can't* be in the garden.

6 Fill in the gaps with the correct form of these verbs.

| ~~be~~ | love | lose | work | need | do | know |

1 That can't **be** the right house.
2 Joan's not here. She must _____ the shopping.
3 Paola might _____ where he lives.
4 You must _____ living in London.
5 Josh can't _____ now. His office is closed.
6 I must _____ my memory. I keep forgetting to do things.
7 We may _____ some more milk.

7 a CD3 ▶ 5 Listen to six short recordings of sounds and voices. Write sentences with *must*, *may*, *might*, *could* or *can't* for each recording.
1 The water must be too cold.

b Work in groups. Compare sentences. Are any the same?

c Listen again. Compare sentences with the class.

Get ready … Get it right!

8 Look at the picture. These things all belong to people at the party. Who do you think owns each thing?

9 a Work in groups. Discuss who you think each thing belongs to. Give reasons for your choices.
I think this book could be Karen's. She might be learning to drive.

b Look at p155. Check your answers. How many did you get right?

VOCABULARY 10C AND SKILLS ▸ I do!

Vocabulary phrasal verbs (3)
Skills Reading: a magazine article;
Listening: a radio interview

QUICK REVIEW Describing people Choose three people in the class. Write sentences to describe each person. Don't write the person's name: *He's got short curly hair. He's wearing a striped shirt.* Work in pairs. Take turns to say your sentences. Your partner guesses who the person is: *It might be Johann.*

Reading and Vocabulary

1 Work in groups. Discuss these questions.
1. What is the average cost of a wedding in your country, do you think?
2. Who usually pays for the wedding in your country?
3. What do they spend the money on?

2 a Read the magazine article. Choose the correct words in these sentences.
1. Tony is Olivia's *third/fourth* husband.
2. Ginny *went/didn't go* to Olivia's wedding.
3. Ginny *had/hadn't* been a bridesmaid for Olivia before.
4. Olivia *has/hasn't* kept in touch with her ex-husbands.
5. *More/Fewer* people in the UK are getting married these days.

b Read the article again. What does it say about these numbers? Did any of the numbers surprise you?

£20,000	six hours	£3,300	£15,000
459,000	231,000	45%	12%

3 a Look at the phrasal verbs in bold in the article. Match them to their meanings 1–10. Write the infinitive of the verbs.
1. avoid doing something you don't want to do
   get out of
2. feel better after you have been unhappy or ill
3. increase or rise
4. find some information in a book or on a computer
5. tell someone some information you think they don't know or have forgotten
6. decide or arrange to do something at a later time
7. argue with someone and stop being friendly with them
8. think of an idea, or a solution to a problem
9. end a marriage or relationship
10. find something by accident

b Check in **VOCABULARY 10.3** p150.

For Better, For Worse

Ginny Bell looks at her friend's chances of having a happy marriage.

When Olivia first started going out with Tony, I thought it would never last. Two months later, she told me they were getting married. I thought she should **put** the wedding **off** for a few months until she knew Tony better. As soon as he had proposed to her, Olivia called me and said, "He really is the one." She'd said the same thing about her last three husbands, but I didn't like to **point** this **out** to her.

When Olivia asked me to be her bridesmaid, I tried to **get out of** the whole thing because I didn't want to see her make the same mistake again. However, I couldn't **come up with** a good excuse, so there I was again, standing outside the church wondering how much Olivia's parents had spent this time. A typical wedding in the UK costs about £20,000 and lasts six hours, so that's about £3,300 an hour. Olivia must be a very expensive daughter to have.

At the church Olivia introduced me by saying, "This is Ginny. She's been a bridesmaid at all my weddings." And indeed I had. I hoped that Olivia and Tony would never **split up**, which could cost another £15,000 – the average cost of a divorce if you have to go to court. Fortunately, Olivia **got over** her last three divorces quickly and is still friends with all her ex-husbands.

So what are their chances of a successful marriage these days? The week before Olivia's wedding I **came across** a newspaper report which said that the number of divorces in the UK is still **going up**, while the number of people getting married is falling. I **looked** some figures **up** and found out that in 1971 there were 459,000 weddings in the UK, but in 2009 there were only 231,000 – the lowest figure since 1861. And as for divorce, where you live makes a huge difference. For example, the divorce rate in the UK is about 45%, but in Italy it's only 12%.

When my husband and I were leaving the reception, Olivia came up to say goodbye and said, "You two have never **fallen out**, have you? How can I make this marriage last?" Well, Olivia, what can I say? Move to Italy!

It's such a special day. You only get married for the fourth time once!

HELP WITH VOCABULARY
Phrasal verbs (3)

4 a Read about the four types of phrasal verbs.

- **TYPE 1** phrasal verbs don't have an object.
  You two have never fallen out.

- **TYPE 2** phrasal verbs always have an object. This is always **after** the phrasal verb.
  Olivia got over her divorces quickly.
  Olivia got over them quickly.

- **TYPE 3** phrasal verbs always have an object. If the object is a noun, you can put it **in the middle** or **after** the phrasal verb.
  I looked some figures up.
  I looked up some figures.
  If the object is a pronoun, you must put it **in the middle** of the phrasal verb.
  I looked them up. not *I looked up them.*

- **TYPE 4** phrasal verbs have three words and always have an object. The object is always **after** the phrasal verb.
  I tried to get out of the whole thing.
  I tried to get out of it.

b Work in pairs. Look at the other phrasal verbs in bold in the article. Are they type 1, 2, 3 or 4?

c Check in **VOCABULARY 10.4** p150.

5 Look at the words in brackets. Where can they go in these sentences? Put a tick or a cross in the gaps.

1 Jeanette never got ✗ over ✓ . (her divorce)
2 He always puts _____ off _____ until the last minute. (his homework)
3 You can't put _____ off _____ any longer. (it)
4 Dylan didn't want to go, but he couldn't get out _____ of _____ . (it)
5 Look _____ up _____ in a dictionary. (these words)
6 If you don't know the answer, look up _____ . (it)
7 I came _____ across _____ when I was cleaning. (this)
8 The teacher pointed _____ out _____ to him. (the mistake)
9 I knew Mark was wrong, but I didn't want to point _____ out _____ . (it)

6 Work in pairs. Student A p106. Student B p111.

A *the best man*

B *the wedding cake*

C *the honeymoon*

D *wedding rings*

E *confetti*

F *women proposing*

Listening and Speaking

7 a Work in pairs. Look at wedding traditions A–F. Which do you have in your country? What do you know about them?

b Before you listen, check these words/phrases with your teacher.

| ancestors | propose to someone | kidnap | a vein | a leap year |

c CD3 ▶6 Listen to a radio programme about wedding traditions. Put photos A–F in the order the people talk about them.

8 a CD3 ▶6 Work in pairs. Listen again. Student A, make notes on the wedding traditions in photos A, B and C. Student B, make notes on the wedding traditions in photos D, E and F.

b Work with your partner. Take turns to explain the origins of the wedding traditions in the photos. Did you remember anything that your partner didn't mention?

HELP WITH LISTENING /t/ and /d/ at the end of words

- We don't usually hear /t/ or /d/ sounds at the end of words when the next word starts with a consonant sound.

9 a Look at these sentences. Circle each *t* and *d* in bold that you think you will hear. Cross out the ones you don't think you will hear.

Wendy, firs**t** of all, we shoul**d** start with the mos**t** obvious question. When di**d** our ancestors star**t** getting marrie**d** to each other?
Well, I'm please**d** that things have move**d** on a bi**t** since then.
An**d** wha**t** abou**t** wedding rings? Where di**d** they originate?

b CD3 ▶7 Listen and check your answers.

c Look at Audio Script CD3 ▶6 p169. Listen again and notice when we say and don't say /t/ and /d/ at the end of words.

10 a Think of a wedding you've been to. Make notes on these things.

- when and where
- the bride and groom
- the other guests
- the ceremony
- the reception/meal
- other interesting points

b Work in groups. Take turns to describe the weddings. Which wedding do you think was the most interesting?

REAL WORLD 10D Do you mind?

Real World asking for, giving and refusing permission

Ella | Rebecca

QUICK REVIEW Phrasal verbs Make a list of five phrasal verbs. Work in pairs and swap papers. Take turns to say a sentence that includes a phrasal verb on your partner's list. Listen to your partner's sentences. Are they correct?

1 Work in groups. Discuss these questions.
1. When did you last stay with relatives or friends? Why did you visit them? How long did you stay?
2. When was the last time relatives or friends came to stay with you? Were there any problems? If so, what were they?
3. What are the best and worst things about staying in someone else's house or flat?

2 a VIDEO 10 CD3 8 Look at the photos. Then watch or listen to the conversations. Answer these questions.

Conversation 1
a How long has Ella been asleep?
b How long does Rebecca say that Ella and Mike can stay?
c Why does Rebecca suggest that Ella should talk to Charlie?

Conversation 2
d How long were Mike and Ella away for?
e How far away does Mike's brother live?
f Why can't Mike phone his parents on his mobile?

b Work in pairs. Try to fill in the gaps in Ella and Mike's questions with these words.

| jumper | car | washing machine |
| landline | breakfast | laptop |

1 **Can I** make myself some _____ ?
2 **May I** use your _____ ?
3 **Do you mind if I** borrow a _____ ?
4 **Is it OK if I** use your _____ to upload some photos?
5 **Would you mind if I** borrowed your _____ some time this week?
6 **Do you think I could** use your _____ to call my parents?

c Work in the same pairs. Try to match these responses to the questions in **2b**. Which are: giving permission? refusing permission?

a Yes, of course. Go ahead. The phone's in the front room, by the window.
b Yes, of course you can. Help yourself. You know where everything is.
c No, not at all. They're in the bottom drawer in our bedroom.
d Sorry, it's only insured for Rebecca and myself.
e Actually, I was just going to put some washing in.
f Sorry, I left mine at work.

d Watch or listen again. Check your answers to **2b** and **2c**.

REAL WORLD
Asking for, giving and refusing permission

3 a Look at the ways of asking for permission in bold in **2b**. Which verb form comes after each phrase: infinitive, Present Simple or Past Simple?

1 Can I + _infinitive_ ... ?
2 May I + _____ ... ?
3 Do you mind if I + _____ ... ?
4 Is it OK if I + _____ ... ?
5 Would you mind if I + _____ ... ?
6 Do you think I could + _____ ... ?

b Choose the correct way to give permission for these questions. After which other phrase in **3a** do we say *No, not at all.* to give permission?

1 A Can I make myself some breakfast?
   B *Yes, of course./No, not at all.*
2 A Do you mind if I make myself some breakfast?
   B *Yes, of course./No, not at all.*

c Look at sentences d–f in **2c**. Answer these questions.

1 Do we usually say *no* when we refuse permission?
2 Do we usually give a reason to say why we refuse permission?
3 Which words do we use to be polite when we refuse permission?

d Check in REAL WORLD 10.1 p151.

Charlie   *Mike*

HELP WITH LISTENING
Intonation (3): asking for permission

4 CD3 ▶9 Listen to the questions in **2b** said twice. Which sounds more polite, a or b?

1 a (b)   3 a b   5 a b
2 a b   4 a b   6 a b

5 CD3 ▶10 **PRONUNCIATION** Listen and practise the questions in **2b** and the responses in **2c**. Copy the stress and polite intonation.

Can I make myself some breakfast?

6 a Put these words in order.

1 see / May / written / what / I / you've ?
2 your / use / for / I / dictionary / Can / a moment ?
3 could / borrow / Do / money / you / some / think / I ?
4 of / if / I / a photo / mind / take / you / you / Do ?
5 I / OK / DVD-ROM / Is / your / if / a few days / it / borrow / for ?
6 the USA / Would / I / to call / used / if / you / your / mind / mobile ?

b Work in pairs. Take turns to say the sentences in **6a**. Decide whether to give or refuse permission. If you refuse permission, give a reason.

> May I see what you've written?
>
> Yes, of course. Here you are.

7 Work in pairs. Student A p105. Student B p110.

HELP WITH PRONUNCIATION
Linking in phrasal verbs

1 CD3 ▶11 Listen to these phrasal verbs. Notice the different types of linking. Listen again and practise.

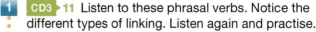

look‿it‿up   get‿out‿of‿it   get‿over/r/‿it
put‿it‿off   give‿it‿away   clear/r/‿out
give‿it‿up   go/w/‿up   see/j/‿off
point‿it‿out   throw/w/‿out   tidy/j/‿up

2 a Work in pairs. Read the conversation. Add the consonant–vowel links and extra linking sounds.

ROB   Hi, Sue. What‿are you doing‿at the weekend?
SUE   We're planning to go/w/‿away.
R   Really? Where are‿/j/‿you‿/j/‿off to?
S   We're‿/j/‿off to Dublin for‿/r/‿a wedding. We have to check in at ten, so we're setting off at eight.
R   Well, this weekend I'm going to tidy‿/j/‿up my‿/j/‿office. I've been putting it off for‿/r/‿ages, but I really need to sort it out.
S   So‿/w/‿are you going to be‿/j/‿in all weekend?
R   Yes, I‿/j/‿am. Do you want me to look after your cat while you're‿/r/‿away?
S   That'd be great, thanks. See you‿/w/‿on Monday!

b Look at Audio Script CD3 ▶12 p170. Then listen and check. Listen again and practise each line of the conversation.

c Practise the conversation in **2a** with your partner.

continue2learn

▶ **Vocabulary, Grammar and Real World**
- **Extra Practice 10 and Progress Portfolio 10** p124
- **Language Summary 10** p150
- **10A–D** Workbook p50

▶ **Reading and Writing**
- **Portfolio 10** Describing people Workbook p82
  Reading a description of a friend
  Writing describing people: organisation, useful phrases

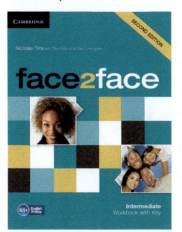

11A Any messages?

Vocabulary things people do at work
Grammar reported speech: sentences

QUICK REVIEW **Asking for, giving and refusing permission** Choose a partner, but don't talk to him/her yet. Imagine you're staying at your partner's house/flat. Think of three things you want to do there. Work in pairs. Take turns to ask for, give or refuse permission.

Vocabulary and Speaking
Things people do at work

1 Match a word/phrase in A to a word/phrase in B. Then check in **VOCABULARY 11.1** p152.

A	B
have a lot of	conferences
work	responsibility
sort out	unsocial hours
organise	people's problems
do	for an audition
go	overtime
run	for the finances
be responsible	a department
deal with	of a company
arrange	shifts
work	customers/clients
be in charge	meetings

2 **a** Write the names of two people you know who have jobs. Think what these people do in their jobs. Use phrases from **1** or your own ideas.

b Work in groups. Tell each other about the people you chose in **2a**. Ask follow-up questions if possible.

Listening

3 **CD3 13** Gabi is a PA (personal assistant) for On The Box, a company that makes TV programmes. Listen to Gabi talking to Fiona, an actress. Answer these questions.

1 Where is Gabi's boss, Max?
2 Where is Fiona?
3 What has happened to Fiona?
4 What is Gabi going to ask Max to do?

Max / Gabi

4 **a** Work in pairs. Try to fill in the gaps in these sentences from Gabi and Fiona's conversation with one word.

1 I can't come to the meeting on _Monday_ .
2 I was in a car _____ .
3 I won't be able to walk on it for a _____ .
4 I've already had one _____ .
5 I'm having another operation on _____ .
6 I still want to be in the _____ .
7 They're going to start filming _____ .
8 You must talk to _____ .

b **CD3 13** Listen and check.

5 **a** **CD3 14** Look at the photo. Gabi is talking to Max the next day. Read sentences a–h. Then listen and put these sentences in the order Gabi says them.

a She said that she'd been in a car accident. _1_
b She said she still wanted to be in the programme.
c I told her that she had to talk to you.
d She told me that she'd already had one operation.
e She said that she was having another operation on Friday.
f I told her they were going to start filming soon.
g She told me she couldn't come to the meeting on Monday.
h She said she wouldn't be able to walk on it for a month.

b Match sentences 1–8 in **4a** to sentences a–h in **5a**.

HELP WITH GRAMMAR
Reported speech: sentences

6 a Look at the sentences in **4a** and **5a**. Notice how the verb form changes in reported speech. Then fill in the table with these verb forms. Use one verb form twice.

> ~~Past Simple~~   Past Perfect   Past Continuous
> would   could   had to   was/were going to

verb form in direct speech	verb form in reported speech
Present Simple	Past Simple
Present Continuous	
Present Perfect Simple	
Past Simple	
am/are/is going to	
will	
can	
must	

b Look again at the sentences in **5a**. Then choose the correct words in these rules.
- We *always/never* use an object (*me*, *her*, etc.) with *say*.
- We *always/never* use an object (*me*, *her*, etc.) with *tell*.
- We *have to/don't have to* use *that* after *say* and *tell* in reported speech.
- Pronouns (*I*, *he*, etc.) and possessive adjectives (*my*, *his*, etc.) *usually/never* change in reported speech.

TIP • The modal verbs *could*, *should*, *would*, *might* and *ought to* don't change in reported speech.

c Check in **GRAMMAR 11.1** p153.

7 **CD3 15** **PRONUNCIATION** Listen and practise the sentences in **5a**. Copy the stress, weak forms and contractions.

She said that /ðət/ she'd been in a car accident.

8 a Gabi also took some other messages for Max yesterday. She is now giving Max the messages. Write what she says in reported speech. Use the verbs in brackets.

1. MR HALL I must talk to Max. (say)
   Mr Hall said (that) he had to talk to you.
2. CARL I'm going to be in New York next week. (tell)
3. SID I didn't understand your email. (say)
4. LINDA WISE I can't come to Monday's meeting. (say)
5. MRS LEE The designs will be ready on Monday. (tell)
6. TED BLACK I'm having a party on Saturday. (say)
7. TED BLACK I want to talk to Max about a new project. (say)
8. MAX'S EX-WIFE I've sold the house. (tell)

b **CD3 16** Listen and check.

HELP WITH LISTENING
/h/ in *he*, *his*, *him* and *her*

9 a **CD3 16** Listen to the beginning of the conversation again. Circle each *h* in bold you hear. Cross out each *h* you don't hear.

GABI Well, Mr Hall said **h**e had to talk to you.
MAX OK, I'll call **h**im later. What's **h**is number?
GABI **H**e only gave me **h**is mobile number. Here it is.
MAX What does **h**e want, anyway? I talked to **h**im last week.
GABI Apparently **h**is wife wants **h**er script back.

b Choose the correct words in these rules.
- We usually hear /h/ in *he*, *his*, *him* and *her* if it follows a *consonant/vowel* sound.
- We don't usually hear /h/ in *he*, *his*, *him* and *her* if it follows a *consonant/vowel* sound.

c Look at Audio Script **CD3 16** p171. Listen to Gabi and Max's conversation again. Notice when we say and don't say /h/ in *he*, *his*, *him* and *her*.

Get ready … Get it right!

10 Write eight sentences about yourself. Four sentences should be true and four should be false. Use these phrases and your own ideas.

- I can/can't …
- I really like …
- I've been to …
- I've never …
- I'm … this weekend.
- I … last year.
- I think I'll …
- Next year I'm going to …

I can play golf quite well.
I really like going to art galleries.

11 a Work in pairs. Tell each other your sentences. Your partner guesses if they're true or false. You can write one word only to help you remember each of your partner's sentences.

b Work with a new partner. Tell each other your first partner's sentences. Use reported speech. Your new partner guesses if they are true or false.

> Bulent said he could play golf quite well.
> I think that's false.
> No, it's true!

c Tell the class two things you found out about your first partner.

11B How did it go?

Vocabulary adjectives (3): jobs
Grammar reported speech: questions, requests and imperatives

QUICK REVIEW Reported speech Think of four things that people have said to you this week. Work in pairs. Tell your partner who the people are and what they said, using reported speech. Ask follow-up questions. A *My sister Annette told me she was going on holiday.* B *Where's she going?*

Vocabulary and Speaking
Adjectives (3): jobs

1 a Work in pairs. Which of these adjectives do you know? Check new words in **VOCABULARY 11.2** p152.

> demanding   well-paid   badly-paid
> temporary   permanent   full-time   part-time
> stressful   challenging   rewarding
> repetitive   lonely   glamorous   dull

b Write two jobs that you would like to do and two that you wouldn't like to do. Think of adjectives from **1a** to describe each job.

c Work in groups. Take turns to say which jobs you chose and why you chose them.

Speaking and Listening

2 a Work in pairs. Discuss these questions.
1 What's the best way to find a job in your town/city?
2 Have you ever had a job interview? If so, how did it go?
3 Which questions are people usually asked at a job interview?

b CD3 17 Look at the photo. Eva is having an audition at On The Box. Listen and fill in the gaps with one or two words.
1 Are you _working_ at the moment?
2 Do you have any acting work in the next _____ ?
3 And what was your last _____ ?
4 What other _____ have you had recently?
5 And where did you _____ ?
6 Are you available to start _____ ?

c Listen again. What are Eva's answers to the questions in **2b**?

d Work in pairs. Compare answers.

3 a CD3 18 Eva is telling her boyfriend, Joe, about the audition. Read sentences a–f. Then listen and put these sentences in order.

a First he asked me if I was working at the moment. *1*
b He wanted to know where I'd studied acting.
c He asked what my last acting job had been.
d He wanted to know whether I was available to start next week.
e He asked me what other parts I'd had recently.
f He also asked if I had any acting work in the next three months.

b Match Max's questions in **2b** to Eva's sentences in **3a**.

HELP WITH GRAMMAR   Reported speech: questions

4 a Look at the reported questions in **3a**. Choose the correct words/phrases in these rules.

• We *use/don't use* the auxiliaries *do*, *does* or *did* in reported questions.
• We use *if* or *whether* to report questions *with/without* a question word.
• We *always/sometimes/never* use an object (*me*, *him*, etc.) with *ask*.
• The changes in the verb forms in reported questions are *the same as/different from* reported sentences.

b Look again at the reported questions in **3a**. Then fill in the gaps with *asked, wanted, whether, question word, subject* or *verb*.

REPORTED WH– QUESTIONS

He/She _____ (me)
He/She wanted to know   + _____ + subject + _____

REPORTED YES/NO QUESTIONS

He/She asked (me)
He/She _____ to know   + *if* or _____ + _____ + verb

c Check in **GRAMMAR 11.2** p153.

5 CD3 ▶19 **PRONUNCIATION** Listen and practise the reported questions in **3a**. Copy the stress and weak forms.

First he asked me if I was /wəz/ working at the moment.

6 a Look at these real questions that people have asked in interviews. Write the questions in reported speech. Use the phrases in brackets.

WHAT NOT TO ASK IN AN INTERVIEW!

1 Can my rabbit come to work with me?
   She asked ... *if her rabbit could come to work with her.*

2 What is your star sign?
   She asked him ...

3 Is it a problem if I'm angry most of the time?
   He asked him ...

4 Will the company pay to look after my horse?
   He asked her ...

5 Do I have to wear a suit for the next interview?
   He wanted to know ...

6 Which job am I applying for?
   He wanted to know ...

7 Have you been in prison too?
   He asked him ...

8 Why am I here?
   She wanted to know ...

9 Why aren't you in a more interesting business?
   She asked them ...

10 Can I come back when I find my glasses?
   She wanted to know ...

b Work in pairs. Compare answers. Which question do you think is the funniest?

7 CD3 ▶20 Max phones Eva later that day. She's got the job! Listen and answer these questions.

1 Where does Eva have to go on Monday?
2 What time does she have to be there?
3 Who is she going to meet?
4 How long is the job going to last?

HELP WITH GRAMMAR
Reported speech: requests and imperatives

8 a Look at these sentences. Which is a request? Which are imperatives?

Can you come to a meeting on Monday?
Be at our offices at ten.
Don't accept any more work.

b Look at how Eva reported what Max said. Then complete the rules with *imperatives* and *requests*.

He asked me to come to a meeting on Monday.
He told me to be at their offices at ten.
He told me not to accept any more work.

- To report _____ , we use:
  asked + object + (*not*) + infinitive with *to*.
- To report _____ , we use:
  told + object + (*not*) + infinitive with *to*.

c Check in **GRAMMAR 11.3** ▶ p153.

9 Eva and Joe are talking later that day. Write Eva's sentences in reported speech.

1 Could you give me a lift tomorrow?
   She asked him to give her a lift tomorrow.
2 Call me at lunchtime.
3 Will you pick me up after the meeting?
4 Don't worry about me.
5 Can you book a table at our favourite restaurant?
6 Don't tell anyone about the job yet.
7 Do you think you could help me learn my lines?

Get ready … Get it right!

10 Choose a partner, but don't work with him/her yet. Write six questions to ask your partner. Choose questions you don't know the answer to. Use these phrases and your own ideas.

- What are you doing …
- How often do you …
- When did you last …
- Do you usually …
- Have you ever …
- Can you …

11 a Work with your partner. Ask and answer your questions. Make notes on your partner's answers.

b Work with a new partner. Tell him/her about your conversation with your first partner. Use reported speech.

> Francesca asked me if I'd ever been to the UK. I told her I'd been there once.

c Tell the class two interesting things you found out about your first partner.

VOCABULARY AND SKILLS
11C Undercover

Vocabulary verb patterns (2): reporting verbs
Skills Reading: a review; Listening: a TV programme

QUICK REVIEW Adjectives to describe jobs
Write five adjectives to describe jobs (*challenging*, *repetitive*, etc.). Then think of a job for each adjective. Work in pairs. Tell your partner your jobs and adjectives. Do you agree with your partner's adjectives?

Speaking, Reading and Vocabulary

1 Work in groups. Discuss these questions.
1 What kinds of TV programmes do you watch? What don't you watch?
2 What's your favourite programme at the moment? Why do you like it?
3 Do you ever watch police dramas? If so, which ones?

2 a Before you read, check these words/phrases with your teacher or in a dictionary.

| an undercover cop | a smuggler | a bug |
| a statue | a warehouse | a trap |

b Read the review of the new TV cop show *Undercover*. Match the people's names to their roles. Who are the people in the photos?

1 Kat   a Rupert's wife
2 Rupert   b other cops
3 Gloria   c an undercover cop
4 Dom   d an artist
5 Glenn and Darren e the art gallery owner
6 Hendrik   f Rupert's son

c Read the review again. Answer these questions.
1 Where is Kat working undercover?
2 Why can the police hear Rupert's phone calls?
3 Who saw Kat go into Rupert's study?
4 Are Kat and Dom in love with each other?
5 What two things are going to happen on Tuesday evening?

3 Tick the verbs you know. Then check new verbs in VOCABULARY 11.3 p152.

invite	offer	admit	refuse
promise	agree	suggest	
remind	warn	threaten	

undercover

Undercover's success is no secret

Undercover is already the best drama we've seen on TV this year. It stars Eva West as Kat Winters, an undercover cop who works for the SCS (Serious Crime Squad). If you didn't see the last episode, here's what you missed.

EPISODE 4: plot summary

Kat is working undercover as a salesperson at a London art gallery owned by Rupert Wilde, who the police believe is an international diamond smuggler. After Kat had worked in the gallery for a while, Rupert and his wife, Gloria, **invited** her to have dinner with their family in their luxury flat above the gallery. Just before dinner, Kat managed to put a bug in the phone in Rupert's private study. However, she didn't know that Gloria had seen her leave the study.

HELP WITH VOCABULARY
Verb patterns (2): reporting verbs

4 a Look at the verbs in bold in the review and underline the verb form that follows them. Then write the infinitive form of the verbs in bold in the table.

invite	+ object + (not) + infinitive with *to*
offer	(+ *not*) + infinitive with *to*
admit	+ verb+*ing*

b Check in VOCABULARY 11.4 p152.

After dinner, Rupert's son, Dom, **offered** to give Kat a lift home. While they were in the car, Dom **admitted** being madly in love with Kat. She was rather shocked by this, particularly when Dom **refused** to drive her home until she **promised** to go out on a date with him. However, Kat needed an opportunity to find out more about the Wilde family, so she **agreed** to have dinner with Dom on Tuesday evening. Dom **suggested** meeting at the gallery at seven.

The next day, two other SCS cops, Glenn and Darren, sat in a van outside the art gallery listening to Rupert's phone calls. They heard him call Hendrik Petersen, a famous Dutch artist. Hendrik **agreed** to deliver three of his statues to Rupert's warehouse at 7.30 p.m. on Tuesday, and **reminded** Rupert to bring the money in used ten-pound notes. Rupert **warned** Hendrik not to tell anyone about their plan and **threatened** to kill him if anything went wrong.

Is Kat walking into a trap? What's going to happen at Rupert's warehouse? Find out in EPISODE 5!

5 **a** Look at these conversations from episode 4 of *Undercover*. Put the sentences in bold in reported speech. Use the verbs in brackets.

DOM ¹**Why don't we go to the Ritz?** (suggest)
1 *Dom suggested going to the Ritz.*
KAT That sounds nice. I've never been there before.
DOM ²**Shall I book a table?** (offer)
KAT Good idea.
DOM And ³**would you like to come to Paris next weekend?** (invite)
KAT Hey, slow down! We haven't even had dinner yet!
DOM Yes, I know, I'm sorry. ⁴**I say some stupid things sometimes.** (admit)
KAT OK. ⁵**Let's talk about Paris after dinner.** (agree)
RUPERT ⁶**Don't be late, Hendrik.** (warn)
HENDRIK Don't worry, ⁷**I'll be there on time.** (promise)
RUPERT ⁸**And don't forget to watch out for the cops.** (remind)
HENDRIK I'll be careful. But if you don't bring the money, ⁹**I'll tell the police everything I know.** (threaten)
RUPERT Sorry, Hendrik, ¹⁰**I don't believe you.** (refuse)

b Work in pairs. Compare sentences.

Listening and Speaking

6 **a** Work in pairs. What do you think is going to happen in episode 5 of *Undercover*?

> I think Hendrik might steal Rupert's money.

b CD3 21 Listen to the beginning of the next episode. Were any of your ideas correct?

c Listen again. Are these sentences true or false?
1 Glenn and Darren are outside the warehouse.
2 They call Kat to tell her what's happening.
3 Rupert and Hendrik meet at the warehouse.
4 Rupert phoned Hendrik earlier that afternoon.
5 Hendrik hasn't got the statues.
6 Gloria threatens to shoot Kat.
7 Gloria agrees to help the police.
8 Dom arrives to take Kat on their date.

HELP WITH LISTENING Missing words

• In informal spoken English we often miss out words when the meaning is clear.

7 **a** Read the beginning of episode 5 of *Undercover*. Notice the missing words in brackets. What kind of words do we often miss out?

DARREN [Are you] Sure this is the place, Glenn?
GLENN Yeah. [The] Warehouse on Tudor Street. [At] Seven thirty.
DARREN [It] Looks closed to me. [Do you] Want a cigarette?
GLENN No, thanks, mate. [I] Gave up last week.
DARREN Yeah, right. [Have you] Heard from Kat recently?

b Look at Audio Script CD3 21 p172. Listen to the first two parts of episode 5 again. Notice the missing words in brackets.

8 Work in pairs. Look again at Audio Script CD3 21 p172. Take turns to say sentences 1–10 in bold in reported speech.

> Darren agreed to wait and see what happened.

9 **a** Work in pairs. Decide what happens at the end of episode 5 of *Undercover*. Try to include all the characters. Make notes on your ideas.

b Work in groups of four with another pair. Compare ideas and discuss the best way to end the episode.

c Tell the class your group's ideas. Which ideas are the best, do you think?

REAL WORLD
11D It's my first day

Real World checking information

QUICK REVIEW Reporting verbs Work in pairs. Who were the characters in the TV drama *Undercover*? What can you remember about episodes 4 and 5? Use reporting verbs (*invite*, *admit*, etc.) where possible: **A** *Dom invited Kat to have dinner with him.* **B** *Yes, and he also admitted falling in love with her.*

1 Work in pairs. Discuss these questions.
1. Which three people do you phone the most? What do you talk about?
2. Do you ever talk in English on the phone? If so, who do you speak to?

2 a VIDEO 11 CD3 22 Look at the photo. Ella has got a new job as a PA at Getaway Holidays. Watch or listen to two phone conversations. Then answer these questions.
1. Why can't the first caller talk to Tanya Wilson?
2. Why does he want to talk to her?
3. How long is he going to be in the UK?
4. Where and when is Andy going on holiday?
5. Why does he want Ella to contact someone at *The Times*?
6. What else does he want Ella to do?

b Work in pairs. Compare answers.

c Watch or listen again. Choose the correct words on Ella's notepad.

MESSAGE FOR TANYA
Bob ¹*Crane / Krane* called from the USA.
Flying to London on ²*Tuesday / Thursday* next week.
Wants to meet for ³*lunch / dinner* to discuss contract.
Arriving at Heathrow on British Airways flight
⁴*BA614 / BA164* from Miami at ⁵*11.15 / 11.50*.

TO DO
– Call Rupert ⁶*Nielson / Nielsen* at The Times.
  Tell him the meeting on Wednesday ⁷*12th / 19th* has been cancelled.
– Email invitations for the ⁸*UK / European* sales conference in ⁹*London / Lisbon*.

*Andy's mobile 07700 ¹⁰*900723 / 900372*

REAL WORLD Checking information

3 a Fill in the gaps with these words.

| ~~name~~ | could | give | talking | catch |
| with | spelt | mean | didn't | say |

1. Sorry, what did you say your __name__ was again?
2. Is that Crane _____ a C?
3. Sorry, I _____ get all of that.
4. Could you _____ it again, please?
5. Do you _____ this Wednesday?
6. And _____ you tell me his surname again?
7. Is that _____ N-i-e-l-s-e-n?
8. Are you _____ about the UK sales conference?
9. Sorry, I didn't quite _____ that.
10. Can you _____ it to me again, please?

b Which sentences in **3a** do we use to ask someone to repeat information? Which do we use to check that the information we have is correct?

c Check in REAL WORLD 11.1 p153.

4 CD3 23 PRONUNCIATION Listen and practise the sentences in **3a**. Copy the stress and polite intonation.
Sorry, what did you say your name was again?

HELP WITH LISTENING
Contrastive stress

- We usually put the main stress on words, numbers or letters that we want to check or correct.

5 **a** **24** Listen to these sentences. Where are the main stresses in Mr Krane's sentence?

ELLA And it arrives at eleven fifty.
MR KRANE No, not eleven fifty, eleven fifteen.

b CD3 **25** Listen to four more pairs of sentences from Ella's conversations. Which words, letters or numbers have the main stress?

c Work in pairs. Look at Audio Script CD3 **25** p173. Practise saying these pairs of sentences. Take turns to be Ella.

6 **a** Choose the correct words.

1
A Hello, ¹(can)/will I help you?
B Yes, can I speak to Mr Smith, please?
A Do you ²mean/say Ron Smith?
B No, Ed Smith.

2
A Can you call Gary on extension 223 and remind him about the meeting?
B Sorry, I didn't ³give/get all of that. Did you ⁴say/tell extension 233?
A No, extension 223.
B And are you ⁵talking/saying about today's meeting?
A No, tomorrow's meeting.

3
A Sorry, I didn't quite ⁶hear/catch that. Can you ⁷give/get me your address again?
B 23 Jerrard Street, SE19.
A Is ⁸this/that Gerrard ⁹with/for a G?
B No, it's ¹⁰with/for a J.

4
A Sorry, ¹¹what/who did you say his name was again?
B It's Trevor Martyn.
A And is that ¹²spelt/said M-a-r-t-i-n?
B No, it's M-a-r-t-y-n.
A And do you ¹³want/like to talk to him ¹⁴about/for this year's conference?
B No, next year's conference.

b Work in pairs. Compare answers. Where are the main stresses in the sentences in bold in **6a**?

c **26** Listen and check.

d Work with your partner. Practise the conversations in **6a**. Take turns to be A and B.

7 Work in new pairs. Student A p106. Student B p111.

HELP WITH PRONUNCIATION
Words ending in -tion, -age and -ture

1 **27** Listen to these sounds and words. Notice how we say the suffixes in bold. Listen again and practise.

1 /ʃən/ audi**tion** prescrip**tion** infec**tion**
2 /ɪdʒ/ man**age** cott**age** encour**age**
3 /tʃə/ na**ture** adven**ture** sculp**ture**

2 **a** Work in pairs. Mark the stress on these words.

reception	collection	promotion	prescription
education	invitation	conversation	information
organisation	pronunciation	examination	
message	village	language	damage
sausage	luggage	package	
future	miniature	temperature	manufacture

b **28** Listen and check. Are the suffixes stressed or unstressed? Which syllable is stressed in words ending in -tion? Listen again and practise.

3 Work in pairs. Practise saying these sentences.

1 There's a prescription for collection at reception.
2 Can you give a message to the cottage in the village?
3 Our organisation manufactures miniature sculptures.
4 We encourage language education in our organisation.
5 I've damaged the package of sausages in my luggage.
6 I managed to get some information on his promotion.
7 We're all going on a nature adventure in the future.
8 Good pronunciation is an invitation to conversation!

continue2learn

■ **Vocabulary, Grammar and Real World**
   ■ **Extra Practice 11 and Progress Portfolio 11** p125
   ■ **Language Summary 11** p152
   ■ **11A–D** Workbook p55

■ **Reading and Writing**
   ■ **Portfolio 11** Telling a story Workbook p84
   Reading a story about an interview
   Writing verb forms in stories

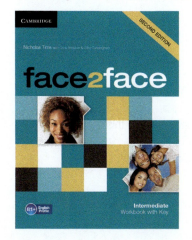

93

12A I wish!

Vocabulary informal words and phrases
Grammar wishes

QUICK REVIEW Checking information Write the names, addresses and phone numbers of two people you know (or you can invent them). Work in pairs. Take turns to say the information. Your partner writes it down. Check any information you are not sure of: *Sorry, I didn't get all of that. Is that spelt H-e-r-n-a-n?*

Vocabulary and Speaking
Informal words and phrases

1 a Work in pairs. Guess the meanings of the words/phrases in bold. Then check your answers in VOCABULARY 12.1 p154.

1 I really **fancy** going away this weekend.
2 I **can't be bothered** to cook this evening.
3 I **don't feel up to** going out after class.
4 I'm completely **broke** at the moment.
5 I often **hang around** for a bit after class.
6 The last film I saw was **rubbish**.
7 I'm really **into** yoga at the moment.
8 It's **up to me** when I take my holiday.
9 I **reckon** it's going to rain tomorrow.
10 I **could do with** a few days off.
11 I'm **sick of** working or studying so hard.
12 I'm **off** to the cinema later.

b Work on your own. Choose six sentences from **1a** that are true for you.

c Work in pairs. Tell your partner your sentences. Ask follow-up questions and try to continue each conversation for 20 seconds.

Listening

2 a Work in pairs. Look at photos A–E. What do you think the people are talking about?

b CD3 29 Listen and match conversations 1–5 to photos A–E.

c Listen again. Fill in the gaps with one or two words.

1 I wish we had a _____.
2 I wish I could come _____.
3 I wish I was on a _____ somewhere.
4 I wish we didn't have to go to this _____.
5 I wish you were coming to the _____ with me.

A *Ryan and Amanda*
B *Dylan and Barbara*

HELP WITH GRAMMAR Wishes

3 a Look at the sentences in **2c**. Then answer the questions.
1 Do these sentences talk about real or imaginary situations?
2 Do they talk about the past or the present/future?

b Look at this sentence. Then answer the questions.

I wish we had a car.

1 Has Juliet got a car?
2 Would she like to have one?

c Look again at the sentences in **2c**. Then fill in the gaps with *Past Continuous*, *Past Simple*, *didn't have to* or *could*.

- To make wishes about states we use: wish + _____ .
- To make wishes about activities happening now we use: wish + _____ .
- To make wishes about abilities or possibilities we use: wish + _____ + infinitive.
- To make wishes about obligations we use: wish + _____ + infinitive.

TIPS • We can say *I wish I/he/she/it* **was** … or *I wish I/he/she/it* **were** …: *I wish I was/were on a beach somewhere.*
• We often use the second conditional to give reasons for wishes: *I wish we had a car. If we had one, I wouldn't spend half my life waiting for buses.*

d Check in GRAMMAR 12.1 p155.

C Jason and Tina
D Molly and Patrick
E Lenny and Juliet

4 **a** Fill in the gaps with the correct form of the verbs in brackets.

1 I wish I _____ (can) find a job.
2 I wish it _____ (not be) so cold in this flat.
3 I wish I _____ (not have to) mark all these exams.
4 I wish I _____ (have) a new dress for the party.
5 I wish we _____ (stay) at home this evening.
6 I wish the bus stop _____ (be) closer to our flat.
7 I wish he _____ (can) come to the pub with us.
8 I wish I _____ (not have to) finish this report.
9 I wish he _____ (like) musicals.
10 I wish I _____ (sit) in a beach bar right now.

b CD3 30 PRONUNCIATION Listen and check. Listen again and practise.

I wish I could find a job.

c Work in pairs. Which people in photos A–E do you think said the sentences in **4a**? There is one sentence for each person.

5 Write sentences with *I wish* for these situations.
1 I have to study all evening.
   I wish I didn't have to study all evening.
2 I'm sitting in a traffic jam.
3 We have to get up at six o'clock every day.
4 I can't afford to go on holiday this year.
5 We live in a very dangerous neighbourhood.
6 My wife's working late this evening.
7 I don't know how to sail.

6 **a** Fill in the gaps in these second conditionals with the correct form of the verbs in brackets.

a If I *could* (can) sail, I *'d live* (live) on a boat all summer.
b I _____ (meet) up with friends tonight if I _____ (not have) an exam tomorrow.
c If there _____ (not be) so much traffic, I _____ (be) home by now.
d If I _____ (can) afford a holiday, I _____ (go) to Turkey.
e I _____ (take) her out to a nice restaurant if she _____ (not have to) work.
f We _____ (not have to) leave home so early if we _____ (live) closer to the office.
g If we _____ (live) in a nicer part of town, we _____ (go out) at night more often.

b Work in pairs. Compare answers. Then match the sentences in **5** to the sentences in **6a**.

Get ready … Get it right!

7 **a** Write six wishes for you. Use these ideas or your own.

- lifestyle
- languages
- money
- possessions
- skills and abilities
- home
- work or studies
- relationships
- sport

I wish I had more free time.

b Think about how your life would be different if your wishes came true.

If I had more free time, I'd write a book.

8 **a** Work in groups. Tell each other about your wishes and how your life would be different if they came true. Ask follow-up questions if possible. Which are the most interesting or surprising wishes?

I wish I could speak Spanish fluently. If I could, I'd go and work in South America.

Really? Which country would you go to?

b Tell the class about the most interesting or surprising wishes in your group.

12B Important moments

Vocabulary phrases with *get*
Grammar third conditional

QUICK REVIEW Wishes Write one thing you wish: you had, you could do, you didn't have to do: *I wish I had a scooter.* Think of reasons for your wishes: *If I had a scooter, I could get to school quicker.* Work in pairs. Tell your partner about your wishes and your reasons.

Vocabulary and Speaking
Phrases with *get*

1 a Look at the table. Notice the different meanings of *get*. Tick the phrases you know in the table.

get = receive/obtain	**get** = become
get something to eat/drink	get lost
get a job	get depressed/angry

get = travel/arrive	other phrases with **get**
get home	get on well with someone
get here/there	get to know someone

Carol and Owen

b Work in pairs. Fill in the gaps in the table with these phrases. Then check in **VOCABULARY 12.2** ▶ p154.

> get fed up with something   get in touch with someone
> get around   get a message   get back from somewhere
> get rid of something   get into trouble
> get a present   get to work   get a phone call
> get better/worse at something   get older

c Work in the same pairs. Which other phrases with *get* do you know?

get on someone's nerves
get annoyed about something

2 a Write three true sentences and three false sentences about yourself using phrases from **1a** and **1b**.

I get on really well with my neighbours.
I used to get into trouble a lot at school.

b Work in pairs. Take turns to say your sentences. You can ask your partner two questions about each sentence. Guess which of your partner's sentences are false.

Listening

3 **CD3 ▶ 31** Look at the photos. Then listen to Carol, Anthony and Michelle talking about important moments in their lives. Choose the correct answers.

1 Carol met her husband *in the USA/at a party*.
2 Owen couldn't fly home because *he lost his passport/the airport was closed*.
3 Anthony *got into financial trouble/lost his job*.
4 He now lives in *London/the country*.
5 Michelle used to *work very hard/get into trouble* at school.
6 She *has competed/wants to compete* in the Olympics.

4 a Work in pairs. Who said these sentences: Carol, Anthony or Michelle?

a If I'd stayed at home, I wouldn't have met my husband.
b If I hadn't lost my job, I wouldn't have started my own business.
c He'd have flown home that day if the weather hadn't been so bad.
d If I hadn't won that race, I'd never have become a serious athlete.
e I wouldn't have left London if I'd stayed with the ad agency.
f If I hadn't started doing this, I'd have got into a lot more trouble.

b **CD3 ▶ 31** Listen again and check. Put the sentences in **4a** in the order you hear them.

Anthony

Michelle

HELP WITH GRAMMAR Third conditional

5 a Look at this sentence. Answer the questions.

if clause	main clause
If I'd stayed at home,	I wouldn't have met my husband.

1 Does the sentence talk about the past or the present?
2 Does this sentence talk about something that is real or imaginary?
3 Did Carol stay at home?
4 Did she meet her husband?

b Look at the third conditionals in **4a**. Then choose the correct words in these rules.
- In the *if* clause we use the *Past Simple/Past Perfect*.
- In the main clause we use *'d*, *would* or *wouldn't* + *have* + *Past Simple/past participle*.
- The *if* clause *is always first/can be first or second* in the sentence.

c Check in GRAMMAR 12.2 p155.

HELP WITH LISTENING Third conditional

6 a CD3 32 Listen to these third conditionals. Notice how we say the contractions (*I'd*, etc.) and the weak form of *have*.

If I'd stayed at home, I wouldn't have /əv/ met my husband.
If I hadn't lost my job, I wouldn't have /əv/ started my own business.

b CD3 33 Listen and write the sentences you hear. You will hear each sentence twice.

7 CD3 34 PRONUNCIATION Listen and practise. Copy the contractions and the weak form of *have*.

if they'd wanted to →
They'd have /əv/ come to the party if they'd wanted to.

8 a Fill in the gaps in these third conditionals with the correct form of the verbs.

1 If her friend _hadn't introduced_ (not introduce) them, they _wouldn't have_ met. (not meet)
2 She _____ (become) a serious athlete if she _____ (come) last.
3 If the agency _____ (not get) into financial trouble, he _____ (not start) his own business.
4 He _____ (stay) in London if he _____ (not lose) his job.
5 If he _____ (go back) to Boston, he _____ (not see) her again.

b Work in pairs. Compare answers. Then match the sentences to the people in photos A–C.

9 Write third conditionals for these situations.

1 I overslept so I was late for work.
If I hadn't overslept, I wouldn't have been late for work.
2 They got lost because they didn't take a map.
3 Roberta was exhausted so she didn't go out.
4 Paula was ill so she didn't go to school.
5 Kevin got depressed because his wife left him.
6 I didn't call you because I lost my phone.

Get ready … Get it right!

10 a Think about three important moments in your life. Use these ideas or your own.
- people you've met
- places you've visited
- exams you've taken
- having children
- getting or losing jobs
- choosing what to study

b Write three third conditionals about how your life would have been different if these things hadn't happened.

11 Work in pairs. Tell each other about the important moments in your life. Ask follow-up questions.

VOCABULARY 12C AND SKILLS > Superheroes

Vocabulary word building (3): word families
Skills Listening: a radio interview; Reading: a magazine article

QUICK REVIEW Third conditional Write three sentences with *because* about good or bad things that happened to you last week: *On Friday I was late for work because I missed the train.* Work in pairs. Swap sentences. Make third conditionals from your partner's sentences: *If you hadn't missed the train on Friday, you wouldn't have been late for work.*

Speaking and Listening

1 Work in groups. Discuss these questions.
1 Look at the photo of Spider-Man. What superpowers does he have?
2 Have you seen any of the Spider-Man films? If so, did you like them? Why?/Why not?
3 What other superheroes do you know? What superpowers do they have?
4 Look at the photo of Stan Lee. What do you think he did?

Spider-Man

Stan Lee

2 a CD3 35 Listen to an interview with the writer, Robin Baker. Put topics a–e in the order he talks about them.
a Stan Lee's other superhero characters.
b Why Spider-Man is different from other superheroes.
c How Spider-Man got his name.
d Stan Lee and his characters' movies.
e Spider-Man's superpowers.

b Listen again. Are these sentences true or false?
1 Stan Lee's comic *The Fantastic Four* saved his company.
2 He thought of the idea for Spider-Man when he saw a spider walking up a wall.
3 Spider-Man was the first name that Stan Lee thought of.
4 Spider-Man doesn't have problems like normal people.
5 He got his superpowers when he was bitten by a spider.
6 Stan Lee is usually a newspaper seller in his characters' movies.

HELP WITH LISTENING
Sentence stress and weak forms: review

3 a Work in pairs. Look at the beginning of the interview. Mark the stressed words and circle the weak forms.

Hello (and) welcome (to) the programme. Stories of superheroes have entertained us for nearly eighty years, and one of the most popular of these is Spider-Man. Today I'm talking to the author Robin Baker, whose new book, *Superhero*, tells the story of Spider-Man's creator, Stan Lee. Welcome to the programme, Robin.

b Look at Audio Script CD3 35 p174. Read and listen to the beginning of the interview. Check your answers.

c Listen to the whole interview again. Follow the sentence stress and weak forms.

Reading and Vocabulary

4 a Look at the photo on p99. What is the man doing? Why is he doing this, do you think?

b Before you read, check these words with your teacher or in a dictionary.

| a coma | a rope | equipment | a skyscraper |

c Read about Alain Robert. Match these topics to paragraphs 1–6.
a A childhood adventure
b The real Spider-Man 1
c Danger and police
d A terrible fall
e Why he likes climbing
f Three amazing climbs

d Read the article again. Answer these questions.
1 Why did he climb up the side of the building where his family lived?
2 Why were the doctors wrong?
3 Why is his style of climbing so dangerous?
4 Why does he usually get arrested?
5 What did he do for the first Spider-Man movie?
6 What happened after he climbed the Jin Mao Building?
7 Why does he climb?

The real Spider-Man

1 Alain Robert has climbed about 100 of the world's tallest buildings, including the Empire State Building in New York, the Eiffel Tower in Paris and the Petronas Twin Towers in Malaysia. It's not surprising people call him 'The real Spider-Man'.

2 Alain began climbing on the cliffs near where he lived in Valence, France. One day, when he was 12, he got home and realised that he'd forgotten his keys. So he climbed up the side of the building and into his family's flat through the window – which was eight floors up. That was when he decided to become a professional climber.

3 In his teens he climbed all the difficult mountains in the Alps and found them "rather **disappointing**". However, he did have a few bad falls. In 1982 he fell 15 metres and was in a coma for five days. Doctors said he'd never climb again. Alain was back on a mountain after only six months.

4 In 1994 he climbed his first skyscraper, in Chicago, and realised he **enjoyed** doing what seemed impossible. He climbs without ropes or **protective** equipment – just with his hands and feet. He's always very **careful**, of course, but admits that the danger is part of the **attraction**. Also he usually climbs without permission, which means he often gets arrested. "That's no problem," says Alain. "I **prefer** staying in prison to staying in hospital."

5 For the release of the first Spider-Man film in 2002, Alain climbed the tallest skyscraper in Venezuela wearing a Spider-Man costume and was watched live on TV by over 10 million people. He also climbed the 88-storey Jin Mao Building in Shanghai in 2007, again dressed as Spider-Man, after which he was arrested and held in prison for five days. And in 2011 he climbed the tallest building in the world, the 828-metre Burj Khalifa Tower in Dubai, in just over six hours.

6 However, Alain doesn't climb buildings just to provide **entertainment** for the public. For him, climbing is a form of **relaxation**, but there's also a deeper meaning to what he does. "It gives me a sense of what is important on Earth," he says. "When you're facing your own death, money is not that important."

HELP WITH VOCABULARY
Word building (3): word families

5 **a** Work in pairs. Fill in the gaps in the table with the words in bold in the article. Write the infinitive form of the verbs.

verb	noun	adjective
disappoint	disappointment	disappointed, *disappointing*
	enjoyment	enjoyable
protect	protection	
care	care	, careless
attract		attractive
	preference	preferable
entertain		entertaining
relax		relaxing, relaxed

b Look at the table again. Underline the suffixes in the nouns and adjectives.

disappoint**ment**, disappoint**ed**, disappoint**ing**

c Do we use these suffixes to make nouns (N) or adjectives (A)?

| -ment N | -ing A | -ed | -able | -ion |
| -ive | -ful | -less | -ence | -ation |

d Check in VOCABULARY 12.3 ▶ p154.

6 **a** Work in pairs. Look at the verbs in the table. Fill in the gaps with the correct nouns and adjectives.

verb	noun	adjective
create	*creation*	*creative*
pollute		
employ		
embarrass		
depend		
harm		
predict		
confuse		
reserve		

b Check in VOCABULARY 12.4 ▶ p154.

7 Work in pairs. Take turns to say a verb. Your partner says the noun and adjective(s).

create — creation, creative

8 Create your own superhero! Work in groups. Look at p114.

HELP WITH PRONUNCIATION Review quiz

 Work in pairs or groups. Do the pronunciation quiz!

1 Circle the word endings that we <u>don't</u> say with a /ə/ sound. (2 points)

kind**ness**   man**age**   danger**ous**   adven**ture**
argu**ment**   honest**y**   promo**tion**

2 Which adjective in each group has a different stress pattern? (2 pts)
   a   relaxed   concerned   frightened
   b   exhausted   terrified   embarrassed

3 Match each word 1–3 to a word a–c with the same *ear* sound. (3 pts)
   1   b**ear**d   a   w**ear**ing
   2   b**ear**   b   h**ear**d
   3   **ear**thquake   c   disapp**ear**

4 Look at the letters in bold. Are the sounds the same or different? (6 pts)
   a   a g**o**rg**eo**us **j**acket
   b   a **u**niversity st**u**dent
   c   an intermedi**a**te certific**a**te
   d   a stubb**or**n w**or**kaholic
   e   en**ough** st**u**ff
   f   alth**ough** it's a dr**ough**t

5 Write the extra linking sounds in these phrasal verbs. (3 pts)
   clear‿out   go‿up   see‿off

6 Look at this sentence. Do we say the words in pink in their strong or weak forms? (4 pts)
   We were trying to find out who this email was from.

 CD3▶36 Listen and check your answers. How many points did you get? Listen again and practise.

continue2learn

■ **Vocabulary, Grammar and Real World**
   ■ **Extra Practice 12 and Progress Portfolio 12** p126
   ■ **Language Summary 12** p154
   ■ **12A–C** Workbook p60

■ **Reading and Writing**
   ■ **Portfolio 12** Life changes Workbook p86
   Reading descriptions of important moments
   Writing common mistakes; an important moment

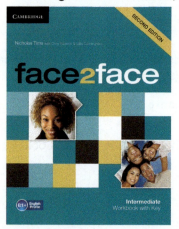

Work in groups of four. Read the rules. Then play the game!

Rules

You need: One counter for each student; one dice for each group.

How to play: Put your counters on **START**. Take turns to throw the dice, move your counter and read the instructions on the square. The first student to get to **FINISH** is the winner.

Grammar and **Vocabulary** **squares:** The first student to land on a Grammar or Vocabulary square answers question 1. The second student to land on the same square answers question 2. If the other students think your answer is correct, you can stay on the square. If the answer is wrong, you must move back to the last square you were on. If a third or fourth student lands on the same square, he/she can stay on the square without answering a question.

Talk about squares: If you land on a Talk about square, talk about the topic for 30 seconds. Another student can check the time. If you can't talk for 30 seconds, you must move back to the last square you were on. If a second or third student lands on the same square, he/she also talks about the same topic for 30 seconds.

End of Course Review

FINISH

38. What are the opposites of these words?
1 painful, correct, common, polite
2 responsible, useless, appear, reliable

37. MOVE BACK TWO SQUARES

36. Correct the mistake in this sentence.
1 His phone's not as older as mine.
2 This house is the same size than ours.

35. Talk about the house or flat you lived in when you were a child.

30. Make a sentence with *I wish …* for this situation.
1 I don't have a laptop.
2 I have to go to a meeting.

31. MOVE FORWARD TWO SQUARES

32. Do we use *make* or *do* with these words/phrases?
1 a course, up your mind, money, exercise
2 a noise, a degree, progress, an exam

33. Talk about what you did on your last birthday.

34. Put this question into reported speech.
1 What are you doing?
2 Does Jim work in the city centre?

29. Make nouns from these adjectives.
1 sad, dangerous, popular, healthy
2 difficult, kind, patient, possible

28. Talk about your last holiday.

27. Which verb pattern follows these verbs?
1 refuse, admit, remind
2 invite, suggest, agree

26. Say eight:
1 body movements and responses
2 adjectives to describe jobs

25. MOVE FORWARD THREE SQUARES

20. Talk about your favourite musical experiences.

21. Put this sentence into the passive.
1 Someone's stolen my phone.
2 Someone's repairing my car.

22. Which verb form comes after these verbs?
1 keep, need, make, will
2 let, seem, would, finish

23. Talk about street food you like or don't like.

24. Do we use *do*, *to do* or *doing* with these phrases?
1 be useless at, manage, could
2 know how, be able to, be no good at

19. Correct the mistake in this sentence.
1 I've been visiting six countries so far.
2 He's been working here since two years.

18. Which prepositions?
1 take part … sth, protest … sth, go … strike
2 keep … touch … sb, get hold … sb

17. MOVE BACK THREE SQUARES

16. What's the question tag?
1 You went out last night, … ?
2 He doesn't know her, … ?

15. Say eight:
1 adjectives to describe feelings
2 character adjectives

10. Do we use *travel*, *get* or *go on* with these phrases?
1 first class, a cruise, on a bus
2 a trip, on your own, a taxi

11. Talk about a job you've done or would like to do.

12. Do these verbs usually describe states or activities?
1 watch, seem, own, eat
2 prefer, buy, cook, need

13. Make adjectives from these verbs.
1 disappoint, protect, relax, care
2 attract, predict, relax, entertain

14. Talk about what you would do if you had more free time.

9. MOVE FORWARD TWO SQUARES

8. Say eight words/phrases for:
1 health problems or symptoms
2 bad weather or natural disasters

7. Talk about things that tourists can do in your town, city or country.

6. Correct the mistake in this sentence.
1 If I'd be younger, I'd go travelling.
2 Can you tell me what time does it start?

5. Say the strong adjectives for these gradable adjectives.
1 hot, surprised, tired, bad
2 big, dirty, small, hot

START

1. Which prepositions do we use with these adjectives?
1 good, nervous, interested, upset
2 keen, fed up, worried, scared

2. Make a question with *How long … ?*
1 She's been living in Rome **for a year**.
2 I've had my car **since 2010**.

3. Talk about what makes you happy.

4. MOVE FORWARD THREE SQUARES

101

Pair and Group Work: Student/Group A

1A 9 p7

a Work on your own. Make questions with these words. Which questions have a preposition at the end? Which are subject questions?

1 from / parents / do / your / Where / come ?
Where do your parents come from?
2 you / about / friends / your / and / do / What / argue ?
3 radio station / to / normally / listen / do / Which / you ?
4 do / on / Who / with / holiday / usually / go / you ?
5 in / home / first / gets up / Who / your ?
6 your / most of / does / home / the cooking / Who / in ?

b Work with your partner. Ask and answer the questions. Ask follow-up questions if possible.

3B 7 p25

a Work on your own. Read about Polly Kirby's job.

I've been writing guide books for ¹_____ years. I've written three books and now I'm working on a book about Kenya. I've been living in Africa since ²_____ and I really love it here. I've been travelling around Kenya for two weeks and I've visited ³_____ different places so far. At the moment I'm on a guided tour to Mount Kilimanjaro. I've wanted to climb this mountain since I arrived in Africa. We've been walking since ⁴_____ and I'm absolutely exhausted. We've travelled about 15 km today and I've seen ⁵_____ elephants! My guide, Shola, has been doing this job for 30 years. He's climbed Kilimanjaro ⁶_____ times this year. I've only known him for three days, but we're already good friends.

b Work with a student from group A. Make questions with *How long ... ?* or *How many ... ?* to complete the text. Use the Present Perfect Continuous and Present Perfect Simple.

1 *How long has Polly been writing guide books?*

c Work with a student from group B. Ask and answer the questions. Fill in the gaps in the text. You start.

d Compare your texts and check your answers.

2D 8 p21

a Work on your own. Imagine you have this problem. Then think of one thing you've tried to do to solve the problem.

> Your cousin got divorced recently and moved out of his house, so you invited him to stay for a few days. It's now six weeks later and he's still living with you. He isn't working at the moment, so he just stays at home and watches TV all day. He's driving you crazy and you want him to move out.

b Work with a student from group B and group C. Take turns to explain your problems, show concern and give advice. Whose advice is the best, do you think?

> I've got a bit of a problem.
>
> Oh, dear. What's the matter?
>
> Well, my cousin got divorced recently ...

c Tell the class the best piece of advice you received.

3A 7 p23

a Work on your own. Fill in the gaps with *you* and the correct form of these verbs. Use the Present Perfect Simple or Past Simple.

| ~~see~~ | have | decide | go away |
| know | study | watch | speak |

1 What's the best film *you've seen* recently?
2 _____ ever _____ a really bad holiday?
3 _____ any sport on TV last week?
4 _____ what to do this weekend yet?
5 How long _____ the other students in the class?
6 _____ for the weekend last month?
7 _____ to anyone in your family today?
8 Is this the first time _____ English in a language school?

b Work with your partner. Ask and answer the questions. Ask follow-up questions if possible.

Pair and Group Work: Student/Group A

5B 3 p41

a Work on your own. Fill in the gaps with *away*, *through*, *out* or *up*.

1 Which room in your house do you need to clear _out_?
2 Who tidies _____ the house in your family?
3 Do you tend to keep everything or do you give things _____?
4 When did you last sort _____ your photos, DVDs or music?
5 Do you put your clothes _____ before you go to bed?
6 How often do you go _____ your drawers and throw things _____?
7 What was the last thing you threw _____?

b Work in pairs. Ask and answer the questions. Who is tidier, you or your partner?

5C 5 p43

a Work on your own. Put the verbs in brackets in the correct form. There may be more than one possible answer.

1 Do you enjoy _____ (go) to birthday parties?
2 Have you ever helped someone _____ (organise) a birthday party?
3 Would you rather _____ (have) your birthday at a different time of the year?
4 Have you ever forgotten _____ (buy) someone in your family a birthday present?
5 Did your parents make you _____ (thank) your relatives for your birthday presents?
6 What do you think the class should _____ (give) your teacher on his/her birthday?

b Work with your partner. Ask and answer the questions. Ask follow-up questions.

6A 11 p47

a Work on your own. Read about a problem you have. Think of three ways you can deal with the problem and decide what will happen if you choose each of these options.

> You're doing a medical degree and you're in the third year of a five-year course. However, you have money problems. You need £9,000 to pay for next year's course, but you haven't got the money. Your parents have already lent you £3,000 and you also owe the bank £6,000.

get a part-time job → not have enough time to study

b Work with a student from group B and group C. Take turns to talk about your problem and your options. Discuss what will happen if you choose each option. Your partners can also suggest other options.

> If I get a part-time job, I won't have enough time to study.

> Why don't you … ?

> If I do that, …

c Decide what to do. Does your group think you've made the right decision?

6C 8 p51

a Work with a student from group A. Write the correct synonym for the words in bold.

pleasant

1 Do you expect people you meet to be **nice** and easy to talk to?
  a Yes, always. b Sometimes. c No, not usually.
2 How **content** do you feel about your life?
  a Very. b Quite. c Not very.
3 How often do you **make a decision** about something based on your intuition?
  a Usually. b Sometimes. c Hardly ever.
4 When did you last **talk to** a stranger, for example in a queue or on a train?
  a Last week. b Last month. c More than a month ago.
5 Do you ever feel **frightened** when you're going to do something new?
  a Yes, usually. b Yes, sometimes. c No, not usually.
6 Do you think you're a **lucky** person?
  a Yes, definitely. b Sometimes. c No, not really.

b Work with a student from group B. Ask and answer the questions. Say the three possible answers when you ask your questions.

c Give your partner 3 points for every a answer, 2 points for every b answer and 1 point for every c answer. What is his/her score?

d Tell your partner his/her score. Then look at p155. Who is luckier, you or your partner?

103

Pair and Group Work: Student/Group A

5D 6 p45

a Work on your own. You want to buy these things. Decide how you can explain them to a sales assistant.

b Work with your partner. You are a customer. Your partner is a sales assistant. Describe the four things in **a** you want to buy from his/her shop. Write the English words for each thing under the pictures. **Don't look at your partner's book.**

c You are a sales assistant. Your partner is a customer. Look at these things in your shop. Listen to your partner describe the things he/she wants to buy. When you understand which thing he/she is describing, tell him/her the English word. **Don't show your partner the pictures.**

a fan   a cool bag   cotton buds

ear plugs   washing-up liquid

a pan scourer   furniture polish   a duster

d Work in pairs. Check your answers. Did you write the correct words?

7C 6 p59

a Work on your own. Fill in the gaps in these questions with *a*, *an*, *the* or – (= no article).

1 Do you know anyone who has just bought _____ new laptop?
2 When did you last have _____ problem with your computer? Did you manage to solve _____ problem yourself?
3 Which do you like best, _____ Italian food or _____ Chinese food?
4 Where's _____ best place for tourists to visit in _____ south of your country?
5 Would you prefer to go on holiday to _____ USA or _____ South Africa?
6 What is/was the best thing about going to _____ school?
7 Do you know anyone who's _____ singer or _____ actor?

b Work with your partner. Ask and answer the questions. Ask follow-up questions if possible.

9B 10 p73

a Work with a student from group A. Choose the correct auxiliaries in the news summary.

> Hello, here is (your name) with the news headlines. The USA ¹**has/has been** had more bad weather today. Tornadoes ²**have/have been** hit towns and cities in Texas, and hundreds of homes ³**have/have been** destroyed. Over 50 people ⁴**have/have been** injured, but so far nobody ⁵**has/has been** died.
>
> The England footballer Phil West ⁶**has just/has just been** told the media that he's getting married next year. Phil and his girlfriend, Sally, ⁷**have/have been** already decided where to have the wedding, but so far the location ⁸**has/has been** kept a secret.

b Practise reading the news summary to your partner from group A.

c Work in pairs with a student from group B. Take turns to read your news summary without stopping. Make brief notes on your partner's news summary.

d Work with your partner from group A. Compare notes. What were group B's news stories about?

7B 6 p57

a Work on your own. Fill in the gaps with the correct form of the verbs in brackets.

1 What _____ you _____ (do) if you suddenly _____ (become) incredibly rich?
2 If you _____ (not study) English, which language _____ you _____ (like) to study?
3 If you _____ (have to) sing in a karaoke bar, which song _____ you _____ (sing)?
4 How _____ your life _____ (be) different if you _____ (live) in the USA?
5 If you _____ (can) have dinner with a famous actor or actress, who _____ you _____ (choose)?

b Work with your partner. Ask and answer the questions. Continue the conversation if possible.

10D 7 p85

a Work on your own. Read the information about conversations 1 and 2. Decide what you want to say in each conversation.

1 You are staying with student B for a few days. Make questions to ask permission to do these things.
- make yourself something to eat
- phone your friend in Kenya
- borrow his/her car tomorrow evening
- use his/her computer to check your email
- invite your cousin to stay the night on Saturday
- have a shower

2 Student B is staying with you for a few days. He/She is going to ask permission to do these things. Decide if you want to give or refuse permission. If you want to refuse permission, think of a reason why.
- watch a DVD this evening
- borrow £100 until next week
- make himself/herself a cup of tea
- stay an extra couple of days
- give his/her sister a call
- invite some of his/her friends to come round for dinner tomorrow

b Work with your partner. Role-play the conversations. You start conversation 1. Your partner starts conversation 2.

c Tell the class which things your partner refused permission for and why.

3C 7 p27

a Read the fact file about a voluntourism holiday. You are going to tell the other students in your group about the holiday. Make notes on the main points.

PLACE	Cambodia, southeast Asia
TYPE OF WORK	help to build a new medical centre for the area with people from the local community
ACCOMMODATION AND FOOD	stay in own room in local villagers' homes; share meals with their host family
FREE TIME	go hiking in the jungle with a local guide from the village; relax on beautiful beaches
OTHER INFORMATION	You must be physically fit and healthy. The project is in a remote area of the country – no internet, phone, TV, etc.

b Work in your groups. Close your books. Take turns to tell your group about the holiday.

c Choose which holiday you'd like to go on. Give reasons for your choices.

d Tell the class which holiday you've chosen. Which holiday is the most popular?

9A 9 p71

a Work with a student from group A. Write sentences to describe these words/phrases. Use *who*, *that*, *which* or *where*. Check words you don't know in a dictionary.

> a lifeguard   a garage   a blender
> a memory stick   a vegetarian   an optimist
> a residential area   an estate agent

A person who saves people's lives at the beach.

b Work in groups of four with a pair from group B. Take turns to say your sentences. Guess the other pair's words. Which pair guessed the most words correctly?

Pair and Group Work: Student/Group A

8A 9 p63

a Work in pairs with a student from group A. Write questions with these words. Put the verbs in the correct active or passive form. Use *by* if necessary.

1 In which year / New Orleans / destroy / Hurricane Katrina?
 a In 2001. b **In 2005.** c In 2009.
2 What percentage of people who / kill / lightning every year are male?
 a 50%. b 70%. c **85%**
3 Which of these countries / have / the most tornadoes in the last 20 years?
 a Mexico. b **The USA**. c Cuba.
4 Which country / hit / the world's biggest earthquake in 1960?
 a China. b The USA. c **Chile**.
5 Which country / have got / the largest number of active volcanoes in the world?
 a **Indonesia**. b Japan. c The Philippines.
6 What percentage of the Earth's surface / cover / water?
 a About 60%. b **About 70%**. c About 80%.

b Work in a group of four with a pair from group B. Ask and answer the questions. Say the three possible answers when you ask your questions. (The correct answers are in bold.)

c Which pair got more answers right?

10C 6 p83

a Work on your own. Fill in the gaps with the correct form of these phrasal verbs.

| get out of | get over | split up |
| look up | put off | come up with |

1 What do you think is the most common reason why couples _____ ?
2 How long does it usually take you to _____ a bad cold?
3 Are you good at _____ solutions to problems?
4 When did you last try to _____ something you didn't want to do?
5 What was the last word you _____ in a dictionary?
6 Do you usually do things immediately, or do you _____ them _____ until the last minute?

b Work with your partner. Ask and answer the questions. Ask follow-up questions if possible.

9D 9 p77

a Work on your own. Read the information for conversations 1 and 2. Decide what you want to say in each conversation.

> 1 You are a doctor. Your next patient has just moved to this town and you haven't seen him/her before. Firstly, find out a few things about him/her (job, family, etc.). Then ask what his/her symptoms are. Finally, decide on the correct treatment.

> 2 You are a patient. You have already seen your doctor twice this month, but he/she wasn't very helpful (last time he/she told you to take some paracetamol). Decide what your symptoms are and how long you've had them. Also decide if you've had these symptoms before.

b Work with your partner. Role-play the conversations. You start conversation 1. Your partner starts conversation 2.

c Tell the class about the treatment your doctor suggested. Were you happy with your doctor's advice? Why?/Why not?

11D 7 p93

a Work on your own. Read this information. Underline the main points and plan what you are going to say.

> Your name is Chris Baker and you work for a travel company called East Coast Breaks in California, USA. You are going to call Getaway Holidays in the UK. You want to speak to Tanya Wilson. You have already arranged a meeting with Tanya at 3.15 p.m. on Friday. You are arriving at Gatwick Airport, London, at 12.35. Your flight number is BA 4517. You would like someone to pick you up at the airport. Your work phone number is 001 212 555 1229.

b Look again at the information you underlined in **a**, then phone Tanya Wilson. If she isn't there, leave a message with her PA.

c You are Bob Krane's PA at Miami Hotels Ltd in Florida, USA. Mr Krane is in a meeting at the moment. Answer the phone and take a message for him. Check information when you need to.

d Work with your partner. Check his/her message. Is it correct?

Pair and Group Work: Student/Group B

1A 9 p7

a Work on your own. Make questions with these words. Which questions have a preposition at the end? Which are subject questions?

1 to / you / music / What / do / kind of / listen ?
   What kind of music do you listen to?
2 you and your friends / What / about / talking / do / like ?
3 the / you / do / go to / with / usually / cinema / Who ?
4 to / you / countries / want / to / Which / go / do ?
5 home / goes / Who / in / bed / your / last / to ?
6 home / the most / watches / your / in / Who / TV ?

b Work with your partner. Ask and answer the questions. Ask follow-up questions if possible.

3B 7 p25

a Work on your own. Read about Polly Kirby's job.

I've been writing guide books for four years. I've written ^a_____ books and now I'm working on a book about Kenya. I've been living in Africa since I left university and I really love it here. I've been travelling around Kenya for ^b_____ and I've visited six different places so far. At the moment I'm on a guided tour to Mount Kilimanjaro. I've wanted to climb this mountain since ^c_____. We've been walking since 7 a.m. and I'm absolutely exhausted. We've travelled ^d_____ km today and I've seen about 15 elephants! My guide, Shola, has been doing this job for ^e_____. He's climbed Kilimanjaro nine times this year. I've only known him for ^f_____, but we're already good friends.

b Work with a student from group B. Make questions with *How long … ?* or *How many … ?* to complete the text. Use the Present Perfect Continuous and Present Perfect Simple.

  a *How many books has she written?*

c Work with a student from group A. Ask and answer the questions. Fill in the gaps in the text. Your partner starts.

d Compare your texts and check your answers.

2D 8 p21

a Work on your own. Imagine you have this problem. Then think of one thing you've tried to do to solve the problem.

> You've got some new neighbours and they're very friendly. However, they come round to your house every day asking for help, or just a chat. They usually stay for at least an hour each time. You work at home, and your neighbours' visits are starting to get on your nerves.

b Work with a student from group A and group C. Take turns to explain your problems, show concern and give advice. Whose advice is the best, do you think?

> I've got a bit of a problem.
>
> Oh, dear. What's the matter?
>
> Well, I've got some new neighbours …

c Tell the class the best piece of advice you received.

3A 7 p23

a Work on your own. Fill in the gaps with *you* and the correct form of these verbs. Use the Present Perfect Simple or Past Simple.

| ~~miss~~ | go on | get | have |
| do | study | see | complete |

1 *Have you* ever *missed* a plane?
2 How long _____ your mobile?
3 _____ anything special on your last birthday?
4 _____ any long journeys lately?
5 _____ anything good on TV this week?
6 How many emails _____ yesterday?
7 _____ the Workbook for this lesson yet?
8 Is this the first time _____ the Present Perfect Simple?

b Work with your partner. Ask and answer the questions. Ask follow-up questions if possible.

Pair and Group Work: Student/Group B

5B 3 p41

a Work on your own. Fill in the gaps with *away*, *through*, *out* or *up*.

1 Do you always put things *away* after you use them?
2 How often do you clear _____ your wardrobe?
3 When did you last tidy _____ your bedroom?
4 Do you throw _____ clothes and shoes that you never wear?
5 Who takes _____ the rubbish in your family?
6 Do you usually go _____ your homework to check for mistakes?
7 When was the last time you sorted _____ your notes from class?

b Work in pairs. Ask and answer the questions. Who is tidier, you or your partner?

6A 11 p47

a Work on your own. Read about a problem you have. Think of three ways you can deal with the problem and decide what will happen if you choose each of these options.

> Yesterday you were in a department store and you saw your friend's wife, Kathy, put some make-up and a skirt in her bag and walk out of the shop without paying for them. Kathy and her husband are quite rich, but you know they're having problems with their marriage.

tell the police → Kathy will be arrested

b Work with a student from group A and group C. Take turns to talk about your problem and your options. Discuss what will happen if you choose each option. Your partners can also suggest other options.

> If I tell the police, Kathy will be arrested.

> Why don't you … ?

> If I do that, …

c Decide what to do. Does your group think you've made the right decision?

5C 5 p43

a Work on your own. Put the verbs in brackets in the correct form. There may be more than one possible answer.

a What would you like _____ (do) on your next birthday?
b Do you know anyone who hates _____ (celebrate) his or her birthday?
c Do you need _____ (buy) a birthday present for anyone soon?
d When you were a child, did your parents let you _____ (stay) up very late on your birthday?
e What do you want your family _____ (get) you for your next birthday?
f Have you started _____ (plan) what you're going to do on your next birthday?

b Work with your partner. Ask and answer the questions. Ask follow-up questions.

6C 8 p51

a Work with a student from group B. Write the correct synonym for the words in bold.

> *certain*
> 1 How **sure** are you that your future will be positive?
>   a Very.   b Quite.   c Not very.
> 2 When was the last time something good happened to you **accidentally**?
>   a Last week.   b Last month.   c More than a month ago.
> 3 What kind of **approach** to life do you have?
>   a Very positive.   b Quite positive.   c Generally negative.
> 4 Do you feel **worried** about the future?
>   a No, not usually.   b Yes, sometimes.   c Yes, most of the time.
> 5 How good are you at **dealing with** problems in your daily life?
>   a Very.   b Quite.   c Not very.
> 6 When was the last time you **tried to do** something that you've never done before?
>   a In the last four weeks.   b In the last three months.   c More than three years ago.

b Work with a student from group A. Ask and answer the questions. Say the three possible answers when you ask your questions.

c Give your partner 3 points for every a answer, 2 points for every b answer and 1 point for every c answer. What is his/her score?

d Tell your partner his/her score. Then look at p155. Who is luckier, you or your partner?

Pair and Group Work: Student/Group B

5D 6 p45

a Work on your own. You want to buy these things. Decide how you can explain them to a sales assistant.

b Work with your partner. You are a sales assistant. Your partner is a customer. Look at these things in your shop. Listen to your partner describe the things he/she wants to buy. When you understand which thing he/she is describing, tell him/her the English word. **Don't show your partner the pictures.**

a marker pen   a highlighter   an adapter

a lead   toothpicks

an electric toothbrush   mosquito coils   mosquito repellent

c You are a customer. Your partner is a sales assistant. Describe the four things in **a** you want to buy from his/her shop. Write the English words for each thing under the pictures. **Don't look at your partner's book.**

d Work in pairs. Check your answers. Did you write the correct words?

7C 6 p59

a Work on your own. Fill in the gaps in these questions with *a*, *an*, *the* or – (= no article).

a When did you last get _____ email with _____ photo attachment? Who or what was _____ photo of?
b Which do you like more, _____ cats or _____ dogs?
c What's the worst thing about being in _____ hospital?
d Would you prefer to go on holiday to _____ Australia or _____ UK?
e What's _____ most expensive restaurant in _____ centre of your town or city?
f Are you planning to go to _____ football match next month?
g Is anyone in your family _____ doctor, _____ architect or _____ lawyer?

b Work with your partner. Ask and answer the questions. Ask follow-up questions if possible.

9B 10 p73

a Work with a student from group B. Choose the correct auxiliaries in the news summary.

Hello, here is (your name) with the news headlines. Seven paintings ¹***have/have been*** stolen from the British Gallery in London. The gallery's manager, Brian Lee, ²***has/has been*** asked the public for help in catching the robbers. And we ³***have just/have just been*** told that three men ⁴***have/have been*** arrested in connection with the robbery.

The actor Gary Sanders ⁵***has just/has just been*** arrived in the UK for the opening of his new film, *Better Late Than Never*. The film ⁶***has already/has already been*** seen by over 20 million people in the USA, and the actor ⁷***has/has been*** said that it's the best film he's ever made.

b Practise reading the news summary to your partner from group B.

c Work in pairs with a student from group A. Take turns to read your news summary without stopping. Make brief notes on your partner's news summary.

d Work with your partner from group B. Compare notes. What were group A's news stories about?

109

Pair and Group Work: Student/Group B

7B 6 p57

a Work on your own. Fill in the gaps with the correct form of the verbs in brackets.

a If you _____ (not be) in an English class now, where _____ you _____ (be)?

b What _____ you _____ (do) if you _____ (find) someone's personal diary?

c If you _____ (have to) go and live on your own for a month, which books _____ you _____ (take) with you?

d How _____ your life _____ (change) if you suddenly _____ (become) famous?

e If you _____ (find) someone's mobile phone in a café, what _____ you _____ (do)?

b Work with your partner. Ask and answer the questions. Continue the conversation if possible.

10D 7 p85

a Work on your own. Read the information about conversations 1 and 2. Decide what you want to say in each conversation.

1 Student A is staying with you for a few days. He/She is going to ask permission to do these things. Decide if you want to give or refuse permission. If you want to refuse permission, think of a reason why.
- make himself/herself something to eat
- phone his/her friend in Kenya
- borrow your car tomorrow evening
- use your computer to check his/her email
- invite his/her cousin to stay the night on Saturday
- have a shower

2 You are staying with student A for a few days. Make questions to ask permission to do these things.
- watch a DVD this evening
- borrow £100 until next week
- make yourself a cup of tea
- stay an extra couple of days
- give your sister a call
- invite some of your friends to come round for dinner tomorrow

b Work with your partner. Role-play the conversations. Your partner starts conversation 1. You start conversation 2.

c Tell the class which things your partner refused permission for and why.

3C 7 p27

a Read the fact file about a voluntourism holiday. You are going to tell the other students in your group about the holiday. Make notes on the main points.

VOLUNTOURS

PLACE	Tanzania, east Africa
TYPE OF WORK	work on a wildlife reserve; help scientists to monitor and protect the animals (lions, zebras, giraffes, etc.).
ACCOMMODATION AND FOOD	stay in shared bedrooms in an old farmhouse near the reserve; cook for yourself
FREE TIME	go on trips to villages to meet local people and learn about their way of life; go on safari
OTHER INFORMATION	You will also work on our tree planting programmes and spend time working in our animal hospital.

b Work in your groups. Close your books. Take turns to tell your group about the holiday.

c Choose which holiday you'd like to go on. Give reasons for your choices.

d Tell the class which holiday you've chosen. Which holiday is the most popular?

9A 9 p71

a Work with a student from group B. Write sentences to describe these words/phrases. Use *who*, *that*, *which* or *where*. Check words you don't know in a dictionary.

a jar	a volunteer	a package holiday
a detached house	a football fan	a loft
an internet forum	a workaholic	

A glass container that you put jam in.

b Work in groups of four with a pair from group A. Take turns to say your sentences. Guess the other pair's words. Which pair guessed the most words correctly?

Pair and Group Work: Student/Group B

8A 9 p63

a Work in pairs with a student from group B. Write questions with these words. Put the verbs in the correct active or passive form. Use *by* if necessary.

1 In which year / Japan / hit / a tsunami?
   a In 2007.   b In 2009.   c **In 2011**.
2 What is the fastest wind that / ever record / inside a tornado?
   a 700 km per hour.   b **512 km per hour.**   c 370 km per hour.
3 Which of these natural disasters / kill / more people every year?
   a Landslides.   b Hurricanes.   c **Floods.**
4 What percentage of the Earth's surface / cover / forest?
   a About 3%.   b **About 9%.**   c About 15%.
5 What is the most snow that / ever fall / in a single storm?
   a **4.8 metres.**   b 3.7 metres.   c 2.1 metres.
6 Which of these countries / not affect / a rise in sea levels in the future?
   a Bangladesh.   b **Bolivia.**   c Holland.

b Work in a group of four with a pair from group A. Ask and answer the questions. Say the three possible answers when you ask your questions. (The correct answer is in bold).

c Which pair got more answers right?

10C 6 p83

a Work on your own. Fill in the gaps with the correct form of these phrasal verbs.

| come across   get over   get out of |
| fall out   point out   go up |

a Have you ever tried to _____ going to a wedding or a party?
b Have you and a close friend ever _____?
c What's the best way to _____ your boyfriend or girlfriend leaving you?
d Have prices _____ a lot in your country this year?
e If a friend made a mistake in English, would you _____ it _____ to him or her?
f Have you ever _____ something interesting while you were tidying up your house or flat?

b Work with your partner. Ask and answer the questions. Ask follow-up questions if possible.

9D 9 p77

a Work on your own. Read the information for conversations 1 and 2. Decide what you want to say in each conversation.

1 You are a patient. You've just moved to a new town and you are going to see a doctor for the first time. You have a stressful job (you're a police officer) and you've been having some health problems recently. Decide what your symptoms are and how long you've had them.

2 You are a doctor. You've already seen your next patient twice this month, but you didn't think there was anything wrong with him/her. The last time you saw him/her you told him/her to take some paracetamol. Ask the patient what his/her symptoms are. Then decide what treatment to give (if any).

b Work with your partner. Role-play the conversations. Your partner starts conversation 1. You start conversation 2.

c Tell the class about the treatment your doctor suggested. Were you happy with your doctor's advice? Why?/Why not?

11D 7 p93

a Work on your own. Read this information. Underline the main points and plan what you are going to say.

Your name is Alex Smith and you work for a travel company called FlyTours in Southampton, England. You are going to call a company called Miami Hotels in the USA. You want to speak to Bob Krane, who is the sales director there. You are flying to Miami on the 30th of next month and would like to meet Mr Krane to discuss a new contract for next year. He can call you back on your mobile (0044 7655 443229) between 9.15 and 4.30 tomorrow.

b You are Tanya Wilson's PA at Getaway Holidays in the UK. Tanya is out of the office today. Answer the phone and take a message for her. Check information when you need to.

c Look again at the information you underlined in **a**, then phone Bob Krane. If he isn't there, leave a message with his PA.

d Work with your partner. Check his/her message. Is it correct?

Pair and Group Work: Other activities

1A 3 p6

a Read the rest of the article. Compare the top ten list in the article with your list from **2b**. How many reasons are in the same place in both lists?

The top ten reasons for happiness

1 YOUR GENES
Some people are simply born happier than others. In a study of 4,000 adult twins, differences in their genes were the main reasons for their different levels of happiness.

2 BEING MARRIED
All studies show that married couples are happier than single people. Just living together without being married doesn't have the same effect.

3 FRIENDS AND FAMILY
People with large families and lots of close friends are usually happier than people who have a lot of money and live on their own.

4 NOT WANTING MORE THAN YOU'VE GOT
People who expect to have a successful career, lots of money and the perfect relationship aren't as happy as people who accept what they've got.

5 HELPING OTHERS
Studies by psychologists in different countries show that when you help other people, it's not only good for them, it also makes you feel happier.

6 RELIGION
Four out of five studies show a positive link between religion and happiness. Very religious people usually live longer too.

7 BEING ATTRACTIVE
Attractive people believe they're very happy – maybe because they also have good genes and are therefore healthier. Cosmetic surgery does not have the same effect!

8 GROWING OLD
Studies show that old people are happy as often as young people and are unhappy less often. This is probably because they spend more time doing the things they enjoy.

9 MONEY
When you're poor, money can buy you some happiness. However, when people have enough money to live comfortably, more money doesn't make them happier.

10 INTELLIGENCE
Surprisingly, this has very little effect on happiness. Being able to get on well with people is much more important than how intelligent you are.

Adapted from the *Daily Mail*

b Work in groups. Discuss these questions.
1. Are the reasons in the article true for people you know? Give examples if possible.
2. Do you disagree with anything in the article? If so, why?
3. Are there any other reasons for happiness that you think should be in the article?

1C 8 p11

a Work with your partners. You are going to start a club for your school, university or local community. Discuss what sort of club you would like to start. Use one of these ideas or your own.

drama	singing and dancing		
books	animation	film	art
sports	nature	TV	English
food and drink	travel		
video games	cycling	hiking	

b Work with the same partners. Decide on these things. Make notes on what you have decided.
- the name of the club
- what people are going to do in the club
- when, where and how often you'll meet
- why people should join your club
- how you're going to advertise the club
- any other ideas

c Work in new groups or with the whole class. Take turns to talk about your club. Use your notes and ideas from **b**.

d Decide which of the other clubs you want to join. Which club is the most popular?

Pair and Group Work: Other activities

2D 8 p21

a Work on your own. Imagine you have this problem. Then think of one thing you've tried to do to solve the problem.

> Your husband/wife goes out with friends a lot in the evenings. You often have to work late and he/she is usually out when you get home, so you have to cook dinner and eat on your own. You'd like him/her to stay at home more often in the evenings so you can spend some time together.

b Work with a student from group A and group B. Take turns to explain your problems, show concern and give advice. Whose advice is the best, do you think?

> I've got a bit of a problem.

> Oh, dear. What's the matter?

> My husband/wife goes out with friends a lot …

c Tell the class the best piece of advice you received.

6A 11 p47

a Work on your own. Read about a problem you have. Think of three ways you can deal with the problem and decide what will happen if you choose each of these options.

> You work for a big company that has offices all over the country. You're very good at your job and you like your colleagues, but your new boss, Colin, never gives you any interesting work. Your old boss, Maria, is now Colin's manager.

look for another job → might have to move house

b Work with a student from group A and group B. Take turns to talk about your problem and your options. Discuss what will happen if you choose each option. Your partners can also suggest other options.

> If I look for another job, I might have to move house.

> Why don't you … ?

> If I do that, …

c Decide what to do. Does your group think you've made the right decision?

3C 7 p27

a Read the fact file about a voluntourism holiday. You are going to tell the other students in your group about the holiday. Make notes on the main points.

PLACE	Fiji, south Pacific
TYPE OF WORK	teach English to children aged 6–11 with help from local teachers; help with art classes, sports and school trips
ACCOMMODATION AND FOOD	stay in school buildings; share a room with 3 people; food provided by school
FREE TIME	go swimming, diving or snorkelling to the coral reefs; climb volcanoes with a guide
OTHER INFORMATION	Many of the children are from poor families so your work will make a real difference in their lives.

b Work in your groups. Close your books. Take turns to tell your group about the holiday.

c Choose which holiday you'd like to go on. Give reasons for your choices.

d Tell the class which holiday you've chosen. Which holiday is the most popular?

4A 10 p31

a Work on your own. Think of your best ever musical experience. Make notes on what happened. Use these ideas or your own.

- what the experience was (a concert, a club night, etc.)
- where and when this happened
- where you were living at the time
- what you were doing around that time (work, studies, etc.)
- who you were with on that day
- the main events of the story
- what you did afterwards
- any other interesting information

b Work in your groups. Take turns to talk about your experience. Ask questions to find out more information. Which experience is the most interesting?

113

1D 7 p13

a Work with your partner. Write questions with question tags to check information you think you know about six other students in the class.

SILVIO → *You live near the school, don't you?*
ISMAY → *You didn't study here last year, did you?*

b Ask the students your questions. Is your information about them correct? Ask follow-up questions if possible.

> Silvio, you live near the school, don't you?

> Yes, I do.

> Whereabouts exactly?

c Tell the class two things you found out about other students.

4B 10 p33

a Work on your own. Think of an interesting journey you've been on. Make notes on these things. Think about when you can use the Past Simple, Past Continuous and Past Perfect.

- when the story happened
- the reason for the journey
- where the journey started
- what you had done before you set off
- what happened on the journey
- what you were doing during the journey
- what you did when you arrived
- any other interesting things about the story

b Work in your groups. Take turns to tell your story. Ask questions to find out more information. Which story is the most interesting?

c Tell the class about the most interesting story in your group.

9C 9 p75

a Work on your own. Think of two things that you've done that are true and two things that are false. Write one or two words only to help you remember each thing.

b Work in your groups. Take turns to tell the group your things from **a**. You can ask each person one question about each thing. What is each person lying about, do you think?

c Tell the class who was the worst liar in the group. How did you know he/she was lying? Who was the best liar in the group?

12C 8 p99

a Work in your groups. Create your own superhero! Choose your hero's superpowers. Use these ideas or your own.

has super strength/speed	can read minds
has X-ray vision	can become invisible	can fly
can travel in time	can turn into an animal
is indestructible	can breathe underwater

b Make notes on these things.

- your superhero's name and where he/she lives
- how he/she got his/her superpowers
- what he/she wears
- what his/her normal life is like
- any weaknesses he/she has
- his/her enemies

c Work with students from different groups. Take turns to describe your superhero. Which is the best?

Extra Practice 1

Language Summary 1 p127

1A p6

1 Choose the correct words.

1 go to/*meet up* with friends
2 do/go exercise
3 go/visit relatives
4 go out/have for a drink
5 have/do a lie-in
6 go out/go to gigs
7 meet up/tidy up the flat
8 meet/chat to friends online
9 have/visit a quiet night in
10 do/go yoga
11 go to/go out art galleries
12 have/visit people round for dinner

2 Make questions about the words in bold.

1 I live **in London**.
   Where do you live?
2 I was born **in 1996**.
3 Alice worked **in London**.
4 **Her mum** lived in Rome.
5 He's talking about **the party**.
6 I've known them **for a year**.
7 She went out with **Dave**.
8 Kevin leaves home **at 8.30**.
9 **Gabi** gets home at 6.00.
10 Jim's been to **ten** countries.

1B p8

3 Fill in the gaps with these words.

~~love~~	right	awful	drive
all	nerves	on	in
mind	stand		

1 I really *love* eating out.
2 I'm very interested _____ art.
3 I'm not very keen _____ sport.
4 I think tennis is all _____ .
5 Call centres _____ me crazy.
6 I don't like flying at _____ .
7 I don't _____ getting up early.
8 I really can't _____ sitting in traffic jams.
9 I think most reality TV programmes are _____ .
10 Waiting in queues really gets on my _____ .

4 Make these sentences negative by changing the underlined words/phrases.

1 I <u>think</u> I'll go out tonight.
   I don't think I'll go out tonight.
2 <u>All</u> of my friends like football.
3 <u>Everyone</u> I know has a car.
4 I <u>usually</u> work on Saturdays.
5 I <u>love</u> travelling by train.
6 I <u>always</u> study at the weekend.
7 I <u>bought</u> a laptop last month.
8 <u>There's a</u> café in my street.
9 Kim<u>'s been</u> there before.
10 They<u>'re watching</u> TV.

1C p10

5 Write the vowels (*a, e, i, o, u*) in these adjectives. Do they describe positive (P) or negative (N) feelings?

1 a nn o y e d   N
2 sh _ ck _ d
3 str _ ss _ d
4 c _ nc _ rn _ d
5 r _ l _ x _ d
6 d _ s _ pp _ _ nt _ d
7 c _ lm
8 sc _ r _ d
9 _ mb _ r _ ss _ d
10 pl _ _ s _ d
11 c _ nf _ s _ d
12 gl _ d
13 _ ps _ t
14 s _ t _ sf _ _ d

6 Choose the correct prepositions.

1 I'm good by/*at* …
2 I'm frightened with/of …
3 I'm happy by/with …
4 I'm annoyed at/from …
5 I'm fed up for/with …
6 I'm bored with/about …
7 I'm surprised by/on …
8 I'm nervous about/by …
9 I'm angry with/for …
10 I'm upset from/about …
11 I'm bad for/at …
12 I'm worried of/about …

1D p12

7 Fill in the gaps with the correct question tags and complete the short answers.

A Carla's Spanish, ¹ *isn't she* ?
B Yes, ² *she is* .

A You don't eat meat, ³ _____ ?
B No, ⁴ _____ .

A Rob called you, ⁵ _____ ?
B Yes, ⁶ _____ .

A You're a doctor, ⁷ _____ ?
B No, ⁸ _____ , actually. I'm a dentist.

A Jack likes jazz, ⁹ _____ ?
B Yes, ¹⁰ _____ .

A Tom's met her, ¹¹ _____ ?
B Yes, ¹² _____ .

A Anita didn't call, ¹³ _____ ?
B Yes, ¹⁴ _____ actually. She left you a message.

A You haven't seen Jo, ¹⁵ _____ ?
B No, ¹⁶ _____ .

A They've moved house, ¹⁷ _____ ?
B Yes, ¹⁸ _____ .

Progress Portfolio 1

Tick the things you can do in English.

☐ I can talk about weekend activities.
☐ I can ask and answer questions about the past, the present and the future.
☐ I can talk about things I like and don't like.
☐ I can describe feelings.
☐ I can use question tags to check information.

Extra Practice 2

Language Summary 2 p129

2A p14

1 Choose the correct verbs.

I ¹(spend)/do a lot of time at work because I sometimes have to ²take/meet important deadlines. Some people say that I must ³have/be a workaholic because I ⁴spend/work very long hours, but I never ⁵take/have work home with me. I think it's very important to ⁶have/spend time to relax and I always ⁷be/have time off work when I need it. Yes, I can ⁸be/have under pressure at work sometimes, but I'm lucky because I ⁹have/meet good working conditions and I don't usually have to ¹⁰take/work overtime.

2 Rewrite these sentences using the words in brackets. Begin each sentence with You ... .

1 You must tell him. (have to)
  You have to tell him.
2 You should apologise to him. (ought)
3 You can't go into that room. (not allowed)
4 People expect you to wear a tie. (supposed)
5 You're not allowed to tell your father. (mustn't)
6 You can leave work early on Fridays. (be able to)
7 It isn't necessary for you to call him back. (not have to)
8 You can wear jeans in the office. (allowed)

2B p16

3 Which word is the odd one out? Why?

1 avocado (beef) lettuce
2 flour fry grill
3 peach pineapple cucumber
4 herbs bakes spices
5 coconut boil barbecue
6 hot dog red pepper lamb
7 onions beans pie
8 sauce cream noodles

4 Put the verbs in brackets into the Present Simple or Present Continuous.

A What ¹ *are* you *doing* ? (do)
B I ² _____ (make) a pie.
  ³ _____ you _____ (want) some?

A I ⁴ _____ (think) street food ⁵ _____ (become) more popular these days.
B Oh, I ⁶ _____ (never eat) street food. I ⁷ _____ (prefer) going to restaurants.

A I ⁸ _____ (work) in a café for a few weeks.
B ⁹ _____ you _____ (like) working there?
A I enjoyed it at first, but now it ¹⁰ _____ (get) a bit boring.

2C p18

5 Choose the correct words.

1 fall sleep/(asleep)
2 fall/have a nap
3 get back to sleep/asleep
4 be wide wake/awake
5 have trouble sleep/sleeping
6 be fast sleep/asleep
7 have/sleep insomnia
8 be a heavy sleep/sleeper

6 Write the strong adjectives.

1 good → fa*ntastic*
2 big → en_____
3 frightened → te_____
4 angry → fu_____
5 interested → fa_____
6 beautiful → go_____
7 tired → ex_____

7 Choose the correct adverbs. Sometimes both are possible.

1 very/absolutely good
2 extremely/absolutely big
3 fairly/really expensive
4 very/absolutely awful
5 incredibly/extremely cold
6 fairly/really boiling

2D p20

8 Fill in the gaps with these words/phrases.

| ~~the matter~~ | I'd | worth a try |
| I'm sorry | could be | should |

A What's ¹ *the matter* ?
B I'm very stressed at work.
A Oh, ² _____ to hear that. Maybe you ³ _____ talk to your boss.
B Well, it's ⁴ _____ , I guess.
A And ⁵ _____ start looking for another job.
B Yes, you ⁶ _____ right.

| good idea | I've tried |
| ought to | you tried | a shame |

A What's wrong?
B I've lost my mobile phone.
A Oh, dear. What ⁷ _____ . Have ⁸ _____ calling it?
B Yes, ⁹ _____ that, but it's switched off.
A Perhaps you ¹⁰ _____ contact the phone company.
B Yes, that's a ¹¹ _____ . I'll do that now.

Progress Portfolio 2

Tick the things you can do in English.

☐ I can talk about work.
☐ I can talk about things I am expected to do and have permission to do.
☐ I can describe things that are happening now or around now.
☐ I can talk about routines and things that are permanent.
☐ I can show concern, give and respond to advice.

Extra Practice 3

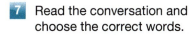
Language Summary 3 p132

3A p22

1 Match the phrasal verbs in A to words/phrases in B.

A	B
set off	at reception
pick up	the UK
get around	early
check in	your parents
check out	for a week
look after	at 10 a.m.
go away	problems
deal with	a cat
get back	a holiday
put up with	at the airport
see them off	from Spain
look forward to	a lot of noise

2 Choose the correct words.

A ¹*Did/Have* you ever ²*go/been* to the USA?
B Yes, I ³*went/'ve been* there twice. I ⁴*'ve visited/visited* Miami in 2005 and two years ago I ⁵*went/'ve been* to New York.
A ⁶*Did/Have* you ⁷*enjoy/enjoyed* New York?
B Yes, I ⁸*had/'ve had* a brilliant time there.

A Where's Jack?
B He's just ⁹*been/gone* out.
A ¹⁰*Did/Has* he ¹¹*say/said* where he was going?
B No, he ¹²*didn't/hasn't*. But his brother ¹³*phoned/has phoned* a few minutes ago, so maybe he's ¹⁴*been/gone* to see him.

3B p24

3 Fill in the gaps with *travel*, *get* or *go on*.

1 *get* back from somewhere
2 _____ a trip
3 _____ a taxi home
4 _____ independently
5 _____ off a bus
6 _____ a cruise
7 _____ economy class
8 _____ a guided tour
9 _____ light

4 Correct the mistakes in these sentences.

since

1 We've been married ~~for~~ 2003.
2 Marco and Luis has been studying English for three years.
3 My son's been having this bike for six months.
4 She's working for the company since July.
5 They've been living in their flat since ten years.
6 I've been liking this band since I was a child.
7 We've been waiting for the train since two hours ago.
8 I've knew my boss for five years.

5 Make questions about the words in bold using *How long … ?* or *How many … ?*.

1 He's been to **fifteen** countries.
   How many countries has he been to?
2 She's been living in Moscow **for a year**.
3 They've been chatting online **since 6 o'clock**.
4 He's visited **three** art galleries this month.
5 I've had **eight** English teachers in my life.
6 I've had my laptop **for a month**.
7 He's worked for **six** companies.
8 She's been working **since 7 a.m.**

3C p26

6 a Are these words nouns (N) or adjectives (A)?

1 kind *A*
2 healthy
3 fame
4 honest
5 sadness
6 patient
7 nature
8 comfort
9 fashionable
10 traditional
11 activity
12 popular
13 confidence
14 possible
15 modesty
16 adventurous

b Change the nouns into adjectives and the adjectives into nouns.

kind > kindness

3D p28

7 Read the conversation and choose the correct words.

A Do you ¹(*know*)/*have* any good places to eat near the hotel?
B I'd ²*recommend/recommending* The Garden Restaurant. It's really nice and quite cheap.
A That ³*sound/sounds* good. And what's the ⁴*better/best* way to ⁵*go/get* around the city?
B Well, ⁶*it/it's* probably best ⁷*take/to take* taxis. And you really must ⁸*to go/go* to the National Art Gallery ⁹*to see/for to see* the Picassos.
A That's good ¹⁰*to know/knowing*. Have you got any other ¹¹*recommends/tips*?
B Well, you ¹²*can/should* definitely go on a boat trip along the river, but don't ¹³*bother/worry* going to the City Museum. It isn't really worth ¹⁴*see/seeing*.
A Yes, I've heard ¹⁵*it/that* before.
B And I wouldn't ¹⁶*buy/buying* souvenirs on the street. They're often very bad quality.
A Thanks, ¹⁷*that/that's* really useful. See you next week!

Progress Portfolio 3

Tick the things you can do in English.

☐ I can talk about travel.
☐ I can talk about past and recent events.
☐ I can say how long something has been happening.
☐ I can say and ask how many things have been completed.
☐ I can describe holidays.
☐ I can ask for, make and respond to recommendations.

Extra Practice 4

Language Summary 4 p135

4A p30

1 Choose the correct words.

I'm a ¹*big*/*large* fan of a band called *OutThere*. They've just ²*bought*/*released* their first single and I've already downloaded it ³*on*/*onto* my phone. I've also ⁴*seen*/*been* them play ⁵*alive*/*live* lots of times. Last week they ⁶*did*/*made* their first ever gig in London. I was a bit nervous when they went ⁷*stage*/*onstage*, but the audience loved them and they ⁸*did*/*made* three encores. Next month they're ⁹*doing*/*going* on tour – and maybe next year they'll ¹⁰*have*/*release* an album in the charts!

2 Put the verbs in the Past Simple or Past Continuous.

Once, when I ¹ _was_ (be) quite young, I ² _____ (walk) by a lake in a park and I ³ _____ (fall) into the water. I ⁴ _____ (not know) how to swim, and as I ⁵ _____ (wear) a lot of clothes I ⁶ _____ (start) going under the water. Luckily two men ⁷ _____ (run) around the park and they ⁸ _____ (see) me. One of them ⁹ _____ (jump) into the water and ¹⁰ _____ (pull) me out. I ¹¹ _____ (start) taking swimming lessons the next day!

3 Change the underlined verbs to *used to* + infinitive if possible.

1 Tim <u>hated</u> going to school.
   Tim used to hate going to school.
2 He <u>started</u> school in 1998.
3 He <u>went</u> to school by bus.
4 He <u>got</u> into trouble a lot.
5 He <u>did</u> a lot of sports.
6 He <u>changed</u> schools in 2006.
7 He <u>played</u> video games a lot.
8 He <u>left</u> school when he was 16.
9 He <u>got</u> a job in a café.
10 He <u>enjoyed</u> working there.
11 He <u>worked</u> 50 hours a week.
12 He <u>became</u> the manager in 2010.

4B p32

4 Find 10 character adjectives. (→↓).

A	M	B	I	T	I	O	U	S	D
G	O	R	B	S	J	R	T	P	E
G	G	A	S	E	E	G	E	S	T
R	E	V	I	N	B	A	W	Z	E
E	N	E	Q	S	T	N	C	I	R
S	E	N	S	I	T	I	V	E	M
S	R	V	G	B	O	S	X	S	I
I	O	P	E	L	M	E	A	N	N
V	U	A	N	E	V	D	L	R	E
E	S	T	U	B	B	O	R	N	D

5 Fill in the gaps with the Past Simple or the Past Perfect of the verbs in brackets.

1 By the time she _met_ (meet) Jack, he _____ (be) married three times.
2 Kim _____ (not be) tired because she _____ (already have) a few hours' sleep.
3 When I got home I _____ (realise) that I _____ (leave) my keys at the office.
4 She _____ (buy) me a book but I _____ (already read) it.
5 By the time we _____ (get) home, Ben _____ (go) to bed.

4C p34

6 Fill in the gaps with these words.

peckish	wander	carriage
appear	check out	
well-known	highlight	

1 I'm a bit _____. I think I'll have a sandwich.
2 That actor is very _____.
3 I often _____ around the park in my lunch break.
4 The _____ of our trip was a visit to the Taj Mahal.
5 You really must _____ that new exhibition.
6 We _____ to be lost.
7 There weren't many people in our _____.

4D p36

7 Make sentences with these words.

1 at times / optimistic / not / He's / very .
   He's not very optimistic at times.
2 a lot of TV / Generally speaking, / rather / old people / watch / tend to .
3 be / a bit / Traffic jams / at times / can / annoying .
4 some / be / noisy / a bit / Perhaps / can / neighbours .
5 very / my / reliable / friends / On the whole, / aren't .
6 a bit / too / Generally speaking, / people / fast / tend to / young / drive / most .
7 aggressive / can / at times / boys / be / teenage / Some / quite .
8 tend to / boring / most / rather / On the whole, / soap operas / be .
9 a bit / the news / be / at times / Watching / can / depressing .
10 quite / tends to / grandfather / be / My / stubborn .

Progress Portfolio 4

Tick the things you can do in English.

☐ I can talk about music.
☐ I can tell stories about things that happened in the past.
☐ I can describe people's character.
☐ I can guess the meaning of some words from the context.
☐ I can understand a radio interview.
☐ I can soften the way I express my opinions.

Extra Practice 5

Language Summary 5 p138

5A p38

1 Complete the words.

1 I live in the city ce _n t r e_ .
2 My aunt lives in a nice little c _ tt _ g _ in the co _ _ t _ y .
3 The car's in the g _ r _ e .
4 We live on the top fl _ _ _ of an ap _ _ tm _ t b _ _ k .
5 Their house has a b _ lc _ _ y and a big l _ f _ .
6 We want to buy a de _ _ ch _ _ house in the s _ b _ b _ .
7 I live in a te _ _ ac _ house in a lively ne _ _ bo _ _ h _ _ d .

2 Correct the mistakes in these sentences.

   taller

1 He's ~~more tall~~ than I thought.
2 Your flat is bigger as mine.
3 This flat isn't as nicer as ours.
4 Your boyfriend's new car is the same than John's.
5 This hotel is similar as the one we stayed in last year.
6 It's certainly different for all the other hotels.
7 She's as older as I am.
8 He's least patient than me.
9 I have bit more free time than I used to.
10 This room's a bit noisyer than the other one.
11 Paul's definitely the worse driver I've ever seen.

5B p40

3 Choose the correct verbs.

1 Please (put)/sort away your toys.
2 He took/tidied out the rubbish.
3 You really need to go/throw away some of this junk.
4 Shall I sort/give this jacket away or throw/tidy it out?
5 I need to clear/go through all my English notes.
6 I have to sort/take out my study.
7 When Liz comes/takes back, tell her to sort/tidy up her room.
8 Please put/clear out the garage.

4 Cross out the verb form that is **not** possible. Sometimes both verb forms are possible.

A What ¹~~will you do~~/are you doing at the weekend?
B ²I'm going to visit/I'm visiting my brother in London. It's his 21st birthday and ³he'll have/he's having a big party by the river.
A That sounds nice. How many people ⁴will be/are being there?
B About a hundred. And my sister ⁵is going to fly/is flying in from Italy for the party.
A Well, I'm sure ⁶you're having/you'll have a great time.
B Yes, I hope so. Oh dear, we'd better go. I think ⁷it's raining/it's going to rain soon.
A OK, ⁸I'll get/I'm getting my umbrella.

5C p42

5 Fill in the gaps with the correct form of the verbs in brackets.

I needed ¹ _to find_ (find) somewhere to live, so I asked the estate agent ² _____ (look) for two-bedroom flats. He kept ³ _____ (show) me ones that seem ⁴ _____ (be) far too expensive, but my parents said they would ⁵ _____ (lend) me some money. I don't mind ⁶ _____ (borrow) from them, so I decided ⁷ _____ (rent) a nice little flat near the park. I really enjoy ⁸ _____ (live) here – and I must remember ⁹ _____ (pay) my parents back one day!

5D p44

6 Write the letters in these materials.

1 t _i_ n   7 m _ t _ l
2 p _ p _ r   8 r _ b _ _ r
3 g _ _ ss   9 c _ r _ b _ _ d
4 w _ _ l   10 c _ t _ _ n
5 st _ _ l   11 pl _ _ t _ c
6 w _ _ d   12 le _ _ h _ r

7 Read these conversations in a department store. Fill in the gaps with these words.

~~need~~	forgotten	what
stuff	looking	type
remember	made	use (x2)
mean (x2)	called (x2)	

SA Do you ¹ _need_ any help?
C Yes, please. I can't ² _____ what they're ³ _____ , but you ⁴ _____ them when it's noisy.
SA Do you ⁵ _____ ear plugs?
C Yes, that's right. Thanks.

SA Can I help you?
C Yes, please. I need some ⁶ _____ for cleaning furniture. It's a ⁷ _____ of liquid. I'm sorry, I've ⁸ _____ what it's called.
SA Is this what you're ⁹ _____ for? Furniture polish?
C Yes, that's it. Furniture polish.

SA Do you need anything else?
C Yes, but I don't know ¹⁰ _____ they're ¹¹ _____ in English. You ¹² _____ them to clean your teeth after a meal.
SA Do you mean a toothbrush?
C No, they're ¹³ _____ of wood.
SA Oh, you ¹⁴ _____ toothpicks.

Progress Portfolio 5

Tick the things you can do in English.

☐ I can describe homes.
☐ I can compare two or more people and things.
☐ I can talk about future arrangements and plans.
☐ I can make predictions about the future.
☐ I can describe things I need and say what they are used for.

Extra Practice 6

Language Summary 6 p141

6A p46

1 Fill in the gaps with the correct form of *make* or *do*.

1 I'm good at _making_ decisions.
2 I think you've _____ a mistake.
3 I have to _____ some work.
4 I've never _____ a cake.
5 I hate _____ the housework.
6 We've _____ our homework.
7 You must _____ up your mind.
8 I don't mind _____ exams.
9 I have to _____ some washing.
10 I'd like _____ a law degree.
11 Please don't _____ a noise.
12 I need _____ an appointment.

2 Look at these sentences about the future. Put the verbs in brackets in the correct form.

1 If I _see_ (see) him, I _'ll give_ (give) him the message.
2 When Joe _____ (get) home, I _____ (tell) him you called.
3 I _____ (phone) Eva before I _____ (go) to work.
4 We _____ (not go) out if you _____ (not come) with us.
5 I _____ (not go) to the gig unless you _____ (come) too.
6 As soon as I _____ (finish) this email, I _____ (help) you.
7 We _____ (wait) here until you _____ (get) back.
8 If we _____ (need) any help, we _____ (give) you a call.

6B p48

3 Complete these sentences with a reflexive pronoun.

1 Ouch! I've just cut _myself_ !
2 My parents usually go on holiday by _____ .
3 Our daughter wrote it _____ .
4 Did you make the pie _____ ?
5 He likes travelling by _____ .
6 Dave and I always cook for _____ when we go camping.
7 Did you and Gary go walking in the mountains by _____ ?

4 Make sentences with these words.

1 an umbrella / rains / in case / Take / it .
   Take an umbrella in case it rains.
2 gets / him / when / He / angry / with / agree / don't / people / extremely .
3 You / it / like / to / don't / take / back / if / can / you / the shop / it .
4 in case / something up / always / want / a dictionary / I / have / I / in / to look / my bag .
5 ought to / lost / You / get / take / in case / a map / you .
6 every / have / you / If / you / kids, / them / read / should / night / to .
7 you / When / instead / to sleep, / a book / can't / read / get .
8 healthy, / fast food / want / If / don't / you / eat / to stay .
9 I / you / to call / your / in case / phone number / me / need / Give .

5 Do sentences a and b have different meanings? If so, how are they different?

1 a If I'm too tired, I go home.
  b If I'm too tired, I'll go home.
2 a I'll take the car if it rains.
  b I'll take the car in case it rains.
3 a When she's late, she calls us.
  b If she's late, she calls us.
4 a If he can't do it, I might help.
  b If he can't do it, I'll help.
5 a I'll carry it if it's not too big.
  b I'll carry it unless it's too big.

6C p50

6 Write the synonyms.

1 notice   s _p o t_
2 accidentally b _____ c_____
3 frightened   s _____
4 sure   c _____
5 deal with   c _____ w_____
6 lucky   f _____
7 satisfied   c _____
8 choose   p _____
9 nice   p _____
10 behave   a _____

6D p52

7 Read the conversation between Ian, Rebecca, Lisa and Duncan. Choose the correct words.

I We need to discuss how to spend the money we [1]*did/**made*** from the festival.
L May I [2]*do/make* a suggestion?
I Yes, of course.
L How about [3]*use/using* the money to repair the village hall?
D Yes, that sounds [4]*as/like* a good idea.
R Sorry, I don't think we should [5]*do/doing* that. For [6]*a/one* thing, a lot of people don't use the village hall.
I What about [7]*spend/spending* the money on some new trees?
D Yes, that's not a [8]*good/bad* idea.
L [9]*Can/Do* I just say [10]*something/anything* here?
I Of course, Lisa.
L Have you thought [11]*for/of* asking people in the village what they think? We [12]*must/could* ask them to post their ideas on the website.
R [13]*What/That* a great idea!
I Well, [14]*it/it's* worth [15]*try/a try*.

Progress Portfolio 6

Tick the things you can do in English.

☐ I can talk about things that are possible in the future.
☐ I can talk about things that are always true.
☐ I can use some synonyms.
☐ I can ask to speak and make suggestions in a discussion.
☐ I can agree and disagree with people and give my opinion.

Extra Practice 7

Language Summary 7 p143

7A p54

1 Fill in the gaps with the correct form of these verbs.

~~put~~	make	do	encourage
have	achieve	dream	
go	take	mess up	

1 They _put_ a lot of effort into everything they do.
2 If you work very hard, you will _____ your goals.
3 My dad has always _____ me to become a writer.
4 I'd like _____ the opportunity to travel more.
5 You should _____ the most of every opportunity you get.
6 I think I _____ my English exam yesterday.
7 I used to _____ of becoming a famous footballer.
8 Whatever I do, it always seems _____ wrong.
9 Sorry you didn't win, but you _____ your best.
10 Have you ever _____ part in a competition?

2 Rewrite these sentences using the words in brackets.

1 Matt can sail. (know how)
   Matt knows how to sail.
2 Karen can't cook Japanese food. (have no idea)
3 We couldn't understand what he was saying. (not be able to)
4 Henrietta can't read maps. (be no good at)
5 We got to the meeting on time. (manage)
6 Christopher can play football very well. (be really good at)
7 Mark can't play video games. (be useless at)
8 My mum couldn't speak Italian. (not have a clue how)
9 My parents can pick us up from the airport. (be able to)
10 My brother can't keep a secret. (find it impossible)

7B p56

3 Complete the words in this conversation.

A Oh no! Someone ¹co_pied_ me in on an email and when I opened the ²at_____ my laptop ³cr_____ !
B I think you've got a ⁴vi_____. Did you ⁵ba_____ up all your important ⁶do_____ ?
A Yes, I always copy them onto this ⁷me_____ st_____ .
B Well, that's good. I'd restart the computer and then ⁸de_____ the email.
A Thanks. I really hope my ⁹ha_____ -dr_____ is OK because I always ¹⁰st_____ all my photos on it.
B Oh, it's probably fine. But I'd ¹¹in_____ some new anti-virus ¹²so_____ immediately.

4 Write second conditionals with these words.

1 I / help / you if I / have / time.
   I'd help you if I had time.
2 What / you do if you / lose / your mobile?
3 If I / live / in the USA, I / be able to speak English fluently.
4 He / come out tonight if he / not / have to work.
5 If you / can / go anywhere in the world, where / you go ?
6 If I / know / the answer, I / not / need to ask.

7C p58

5 Choose the correct words.

1 I follow her *in*/*on* Twitter.
2 To get to the homepage, click on this *link*/*status*.
3 I've just uploaded a new *profile*/*forum* for my Facebook page.
4 When did you last *upload*/*update* your status?
5 Lots of people *downloaded*/*posted* comments on your blog.
6 When did he last *tweet*/*Twitter*?

6 Fill in the gaps with *a*, *an*, *the* or – (= no article).

1 I met _____ film director and _____ actor last week. _____ actor lives in _____ Spain and _____ director lives in _____ USA.
2 Do you prefer _____ burgers or _____ hot dogs?
3 Marco's going to _____ university in _____ UK.
4 Lee's _____ doctor and he works in _____ hospital where my son was born. It's _____ biggest hospital in _____ city.

7D p60

7 Rewrite these direct questions as indirect questions. Use *you* and the words in brackets.

1 Where is he? (know)
   Do you know where he is?
2 When does it start? (could, tell)
3 Where did Pete go? (any idea)
4 Does this bus go to Ely? (know)
5 Should we leave now? (think)
6 Is this Ali's number? (can, tell)
7 What's it called? (any idea)
8 Has she lost her job? (think)

Progress Portfolio 7

Tick the things you can do in English.

☐ I can describe my goals and achievements.
☐ I can talk about people's ability in the present or past.
☐ I can talk about computers.
☐ I can talk about imaginary situations in the present or the future.
☐ I can ask indirect questions.

Extra Practice 8

Language Summary 8 p145

8A p62

1 Find 10 words for bad weather and natural disasters (→↓).

T	E	B	L	I	Z	Z	A	R	D
L	A	N	D	S	L	I	D	E	I
T	R	O	S	T	O	R	M	Z	L
S	T	E	D	O	E	T	H	U	K
U	H	U	R	R	I	C	A	N	E
N	Q	W	O	N	V	L	E	N	F
A	U	E	U	A	E	N	G	O	L
M	A	J	G	D	S	E	A	K	O
I	K	F	H	O	G	P	L	E	O
H	E	A	T	W	A	V	E	N	D

2 Fill in the gaps with the correct active or passive form of the verbs in brackets.

1 Wind can _be used_ (use) to make clean energy.
2 About 300 billion emails _____ (send) every day.
3 People in the UK _____ (send) 30 billion texts every day.
4 My car _____ (repair) at the moment.
5 Tom _____ (drive) his parents to the airport now.
6 I think in the future most jobs _____ (do) by machines.
7 Hurricane Katrina _____ (destroy) New Orleans in 2005.
8 The causes of global warming _____ (know) for years.
9 Several houses _____ (hit) by lightning last night.
10 Climate change should _____ (teach) in schools.

8B p64

3 Write the containers.

1 a b _a g_ of sweets
2 a c _ _ of cola
3 a p _ _ _ _ _ of crisps
4 a j _ _ _ of marmalade
5 a t _ _ _ of cat food
6 a b _ _ _ of ketchup
7 a b _ _ _ of chocolates
8 a c _ _ _ _ of orange juice

4 Cross out the incorrect word/phrase. Sometimes both words/phrases are correct.

1 I haven't got *any/no* money.
2 There weren't *much/many* people at the meeting.
3 My aunt knows *loads of/several* famous people.
4 There aren't *enough/much* cups.
5 There's *a few/a little* jam left.
6 I need *a bit of/a little* time to think about it.
7 There are *plenty of/a bit of* biscuits in the cupboard.
8 Please be quiet! You're making *too much/too many* noise!
9 We've got *lots of/plenty of* time.
10 He's got *loads of/hardly any* Facebook friends.

8C p66

5 Make the opposites of these adjectives by adding a prefix.

1 _un_ usual   11 ____ reliable
2 ____ honest   12 ____ patient
3 ____ correct   13 ____ organised
4 ____ selfish   14 ____ responsible
5 ____ polite   15 ____ considerate
6 ____ loyal   16 ____ similar
7 ____ regular   17 ____ conscious
8 ____ formal   18 ____ possible
9 ____ helpful   19 ____ sensitive
10 ____ mature   20 ____ believable

6 Fill in the gaps with *under-*, *re-*, *over-*, *-ful* or *-less*.

1 I _re_use most of my jam jars.
2 £1,000 for that old car? You're being rather ____-optimistic.
3 Don't worry about the dog. He's completely harm____ .
4 I ____slept and missed my train.
5 It's dangerous to ____estimate the dangers of climate change.
6 Ow! My knee is really pain____ .
7 I need to ____charge my phone.
8 The bill is only £10! I think the waiter has ____charged us.
9 She's a very success____ author.
10 Throw it away. It's use____ .

8D p68

7 Read this conversation. Fill in the gaps with these phrases.

~~Could you~~	What else
it's worth	watch out
good idea	make sure
hadn't thought	just in case
sounds like	really helpful
If I were you	don't forget

A We're planning to drive across Australia. [1] _Could you_ give us some advice?
B Well, [2] _____ your car is in good condition. And of course [3] _____ to take a map.
A OK. [4] _____ do you think we should take with us?
B [5] _____ , I'd take lots of water, sun cream and a hat.
A That [6] _____ good advice.
B And [7] _____ taking a spare can of petrol, [8] _____ .
A Yes, that's a [9] _____ . I [10] _____ of that.
B Also, [11] _____ for kangaroos on the road, particularly in the evening.
A Right, thanks a lot. That's [12] _____ .
B No problem. Have a good trip!

Progress Portfolio 8

Tick the things you can do in English.

☐ I can talk about bad weather and natural disasters.
☐ I can use passive verb forms.
☐ I can talk about quantity.
☐ I can understand a short news report.
☐ I can give, ask for and respond to warnings and advice.

Extra Practice 9

Language Summary 9 p147

9A p70

1 Write the letters in these words connected to health.

1 a w _a_ _r_ d
2 a s _ rg _ _ n
3 an op _ rat _ _ g th _ _ t _ e
4 a sp _ c _ l _ _ t
5 a s _ rg _ _ y
6 a p _ _ sc _ pt _ _ n
7 an i _ f _ _ t _ _ n
8 ast _ m _
9 an a _ _ er _ y
10 a m _ gr _ _ n _

2 a Fill in the gaps with *who*, *that*, *which*, *whose*, *where* or *when*.

1 Coffee and chocolate are things _that_ you should try to avoid.
2 A person _____ body is full of toxins isn't very healthy.
3 Monday was the day _____ I started fasting.
4 A gym is a place _____ you can do exercise.
5 Guarana is a type of plant _____ gives you energy.
6 A personal trainer is someone _____ helps you get fit.
7 Meditation and yoga are things _____ people do to relax.
8 Kim is the doctor _____ I told you about on the phone.

b In which sentences in **2a** can we leave out *who*, *that* or *which*?

9B p72

3 Choose the correct verbs.

1 *go*/*have* on strike
2 *take*/*meet* a target
3 *protest*/*publish* a report
4 *take*/*go* part in a demonstration
5 *reject*/*protest* against something
6 *discover*/*call off* something new
7 *pay off*/*call off* a strike
8 *take*/*meet* somebody to hospital
9 *protest*/*accept* an offer
10 *pay off*/*reject* a debt

4 Tick the verb forms in blue that are correct. Change the ones that are incorrect.

The government [1]*have been published* a survey which shows that drivers don't slow down in bad weather. Over 2,000 people [2]*have already been injured* in accidents this year.

The one-day strike by tube drivers [3]*has called off*. The transport union [4]*has been accepted* a new pay offer, which the government [5]*has increased* by 2%.

A new report [6]*has just published* which shows that the government [7]*has spent* an extra £5 billion on schools this year. This news [8]*has welcomed* by teachers' unions and parents' groups.

9C p74

5 Write the words for body movements and responses.

1 ycr — c_ry_
2 gluha — l_____
3 limes — s_____
4 ahsctrc — s_____
5 wornf — f_____
6 wates — s_____
7 veaw — w_____
8 tcrhets — s_____
9 wany — y_____
10 husbl — b_____
11 alcwr — c_____
12 vesrhi — s_____

6 Choose the correct words.

1 *In spite of*/*Although* I wasn't very hungry, I had a pizza.
2 *Despite*/*Although* feeling tired, I went to my sister's party.
3 She was very angry. *However,*/*Despite,* she didn't show it.
4 I was late for work, *however*/*even though* I left home early.
5 He went out for a run *although*/*in spite of* the rain.
6 I went to my cousin's wedding *although*/*however* I didn't feel very well.

9D p76

7 a Choose the correct words.

DOCTOR

a Hello, Mrs Smith. Now, what [1]*seem*/*seems* to be the problem?
b No, but come back if you're not feeling [2]*good*/*better* in two days.
c And how long have you been [3]*felt*/*feeling* like this?
d Right, let me [4]*having*/*have* a look at you. Yes, your temperature is rather high. I think you've got flu.
e Have you got any other [5]*treatments*/*symptoms*?
f No, but here's a [6]*prescription*/*recipe* for some painkillers.

MRS SMITH

g For about two or three days.
h Yes, I thought so. Do I need some [7]*virus*/*antibiotics*?
i I've got a temperature and I can't [8]*stop*/*keep* sneezing.
j Yes, I've got a runny nose and I keep [9]*get*/*getting* headaches.
k Thanks. Do I need [10]*to make*/*make* another appointment?

b Put the conversation in **7a** in the correct order.

a, i, e, …

Progress Portfolio 9

Tick the things you can do in English.

☐ I can say which person, thing, place and time I'm talking about.
☐ I can talk about things that have happened in the news.
☐ I can use connecting words to join sentences and clauses.
☐ I can talk about health and medical problems with a doctor.

Extra Practice 10

Language Summary 10 p150

10A p78

1 Choose the correct verbs.

LEAH Guess what? Jim's back in the UK! He ¹*got/kept* in touch with me yesterday.
FAY Really? I haven't ²*called/heard* from him for years.
L He's trying to ³*get/keep* hold of people from school. Have you ⁴*got/kept* in touch with anyone?
F No, I've ⁵*kept/lost* touch with most of them, but I ⁶*'m/get* still in touch with Bev. I'll ⁷*leave/give* her a call and ⁸*make/let* her know that Jim's back in town.

2 Rewrite these sentences using the verb form in brackets.

1 I'd agreed to babysit for Jo, but I had to work. (be supposed to)
I was supposed to babysit for Jo, but I had to work.
2 I had planned to go to the gym after work, but I was too tired. (be going to)
3 Liam expected me to help him buy a new laptop, but I was ill. (be supposed to)
4 I'd agreed to take Dave and Tina to the airport, but I forgot! (be supposed to)
5 We had planned to drive to the wedding, but we went by train instead. (be going to)

10B p80

3 Complete the words in these descriptions of people.

1 She's got w _a_ _v_ y hair and she's wearing a fl _ w _ _ y dress.
2 He's wearing a l _ g _ t blue jacket and a s _ r _ p _ d tie.
3 She's got a p _ _ yt _ _ l and she's wearing a pl _ _ n shirt.
4 He's got sh _ _ l _ er-le _ g _ h hair and he's going b _ _ d.
5 She's wearing g _ _ ss _ _ and lots of j _ w _ ll _ _ y.
6 He's got short c _ _ l _ hair – and it's d _ _ d pink!

4 Choose the correct verbs.

A Where's Jo? She isn't in her office. I suppose she ¹*may/can't* be out with a client.
B Well, it's one o'clock, so she might ²*have/be having* lunch.
A Yes, maybe. Or she ³*could/must* be in a meeting.

A You work in a prison, don't you? It ⁴*must/may* be hard work.
B Yes, it is. But I ⁵*can't/might* look for another job soon. I may ⁶*try/be trying* to join the police.

A Is that Paula going for a run?
B It ⁷*might/can't* be her, surely! She hates doing exercise.
A She must ⁸*try/be trying* to get fit before the summer holidays.

10C p82

5 a Fill in the gaps with the correct form of these phrasal verbs.

~~go up~~	get over	put off
come up with		point out
get out of		split up with
look up	fall out	come across

1 The price of petrol *is going up* .
2 My sister and I had an argument and _____ .
3 Can you _____ this *word* for me?
4 The mechanic _____ *the problem* to us.
5 I'm sure we'll _____ *a solution* sooner or later.
6 I _____ *this photo* when I was clearing out the loft.
7 It took Samantha a long time to _____ *her divorce*.
8 Sam's _____ *his girlfriend*.
9 I _____ *the meeting* by pretending to be ill.
10 We had to _____ *the wedding* because my dad was ill.

b Rewrite sentences 3–10 in **5a** using a pronoun instead of the words in blue.

3 *Can you look it up for me?*

10D p84

6 a Choose the correct phrases. Sometimes both are possible.

1 *Do you think I could/May I* borrow your scooter?
2 *May I/Would you mind if I* stayed at your place tonight?
3 *Do you mind if I/Is it OK* use your phone?
4 *Is it OK if I/Can I* use the photocopier?
5 *Can I/Would you mind if I* make myself some tea?
6 *Do you mind if I/Would you mind if I* left early today?

b Match questions 1–6 to answers a–f.

a No, not at all. Go ahead. *3*
b Yes, of course. It's parked outside. Here are the keys.
c Sorry, I'm afraid it's broken.
d No, not at all. What time do you want to leave?
e Yes, of course you can. Help yourself.
f Actually, my parents are staying with us at the moment.

Progress Portfolio 10

Tick the things you can do in English.

☐ I can talk about contacting people.
☐ I explain why I didn't do things I had planned to do or had agreed to do.
☐ I can describe people's clothes and physical appearance.
☐ I can make deductions about the present.
☐ I can ask for, give and refuse permission.

Extra Practice 11

Language Summary 11 p152

11A p86

1 Choose the correct verbs.
1 *be*/*do* in charge of a company
2 *go*/*work* unsocial hours
3 *do*/*go* for an audition
4 *deal with*/*work* customers
5 *work*/*run* a department
6 *arrange*/*sort out* a problem
7 *go*/*organise* conferences
8 *work*/*arrange* meetings
9 *do*/*go* overtime
10 *have*/*run* a lot of responsibility
11 *run*/*work* shifts
12 *have*/*be* responsible for the finances

2 Put these sentences into reported speech. Use the phrases in brackets.
1 "I live in L.A." (He said)
   He said (that) he lived in L.A.
2 "I can't swim." (She told me)
3 "We're going on holiday on Sunday." (They said)
4 "I got your email." (He said)
5 "My brother is going to buy a new car." (He told me)
6 "I'll text you." (She said)
7 "I must go." (She told me)
8 "I've been to Brazil." (He said)
9 "We need to borrow some money." (They told him)
10 "They didn't call." (She said)

11B p88

3 Complete these adjectives that describe jobs. What's the hidden adjective?

	¹W		L		A		D	
	²S				S		F	L
³T		M		O			Y	
	⁴G	L				R		S
	⁵R		W			D		G
⁶D		M			D			G
⁷C					L			G
		⁸L				L	Y	
	⁹P		T		M			

4 Joe is going for a job interview tomorrow. Put his mother's comments into reported speech.
1 "Wear a suit." (tell)
   She told him to wear a suit.
2 "Don't wear trainers." (tell)
3 "Be polite to everyone." (tell)
4 "Don't be late." (tell)
5 "Can you give me a call after the interview?" (ask)
6 "Would you like to come for dinner tomorrow evening?" (ask)

5 Joe is having dinner at his parents' house after the interview. Put their questions into reported speech.
1 "How did it go?" (mum/ask)
   His mum asked (him) how it went.
2 "Have you heard from them yet?" (dad/want to know)
3 "When are they going to contact you?" (mum/ask)
4 "What does the company do?" (dad/want to know)
5 "Do you want to work for them?" (mum/ask)

11C p90

6 Use the verbs in the box to report these sentences.

agree	invite	suggest	admit
threaten	offer	promise	
remind	refuse	warn	

1 "OK, let's buy a new car." (Ian)
   Ian agreed to buy a new car.
2 "Why don't we go to the cinema?" (Fiona)
3 "I won't apologise." (Gabi)
4 "I'll pay for dinner." (Kevin)
5 "I'll pay you back soon." (Zak)
6 "I stole the money." (Mark)
7 "If you don't give it back, I'll tell the police." (Chris → Mark)
8 "Would you like to go for a drink?" (Tom → Ruth)
9 "Don't trust him." (Liz → Ann)
10 "Don't forget to pay the gas bill." (Patricia → Dave)

11D p92

7 Joe is checking information on the phone. Fill in the gaps.

JOE Sorry, ¹ *what* did you say your name ² _____ again?
MATT It's Matt Parker.
J Is ³ _____ Barker ⁴ _____ a B?
M No, with a P. And our address is 22 Stanton Road, Glasgow, GL22 6FR.
J Sorry, I didn't ⁵ _____ all of that. Could you ⁶ _____ it again, please?
M 22 Stanton Road, Glasgow, GL22 6FR. We're arriving at Gatwick on Friday.
J Do you ⁷ _____ this Friday?
M No, next Friday, the 23ʳᵈ. The flight number is BA402 and we get in at 17.45.
J ⁸ _____, I didn't quite ⁹ _____ that. Can you ¹⁰ _____ it to me ¹¹ _____, please?
M We're on flight BA402 and we arrive at 17.45.
J And ¹² _____ you ¹³ _____ me your colleague's name?
M It's Erica Minton.
J Is that ¹⁴ _____ M-i-n-t-e-n?
M No, it's M-i-n-t-o-n.
J OK, I'll give him the message. Thanks for calling. Goodbye.

Progress Portfolio 11

Tick the things you can do in English.

☐ I can talk about things people do at work.
☐ I can report what people say and questions they ask.
☐ I can describe jobs.
☐ I can understand a TV drama.
☐ I can check information.

Extra Practice 12

Language Summary 12 p154

12A p94

1 Fill in the gaps with these words/phrases.

> ~~off~~   rubbish   broke   fancy
> hang around   could do   up to
> really into   reckon   feel
> can't be bothered   sick of

1. I'm _off_ now. Bye!
2. I've been working really hard. I _____ with a day off.
3. Teenagers often _____ together after school.
4. Sorry, I don't _____ up to going out. I'm exhausted.
5. I'd love to go clubbing, but I'm completely _____.
6. I don't mind where we go on holiday, it's _____ you.
7. I think most TV programmes are _____!
8. My son's _____ diving at the moment. He loves it.
9. I really _____ going out for a meal this evening.
10. I _____ he's going to propose to her soon.
11. I'm _____ tidying up after the children.
12. I _____ to go out tonight. I'm too tired.

2 Make wishes about these situations.

1. I can't find my keys.
   I wish I could find my keys.
2. I don't have a job.
3. I have to get up at 5.30 tomorrow morning.
4. I'm working in a fast food restaurant and I hate it!
5. I can't afford a new phone.
6. I get nervous when I meet new people.
7. I have to work all weekend.
8. I'm standing in the rain waiting for a bus.
9. I live next to a railway line and it's very noisy.
10. I'm not going away on holiday this year.

12B p96

3 Choose the correct words. Fill in the gaps with the correct form of *get* and these words/phrases.

> ~~a present~~   rid of   fed up with
> in touch with   back from
> to eat   message   around
> better at   lost

1. Have you _got_ your mother _a present_ for her birthday?
2. They _____ because they didn't take a map.
3. When are you _____ your holiday?
4. We don't need this old table. Shall we _____ it?
5. I'm hungry. Why don't we _____ something _____?
6. I'd _____ living at home so I moved out.
7. I'm trying to _____ an old friend from school.
8. What's the best way to _____ Istanbul?
9. He's _____ playing the piano. He practises for two hours every day.
10. Sorry I didn't call you back. I never _____ your _____.

4 Look at these third conditionals. Put the verbs in brackets in the correct form.

1. If he _'d asked_ (ask) me, I _'d have gone_ (go) with him.
2. If you _____ (not tell) me, I _____ (not know) about it.
3. She _____ (not be) late for the meeting if she _____ (leave) home earlier.
4. Brian _____ (become) a professional footballer if he _____ (not break) his leg.
5. If Sue _____ (know) about the party, she _____ (go).
6. I _____ (finish) my essay by now if my laptop _____ (not crash).
7. If Chris _____ (not go) on holiday to Ibiza, he _____ (not meet) his wife.

12C p98

5 a Write nouns for these verbs.

1. attract — _attraction_
2. enjoy
3. create
4. predict
5. reserve
6. depend
7. protect
8. entertain
9. prefer

b Write the adjectives for the main verbs in **5a**.

attract → attractive

6 a Write two adjectives for each of these verbs.

1. relax — _relaxed_ , _relaxing_
2. disappoint _____ , _____
3. harm _____ , _____
4. pollute _____ , _____
5. confuse _____ , _____
6. care _____ , _____
7. employ _____ , _____
8. embarrass _____ , _____

b Write the nouns for the verbs in **6a**.

relax → relaxation

Progress Portfolio 12

Tick the things you can do in English.

- ☐ I can use some informal words and phrases.
- ☐ I can make wishes about the present and the future.
- ☐ I can talk about imaginary situations in the past.
- ☐ I can understand an interview about someone's career.

Language Summary 1

VOCABULARY

1.1 Weekend activities 1A 1 p6

visit relatives
have a lie-in
go to concerts/gigs/festivals
chat to friends online
have a quiet night in
do yoga
meet up with friends
tidy up the house/the flat
go to museums/art galleries
do exercise
have people round for dinner
go out for a drink/meal

TIP • In the Language Summaries we only show the **main** stress (•) in words and phrases.

 **have a lie-in** when you stay in bed longer than usual in the morning: *I often have a lie-in on Sundays.*

 **have people round for dinner** invite people to your house to have dinner: *We're having Tom's parents round for dinner on Saturday.*

 **tidy up the house/flat** put things back in the places where you usually keep them: *I usually tidy up the flat before I go to work.*

TIPS • A *relative* is a person in your family (an aunt, a grandparent, a cousin, etc.). Your *parents* are your mother and father only.

• A *gig* is an informal word for a concert: *I went to an amazing gig last night.*

• We also use *chat* or *have a chat* to mean 'talk to someone in a friendly and informal way': *He's chatting with some friends. I had a chat with our new neighbour.*

1.2 Likes and dislikes 1B 1 p8

phrases to say you love or like something	phrases to say you don't like something
I (really) love …	I (really) hate …
I'm (really/very/quite) interested in …	I don't like … at all.
I (really) enjoy …	I can't stand …
I'm (really/very/quite) keen on …	… (really) get(s) on my nerves.
I think … is/are great/brilliant/wonderful.	I can't bear /beə/ …
	I'm not (very) keen on …
phrases to say something is OK	… drive(s) me crazy.
I think … is/are all right.	I think … is/are awful/terrible/dreadful.
I don't mind …	

TIPS • *I can't stand* and *I can't bear* mean 'I hate'.

• *Great, brilliant* and *wonderful* all mean 'very good'. *Awful, terrible* and *dreadful* all mean 'very bad'.

• We can use pronouns, nouns or verb+*ing* with the phrases for likes and dislikes: *I really love it. I can't stand football.* **Waiting in queues** *really drives me crazy.*

1.3 Adjectives (1): feelings 1C 1 p10

relaxed /rɪˈlækst/ happy because you aren't worried about anything: *Adela felt very relaxed after her holiday in Spain.*
nervous /ˈnɜːvəs/ worried because of something that is going to happen: *I always get nervous before I speak in public.*
pleased happy or satisfied: *I'm pleased you like the present.*
embarrassed /ɪmˈbærəst/ feel stupid because of something you did or something that happened: *I felt so embarrassed when our son said he didn't like the food.*
angry having a strong negative feeling about someone and wanting to shout at them or hurt them: *I was really angry at him for crashing the car.*
annoyed a bit angry: *I get annoyed when I have to wait in queues.*
fed up annoyed or bored because you have done something for too long: *I'm fed up with working so hard.*
disappointed unhappy because something is not as good as you wanted it to be, or because something hasn't happened: *They were disappointed that only ten people came to their party.*
stressed worried and not able to relax: *He's very stressed about his new job.*
calm relaxed and peaceful: *I always feel very calm after yoga.*
upset unhappy or worried because something bad has happened: *She was very upset when she lost her job.*
scared frightened: *I'm really scared of spiders.*
satisfied pleased because something has happened in the way that you want: *She was very satisfied with her students' work.*
confused when you can't think clearly or understand something: *Matt was confused and didn't know what to do.*
shocked very surprised and upset: *I was shocked by the news of his death.*
glad happy and pleased: *I'm glad you enjoyed the meal.*
concerned worried: *I'm very concerned about the environment.*
depressed unhappy and not able to enjoy anything: *He became very depressed when he lost his job.*

TIPS • We use *-ed* adjectives to describe how people feel: *I was very disappointed when I got my exam results.*

• We use *-ing* adjectives to describe the thing, situation, place or person that causes the feeling: *My exam results were disappointing.*

1.4 Prepositions with adjectives 1C 6 p11

• We often use prepositions with adjectives. The most common prepositions for these adjectives are in **bold**. Other prepositions that we can also use with these adjectives are in brackets ( ).

good **at**	scared **of** (by)
happy **with** (about)	bored **with** (by, of)
interested **in**	frightened **of** (by)
nervous **about** (of)	annoyed **at** (with, by)
keen **on**	bad **at**
worried **about**	satisfied **with** (by)
surprised **by** (at)	embarrassed **by** (about)
upset **about** (by)	concerned **about** (by)
fed up **with** (of)	angry **about** (at) something
pleased **with** (by, about)	angry **with** (at) someone

TIP • After prepositions we use a noun, a pronoun or verb+*ing*.

GRAMMAR

1.1 Question forms 1A 5 p7

AUXILIARIES

- We usually use an auxiliary (*does*, *are*, *did*, *has*, etc.) to make questions.

	question word	auxiliary	subject	verb	
PRESENT SIMPLE	How often	does	Fiona	teach	yoga classes?
PRESENT CONTINUOUS	What	is	Fiona's son	doing	at the moment?
PAST SIMPLE	What	did	Fiona	do	last Sunday?
PRESENT PERFECT SIMPLE	How many songs	has	Maxie	written	?

- We use the auxiliaries **do** and **does** to make questions in the Present Simple: *Who do you work for? What does he do in his free time?*
- We use the auxiliaries **am**, **are** and **is** to make questions in the Present Continuous: *Where am I going? What are you watching? What's he doing?*
- We use the auxiliaries **have** and **has** to make questions in the Present Perfect Simple: *Where have you been? Has he called yet?*

SUBJECT QUESTIONS

- Most questions with auxiliaries ask about the object of a sentence: **A** *How many songs* **has Maxie written? B** *He's written* **about 25 songs**.
- Subject questions ask about the subject of a sentence: **A** *What* makes her husband happy? **B** *Cooking* makes him happy.
- We don't use *do*, *does* or *did* in Present Simple and Past Simple subject questions: *Who visits them most weekends?* not *Who does visit them most weekends?*
- Subject questions have the same word order as positive sentences.
- We can make subject questions with *Who*, *What*, *Whose* and *Which*.

QUESTIONS WITH PREPOSITIONS

- We often put prepositions at the end of questions: *How many countries has he been* **to***? Who does Caroline go to art galleries* **with***?*

TIP • We don't usually put prepositions at the beginning of questions: *What are you talking about?* not *About what are you talking?*

1.2 Positive and negative verb forms, words and phrases 1B 5 p9

	positive	negative
PRESENT SIMPLE	I know	you don't want
PRESENT CONTINUOUS	you're waiting	I'm not feeling
PAST SIMPLE	I waited	I didn't get
PRESENT PERFECT SIMPLE	I've seen	she hasn't flown

I DON'T THINK ...; THERE IS/ARE NO ...

- We often make negative sentences with *I don't think* ...: *I don't think that's right.* not *I think that isn't right. I don't think I could do that.* not *I think I couldn't do that.*
- We can use **no** to make negatives with *there is/there are*: *There aren't any traffic jams.* = *There are* **no** *traffic jams. There isn't a better way to travel.* = *There's* **no** *better way to travel.*

WORDS AND PHRASES

positive	negative	positive	negative
love	hate	everyone	no one
always	never	all	none
usually	hardly ever	both	neither

TIPS • We can say *don't always/usually/often*, but not *don't sometimes/hardly ever/never*.

• We can say *everyone* or *everybody* and *no one* or *nobody*.

• We don't usually use double negatives. We say: *I didn't see anyone.* not *I didn't see no one.*

• We use plural verb forms with *both*: *Both of my sisters* **have got** *cars.* We use singular verb forms with *neither*: *Neither of them* **likes** *driving.*

REAL WORLD

1.1 Question tags 1D 4 p13

- We usually use question tags (*don't you?*, etc.) to check information that we think is correct.
- We usually use the **auxiliary** in question tags: *You live next door to Lisa,* **don't** *you?*
- We only use **pronouns** in question tags: *Barbara went to Liverpool University, didn't* **she***?*
- If the main verb is positive, the question tag is usually **negative**: *It was a great match yesterday,* **wasn't it***?*
- If the main verb is negative, the question tag is usually **positive**: *You haven't ordered any food yet,* **have you***?*
- We often use short answers (*Yes, I do. No, I don't.*, etc.) to say that the information is correct.
- When the information isn't correct, we often use *actually* after the short answer to sound more polite, then give more information: **A** *You've been diving, haven't you?* **B** *No, I haven't,* **actually***. It sounds a bit too dangerous to me.*

TIPS • We can also use *Yes, that's right.* to say that the information is correct: **A** *You're from London originally, aren't you?* **B** *Yes, that's right./Yes, I am.*

• If the main verb is in the positive form of the Present Simple or Past Simple, we use *don't*, *doesn't* or *didn't* in the question tag: *Jim lives in the USA,* **doesn't he***?*

• We say *aren't I?* not *amn't I?*: *I'm late,* **aren't I***?*

Language Summary 2

VOCABULARY

2.1 Collocations (1): work 2A p14

take work home
have time to relax
work long hours
work overtime
be a workaholic

meet deadlines
take time off work
be under (a lot of) pressure at work
spend a lot of time at work
have good working conditions

overtime extra time that you work after your usual working hours: *I have to work overtime tonight.*
a workaholic someone who works too much: *Chris is a real workaholic. He never does anything else.*
a deadline the time when work must be finished: *The deadline for this report is 9 a.m. tomorrow.*
pressure /ˈpreʃə/ difficult situations or problems that make you feel worried or unhappy: *I'm under a lot of pressure at work at the moment.*
working conditions things which affect the quality of your job (working hours, the place you work, holidays, sick pay, etc.): *Working conditions have improved in the last fifty years.*

TIP • We can also say *hit deadlines*: *Jessica's very reliable. She always hits her deadlines.*

2.2 Food and ways of cooking 2B p16

FRUIT, VEGETABLES AND MEAT

a peach   a coconut   a pineapple
an avocado   beans   an onion /ˈʌnjən/
a cucumber   a lettuce /ˈletɪs/   a green/red pepper

lamb /læm/   beef   a hot dog

TIP • *Beef* is meat from cows. *Lamb* is meat from young sheep. Both of these words are uncountable.

OTHER TYPES OF FOOD

peanuts   a chilli   flour /flaʊə/

herbs   spices   sauce

cream   noodles   a pie

WAYS OF COOKING

grill   barbecue   boil

fry   stir fry   bake

TIPS • *Grill* and *barbecue* are also nouns: *a grill, a barbecue*. We boil things in *a saucepan*, fry things in *a frying pan*, stir fry things in *a wok* and bake things in *an oven* /ˈʌvən/.

• We make the adjectives by adding *-ed*, *-d* or *-ied* to the verbs: *grilled fish, barbecued lamb, boiled vegetables, fried sausages, stir fried noodles, baked potatoes.*

2.3 Sleep 2C p18

fall asleep start sleeping: *She fell asleep on the train home.* Also: **be asleep**
wake up stop sleeping: *I woke up at six thirty this morning.*
get to sleep start sleeping, often with some difficulty: *It usually takes me half an hour to get to sleep.*
get back to sleep start sleeping again after you have woken up: *It took me a long time to get back to sleep.*
be wide awake be completely awake: *I was wide awake at 3 a.m. last night.*
be fast asleep be completely asleep: *The children were fast asleep when we got home.*

129

snore /snɔː/ breathe in a noisy way when you are sleeping: *My husband was snoring so loudly I couldn't get to sleep.*
have trouble sleeping find it difficult to sleep well: *I've had trouble sleeping since I lost my job.*
have insomnia not be able to get to sleep: *A lot of people in the UK have insomnia.*
take a sleeping pill take a pill that helps you sleep: *When I can't get to sleep, I often take a sleeping pill.*
have a dream have stories and pictures in your head while you are sleeping: *I had a very strange dream last night.*
have a nightmare have a frightening dream: *I had a terrible nightmare last night.*
be a light/heavy sleeper be someone who wakes up easily/doesn't wake up easily: *Carla's a very heavy sleeper – nothing can wake her up.*
have a nap have a short sleep in the day: *My dad always has a nap after lunch.* Also: **take a nap**

2.4 Gradable and strong adjectives; adverbs   p19

- Strong adjectives already include the idea of *very*, for example, *brilliant* means 'very good'.

gradable adjectives	strong adjectives
good	brilliant, fantastic
bad	terrible, awful /ˈɔːfəl/
tired	exhausted /ɪɡˈzɔːstɪd/, shattered
big	huge /hjuːdʒ/
difficult	impossible
frightened	terrified
surprised	amazed
tasty	delicious /dɪˈlɪʃəs/
small	tiny /ˈtaɪni/
cold	freezing
hot	boiling
beautiful	gorgeous /ˈɡɔːdʒəs/
big	enormous
interested	fascinated
angry	furious /ˈfjʊəriəs/
happy	delighted
dirty	filthy /ˈfɪlθi/

- We can use the adverbs **fairly**, **very**, **extremely** and **incredibly** with gradable adjectives, but not with strong adjectives: *very good* not *very fantastic*; *incredibly hot* not *incredibly boiling*, etc.
- *Fairly* is less strong than *very*. *Incredibly* and *extremely* are stronger than *very*.
- We can use **absolutely** with strong adjectives, but not gradable adjectives: *absolutely terrified* not *absolutely frightened*, etc.
- We can use **really** with both gradable and strong adjectives: *really tired*, *really exhausted*, etc.

TIP • These strong adjectives also mean *very good*: *amazing, excellent, fabulous, incredible, marvellous, superb, terrific, wonderful.*

GRAMMAR

2.1 be able to, be supposed to, be allowed to, modal verbs (1) 2A 4 p15

- *can*, *must*, *have to*, *should* and *ought to* are modal verbs.
- We use **can** and **be able to** to talk about ability or possibility: *People can get their best ideas when they're doing nothing. We're able to continue working when we're travelling.*
- We use **be supposed to** to say a person is expected to do something: *In the UK people are supposed to have a break every four hours.*
- We use **be allowed to** and **can** to say we have permission to do something: *Some French employees are allowed to begin their weekend at 3 p.m. on Thursday. In some American companies, employees can sleep whenever they want.*
- We use **must** and **have to** to say something is necessary: *Rob says he must take more time off work. Lots of people have to take work home.*
- We use **should** and **ought to** to give advice: *People should only work 35 hours a week. We ought to spend more time relaxing.*

TIPS • We can use *have to* or *have got to* to say that something is necessary: *I have to work tonight.* = *I've got to work tonight.* *Have got to* is very common in spoken English.

• *Must* and *have to* have very similar meanings in their positive form: *I must go.* = *I have to go.* *Have to* is more common than *must*.

• We can't use *must* in the past. To say something was necessary in the past, we use *had to*: *I had to go to three meetings yesterday.*

POSITIVE, NEGATIVE AND QUESTION FORMS

- We use **the infinitive** after *can*, *must*, *have to*, *should*, *ought to*, *be able to*, *be allowed to* and *be supposed to*.
- *Can*, *must*, *should* and *ought to* are the same for all subjects.

positive	negative	question
I can go.	I can't go.	Can I go?
You must go.	You mustn't go.	(Must you go?)
He should go.	He shouldn't go.	Should he go?
We ought to go.	We ought not to go.	(Ought we to go?)

- We make negatives and questions of *have to* by using the auxiliaries *do* and *does*: *I don't have to go.*; *Does she have to go?*, etc.
- We make negatives and questions of *be able to*, *be allowed to*, *be supposed to* by changing the form of the verb *be*: *He isn't able to come. You aren't allowed to go. What are we supposed to do?*

TIP • We don't usually use *ought to* in its question form. We usually use *Do you think …* instead: *Do you think I ought to call him?*

MUSTN'T OR DON'T HAVE TO

- We use **don't have to** to say something isn't necessary: *You don't have to wear a suit to work, but you can if you want to.*
- We use **mustn't** to say something is not allowed: *You mustn't send personal emails from the office. You can only send work emails.*

TIP • To say something wasn't necessary in the past, we use **didn't have to**: *I didn't have to work yesterday.* not *I hadn't to work yesterday.*

2.2 Present Continuous and Present Simple 2B 4 p17

- We use the **Present Continuous** for things that:
  a are happening at the moment of speaking: *I'm blogging from a busy street food market. I'm sitting in one of Mexico City's busy parks.*
  b are temporary and happening around now, but maybe not at this exact moment: *Now I'm writing a book about street food. We're working in Mexico for a few days.*
  c are changing over a period of time: *My blog is becoming more popular every year. More and more people are visiting Thailand on holiday these days.*

- We use the **Present Simple** for:
  a habits and routines with *always, sometimes, never, every day, every year,* etc.: *I always try the street food wherever I go. I come here every year.*
  b things that are permanent, or true for a long time: *I live in London. People still eat a lot of street food in Indonesia.*
  c verbs that describe states (*be, have got, want,* etc.): *The country's capital has got some fantastic street food. If you want to make the perfect burrito, start with a freshly-made flour tortilla.*

ACTIVITY AND STATE VERBS

- Activity verbs talk about activities and actions. We can use activity verbs in the Present Simple and the Present Continuous (and other continuous verb forms): *I watch TV every evening. I'm watching TV now.* Typical activity verbs are: *watch, talk, spend, eat, learn, buy, cook, take, happen.*

- State verbs talk about states, feelings and opinions. We don't usually use state verbs in the Present Continuous (or other continuous verb forms): *I like burritos.* not *I'm liking burritos.*

- Learn these common state verbs.

'be and have' verbs	'think and know' verbs	'like and hate' verbs	senses	other verbs
be	think	like	see	hope
have (got)	know	love	hear	seem
own	believe	hate	taste	need
belong	understand	prefer	smell	cost
	remember	want	touch	agree
	forget			weigh
	mean			contain

TIPS • We often use *can* with verbs that describe the senses to talk about what is happening now: *I can hear a noise outside. I can't see anything.*

- Some verbs can be both activity verbs and state verbs:
I'm having dinner at the moment. (activity)
They have two children. (state)
What are you thinking about? (activity)
I think football is boring. (state)

- We often use *still* with the Present Simple and Present Continuous to mean something that started in the past and continues in the present: *People still eat a lot of street food in Indonesia. I'm still waiting for him to call me.*

Present Continuous

- We make the Present Continuous **positive** and **negative** with: **subject** + **be** + (**not**) + **verb+ing**
I'm (not) working at the moment.
You/We/They are/aren't writing a blog.
He/She/It's/isn't becoming more popular.

- We make Present Continuous **questions** with:
(**question word**) + **am, are** or **is** + **subject** + **verb+ing**
What am I doing here?
Who are you/we/they talking to?
Is he/she/it working today?

Present Simple

- For *I/you/we/they*, the Present Simple **positive** is the same as the infinitive.

- For *he/she/it*, we add *-s* or *-es* to the infinitive: *he lives; she goes; it works.*

- We make the Present Simple **negative** with:
subject + **don't** or **doesn't** + **infinitive**
I/You/We/They don't live here.
He/She/It doesn't work.

- We make Present Simple **questions** with:
(**question word**) + **do** or **does** + **subject** + **infinitive**
Where do I/you/we/they live?
Does he/she/it work?

REAL WORLD

2.1 Showing concern, giving and responding to advice 2D 4 p20

showing concern

Oh, dear. What's the matter?   Oh, I'm sorry to hear that.
I can see why you're upset.   Yes, I see what you mean.
Oh, how awful!   Oh, dear. What a shame.

giving advice

Have you tried talking to him about it?
Perhaps you ought to spend more time together.
Maybe you should sleep in separate rooms.
Why don't you talk to her about it?
I'd take her out for a really nice meal.

responding to advice

Yes, you could be right.   Yes, that's a good idea.
Well, it's worth a try, I guess. I might try that.
I've tried that, but …

- After *Have you tried …* we use **verb+ing**: *Have you tried talking to him about it?*

- After *you ought to …*, *you should …*, *Why don't you …*, and *I'd* (= *I would*) *…* we use **the infinitive**: *Perhaps you ought to spend more time together.*

- We often use *What should I do?* or *What do you think I should do?* to ask for advice.

Language Summary 3

VOCABULARY

3.1 Phrasal verbs (1): travel 3A p22

TIP • sb = somebody; sth = something.

set off start a journey: *They set off at 5 a.m.*
get around travel to different places in the same town/city/area: *What's the cheapest way to get around?*
deal with sth do something in order to solve a problem or achieve something: *I have to deal with a lot of difficult customers as part of my job.*
check in go to the reception desk of a hotel to say you have arrived and to get the key to your room: *Have you checked in yet?*
check out go to the reception desk of a hotel to pay your bill before you leave: *We checked out early this morning.*
see sb off go to the place where somebody is leaving from (for example, an airport or a station) to say goodbye to them: *My parents came to see me off at the airport.*
pick sb up go to a place where somebody is waiting and take them where they want to go: *Can you pick me up from the station?*
get back (to/from a place) return to a place after you have been somewhere else: *When did you get back from Brazil?*
put up with sth accept a situation or a problem that you don't like because you can't change it: *I don't know how you put up with all this noise.*
look after take care of something or someone (a pet, a plant, a baby, etc.): *Could you look after our cat when we're on holiday?*
go away leave your home to spend time somewhere else, usually for a holiday: *We're going away in June.*
look forward to sth feel happy and excited about something that is going to happen: *I'm really looking forward to my holiday.*

set off   see off

pick up   check in

TIPS • You also *check in* at an airport (or online) before you fly somewhere.

• We say *get (back) home* not ~~get (back) to/from home.~~

• We often use verb+*ing* after *look forward to*:
*I'm looking forward to **seeing** you.*

3.2 Phrases with *travel, get* and *go on* 3B p24

travel
- on your own
- independently
- first/business/economy class
- together/separately
- light

get
- into/out of a car
- back from somewhere
- here/there by (10.30)
- on/off a bus/plane/train
- a taxi home/to work

go on
- a trip
- a guided tour
- a journey
- a cruise
- a package holiday

independently without the help of other people: *I don't like package holidays. I prefer travelling independently.*
first class the best and most expensive way to travel: *Famous people usually travel first class.*
economy class the cheapest way to travel: *I don't have much money so I always fly economy class.*
travel light travel with a very small amount of luggage: *I always travel light. I only take hand luggage.*
a trip when you go to a place for a short time and then come back: *I went on a business trip to Berlin last month.*
a guided tour /tʊə/ when you travel to lots of places in a city or country and a guide tells you about the interesting things you can see: *We're going on a guided tour of London.*
a journey /ˈdʒɜːni/ when you travel from one place to another place: *We went on a journey across Europe.*
a cruise /kruːz/ a holiday on a ship when you sail from place to place: *We're going on a Mediterranean cruise next month.*
a package /ˈpækɪdʒ/ **holiday** a holiday where everything is included in the price: *A lot of British people go on package holidays to Spain every summer.*

TIPS • *Travel* is usually a verb. When we want to use a noun, we usually use *journey* or *trip*: *How was your journey/trip?* not ~~How was your travel?~~

• *Get* has many different meanings in English: *get back* = arrive back; *get a taxi* = take a taxi, etc.

• You can also *get on/off a bike, a scooter* and *a motorbike*.

• *By* + time means 'at or before': *I'll get there by 2.30.* = I'll get there at 2.30 or earlier.

3.3 Word building (1): suffixes for adjectives and nouns 3C 5 p27

- We sometimes make adjectives from nouns, or nouns from adjectives, by adding an ending (a suffix), for example *happy → happiness*.

adjective	noun	suffix	noun	adjective	suffix
kind sad lazy	kindness sadness laziness	-ness	danger adventure fame	dangerous adventurous famous	-ous
patient confident important	patience confidence importance	-ce	comfort knowledge fashion	comfortable knowledgeable fashionable	-able
difficult honest modest	difficulty honesty modesty	-y	nature tradition music	natural traditional musical	-al
popular active possible	popularity activity possibility	-ity	health noise tourist	healthy noisy touristy	-y

TIP • When the adjective or noun ends in *-t*, *-y* or *-e*, we sometimes have to change the spelling: *patient → patience*, *lazy → laziness*, *nature → natural*, etc.

GRAMMAR

3.1 Present Perfect Simple 3A 3 p23

- We use the **Present Perfect Simple** for experiences that happened some time before now, but we don't know or don't say when they happened: *I've worked in the USA and in Europe. We've been away together a few times.* To give more information about an experience we use the **Past Simple**: *I really enjoyed my time there too. Each time there was a problem back at the hotel.*

- We use the **Past Simple** to say when something happened: *My wife and I started working in the hotel industry 19 years ago. Three days ago a guy set off on his own into the mountains.*

- We use the **Present Perfect Simple** for something that started in the past and continues in the present: *I've lived in this country for about three years. We've had this place since 2008.*

- We use the **Present Perfect Simple** for something that happened a short time ago, but we don't say exactly when: *I've just been to Banff to pick him up from the hospital. My wife's gone to see some friends off at Manchester airport.*

POSITIVE AND NEGATIVE

- We make the Present Perfect Simple **positive** and **negative** with:
 I/you/we/they + **'ve**, **have** or **haven't** + **past participle**
 he/she/it + **'s**, **has** or **hasn't** + **past participle**

 I/You/We/They've/haven't worked in Canada.
 He/She/It's/hasn't been to South America.

QUESTIONS

- We make Present Perfect Simple **questions** with:
 (question word) + **have** or **has** + **subject** + **past participle**
 How long have I/you/we/they lived here?
 Has he/she/it been there before?

FOR AND SINCE

- We use **for** with a period of time (how long): *I've lived in this country for about three years.*
- We use **since** with a point in time (when something started): *We've had this place since 2008.*

TIPS • We can also use **for** with the Past Simple: *I lived in Colombia for six years.* (I don't live there now.)

• We don't usually use *during* with the Present Perfect Simple: *I've been here for a week.* not *I've been here during a week.*

BEEN AND GONE

- *Go* has two past participles, *been* and *gone*.
- We use **been** to mean 'go and come back': *I've just been to Banff to pick him up from the hospital.* (I'm back at the place I started from now.)
- We use **gone** to mean 'go, but not come back yet': *My wife's gone to see some friends off at Manchester airport.* (She's not back yet.)

ADVERBS AND TIME PHRASES

- We can use these words/phrases with the **Present Perfect Simple**: *never, ever, recently, lately, before, this week, just, yet, already*: *I've never been to Russia.*, etc.

- We must use the **Past Simple** with phrases that say a definite time (*two years ago, in 1997, last week, at 10 o'clock*, etc.): *I went there two years ago.* not *I've been there two years ago.*

- We use **just** to say something happened a short time ago. We don't use *just* in negative sentences: *Jo's just phoned. Has Jo just phoned?* not *Jo hasn't just phoned.* We put *just* before the past participle.

- We use **yet** to say something hasn't happened, but we think it will happen in the future. We don't use *yet* in positive sentences: *He hasn't finished it yet. Have you finished it yet?* but not *I've finished it yet.* We put *yet* at the end of the sentence or clause.

- We use **already** to say something happened some time in the past, maybe sooner than we expected. We don't use *already* in negative sentences: *We've already seen it. Have you already seen it?* but not *I haven't already seen it.* We put *already* before the past participle.

- **Recently** and **lately** mean 'not long ago': *I haven't been to London recently/lately.*

- After **this is the first time**, **this is the second time**, etc. we use the Present Perfect Simple: *This is the first time we've been here.* not *This is the first time we are here.*

TIP • We also use the Present Perfect Simple with *this week/month/year*, etc. and with *this morning*, *this afternoon*, etc. if it is still that time of day. Compare these sentences:
A *Have you seen Bob this morning?* (It is still morning.)
B *Did you see Bob this morning?* (It is now afternoon or evening.)

3.2 Present Perfect Continuous and Present Perfect Simple 3B 5 p25

- We usually use the **Present Perfect Continuous** to talk about an **activity** that started in the past and continues in the present: *The company has been publishing guide books for 40 years.*

- We usually use the **Present Perfect Simple** to talk about a **state** that started in the past and continues in the present: *The book has been a best-seller since it was published in 1973.*

TIPS • We often use the Present Perfect Continuous with verbs that talk about longer activities: *learn, rain, try, play, work, read, wait*, etc.: *I've been learning English for five years.*

• We don't usually use the Present Perfect Continuous with verbs that talk about short actions: *start, find, lose, break, buy, stop*, etc.: *I've started a course.* not *I've been starting a course.*

• With some verbs, both verb forms are possible: *I've lived/been living here for five years. He's worked/been working in Australia since 2011.*

Present Perfect Continuous

- We make the Present Perfect Continuous **positive** with:
  I/you/we/they + 've or have + been + verb+*ing*
  he/she/it + 's or has + been + verb+*ing*
  They've been travelling since 1972.
  The company has been publishing guide books for 40 years.

- We make the Present Perfect Continuous **negative** with:
  I/you/we/they + haven't + been + verb+*ing*
  he/she/it + hasn't + been + verb+*ing*
  I haven't been sleeping very well lately.
  He hasn't been working here for very long.

TIPS • We often use the Present Perfect Continuous to talk about the **activity** we have been doing: *I've been doing my homework.* (We don't know if the homework is finished or not.)

• We often use the Present Perfect Simple to say an activity is **finished**: *I've done my homework.* (The homework is finished now.)

HOW LONG … AND HOW MANY …

- We usually use the **Present Perfect Continuous** to say **how long** an activity has been happening: *Their television company, Lonely Planet TV, has been making programmes since 2004.*

- We usually use the **Present Perfect Simple** to say **how many** things are finished: *Lonely Planet has published over 650 guidebooks since the company began.*

Questions with *How long* … ? and *How many* … ?

- We make **Present Perfect Continuous** questions with *How long* … ? with:
  How long + have + I/you/we/they + been + verb+*ing*
  How long + has + he/she/it + been + verb+*ing*
  How long have you been waiting here?
  How long has Lonely Planet been publishing guide books?

- We make **Present Perfect Simple** questions with *How many* … ? with:
  How many + have + I/you/we/they + past participle
  How many + has + he/she/it + past participle
  How many countries have you visited?
  How many books has Lonely Planet published?

TIP • We can also make questions with the Present Perfect Simple and *How much* (+ noun) … ?: *How much money have you spent so far?*

REAL WORLD

3.1 Asking for and making recommendations 3D 3 p28

asking for recommendations

Do you know any good places to stay/eat?
What's the best way to (get around)?
What else is worth seeing?
What about (places outside Delhi)?
Have you got any other tips?

recommending things

It's probably best to (use rickshaws).
I'd recommend (the trains).
You should definitely see (the Red Fort).
That's well worth seeing.
You really must go to (Agra) to see (the Taj Mahal).

not recommending things

Don't bother going to (the museums).
It isn't really worth visiting, (I don't think).
Don't drink anything with ice in it.
I wouldn't eat any salads.

responding to recommendations

That's good to know.
That sounds good.
Thanks, that's really useful.
Yes, I've heard that before.

- After *It's (well/not) worth* … we use **verb+*ing***: *That's well worth **seeing**.*

- After *Don't bother* … we use **verb+*ing***: *Don't bother **going** to the museums.*

- After *I'd/I wouldn't* … we use **the infinitive**: *I'd **recommend** the trains.*

Language Summary 4

VOCABULARY

4.1 Collocations (2): music 4A p30

do/play a concert/a gig
be a big fan of a singer/band
release a new single/album/CD
do an encore
download a track onto my phone
be/go on tour
have an album/a CD in the charts
see someone play live
be/go onstage

> **a gig** (informal) a concert (rock, pop, jazz, etc.): *I went to a brilliant gig last night.*
> **a fan** a person who likes a particular band, singer, sports team, etc.: *I'm a big fan of Coldplay. My brother's a Manchester United fan.*
> **a single** a CD or record that has only one main song: *Have you heard Madonna's new single?*
> **an album** a collection of songs or pieces of music on a CD or a record, or that you can download from the internet: *The Beatles' first album was called 'Please Please Me'.*
> **release** make a CD, film, etc. available for the public to buy or see: *Their first album was released last week.*
> **an encore** an extra song or piece of music that is performed at the end of the show, usually because the audience shouts for it: *When I saw U2 at Wembley, they did three encores.*
> **a track** a song or piece of music on a CD or record, or that you can download from the internet: *I downloaded this track from the band's website.*
> **on tour** when a band or singer is on tour, they travel from one city or country to another and play concerts in each place: *Bands can make a lot of money when they go on tour.*
> **the charts** official lists that show which singles and albums have sold the most copies each week: *Lady Gaga has two albums in the charts.*
> **play live** /laɪv/ play in front of an audience: *Have you ever seen the Rolling Stones play live?*
> **be onstage** be on a stage in a concert hall or a theatre: *What time are the band onstage?*

TIPS • We can also use *tour* as a verb: *My favourite band are touring at the moment.*

• We can also use *live* to talk about TV programmes or sporting events that we can see at the same time as they are happening: *The World Cup final is shown live in over 160 countries.*

• We often use *a venue* /ˈvenjuː/ to talk about a place where bands or singers play concerts: *There are lots of great venues in London.*

4.2 Adjectives(2): character 4B p32

Adventurous people like visiting new places and having new experiences.
Talented people have a natural ability to do something, like paint, write, play music, etc.
Sensible /ˈsensɪbəl/ people can make good decisions based on reasons and facts.
Sensitive people are able to understand other people's feelings and problems, and help them in a way that does not upset them.
Brave people are not frightened in dangerous or difficult situations.
Determined /dɪˈtɜːmɪnd/ people want to do something very much and don't allow anything to stop them.
Reliable /rɪˈlaɪəbəl/ people always do what you want or expect them to do.
Independent people don't want or need other people to do things for them.
Organised people plan things well and don't waste time.
Stubborn /ˈstʌbən/ people won't change their ideas or plans when other people want them to.
Ambitious /æmˈbɪʃəs/ people want to be very successful or powerful.
Confident people are sure that they can do things successfully or well.
Practical people are good at planning things and dealing with problems.
Generous /ˈdʒenərəs/ people like giving money and presents to other people.
Mean people don't like spending money or giving things to other people.
Responsible /rɪˈspɒnsɪbəl/ people behave sensibly and can make good decisions on their own.
Aggressive people behave in an angry or violent way towards other people.
Optimistic people always think that good things will happen in the future.
Pessimistic people always think that bad things will happen in the future.

TIP • Someone who is optimistic is *an optimist*. Someone who is pessimistic is *a pessimist*.

 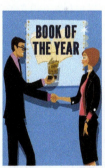 

He's adventurous.   She's talented.   She's generous.

He's brave.   He's stubborn.   She's organised.

4.3 Guessing meaning from context
4C p35

- Sometimes you can guess the meaning of a word by:
  a deciding which part of speech it is (noun, verb, adjective, etc.).
  b understanding the rest of the sentence and the general meaning of the text.
  c recognising a similar word in your language, or another language you know.

1 **wandered** (regular verb) walked around slowly: *Have you ever wandered around an art gallery?*
2 **well-known** (adjective) famous: *We looked at paintings by well-known artists.*
3 **bizarre** /bɪˈzɑː/ (adjective) strange: *Nothing is too bizarre for this museum.*
4 **highlight** (noun) most interesting part: *The highlight of this museum is Imelda Marcos's massive shoe collection.*
5 **appear** (regular verb) seem: *The sculptures appear to be frozen in time.*
6 **carriages** /ˈkærɪdʒɪz/ (noun) parts of a train that people travel in: *There are 930 trains with over 14,000 carriages.*
7 **peckish** (adjective) a bit hungry: *Are you feeling a bit peckish?*
8 **set up** (irregular phrasal verb) started (for a business, company, museum, etc.): *The museum was set up by a man called Hamburger Harry.*

TIP • Be careful of words/phrases that are 'false friends' in your language. For example, *sensible* in Spanish means *sensitive* and *fast* in German means *almost*.

> **check out** (regular phrasal verb) go to a place to see what it is like: *You should check out The Museum of Bad Art.*
> **massive** (adjective) very big: *Imelda Marcos's massive shoe collection.*
> **displayed** (regular verb) organised in a way that they can be seen by the public: *749 pairs are now displayed in the museum.*
> **sculptures** (noun) a piece of art made out of stone, wood, metal or concrete: *He placed about 300 life-size concrete sculptures of real people on the sea bed.*
> **breathtaking** (adjective) extremely exciting, beautiful or surprising: *The sight of brightly-coloured tropical fish swimming between the sculptures is absolutely breathtaking.*
> **miniature** /ˈmɪnɪtʃə/ (adjective) very small, particularly for something that is usually much bigger: *Why not take him to visit the largest miniature railway museum in the world?*
> **track** (noun) The long pieces of metal on the ground that a train travels on: *The museum has 13,000 metres of track.*
> **impressive** (adjective) admired and respected, often because it's special, important, or very large: *It's an impressive sight.*

GRAMMAR

4.1 Past Simple and Past Continuous
4A p31

- We use the **Past Simple** for:
  a a single completed action in the past. *My boyfriend **bought** tickets to see her play live. Then I **moved** to London.*
  b a repeated action or habit in the past. *I **listened** to her second album all the time. I **practised** for hours every day.*
  c a state in the past. *My boyfriend **wanted** to sell it on eBay. I **loved** dance music.*

- We use the **Past Continuous** for:
  a an action in progress at a point of time in the past. *Five years ago I **was living** in New York. Twenty minutes later I **was standing** in front of 1,000 people.*
  b the background events of a story. *All the fans **were singing** along. All the clubbers **were dancing** and **having** a good time.*
  c an action in progress when another (shorter) action happened. *While I **was playing** my last track, the manager came over and congratulated me. While she **was doing** an encore, she threw her shoes into the crowd.* Look at this diagram.

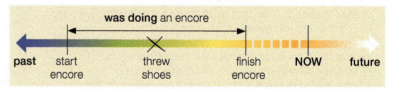

TIPS • We can also use the Past Continuous when the longer action is interrupted: *While we were having a picnic, it started to rain.*

• We can use *when* or *while* with the Past Continuous: *He phoned me when/while I was waiting for the train.* We don't usually use *while* with the Past Simple: ~~*While he phoned me, I was waiting for a train.*~~

Past Simple

- We usually make the Past Simple **positive** of regular verbs by adding *-ed* or *-d* to the infinitive: *work → worked, live → lived*, etc. There are no rules for irregular verbs. There is an Irregular Verb List on p175.
  *I **stayed** at home and **watched** TV.*
- We make the Past Simple **negative** with:
  subject + **didn't** (= did not) + **infinitive**
  *He **didn't go** to work yesterday.*
- We make Past Simple **questions** with:
  (question word) + **did** + **subject** + **infinitive**
  *What time **did** he **call** you?*

Past Continuous

- We make the Past Continuous **positive** and **negative** with:
  subject + **was, were, wasn't** or **weren't** + **verb+ing**
  *I/He/She/It **was/wasn't working** when you called.*
  *We/You/They **were/weren't living** in Australia in 2010.*
- We make Past Continuous **questions** with:
  (question word) + **was** or **were** + **subject** + **verb+ing**
  ***Was** I/he/she/it **waiting** for you?*
  *What **were** you/we/they **doing** at 2 p.m. yesterday?*

4.2 used to 4A 6 p31

- We can use *used to* or the Past Simple to talk about **repeated** actions, habits or states in the past:
I went/used to go to a lot of gigs.
I listened/used to listen to her second album all the time.
Back then I was/used to be one of Lady Gaga's biggest fans.

- We can't use *used to* to talk about **one** action in the past:
That night she sang for over two hours. not *That night she used to sing for over two hours.*

TIP • We can only use *used to* to talk about the past. To talk about habits or repeated actions in the present, we use *usually* + Present Simple. Compare these sentences:
I used to work at the weekend. (I don't work at the weekend now.)
I usually work at the weekend. (I work at the weekend now.)

POSITIVE AND NEGATIVE

- We make **positive** sentences with *used to* with:
subject + used to + infinitive
He used to live in Dublin when he was a teenager.

- We make **negative** sentences with *used to* with:
subject + didn't + use to + infinitive
We didn't use to go clubbing very often.

QUESTIONS

- We make **questions** with *used to* with:
(question word) + did + subject + use to + infinitive
Did you use to go out a lot when you lived in New York?
Where did you use to live when you were young?

TIPS • *Used to* is the same for all subjects:
I/You/He/She/We/They used to live in Ireland.

• Notice how we spell the negative and question forms: *didn't use to* not *didn't used to*; *did you use to* not *did you used to*.

• In the negative we can say *didn't use to* or *never used to*: *I never used to go to gigs when I was young.*

• The short answers to yes/no questions with *used to* are:
Yes, I did./No, I didn't.; Yes, he did./No, he didn't., etc.

4.3 Past Perfect 4B 5 p32

- When there is more than one action in the past, we often use the Past Perfect for the action that happened **first**.

second action (Past Simple)	first action (Past Perfect)
Cho joined the expedition after	Luke had gone back to the UK.
He also read messages that	people had sent him.
Ed calculated that	he'd walked about 6,000 miles.

- Compare these sentences:
1 *When I turned on the TV, the programme started.*
First I turned on the TV, then the programme started almost immediately.
2 *When I turned on the TV, the programme had started.*
First the programme started, then I turned on the TV.

TIPS • If the order of past events is clear from the context, we don't usually use the Past Perfect: *We had dinner, watched TV and then went to bed.*

- We don't always use the Past Perfect with **before** and **after** because the order of events is clear: *We (had) finished eating before they arrived. I went home after the meeting (had) finished.*

POSITIVE AND NEGATIVE

- We make the Past Perfect **positive** with:
subject + had or 'd + past participle
They had planned to do the whole walk together.

- We make the Past Perfect **negative** with:
subject + hadn't + past participle
He hadn't been to the Amazon jungle before.

TIP • The Past Perfect is the same for all subjects: *I/You/He/She/It/We/They had already arrived when John got home.*

QUESTIONS

- We make Past Perfect **questions** with:
(question word) + had + subject + past participle
What had he done before he became an explorer?

TIPS • The short answers to Past Perfect yes/no questions are: *Yes, I had./No, I hadn't.*, etc.

• We often use the Past Perfect after *realised*, *thought*, *forgot* and *remembered*: *I realised I'd left my wallet at home.*

• We often use **by the time**, **when**, **as soon as**, **because** and **so** to make sentences with the Past Perfect and Past Simple:
The party had finished by the time he arrived.

• We use the same adverbs and time phrases with the Past Perfect as we do with the Present Perfect Simple: *Tracy had just/already finished it.* See **GRAMMAR 3.1** p133 for more information on adverbs and time phrases.

REAL WORLD

4.1 Softening opinions and making generalisations 4D 3 p36

- Sometimes English speakers soften the way they express their opinions so that they don't sound rude or offensive.

- We often use these phrases in **bold** to soften our opinions:

Some of them can be **quite** aggressive **at times**.
On the whole, most fans just want to see a good game.
Footballers **tend to** earn **rather** a lot of money.
That's **not very** sensible behaviour, is it?
Generally speaking, most footballers are just normal people.
Perhaps some people **can** take it **a bit** too seriously.

- After **tend to** we use **the infinitive**: *He tends to be a bit mean.*

- *Rather*, *quite*, *not very* and *a bit* usually come **before** an adjective: *They can get quite/rather/a bit noisy at times.*

- We often put **generally speaking** and **on the whole** at the beginning of a sentence: *Generally speaking/On the whole, most football fans aren't violent at all.*

- We often use **not very** + **positive adjective** to criticise someone or something politely:
That's not very sensible behaviour. (That's stupid behaviour.)
He wasn't very polite. (He was rude.)

Language Summary 5

VOCABULARY

5.1 Homes 5A 1 p38

HOMES AND BUILDINGS

an apartment block

a cottage /ˈkɒtɪdʒ/

a detached /dɪˈtætʃt/ house

a terraced /ˈterɪst/ house

TIP • We can say *an apartment block*, *an apartment building* or *a block of flats*.

PARTS OF A HOME

a balcony

a garage /ˈgærɑːʒ/

a loft

a study

a roof

stairs

TIP • We can also say *upstairs* and *downstairs* to talk about the floor above or below where we are now: *I think you left your wallet upstairs. If you're going downstairs, can you make some tea?*

LOCATION

in the city centre
in the country
in the suburbs
in a quiet/lively/friendly neighbourhood
in a residential area
on the ground/first/top floor

a suburb /ˈsʌbɜːb/ an area where people live outside the centre of a city: *They lived in a suburb of New York. People who live in the suburbs have to commute into the city.*
a neighbourhood /ˈneɪbəhʊd/ the area of a town or city that is around someone's home: *I live in a quiet neighbourhood.*
lively /ˈlaɪvli/ a lively neighbourhood has a lot of places to go (cafés, restaurants, clubs, etc.) and a lot of interesting things happening in it: *We live in a very lively neighbourhood.*
a residential area a part of town with a lot of houses or flats, but no offices, big shops or factories: *My parents live in a residential area just outside the city centre.*

TIPS • In the UK the suburbs often have a lot of detached houses and are usually quite expensive places to live.

• *the ground floor* [UK] = *the first floor* [US]; *the first floor* [UK] = *the second floor* [US], etc.

• We can also say *a ground-floor flat*, *a top-floor flat*, etc.

5.2 Phrasal verbs (2) 5B 2 p40

clear sth out tidy a room, cupboard, etc. and get rid of the things in it that you don't want any more: *I'm going to clear out the garage this weekend.*
sort sth out arrange or organise things that are not in order or are untidy: *I need to sort out my notes – I can't find anything!*
give sth away give something to someone without asking for money: *I didn't need my old TV so I gave it away.*
throw sth away or **throw sth out** put something in the rubbish bin that you don't want any more: **A** *What should I do with this lamp?* **B** *Throw it away/out, it's broken.*
take sth out remove something from a place: *Can you take the rubbish out for me, please?*
tidy (sth) up make a room or place tidy by putting things back in the place where you usually keep them: *I always tidy up before I go to bed.*
put sth away put something in the place where you usually keep it: *Don't leave your clothes on the floor – put them away.*
come back return to a place: *John's on holiday, but he's coming back tomorrow afternoon.*
go through sth carefully look at things to find something or to see if you want to keep them: *I went through everything in these boxes and threw away a lot of junk.*

throw away/out

put away

5.3 Verb patterns (1) 5C 4 p43

- When we use two verbs together, the form of the second verb usually depends on the first verb: start **singing**; decided **to make**; can't **celebrate**; tell their children **to make**; make it **shine**, etc. This is called a verb pattern.

start like begin love keep enjoy finish mind prefer hate continue	+ verb+ing (doing)
decide remember forget try start like begin love need would like want plan prefer hate continue learn seem	+ infinitive with to (to do)
can might could should would will must would rather	+ infinitive (do)
tell ask help allow teach would like want pay	+ object + infinitive with to (sb/sth to do)
make help let	+ object + infinitive (sb/sth do)

TIPS • The verbs in blue in the table have more than one verb pattern. Both verb patterns have the same meaning: *I started to write an email. = I started writing an email.*

• In British English, *like/love/hate* + verb+*ing* is more common: *I like/love/hate watching golf.* In American English, *like/love/hate* + infinitive with *to* is more common: *I like to watch golf.*

5.4 Materials 5D 1 p44

wool, rubber, metal, cardboard

plastic, leather, paper, cotton

wood, tin, glass, steel

GRAMMAR

5.1 Making comparisons 5A 5 p39

COMPARATIVES AND SUPERLATIVES

- We use comparatives (*bigger*, *more expensive*, etc.) to compare two things.
- We use superlatives (*biggest*, *most expensive*, etc.) to compare three or more things.

1-syllable adjectives; 2-syllable adjectives ending in -y

adjective	comparative	superlative
old	old**er**	old**est**
small	small**er**	small**est**
nice	nic**er**	nic**est**
big	big**ger**	big**gest**
noisy	nois**ier**	nois**iest**

TIPS • When the adjective ends in -e, we only add -r or -st: *safe → safer, safest*.

• When the adjective ends in consonant + vowel + consonant, we double the final consonant: *thin → thinner, thinnest*.

• When a two-syllable adjective ends in -y, we change the -y to -i and add -er or -est: *funny → funnier, funniest*.

other 2-syllable adjectives; long adjectives

adjective	comparative	superlative
spacious	**more** spacious	**most** spacious
amazing	**more** amazing	**most** amazing
patient	**more** patient	**most** patient
expensive	**more** expensive	**most** expensive

- *Good*, *bad* and *far* are irregular: *good → better, best; bad → worse, worst; far → further/farther, furthest/farthest*.

- The opposites of *more* and *most* are **less** and **least**: *It's a bit less expensive than the Redland house. It's the least expensive place we've seen.*

- We use **much**, **far** or **a lot** before a comparative to say there's a **big difference**: *That place was much/far/a lot noisier than the other two.*

- We use **slightly**, **a little** or **a bit** before a comparative to say there's a **small difference**: *It seemed slightly/a little/a bit bigger than where we live now.*

TIPS • We use **the**, **possessive 's** or **a possessive adjective** before a superlative: *It had **the** most amazing view. He's Peter**'s** best friend. That's **their** oldest daughter.* The most common form is '*the* + superlative'.

• When we compare two things we use **than** after the comparative: *The back garden was far smaller than I'd expected.*

• We can also use **more** and **most** with nouns: *It's got more space. It's got the most rooms.*

OTHER WAYS TO MAKE COMPARISONS

- We can use **the same** + (noun) + **as** to say two people or things are the same: *It's the same size as our house.*
- We can also use **as** + adjective + **as** to say two people or things are the same: *It was as small as the one we've got now.*
- We can use **similar to** + noun to say two people or things are nearly the same: *It's very similar to where we live now.*
- We can use **not as** + adjective + **as** to say two people or things are not the same: *It's not as big as the other two places.*
- We can also use **different from** + noun to say two people or things are not the same: *It was different from anything else we've seen.*

TIP • We can say *different from* or *different to*: *It was different from/to anything else we've seen.*

5.2 The future: *will*, *be going to*, Present Continuous   5B 6 p41

- We use **will** when we decide to do something at the time of speaking: *OK, I'll throw those away.*
- We use **be going to** when we already have a plan or an intention to do something: *I'm going to sort out the rest of them at the weekend.*
- We use the **Present Continuous** when we have an arrangement with another person: *He's picking them up tomorrow evening after work.*
- We use **be going to** for a prediction that is based on present evidence (something we can see now): *It's going to break the first time she uses it!*
- We use **will** for a prediction that is a personal opinion and is not based on present evidence: *But you'll never listen to them again.*

TIPS • When we use the Present Continuous for future arrangements, we usually know exactly when the arrangements are happening. They are the kind of arrangements we can write in a diary: *I'm having dinner with Richard on Saturday.*

• For how to make the positive, negative and question forms of the Present Continuous, see GRAMMAR 2.2 p131.

• We can also use *be going to* to talk about future arrangements: *What are you going to do tomorrow?*

will
POSITIVE AND NEGATIVE

- We make the positive and negative forms of *will* with:
subject + **'ll**, **will** or **won't** (= will not) + **infinitive**
I'll give you a ring next week.
He won't talk to anyone about it.

TIP • *Will/won't* is the same for all subjects: *I/you/he/she/it/we/they will/won't do it.*

QUESTIONS

- We make questions with *will* with:
(question word) + **will** + **subject** + **infinitive**
Will you use that old printer again?
What will he decide to throw away?

TIPS • We often use *Do you think …?* to make questions with *will*: *Do you think your sister will like this dress?*

• We often use *probably* or *definitely* with *will*: *He'll probably/definitely call you back tomorrow.*

• We often use *might* to mean 'will possibly': *I might finish it this weekend.*

• We also use *will* to talk about future facts and for offers: *I'll be 45 next birthday. I'll help you clear out the study.*

be going to
POSITIVE AND NEGATIVE

- We make the positive and negative of *be going to* with:
subject + **am**, **are** or **is** + (**not**) + **going to** + **infinitive**
I'm/'m not going to keep this jumper.
You/We/They're/aren't going to use it again.
He/She/It's/isn't going to work any more.

QUESTIONS

- We make questions with *be going to* with:
(question word) + **am**, **are** or **is** + **subject** + **going to** + **infinitive**
When am I going to see you again?
Are you/we/they going to move house?
What's he/she/it going to do tomorrow?

TIP • With the verb *go*, we usually say *I'm going to the cinema.* not *I'm going to go to the cinema.* But both are correct.

REAL WORLD

5.1 Explaining what you need   5D 3 p44

saying you don't know the name of something

I'm sorry, I've forgotten what it's called.
I don't know what it's called in English.
I can't remember what they're called.
I'm sorry, I don't know the word for them.

describing what something is used for

It's a thing for (making soup).
It's stuff for (getting marks off your clothes).
You use it when (you get coffee on your shirt).
You use them to (mend your clothes).

describing what something looks like

It's a type of (liquid).
They're made of (metal).
They've got (a hole in the end).
They look like (headphones).

checking something is the right thing

Is this what you're looking for?
Do you mean (a blender)?
Oh, you mean (stain remover).

- We often use *stuff* to talk about **uncountable** nouns we don't know the name of.
- After *It's a thing for …* and *It's stuff for …* we use **verb+ing**.
- After *You use it/them …* we use **the infinitive with to**.

Language Summary 6

VOCABULARY

6.1 make and do   6A 1 p46

make	do
a decision	the cleaning
a mistake	a course
money	homework
friends	nothing
a noise	exercise
dinner	the washing-up
an excuse	the shopping
someone laugh/cry	some work
up your mind	the washing
progress	a degree
a cake	an exam
an appointment	the housework
a mess of something	someone a favour

make an excuse give a reason to explain why you did something wrong (often used in the plural): *You need to stop making excuses and be more responsible.*
make up your mind make a decision: *I can't make up my mind where to go on holiday.*
make progress get closer to achieving or finishing something: *We haven't finished yet, but we're making good progress.*
make an appointment arrange a time and place to meet someone, particularly a doctor, dentist, etc.: *I've made an appointment to see the doctor.*
make a mess of something (informal) do something badly or make a lot of mistakes: *I made a mess of my exam. I only got 23%.*
do the housework do things like washing, cleaning, etc. in order to keep the house clean and tidy: *I can't stand doing the housework.*
do someone a favour do something to help someone: *Could you do me a favour and help me with my homework?*

do the washing-up   do the washing

TIPS • We often use *make* for 'food' words: *make lunch, make dinner, make a cake*, etc.
• We often use *do* for 'study' words: *do homework, do a degree, do an exam*, etc.
• We usually use *do* for jobs connected to the house: *do the cleaning, do the washing*, etc.
• *do the washing-up* [UK] = *do the dishes* [US]

6.2 Reflexive pronouns   6B 7 p49

• We use reflexive pronouns (*myself, yourself*, etc.) when the subject and object are the same people: *It's important that **they** are allowed to enjoy **themselves**.*
• We use *by myself, by yourself*, etc. to mean *alone*: *This means children spend most of their free time studying **by themselves**.*
• We also use reflexive pronouns to emphasise that we do something instead of someone else doing it for us: *We should also encourage children to work things out **themselves**.*

subject pronouns	reflexive pronouns	subject pronouns	reflexive pronouns
I	myself	it	itself
you (singular)	yourself	we	ourselves
he	himself	you (plural)	yourselves
she	herself	they	themselves

TIPS • Some verbs that are reflexive in other languages aren't reflexive in English, for example *meet, relax* and *feel*.
• We can say *on my own, on your own*, etc. instead of *by myself, by yourself*, etc.: *I enjoy living by myself/on my own.* We don't say ~~by my own~~.
• Notice the difference between *themselves* and *each other*:

Nicky and Alice are looking at themselves.   Nicky and Alice are looking at each other.

6.3 Synonyms   6C 6 p51

• We often use synonyms when we are speaking or writing so that we don't repeat words.

choose	pick	concerned	worried
satisfied	content	frightened	scared
lucky	fortunate	make a decision	make up your mind
behave	act	try to do	have a go at doing
notice	spot	talk to someone	chat to someone
by chance	accidentally	nice	pleasant
attitude	approach	enormous	huge
sure	certain	pleased	glad
deal with	cope with	wonderful	brilliant
show	reveal	terrible	awful

TIP • Many synonyms in English have small differences in meaning or use. For example, *chat to someone* is more informal than *talk to someone*.

GRAMMAR

6.1 First conditional 6A 5 p47

- Look at this first conditional. Notice the different clauses.

if clause (if + Present Simple)	main clause ('ll, will or won't + infinitive)
If I **start** teaching again,	**I'll be** exhausted after a year.

- The first conditional talks about the result of a possible event or situation in the **future**.
- The *if* clause talks about things that are **possible**, but not certain: *If I start teaching again, I'll be exhausted after a year.* (maybe I will start teaching again). The main clause says what we think the result will be in this situation (I'm sure I will be exhausted after a year).
- The *if* clause can be first or second in the sentence: *I'll be exhausted after a year if I start teaching again.*
- We make first conditional **questions** with: (question word) + will + subject + infinitive + if … : *What will you study if you do another degree?*
- We often use *might* in the main clause to mean 'will perhaps': *You might not get in this year if you don't apply soon.*
- We can use **unless** to mean 'if not' in the first conditional: *Unless I do it now, I'll be too old.* = *If I don't do it now, I'll be too old.*

6.2 Future time clauses 6A 6 p47

- We can also use sentences with *before*, *as soon as*, *after*, *until* and *when* to talk about the **future**: *I'll ask them before they go on holiday.*
- In these sentences we use **will/won't + infinitive** in the main clause: *I'll make a decision after I talk to him.*
- We use the **Present Simple** in clauses beginning with *before*, *as soon as*, *after*, *until* and *when*: *I won't say anything to them until you decide what to do.*

TIP • We use *when* to say we are certain that something will happen. Compare these two sentences:
A *I'll tell Jo when I see her.* (I'm certain I will see Jo.)
B *I'll tell Jo if I see her.* (Maybe I will see Jo.)

6.3 Zero conditional; conditionals with modal verbs and imperatives; in case 6B 3 p48

ZERO CONDITIONAL

- Zero conditionals talk about things that are **always true**: *If you have children, you want them to be happy.*
- In zero conditionals both verbs are in the **Present Simple**: *If children study all the time, they don't develop in other ways.*

TIP • *If* and *when* have the same meaning in zero conditionals: *If/When I'm stressed, I don't sleep very well.*

ZERO OR FIRST CONDITIONAL

- Compare these sentences:
A *If my children get good grades, I take them to the beach.*
This sentence is a **zero conditional**. It talks about something that is always true. (I take my children to the beach every time they get good grades at school.)
B *If my children get good grades, I'll take them to the beach.*
This sentence is a **first conditional**. It talks about one specific time in the future. (I'll take my children to the beach if they get good grades in their next exam.)

CONDITIONALS WITH MODAL VERBS AND IMPERATIVES

- We can use modal verbs (*should*, *can*, etc.) in the main clause of conditionals: *If parents want their children to be happy, they **shouldn't** put too much pressure on them. If you criticise children for not getting good grades, they **can** feel like they're failures.*
- We can also use imperatives (*praise*, *don't give*, etc.) in the main clause of conditionals: *If you want to help your children, **praise** the effort they make.*
- In these conditionals we use the Present Simple in the *if* clause: *If you **need** some help, ask me.*

TIP • We can use other modal verbs (*must*, *have to*, *might*, etc.) in conditionals: *If you don't understand, you must ask the teacher.*

IN CASE

- We use *in case* to say that we are prepared for something that might happen: *Students are scared of answering questions **in case** they get them wrong. I'll take an umbrella **in case** it rains.*
- *In case* and *if* have different meanings. Compare these sentences:
MIKE *I'll buy some food in case I get hungry.*
Mike is definitely going to buy some food so that he is prepared if he gets hungry in the future.
JAMES *I'll buy some food if I get hungry.*
James might buy some food, but only if he gets hungry in the future.

REAL WORLD

6.1 Discussion language 6D 4 p52

asking to speak	ways of agreeing
May I make a suggestion? Can I make a point here? Can I just say something here?	Yes, that sounds like a good idea. Well, it's (definitely) worth a try. Yes, that's not a bad idea. Yes, that could work. What a great/brilliant idea!
making suggestions	
How about (having some live music)? We could (hire some professional musicians). What about (charging people five pounds each)? Have you thought of (asking the school to put on a musical)? I suggest we (have some competitions).	**ways of disagreeing** I'm not sure about that. For one thing, … Sorry, I don't think we should do that. I'm not sure that's a good idea.

Language Summary 7

VOCABULARY

7.1 Goals and achievements 7A p54

achieve your goals succeed in doing the things that you want to do in life, especially after a lot of work: *If you work hard, you will achieve your goals.*
put a lot of effort into sth use a lot of physical or mental activity in order to achieve something: *She puts a lot of effort into everything she does.* Also: **make an effort to do sth**
do your best make the greatest effort possible: *It doesn't matter if you don't win, just try to do your best.*
have an opportunity be in a situation that makes it possible for you to do something that you want to do: *Henry was very happy to have the opportunity to work in Hollywood.*
mess sth up (informal) do something wrong or badly: *I really messed up that job interview.*
dream of sth imagine something that you would like to happen: *I've always dreamed of living on a beautiful island.*
encourage /ɪnˈkʌrɪdʒ/ talk or behave in a way that makes somebody else more confident to do something: *My friends encouraged me to write a novel.*
take part in sth be involved in an activity with other people: *All the children took part in the competition.*
make the most of sth get the maximum use, benefit or enjoyment from something, often because it may not last long: *It's a beautiful day – let's make the most of it.*
go wrong change or end in a bad or negative way: *Whatever I try to do, it always goes wrong.*

TIP • We say *have an/the opportunity to do something* not ~~have a/the possibility to do something.~~

7.2 Computers (1) 7B p56

a password a secret combination of letters or numbers which you use when you log onto a computer website.
install software (onto a computer) put a computer program onto a computer so that the computer can use it.
back sth up copy documents, files, etc. from a computer onto a memory stick, another computer, online, etc.
store put or keep things in a particular place so you can read or use them in the future.
a hard drive part of a computer that stores information.
a memory stick a small piece of equipment that you use for storing information or photos. Also **a USB drive** or **a USB stick**
spam unwanted emails, usually advertisements.
an attachment a document, picture, etc. sent with an email.
a virus /ˈvaɪrəs/ a computer program which can make copies of itself and stops a computer from working normally.
crash when a computer or a website suddenly stops working.
copy sb in (on an email) send somebody a copy of an email that you are sending to somebody else.
forward sth to sb send an email you have received to somebody else's computer.
delete remove a document, email, etc. from a computer.
print (out) produce a copy of a document, etc. on paper.
scan use a machine to put a document, etc. into a computer.
WiFi a wireless way of connecting computers to the internet in a public place (a café, a train, etc.).

7.3 Computers (2) 7C p58

A social networking site is a website such as Facebook, Google+, etc. that is designed to help people communicate and share information, photos, etc. with a group.
When you **update your status**, you add a new comment to your page on a social networking site. Also: **update your (Facebook) page** and **a status update**
A profile is the personal information (interests, married, etc.) you add to your page on a social networking site.
When you **upload** something, you copy or move photos, documents, etc. to a website. (opposite: **download**)
A forum is a website or part of a website where people can discuss particular topics. Also: **a message board**
When you **post a comment** on a website, forum, etc. you write something for other people to read.
When you **tweet**, you write a message on Twitter for other people to read. Also: **a tweet** (noun)
When you **follow** somebody **on** Twitter, you are automatically sent messages from this person when they tweet.
A link is a connection between two pages on the internet.

7.4 Use of articles: *a, an, the,* no article 7C p59

• We use *a* or *an*:
  a when we don't know, or it isn't important, which one: *Many of them can't go* **a day** *without checking for status updates.*
  b with jobs: *If you're* **a designer** *working in Dublin …*
  c to talk about a person or thing for the first time: *… you have* **a new person** *to add to your collection of friends.*

• We use *the*:
  d to talk about the same person or thing for the second/third/fourth, etc. time: *But do you really want to be friends with* **the person***?*
  e when there is only one (or only one in a particular place): *Social networking sites are one of the most amazing success stories of* **the internet***.*
  f with countries that are groups of islands or states: *According to a children's charity in* **the UK** *…*
  g with superlatives: **The largest** *number of active social relationships is 150.*

• We don't use an article:
  h for most towns, cities, countries and continents: *… or an engineer who's moving to* **Egypt** *…*
  i to talk about people or things in general: *But what effect is this having on* **society***?*
  j for some public places (school, hospital, university, college, prison, etc.) when we talk about what they are used for in general: *You don't have to be at* **school** *or university to use social networking sites.*

TIP • We use *the* with public places when we talk about the building: *She works in the school opposite the park. He's gone to the hospital to visit his father.*

GRAMMAR

7.1 Ability   7A 4 p55

- These phrases talk about things you **can** or **could** do:
  be quite/very/really good at (doing sth): *She's very good at encouraging people.*
  be able to (do sth): *I was able to give a good performance.*
  know how (to do sth): *He knows how to do some really amazing tricks.*
  find sth quite/very/really easy (to do): *I found some of the tricks quite easy to learn.*
  manage to (do sth): *I managed to do all the tricks without messing them up.*

- These phrases talk about things you **can't** or **couldn't** do:
  not have a clue how (to do sth): *I didn't have a clue how to sing opera.*
  find sth impossible (to do): *I found it impossible to breathe and sing at the same time.*
  be useless at (doing sth): *I was useless at learning languages at school.*
  have no idea how (to do sth): *I had no idea how to do any magic tricks.*
  be no good at (doing sth): *I'm no good at doing card tricks.*
  not be able to (do sth): *I was disappointed that I wasn't able to win.*

TIPS • We use *manage to do sth* to talk about something you do successfully, but is difficult.

- We can also say *be **brilliant/great/excellent/not bad** at doing sth* and *be **hopeless/bad/terrible/awful/rubbish** at doing sth.*

- We can also say *find something **difficult/hard** to do.*

+ infinitive (do)	+ infinitive with *to* (to do)	+ verb+*ing* (doing)
(not) be able to can could	not have a clue how find something impossible/ quite easy have no idea how know how manage	be quite/very/ really good at be useless at be no good at

TIP • We can also use a noun or a pronoun after *be good at, be useless at,* etc.: *Tim's hopeless at tennis, but Ian's brilliant at it.*

7.2 Second conditional   7B 3 p56

- We use the second conditional to talk about **imaginary** situations: *If I lost my laptop, I'd probably lose my job!* (I don't think this will ever happen to me.)
- The second conditional talks about **the present or future**.
- We often use the second conditional to talk about the opposite of what is true or real: *If we didn't have WiFi, this place would be empty.* (But we have WiFi, so this is an imaginary situation.)

POSITIVE AND NEGATIVE

if clause (*if* + Past Simple)	main clause (*'d, would* or *wouldn't* + infinitive)
If I **lost** my laptop, If the internet **didn't exist**,	I'**d** probably **lose** my job! I **wouldn't have** a business.

- Compare these sentences:
  A *If I **have** enough money, I'**ll buy** a new laptop.*
  This is a real possibility (the person <u>might</u> buy a new laptop).
  B *If I **had** enough money, I'**d buy** a new laptop.*
  This is an imaginary situation (the person <u>can't</u> buy a new laptop).

TIPS • The *if* clause can be first or second in the sentence: *We'd lose a lot of customers if our website crashed. If our website crashed, we'd lose a lot of customers.*

- We can say *If I/he/she/it **was** …* or *If I/he/she/it **were** …* in the second conditional: *If I was/were rich, I'd buy a big house.*
- We can use **might** + infinitive in the main clause of the second conditional to mean 'would perhaps': *If they turned off their computers, they might make some new friends.*
- We can use **could** + infinitive in the main clause of the second conditional to mean 'would be able to': *If we didn't have online meetings, I could travel a bit more.*

QUESTIONS

- We often make questions in the second conditional with *What would you do if … ?*: *What would you do if you lost your laptop?*
- We can also make *yes/no* questions in the second conditional: *If someone asked you to lend them your computer, would you do it?*
- The short answers to these *yes/no* questions are: *Yes, I would./No, I wouldn't.* We can also say *(Yes,) I might.*

REAL WORLD

7.1 Indirect and direct questions   7D 3 p60

- In more formal situations we often use indirect questions because they sound more polite: *Could you tell me what time it starts?* sounds more polite than *What time does it start?*

indirect question phrase	question word or *if/whether*	main clause (positive verb form)
Could you tell me	what time	it starts?
Have you any idea	if	he's been invited?
Can you tell me	when	they're arriving?
Do you know	whether	we've booked them a hotel room?

- We use *if* or *whether* in indirect questions when there isn't a question word. *If* and *whether* are the same: *Have you any idea if/whether we asked him to come?*
- We don't use *if* or *whether* with **Do you think …?**: *Do you think we should email everyone again?* not *Do you think if/whether we should email everyone again?*
- In indirect questions, the main verb is in the positive form. We say: *Can you tell me when they're arriving?* not *Can you tell me when are they arriving?*

Language Summary 8

VOCABULARY

8.1 Bad weather and natural disasters
8A p62

a storm very bad weather with lots of rain, snow, wind, etc.: *There was a terrible storm last night*.
thunder the loud noise that comes from the sky during a storm: *Last night I was woken up by the thunder*. Also: **a thunderstorm**
lightning a bright light in the sky caused by electricity during a storm, usually followed by thunder: *A man was hit by lightning last night*.
a gale a very strong wind: *There will be gales in the south tonight*.
a hurricane (= **a typhoon** /taɪˈfuːn/ or **a cyclone**) a violent storm with extremely strong winds: *Dozens of houses were destroyed by last night's hurricane*.
a tornado (US: **a twister**) an extremely strong and dangerous wind that blows in a circle and destroys buildings: *There are often tornados in the Caribbean in the summer*.
a heat wave a period of unusually hot weather that continues for a long time: *The heat wave in Texas has been going on for over a month*.
a blizzard a very bad snow storm with strong winds: *We got stuck in a blizzard for six hours*.
a flood /flʌd/ when a lot of water covers an area that is usually dry, especially when it rains a lot or a river becomes too full: *There have been floods in many parts of India*.
an earthquake /ˈɜːθkweɪk/ a sudden violent movement of the Earth's surface, often causing a lot of damage: *In 1906 parts of San Francisco were destroyed by a huge earthquake*.
a tsunami an extremely large wave that can cause a lot of damage when it hits the coast: *The tsunami in Asia was one of the most powerful ever recorded*.
a drought /draʊt/ a long period of time with no rain and not enough water for plants and animals: *The drought in north Africa has continued for over six months*.
a landslide when a large quantity of rocks and earth falls down the side of a mountain: *The landslide closed the road through the mountains for over a month*.

TIPS • The adjective for *storm* is *stormy*: *It was a very stormy night*.
• We say *thunder and lightning* not ~~lightning and thunder~~.
• *Flood* is a noun and a verb: *The whole village was flooded*.

8.2 Containers **8B** p64

a bottle   a bag   a tin   a box

a can   a carton   a jar   a packet

COMMON COLLOCATIONS
a bottle of milk, beer, ketchup, olive oil, lemonade
a bag of sweets, potatoes, crisps [US: chips]
a tin of tuna, biscuits, cat food, soup, beans
a box of chocolates, tissues
a can of beer, lemonade
a carton of milk, orange juice, soup
a jar of honey, jam, marmalade
a packet of biscuits, sweets, soup, beans, tissues, crisps

TIPS • We usually use *a tin* for food (*a tin of tomatoes*) and *a can* for drink (*a can of cola*).
• *Marmalade* is made from citrus fruit (oranges, etc.). *Jam* is made from soft fruit (strawberries, etc.).

8.3 Word building (2): prefixes and opposites **8C** p67

• We often use the prefixes *un-*, *dis-*, *im-*, *in-* and *ir-* to make opposites of words.

prefix	examples
un-	unconscious unusual uncommon unbelievable unselfish unreliable unambitious unhelpful
dis-	disappear dishonest disorganised disloyal dissimilar
im-	impossible impatient impolite immature
in-	incorrect inconsiderate informal insensitive
ir-	irresponsible irregular

TIPS • We can use these prefixes to make opposites of adjectives and verbs: *unconscious*, *dishonest* (adjectives); *undo*, *disappear* (verbs).
• Adjectives beginning with *p* usually take the prefix *im-*: *patient* → *impatient*.
• Adjectives beginning with *r* usually take the prefix *ir-*: *responsible* → *irresponsible*.

8.4 Word building (2): other prefixes and suffixes **8C** p67

• We often use other prefixes and suffixes to change the meaning of words.

prefix/suffix	meaning	examples
under-	not enough	underestimate underpaid undercharge underuse
re-	do something again	reattach repaid rewrite recharge remarry replay reuse
over-	too much	over-optimistic overpaid oversleep overcharge overuse
-ful	with	hopeful painful careful successful playful useful
-less	without	harmless painless sleepless careless useless

145

GRAMMAR

8.1 The passive 8A 4 p63

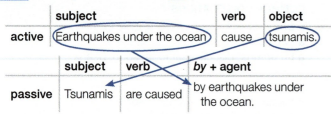

	subject	verb	object
active	Earthquakes under the ocean	cause	tsunamis.

	subject	verb	by + agent
passive	Tsunamis	are caused	by earthquakes under the ocean.

- In **active** sentences the focus is on the person or thing doing the action (earthquakes under the ocean). In **passive** sentences the focus is on the result of the action (tsunamis).
- In passive sentences we can use '**by** + the agent' to say what or who does the action.
- We often use the passive when we are more interested in what happens to someone or something than in who or what did the action: *Droughts often happen because all the trees have been cut down.*
- We make the passive with: **subject** + **be** + **past participle**

verb form	be	past participle
Present Simple	am/are/is	caused
Present Continuous	am/are/is being	caused
Present Perfect Simple	have/has been	cut down
Past Simple	was/were	killed
be going to	am/are/is going to be	hit
will	will be	flooded
can	can be	caused

- We make negative passive sentences by using the negative form of *be*: *it **isn't** caused, they **haven't been** cut down*, etc.

TIP • We can use other modal verbs (*could, must, should*, etc.) in passive verb forms: *Many people could be made homeless.*

8.2 Quantifiers 8B 6 p65

quantity	plural countable nouns (*bottles, tins*, etc.)	uncountable nouns (*rubbish, stuff*, etc.)
nothing	not any no	not any no
a small quantity	not many hardly any several a few	not much a bit of hardly any a little
a large quantity	a lot of/lots of loads of plenty of	a lot of/lots of loads of plenty of
more than we want	too many	too much
less than we want	not enough	not enough
the correct quantity	enough	enough

- *Not many, hardly any* and *not much* have a negative meaning. *Several, a few, a bit of* and *a little* have a positive meaning. *Several* is usually more than *a few*.

SOME, ANY, MUCH, MANY

- We usually use *some* in positive sentences: *I've found some coffee.*
- We usually use *any* in negative sentences and questions: *There isn't any sugar. Is there any milk?*
- We don't usually use *much* or *many* in positive sentences: *There's a lot of stuff here.* not *There's much stuff here.*
 I've got lots of old books. not *I've got many old books.*

TIPS • We use *some* and *any* with plural countable nouns (*biscuits, beans*, etc.) and uncountable nouns (*pasta, milk*, etc.).

• We often use *some* in questions with *Would you like …?*: *Would you like some coffee?*

REAL WORLD

8.1 Warnings and advice 8D 3 p68

- We give warnings when we think something might be dangerous.

asking for advice

Could you give me some advice?
What (else) do you think we should take with us?
What should we do if we get lost?
Do you think it's a good idea to tell someone where we're going?

giving advice

If I were you, I'd buy a new tent.
Make sure you take plenty of warm clothes.
It's a good idea to take some waterproof clothing **in case** it rains.
Don't forget to take a map.
It's worth taking a compass, **just in case**.
You'd better take a torch in case you have to walk in the dark.

giving warnings

Don't wear new boots **or else** you'll get blisters.
Whatever you do, don't lose sight of each other.
Be careful when you're crossing rivers.
Watch out for wolves.

responding to advice or warnings

That's really useful, thanks.
That's a good idea. I hadn't thought of that.
Right, thanks. That's really helpful.
That sounds like good advice.

- After *If I were you, I'd …* and *You'd better …* (= you had better) we use **the infinitive**: *If I were you, I'd buy a new tent. You'd better take a torch.*
- After *It's a good idea …* and *Don't forget …* we use the **infinitive with *to***: *It's a good idea to take some waterproof clothing. Don't forget to take a map.*
- After *It's worth …* , we use **verb+*ing***: *It's worth taking a compass.*
- After *Whatever you do, …* we use **the imperative** (usually the negative imperative): *Whatever you do, don't lose sight of each other.*

Language Summary 9

VOCABULARY

9.1 Health   9A 6 7 p71

A **surgeon** /ˈsɜːdʒən/ is a doctor who does operations.
An **operating theatre** is the place where you have an operation.
Asthma /ˈæsmə/ is an illness which makes it difficult for you to breathe.
A **specialist** is a doctor who knows a lot about one area of medicine.
The **A&E department** is the part of a hospital where you go if you have an emergency. (**A&E** = Accident and Emergency)
An **allergy** /ˈælədʒi/ is a medical problem that some people get when they eat, breathe or touch certain things.
A **migraine** is an extremely painful headache *that/which* can also make you feel sick.
A **ward** is a big room with beds in a hospital *where* patients receive medical treatment.
A **surgery** /ˈsɜːdʒəri/ is a building or an office *where* you can go and ask a GP or a dentist for medical advice.
A **GP** is a doctor *who/that* gives medical treatment to people *who/that* live in a particular area. (**GP** = general practitioner)
A **prescription** is a piece of paper *that/which* the doctor gives you so that you can get the medicine you need.
An **infection** is a disease in part of your body *that/which* is caused by bacteria or a virus.

TIP • We can also say that we are *allergic* /əˈlɜːdʒɪk/ *to* something: *My sister is allergic to nuts.*

9.2 Collocations (3): the news   9B 2 p72

pay off a debt
take part in a demonstration
protest against something
take somebody **to hospital**
publish a report
meet a target
discover something new
accept/reject an offer
go on strike
call off a strike

a debt /det/ money which is owed to somebody else: *The company has huge debts.* Also: **be in debt**
pay off pay back money you owe to a bank, a person, etc.: *A lot of countries are finding it hard to pay off their debts.*
a demonstration when a group of people stand or walk somewhere to show that they disagree with or support something: *30,000 people took part in the demonstration.*
protest say or show that you disagree with something: *A large crowd were protesting against the war.*
a target something you want to achieve: *The company has already met its sales target for the year.*
discover find information, a place or an object for the first time: *Scientists have discovered a new way to predict earthquakes.*
reject not accept: *The workers rejected the pay offer.*
a strike a period of time when people don't go to work because they want more money, better working conditions, etc.: *The postal workers' strike is now in its fifth day.*
call sth off cancel something that was planned: *The match was called off because of bad weather.*

TIP • People who take part in a demonstration are called *demonstrators*. People who protest against something are called *protesters*.

9.3 Body movements and responses   9C 1 p74

cry   laugh   smile   yawn

wave   shiver   blush   stretch

scratch   crawl   frown   sweat

TIP • If you have *an itch*, you want to scratch it.

9.4 Connecting words   9C 4 p75

- *Although* /ɔːlˈðəʊ/, *even though* /ˌiːvənˈðəʊ/, *despite*, *in spite of* and *however* are similar in meaning to *but*.

- We use *although*, *even though*, *despite* and *in spite of* to contrast **two clauses in the same sentence**: *Although/Even though we don't enjoy crying, it's actually good for us. Despite/In spite of appearing rude, they could be yawning so they can listen more closely to what you're saying.*

- We use *however* to contrast **two sentences**. We put a comma (,) after *however*: *Scientists have shown that people are more likely to forgive you if you blush. However, people might not forgive you so easily if you don't blush at all!*

- After *despite* and *in spite of* we usually use **a noun** or **verb+ing**: *In spite of* this knowledge*, …; Despite* appearing rude*, …*

- After *although* and *even though* we usually use **a clause**: *Although/Even though* we don't enjoy crying*, …*

TIPS • *Even though* is usually stronger than *although*.

• We can put *although*, *even though*, *despite* and *in spite of* at the beginning or in the middle of a sentence. We usually put *however* at the beginning of a sentence.

• In spoken English, we often use *though* /ðəʊ/ instead of *although* or *even though*. We usually put *though* at the end of a sentence: **A** *I enjoyed the film.* **B** *Me too. I didn't like the ending, though.*

9.5 Health problems, symptoms and treatment 9D p76

health problems	asthma an allergy hay fever flu a migraine an infection a virus food poisoning a cold
symptoms	a runny nose a blocked-up nose wheezy sneeze be sick throw up a sore throat /θrəʊt/ a temperature /ˈtemprətʃə/ a cough /kɒf/ a rash diarrhoea a stomach ache /ˈstʌməkeɪk/
treatment	antibiotics penicillin painkillers paracetamol cough medicine

hay fever an illness with symptoms similar to a cold that is caused by flowers or grass in the spring and summer.
a virus /ˈvaɪrəs/ a very small living thing which can cause illnesses, disease and infections.
food poisoning when you eat some food that is bad and makes you ill.
a runny nose when your nose produces liquid all the time, usually when you have a cold.
a blocked-up nose when you can't breathe through your nose.
wheezy when you breathe noisily and with difficulty, particularly when you have asthma or an allergy.
sneeze when you blow air down through your nose suddenly, for example when you have a cold.
throw up (informal) be sick, vomit.
diarrhoea /daɪəˈrɪə/ when you have to go to the toilet all the time.
a rash a group of small red spots on the skin, often caused by allergies, that you want to scratch.
penicillin /penəˈsɪlən/ a type of antibiotic.
paracetamol /pærəˈsiːtəmɒl/ a type of painkiller.

TIPS • We can say *I've got **a** stomach ache.* or *I've got stomach ache*. We can also say *I've got **a** toothache*. or *I've got toothache*. and *I've got **a** headache*. but not *I've got headache*.

• We can use *be sick* to mean 'be ill' or 'vomit/throw up'. In American English, *be sick* is more common than *be ill*: *Sorry, I can't come to work today. I'm ill.* (UK) *I'm sick.* (US)

• *Sneeze* is a noun and a verb. When a person sneezes, we often say *Bless you!*

hay fever

a sore throat

a temperature

a stomach ache

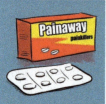
painkillers

cough medicine

GRAMMAR

9.1 Relative clauses with *who*, *that*, *which*, *whose*, *where* and *when* 9A 4 p71

• We often use relative clauses to say which person, thing, place, etc. we are talking about.
• In relative clauses we use:
  a **who** or **that** for people: *The woman **who** I was sharing a room with … . I'm the type of person **that** eats three meals a day.*
  b **that** or **which** for things: *The food **that** we usually eat contains toxins **which** stay in our bodies.*
  c **where** for places: *I was taken to the guest house **where** everyone was staying.*
  d **whose** for possessives: *The woman **whose** fasting programme we were following … .*
  e **when** for times: *This was also **when** I started getting really hungry.*

TIPS • We usually use *who* for people (*that* is also correct).
• We usually use *that* for things (*which* is also correct).
• We don't use *what* in relative clauses: ~~The food **what** we usually eat~~ … . We can use *what* to mean 'the thing/things that': *Now I'm much more careful about **what** I eat.* (= the things that I eat)

LEAVING OUT WHO, THAT, WHICH

• We can leave out *who*, *that* or *which* when it isn't the subject of the relative clause.
• Compare the relative clauses in these sentences:
  A *I'm the type of person that eats three meals a day.*
  In this sentence we must use *that* because it is the subject of the relative clause.
  B *The food (that) we usually eat contains toxins.*
  In this sentence we can leave out *that* because it is the object of the relative clause (*we* is the subject).

TIPS • We never leave out *whose* in relative clauses.
• We can usually leave out *where* if we add a preposition at the end of the relative clause: *That's the café **where** I met my wife.* → *That's the café I met my wife **in**.*
• We can only leave out *when* if the time reference is clear: *Monday's the day (when) I play tennis.*

That's the man **who** stole my phone!

That's the house **where** I was born.

9.2 Present Perfect Simple active and passive for recent events   9B 4 p73

- We use the Present Perfect Simple for giving news about something that happened a short time ago, but we don't say exactly when.
*World leaders **have met** to discuss the global economy.
A new report on the environment **has** just **been published**.*

- We make the **Present Perfect Simple active** with:
I/you/we/they + 've, have or haven't + past participle
he/she/it + 's, has or hasn't + past participle

  The UK has failed to meet its targets.
  We haven't met our targets yet.

- We make the **Present Perfect Simple passive** with:
I/you/we/they + 've, have or haven't + been + past participle
he/she/it + 's, has or hasn't + been + past participle

  At least forty people have been arrested.
  Some of the items still haven't been examined.

- We often use passive verb forms in radio and TV news reports and newspaper articles.

- When we say the exact time something happened, we must use the Past Simple active or passive: *Gareth Jones found the treasure five days ago.*

JUST, YET, ALREADY, STILL

- We use *just* to say something happened a short time ago. We put *just* after the auxiliary: *The ministers have just had a meeting. A new report has just been published.*

- We use *yet* to say something hasn't happened, but we think it will happen in the future. We put *yet* at the end of the sentence or clause: *We haven't met our targets yet. Why haven't we heard anything from the government yet?*

- We use *already* to say something happened some time in the past, maybe sooner than we expected. We put *already* after the auxiliary: *Experts have already examined most of the items. CO_2 has already been reduced by 2.7%.*

- We use *still* to say something started in the past and continues in the present. We put *still* before the auxiliary: *Some of the items still haven't been examined.*

TIPS • We don't use *just* or *already* in negative sentences: *I've just seen him.* not *I haven't just seen him.*; *The meeting has already finished.* not *The meeting hasn't already finished.*

• We don't use *yet* in positive sentences: *She hasn't told him yet. Has she told him yet?* but not *She's told him yet.*

• We only use *still* in negative sentences with the Present Perfect Simple: *Some of the items still haven't been examined.* not *Some of the items still have been examined.*

REAL WORLD

9.1 What doctors say   9D 2 p76

Now, what seems to be the problem?
How long have you been feeling like this?
Do you know if you're allergic to anything?
What have you eaten recently?
Come back if you're not feeling better in two days.
Have you been taking anything for them?
Have you got any other symptoms?
Right, let me have a look at you.
I'm just going to take your temperature.
Here's a prescription for some painkillers.

9.2 What patients say   9D 5 p76

I'm not feeling very well.
I haven't been feeling very well recently.
I've got a terrible stomach ache.
My chest hurts.
I keep getting really bad headaches.
I can't stop sneezing.
I'm allergic to penicillin.
Do I need some antibiotics?
How often should I take them?
Do I need to make another appointment?

- We use *I keep …* and *I can't stop …* for things that happen lots of times. We don't want these things to happen.

- After *I keep …* and *I can't stop …* we use **verb+ing**: *I keep **waking up** at night. I can't stop **sneezing**.*

TIPS • We can use *-ache* to talk about a pain in your head, tooth, stomach, back or ear (*headache, toothache, stomach ache, backache, earache*): *I've got a terrible headache.*

• For other parts of the body, we use *My … hurts*: *My knee hurts.* not *I've got kneeache.*

• We can also say *I've got a pain in my …* : *I've got a pain in my knee.*

Language Summary 10

VOCABULARY

10.1 Contacting people   10A p78

get hold of sb contact somebody, often with difficulty: *Did you manage to get hold of Mrs Edwards?*
let sb know sth tell somebody some information: *Let me know when you get there.*
be in touch /tʌtʃ/ **with sb** communicate regularly with somebody by phone, email, letter, etc.: *Are you still in touch with any of your old school friends?*
lose touch with sb not be in touch with somebody any more, usually because they have moved house, changed job, etc.: *I lost touch with Tim after he moved to Australia.*
keep in touch with sb or **stay in touch with sb** not lose touch with somebody: *I hope we keep in touch while you're in the USA.*
get in touch with sb contact somebody by writing, emailing or phoning them: *I'm trying to get in touch with somebody from the office.*

TIPS • We can say *be/keep/lose/get in* **touch** *with somebody* or *be/keep/lose/get in* **contact** *with somebody*: *I'm still in touch/contact with my old boss.*

• We can also say *get* **back** *in touch with somebody*, which means 'communicate with somebody again after a long time'.

10.2 Describing people   10B p80

APPEARANCE

 dyed hair
 shoulder-length hair
 straight hair
 curly hair
 wavy hair

 her hair up
 a ponytail
 going bald /bɔːld/
 a dark blue jacket
 a light blue jacket

 a striped tie
 a flowery dress
 a plain shirt
 glasses
 jewellery /dʒuːəlriː/

AGE

• We often use *in his/her teens/early twenties/mid-thirties/late forties*, etc. to talk about someone's approximate age.

TIP • We use *The person/man/woman/one* **with** … + (red) hair, glasses, a beard, etc., but *The person/man/woman/one* **in** … + clothes: *She's the woman* **with** *long wavy hair and glasses. He's the one* **in** *a blue suit.*

10.3 Phrasal verbs (3): meanings
10C p82

get out of sth avoid doing something you don't want to do: *I tried to get out of the whole thing.*
get over sth feel better after you have been unhappy or ill: *Olivia got over her last three divorces quite quickly.*
go up increase or rise: *The number of divorces in the UK is still going up.*
look sth up find some information in a book or on a computer: *I looked some figures up.*
point sth out tell someone some information you think that they don't know or have forgotten: *I didn't like to point this out to her.*
put sth off decide or arrange to do something at a later time: *She should put the wedding off.*
fall out (with sb) argue with somebody and stop being friendly with them: *You two have never fallen out.*
come up with sth think of an idea or a solution to a problem: *I couldn't come up with a good enough excuse.*
split up (with sb) end a marriage or relationship: *I wondered how long it would be before Olivia and Tony split up.*
come across sth find something by accident: *I came across a newspaper report.*

10.4 Phrasal verbs (3): grammar
10C p83

• Phrasal verbs have two or three words: *wake up, look after, get on with*, etc. Look at the differences between the four types of phrasal verbs.

TYPE 1 phrasal verbs don't have an object (*fall out, split up, go up*, etc.):
You two have never fallen out.

TYPE 2 phrasal verbs always have an object (*get over sth, come across sth*, etc.). The object is always **after** the phrasal verb:
Olivia got over her divorces quickly.
Olivia got over them quickly.

TYPE 3 phrasal verbs always have an object (*look sth up, put sth off, point sth out*, etc.). If the object is a noun, you can put it **in the middle** or **after** the phrasal verb:
I looked some figures up.
I looked up some figures.

If the object is a pronoun, you must put it **in the middle** of the phrasal verb:
I looked them up. not *I looked up them.*

TYPE 4 phrasal verbs have three words and always have an object (*get out of sth, come up with sth*, etc.). The object is always **after** the phrasal verb:
I tried to get out of the whole thing.
I tried to get out of it.

TIP • We can sometimes add a preposition to some type 1 phrasal verbs to make them type 4 phrasal verbs: *I've never fallen out* **with** *my brother. Georgina has just split up* **with** *her boyfriend.*

GRAMMAR

10.1 was/were going to, was/were supposed to   10A 5 p79

- We use *was/were going to* to talk about plans we made in the past which didn't happen, or won't happen in the future. Look at these sentences.
  We **were going to visit** the Bradleys later that year, but we didn't go for some reason.
  (They planned to visit the Bradleys, but they didn't.)
  We **were going to spend** our anniversary in the cottage in Wales where we had our honeymoon, but it was already booked.
  (They planned to spend their anniversary in the cottage in Wales, but now they aren't going to go there.)

- We use *was/were supposed to* to talk about things we agreed to do, or other people expected us to do, but we didn't do. Look at these sentences.
  Tom **was supposed to book** the cottage months ago, but he forgot.
  (Tom agreed to book the cottage, but he didn't book it.)
  I **was supposed to call** you back, wasn't I? Sorry, Leo, I was out all day.
  (Leo expected his mother to call him back, but she didn't.)

- After *was/were going to* and *was/were supposed to* we use **the infinitive**: It was going to **be** a surprise party. I was supposed to **call** you back.

TIP • We often use *was/were going to* or *was/were supposed to* to apologise for not doing something. We usually give a reason: *Sorry, I was going to call you back last night, but I didn't get home until late.*

10.2 Modal verbs (2): making deductions   10B 3 p81

- We often use the modal verbs *must*, *might*, *could*, *may* and *can't* to make deductions in the present.

- We use *must* to talk about something that we believe is true: *He must be talking to some guests in the other room. He must know that speech by now.*

- We use *could*, *may* or *might* to talk about something that we think is possibly true: *He might be in the bathroom. He may want to be on his own for a bit. He could be picking people up from the station. It could be the guy that moved to New York.*

- We use *can't* to talk about something that we believe isn't true: *That can't be her real hair colour. He can't be having a cigarette.*

- When we know something is definitely true, or is definitely not true, we don't use a modal verb: *He's practising his speech in front of the mirror. No, that isn't Derek Bradley.*

- To make deductions about **states** we use:
  modal verb + infinitive
  He must know that speech by now.

- To make deductions about **something happening now** we use: modal verb + be + verb+ing
  He must be talking to some guests in the other room.

TIP • We don't use *can* or *mustn't* to make deductions: *It could be him.* not *It can be him.* *He can't be a millionaire.* not *He mustn't be a millionaire.*

REAL WORLD

10.1 Asking for, giving and refusing permission   10D 3 p84

ASKING FOR PERMISSION

Can I (make myself some breakfast)?
May I (use your washing machine)?
Do you mind if I (borrow a jumper)?
Is it OK if I (use your laptop to upload some photos)?
Would you mind if I (borrowed your car some time this week)?
Do you think I could (use your landline to call my parents)?

- After *Can I …?*, *May I …?* and *Do you think I could …?* we use the **infinitive**: *May I use your phone?*

- After *Do you mind if I …?* and *Is it OK if I …?* we use the **Present Simple**: *Do you mind if I watch TV? Is it OK if I borrow your bike?*

- After *Would you mind if I …?* we use the **Past Simple**: *Would you mind if I used your motorbike this weekend?*

GIVING PERMISSION

- We usually give permission by saying: *Yes, of course.*; *Sure, go ahead.*; *Help yourself.*, etc.

- *Do you mind if I …?* and *Would you mind if I …?* mean 'Is it a problem if I do this?'. To give permission for these phrases, we usually say: *No, not at all.* (= It's not a problem for me if you do this.) Compare these conversations.

1 A *Can I make myself a sandwich?*
   B *Yes, of course.*
2 A *Do you mind if I make myself a sandwich?*
   B *No, not at all.*

REFUSING PERMISSION

- We don't usually say *no* to refuse permission because it isn't polite.

- To refuse permission politely, we often say *Sorry, …* or *Actually, …* then we give a reason: *Actually, I was just going to put some washing in. Sorry, it's only insured for Rebecca and myself.*

TIPS • We can also ask permission for other people to do things: *Can John stay for dinner? Is it OK if Luis uses your computer?*

• *Would you mind if I …?* is a very polite way to ask for permission. We often use this phrase if we don't know the other person very well or if we have a big favour to ask: *Would you mind if I stayed for a few days?*

• We can also use *Could I …?* or *Is it all right if I …?* to ask for permission: *Could I borrow your pen? Is it all right if I sit here?*

Language Summary 11

VOCABULARY

11.1 Things people do at work 11A p86

have a lot of responsibility
work unsocial hours
sort out people's problems
organise conferences
do overtime
go for an audition
run a department
be responsible for the finances
deal with customers/clients
arrange meetings
work shifts
be in charge of a company

> **unsocial hours** the times of the day or week when most people don't have to work, for example at night, at the weekend, etc.: *I'm fed up with working unsocial hours.*
> **overtime** the time you work after the usual time needed or expected in a job: *We get paid more for working overtime.*
> **an audition** /ɔːˈdɪʃən/ when someone does a short performance to try and get a job as an actor, singer, etc.: *Hugo's just gone for an audition for a part in a TV drama.*
> **run a department** organise or manage a part of a business, company, school, etc.: *She's been running the advertising department for two years.*
> **finances** /ˈfaɪnænsəz/ the money that a company or person has: *This department is responsible for the company's finances.*
> **a shift** a period of work in a hospital, factory, etc.: *Ambulance drivers usually have to work shifts.*
> **be in charge of sth** be responsible for a group of people, or an activity: *He's in charge of 15 people in his department.*

TIP • You can *do overtime* or *work overtime*.

11.2 Adjectives (3): jobs 11B p88

A **demanding** job needs a lot of time and energy.
In a **well-paid** job you earn a lot of money.
In a **badly-paid** job you don't earn very much money.
You have a **temporary** job for just a short time.
You have a **permanent** job for a long time.
If you have a **full-time** job, you work every day in the working week (usually Monday to Friday).
If you have a **part-time** job, you only work part of the week.
If you have a **stressful** job, you worry about it a lot.
A **challenging** job is very difficult, but in an enjoyable way.
A **rewarding** job makes you feel satisfied when you do it well.
In a **repetitive** job you do the same things again and again.
If you have a **lonely** job, you work on your own and don't see or talk to many people.
A **glamorous** job is very exciting and attractive because it is connected with fame or success.
A **dull** job is very boring.

TIP • We can also say *I work full-time.* and *I work part-time.*

a stressful job

a repetitive job

11.3 Reporting verbs 11C p90

invite ask somebody to go to an event (a meal, a concert, etc.): *"Would you like to have dinner with us tonight?"* → *He invited her to have dinner with them.*
offer ask someone if they would like you to do something for them: *"Can I give you a lift home?"* → *He offered to give her a lift home.*
admit agree that something is true, especially when you don't want to: *"It's true. I'm madly in love with you."* → *He admitted being madly in love with her.*
refuse say you won't do or accept something: *"I won't drive you home."* → *He refused to drive her home.*
promise tell somebody you will certainly do something: *"I'll go on a date with you."* → *She promised to go on a date with him.*
agree accept a suggestion or idea: *"OK, I'll have dinner with you."* → *She agreed to have dinner with him.*
suggest say a possible plan, action or idea for other people to think about: *"Let's meet at the gallery at seven."* → *He suggested meeting at the gallery at seven.*
remind make somebody think of something they have forgotten: *"Don't forget to bring the money."* → *He reminded him to bring the money.*
warn tell somebody about a possible problem or danger, often in the future: *"Don't tell anyone about our plan."* → *He warned him not to tell anyone about their plan.*
threaten tell somebody you will hurt, kill or cause problems for them if they don't do what you want. *"I'll kill you if anything goes wrong."* → *He threatened to kill him if anything went wrong.*

11.4 Verb patterns (2): reporting verbs 11C p90

• We often use verbs like *offer*, *invite*, etc. to report what people say. These verbs are followed by different verb patterns.

invite remind warn	+ object + (*not*) + infinitive with *to* (sb/sth (not) to do)
offer refuse promise agree threaten	+ (*not*) + infinitive with *to* ((not) to do)
admit suggest	+ verb+*ing* (doing)

Rupert **invited** *her to have* dinner with his family.
Dom **offered** *to give* Kat a lift home.
Dom **admitted** *being* madly in love with Kat.

TIPS • We don't have to report every word people say. It's more important to report the idea: *"OK, it's true. I was the one who crashed your car."* → *He admitted crashing her car.*

• Some reporting verbs can have more than one verb pattern. For example, after *promise*, *agree*, *admit* and *suggest* we can also use *that* + clause: *Kat promised (Dom) that she would go out with him. Dom admitted that he was in love with Kat.*

• We often use *not* with *warn*: *Rupert warned Hendrick **not** to tell anyone about their plan.*

GRAMMAR

11.1 Reported speech: sentences 11A 6 p87

- We use reported speech to tell someone what another person said.
- We usually change the verb form in reported speech. Look at the table.

verb form in direct speech	verb form in reported speech
Present Simple I still want to be in the programme.	**Past Simple** She said she still wanted to be in the programme.
Present Continuous I'm having another operation on Friday.	**Past Continuous** She said that she was having another operation on Friday.
Present Perfect Simple I've already had one operation.	**Past Perfect** She told me she'd already had one operation.
Past Simple I was in a car accident.	**Past Perfect** She said that she'd been in a car accident.
am/are/is going to They're going to start filming soon.	**was/were going to** I told her they were going to start filming soon.
will I won't be able to walk on it for a month.	**would** She said she wouldn't be able to walk on it for a month.
can I can't come to the meeting on Monday.	**could** She told me she couldn't come to the meeting on Monday.
must You must talk to Max.	**had to** I told her that she had to talk to you.

SAY AND TELL

- To introduce reported speech we usually use *say* or *tell*.
- We **never** use an object (*me*, *her*, etc.) with *say*: He said (that) …
- We **always** use an object (*me*, *her*, etc.) with *tell*: He told **me** (that) …
- We don't have to use *that* after *say* and *tell* in reported speech.
- Subject pronouns (*I*, *he*, etc.) and possessive adjectives (*my*, *his*, etc.) usually change in reported speech: "We can't come to your party." → She told me that they couldn't come to my party.

TIPS • The modal verbs *could*, *should*, *would*, *might* and *ought to* don't change in reported speech.

- The Past Simple doesn't have to change to the Past Perfect. It can stay the same: "I met him in 2011." → She said she (had) met him in 2011.

- We don't have to change the verb form if the reported sentence is about something general, or something that is still in the future: "I love classical music." → I told him I love classical music.

- We often change time expressions in reported speech: *tomorrow* → *the next day*; *next week* → *the following week*; *last week* → *the week before*, etc.

11.2 Reported speech: questions 11B 4 p88

- We use reported questions when we want to tell someone what another person asked us.
- We don't use the auxiliaries *do*, *does* or *did* in reported questions: He asked if I had any acting work. not He asked if I did have any acting work.
- We use *if* or *whether* when we report *yes/no* questions: "Are you working at the moment?" → He asked me if/whether I was working at the moment.

- We sometimes use an object (*me*, *him*, etc.) with *ask*: He asked (me) whether I was available to start next week.
- The changes in the verb forms in reported questions are the same as reported sentences: "What other parts have you had recently?" → He asked me what other parts I'd had recently.

REPORTED QUESTIONS

He/She asked (me) He/She wanted to know	question word if/whether	subject + verb

He wanted to know **where** I'd studied acting.
He asked me **if/whether** I was working at the moment.

TIP • The word order in reported questions is the same as in positive sentences: I asked her where her brother was. not I asked her where was her brother.

11.3 Reported speech: requests and imperatives 11B 8 p89

- To report **requests**, we use:
  asked + **object** + (**not**) + **infinitive with to**
  He asked me to come to a meeting on Monday.

- To report **imperatives**, we use:
  told + **object** + (**not**) + **infinitive with to**
  He told me to be at their offices at ten.
  He told me not to accept any more work.

REAL WORLD

11.1 Checking information 11D 3 p92

asking someone to repeat information

Sorry, what did you say (your name) was again?
Sorry, I didn't get all of that.
Could you say it again, please?
And could you tell me (his surname) again?
Sorry, I didn't quite catch that.
Can you give it to me again, please?

checking the information you have is correct

Is that (Crane) with a (C)?
Do you mean (this Wednesday)?
Is that spelt (N-i-e-l-s-e-n)?
Are you talking about (the UK sales conference)?

TIP • We can say *I didn't quite* **catch** *that.* or *I didn't quite* **get** *that.*

153

Language Summary 12

VOCABULARY

12.1 Informal words and phrases
12A 1 p94

fancy (doing sth) want to do something: *I really fancy going away this weekend.*
can't be bothered (to do sth) not want to do something because you don't have enough energy or interest: *I can't be bothered to cook this evening.*
(not) feel up to (doing sth) not feel well enough or have enough energy to do something: *I don't feel up to going out after class.*
be (completely) broke not have any money: *I'm completely broke at the moment.*
hang around spend time somewhere, usually for no particular reason: *I often hang around for a bit after class.*
rubbish very bad quality: *The last film I saw was rubbish.*
be (really) into sth enjoy or like something: *I'm really into yoga at the moment.*
be up to sb it's your decision: *It's up to me when I take a holiday.*
reckon think, have an opinion: *I reckon I'll do quite well in my next English test.*
could do with want or need (food, drink, etc.): *I could do with a few days off.*
be sick of (doing sth) be fed up with doing something: *I'm sick of working so hard.*
be off (to somewhere) go to a place: *I'm off to the cinema later.*

TIP • *I'm off.* = *I'm leaving now. Right, I'm off. See you tomorrow.*

12.2 Phrases with *get* **12B** 1 p96

get = receive/obtain	*get* = become
get something to eat/drink	get lost
get a job	get depressed/angry
get a message	get fed up with something
get a present	get better/worse at something
get a phone call	get older

get = travel/arrive	other phrases with *get*
get home	get on well with someone
get here/there	get to know someone
get around	get in touch with someone
get back from somewhere	get rid of something
get to work	get into trouble

TIPS • We can use other adjectives with *get*: *get upset/tired/annoyed*, etc.
• We also use *get* to mean *buy*: *Could you get me some bread from the shops?*

12.3 Word building (3): word families (1) **12C** 5 p99

● We often make nouns and adjectives by adding suffixes (*-ment*, *-ing*, etc.) to verbs.

verb	noun	adjective
disappoint	disappoint**ment**	disappoint**ed**, disappoint**ing**
enjoy	enjoy**ment**	enjoy**able**
protect	protect**ion**	protect**ive**
care	care	care**ful**, care**less**
attract	attract**ion**	attract**ive**
prefer	prefer**ence**	prefer**able**
entertain	entertain**ment**	entertain**ing**
relax	relax**ation**	relax**ing**, relax**ed**

● We use these suffixes to make nouns: *-ment*, *-ion*, *-ence*, *-ation*.
● We use these suffixes to make adjectives: *-ing*, *-ed*, *-able*, *-ive*, *-ful*, *-less*.

TIPS • Sometimes the verb and the noun are the same: *They really **care** about the environment.* (verb); *He puts a lot of **care** into his work.* (noun)
• We often use *-able* to mean 'can': *It's an enjoyable film.* = People can enjoy it.
• We use *-ful* to mean 'with'. We use *-less* to mean 'without'.

12.4 Word building (3): word families (2) **12C** 6 p99

verb	noun	adjective
create	creat**ion**	creat**ive**
pollute	pollut**ion**	pollut**ed**, pollut**ing**
employ	employ**ment**	employ**ed**, employ**able**
embarrass	embarrass**ment**	embarrass**ed**, embarrass**ing**
depend	depend**ence**	depend**able**
harm	harm	harm**ful**, harm**less**
predict	predict**ion**	predict**able**
confuse	confus**ion**	confus**ing**, confus**ed**
reserve	reserv**ation**	reserv**ed**

GRAMMAR

12.1 Wishes   12A 3 p94

- We often use *I wish …* to talk about **imaginary** situations in the **present or the future**.
- We often use sentences with *I wish …* to talk about the opposite of what is true or real: *I wish we had a car.* (The woman hasn't got a car, but she would like to have one.)
- To make wishes about states we use *wish* + **Past Simple**: *I wish we **had** a car. I wish I **was** on a beach somewhere.*
- To make wishes about activities happening now we use *wish* + **Past Continuous**: *I wish you **were coming** to the theatre with me.*
- To make wishes about abilities or possibilities we use *wish* + **could** + infinitive: *I wish I **could come** with you.*
- To make wishes about obligations we use *wish* + **didn't have to** + infinitive: *I wish we **didn't have to go** to this party.*

TIPS • We can say *I wish I/he/she/it **was** …* or *I wish I/he/she/it **were** …* : *I wish I was taller. = I wish I were taller.*

- We often use the second conditional to give reasons for wishes: *I wish we had a car. If we had one, I wouldn't spend half my life waiting for buses.*
- Notice the difference between *I wish …* and *I hope …* :
  A *I wish you were coming to the party.*
  (I know that you aren't coming = imaginary situation)
  B *I hope you're coming to the party.*
  (I think that you might come = real possibility)
- We can also make sentences with *wish* with *you/he/she/we/they*: *He wishes he lived somewhere hotter. We wish we could afford a holiday.*

12.2 Third conditional   12B 5 p97

- We use the third conditional to talk about **imaginary** situations in the **past**.
- We often use third conditionals to talk about the opposite of what really happened: *If I'd stayed at home, I wouldn't have met my husband.* (She didn't stay at home and so she went to a party and met her husband.)
  If I hadn't lost my job, I wouldn't have started my own business. (He lost his job so he decided to start his own business.)

POSITIVE AND NEGATIVE

if clause (if + Past Perfect)	main clause ('d, would or wouldn't + have + past participle)
If I **'d stayed** at home,	I **wouldn't have met** my husband.
If I **hadn't started** doing this,	I**'d have got** into a lot more trouble.

TIPS • As with other conditionals, in the third conditional the *if* clause can be first or second in the sentence. We use a comma (,) when the *if* clause is first:
If I hadn't won that race, I'd never have become a serious athlete.
I'd never have become a serious athlete if I hadn't won that race.

- We can use **could have** in the main clause of the third conditional to talk about ability: *If I'd been there, I could have helped you.*
- We can also use **might have** in the main clause of the third conditional to mean 'would have perhaps': *If you hadn't got lost, we might have got there on time.*
- We don't usually use *would* in the *if* clause: *If I'd known, I'd have told you.* not *If I would have known, I'd have told you.*
- In spoken English we can say *I'd have* /ˈaɪdəv/ or *I would've* /aɪ ˈwʊdəv/ in the main clause: *"I would've got into a lot more trouble if I hadn't started doing this."*

Answer Key

6C 8 p51

HOW LUCKY ARE YOU?

16–18 points
You're very positive about life and probably think that you're already a very lucky person. When things go badly, you don't worry too much because you know something good is going to happen soon. Why don't you do the lottery next weekend – you might win!

13–15 points
You're quite a lucky person and tend to look on the bright side of life. You know lots of people and have a very busy social life. Try to do something new every month and make sure you have some time to yourself as well.

9–12 points
You think you're lucky in some parts of your life, but not in others, and maybe you worry about the past and the future too much. Try to enjoy the present a little more and listen to your heart when you make decisions, not just your head.

6–8 points
You're not very lucky at the moment and probably expect things to get worse, not better. Why not try to meet some new people and take a few more chances in life? What's the worst that could happen?

10B 9 b p81

baseball cap: Nick Bradley
wedding photos: Peggy
glasses case: Brenda Bradley
speech: Tom
earrings: Jane Lewis
wedding ring: Sheila Jones
football key ring: Leo
driving test book: Karen
London book: Brenda Bradley
wallet: Derek Bradley
watch: Trevor Jones

Audio and Video Scripts

CD1 1

FIONA What makes me happy? Well, I love doing yoga, that's very important to me and I do it every day. I'm also a yoga teacher and I teach classes three times a week. I really enjoy teaching and it never really feels like work. And I love spending time with my son Leo, of course. He's nearly seven now and it's wonderful watching him grow up. At the moment he's playing a video game – it's amazing how good he is, he's much better than I am and he beats me every time. Er, what else? Well, I *love* having a lie-in, which doesn't happen very often, as you can imagine! But last Sunday Leo stayed with his grandparents, so my husband and I didn't get up till midday. It was heaven!

MAXIE Well, um, playing guitar makes me happy. I got my first guitar when I was twelve and now I'm in a band at uni. I started writing my own songs about two years ago and, er, so far I've written about twenty-five songs. Our band isn't famous or anything, but we play every weekend, usually at local pubs or parties, and there's always a really good atmosphere. Oh, and last month I put a video of the band on YouTube and so far it's got over 20,000 hits, which is fantastic! Er, what else? Well, I love visiting new places – that makes me happy too. I've been to six countries so far, and maybe one day we'll play gigs all over the world – now that would be amazing!

CAROLINE What makes me happy? Well, I really enjoy going to art galleries with my twin sister, Mary. We go to an exhibition together once or twice a month and we always have a wonderful time. Another thing that makes me really happy is working in the garden. I've always loved growing plants and flowers, ever since I was a little girl, and this year I've started a small vegetable garden. We often have friends round for dinner and it's nice to eat things we've grown ourselves. But I don't do the cooking, my husband does all that – it's one of the things that makes him happy. I just do the eating! Hm, what else? Well, seeing our grandchildren, of course. They visit us most weekends and we love every minute we spend with them.

CD1 2

Whereabouts do you /dəjə/ live? | How long have you /həvjə/ lived there? | Who lives with you? | What time do you /dəjə/ get up on Sundays? | Why are you /əjə/ studying English? | Where did you /dɪdʒə/ go on holiday last year? | How many countries have you /həvjə/ visited? | Who emails you the most? | What did you /dɪdʒə/ do yesterday evening? | What are you /əjə/ planning to do next weekend?

CD1 3

I don't often visit my grandmother. | No one in my family likes tennis. | My mum hasn't lost her mobile. | I don't think I'll buy a new phone. | There's no doctor in the village. | None of my friends have got cars. | Neither of my brothers likes cooking. | There's no milk in the fridge.

CD1 4

SALLY Sorry I'm late. Did you get my text?
PETER Hi, Sally. Yes, I've ordered you the vegetarian pizza.
S Great, thanks a lot.
ERIC Were you working late?
S No, I go to a drama club on Mondays.
ALICE I didn't know you've joined a drama club.
S I only joined a few weeks ago, but I'm really enjoying it.
P So what do you do exactly?
S Well, first we choose a play, then three months later we put it on at the local theatre. We don't get paid or anything, it's just for fun.
A And what play are you working on at the moment?
S It's a comedy called *The Best Years of our Lives*. It's very funny. I play a confused old lady who's fed up with her husband.
P Well, that shouldn't be too difficult.
S Hey!
E I'd love to come and see you onstage.
A Yeah, me too.
S Hm, I'm not sure about that. I'd feel very nervous if I knew you were all watching me. Anyway, how's your book club going, Eric?
E Oh, it's going very well, thanks.
P So what do you do in your book club?
E Well, every month someone chooses a book and we all read it. Then we meet up a month later at someone's house and talk about what we thought of the book.
S With lots of food and drink, probably.
E Yes, of course. That's the best bit!
A Do you always read the books?
E Yes ... well, I try to, but I don't always finish them. Sometimes I just read the last page to see what happened in the end.
P Well, my brother runs an animation club, which is quite interesting.
S What's that about?
P It's for people who like making animated films – you know, short cartoons, things you might see on YouTube.
A Are you a member?
P No, but I've been to a couple of meetings. They're great fun. People watch each other's films and then talk about how they made them.
S You're interested in that sort of thing, aren't you, Eric?
E Yes, I do some animation on my laptop. Maybe I should go sometime.
P Sure. I'll let you know when the next meeting is.
E Great, thanks.
A Well, I've just joined a glee club.
P Er, what's a glee club?
A Basically it's a club for people who like singing and dancing. We choose some songs and then learn the words and dance steps, and at the end of the year we're going to put on a performance for charity.
P Oh. Are you any good?
A Well, I'm OK at singing, but I'm not the best dancer in the world. They always put me near the back!
E Go on, give us a song, then.
A No, I couldn't sing here, I'd be too embarrassed. Oh, look, here comes the food.
S That was lucky!

VIDEO 1 CD1 5

REBECCA I'm really looking forward to meeting Lisa's new boyfriend. She was telling me all about him last weekend. He sounds really nice. They're very late, though.
CHARLIE They'll be here soon, I'm sure.
LISA Ah, here they are. Hi, Rebecca. Hello, Charlie. How are you?
R We're fine, thanks.
L And how's the most beautiful baby in the world?
C Hi, you must be Daniel. I'm Charlie and this is Rebecca.
DANIEL Hi, nice to meet you. You live next door to Lisa, don't you?
C Yes, I do.
L How long have you lived in this village?
C Oh, about three years now. It's a really nice place to live – apart from the noisy neighbours, of course.
L Hey! *You're* the ones with the baby who cries all night.
R Yeah, that's true. So, Daniel, you're from London originally, aren't you?
D Yes, that's right. I moved out to the country about two years ago.
L So where do you live now?
D In Renfield – you know, about 20 miles away.
C Yes, I know it. And how did you and Lisa meet?
D Well, my brother Alex used to share a flat with Lisa's sister Barbara when they were students.
C Barbara went to Liverpool university, didn't she?
L Yes, she did. Anyway, last month Alex invited me and my sister over to his birthday party, which is where I met Daniel.

R And what do you do, Daniel?
D I work for a water sports company. I teach sailing, canoeing, diving – that sort of thing.
L You've been diving, haven't you?
C No, I haven't, actually. It sounds a bit too dangerous to me.
D Oh, it's not really, not if you know what you're doing. And what do you do, Charlie?
C I work for Getaway Holidays, you know, the package tour company. It's a boring office job, really, but the money's OK.
D Oh, right.
L Well, I know something you two have got in common.
D Oh, what's that?
L You both support Manchester United.
C Really? Well, you'll have to come round and watch a match sometime.
D That would be nice, thanks. It was a great match yesterday, wasn't it?
C Yes, it was. They played really well – and three brilliant goals.
R Isn't it amazing? You put two men together, and after five minutes they're already talking about football.
D It's how we communicate.
C Yeah, and it means we never have to talk about our feelings.
R Very funny.
L I'm getting hungry. You haven't ordered any food yet, have you?
R No, we haven't. We were waiting for you. Shall we go and get some menus?
L Yeah, good idea. You two can talk about football while we're gone.
R And keep an eye on Harry.
C Yeah, of course … Why does that always happen? You don't have any kids, do you?
D No, I don't. One day, maybe.
C Well, I wouldn't hurry if I were you. I haven't had a good night's sleep for six months. What's the matter, little man? Do you want mummy to change you when she gets back? Do you?

CD1 ▶ 7

1 syllable stressed, scared, shocked
● ● worried, frightened
● ● ● annoyed, confused, relaxed, concerned, depressed
● ● ● satisfied, terrified, interested
● ● ● ● excited, embarrassed, exhausted

CD1 ▶ 9

PRESENTER Welcome to *Cover to Cover*. Today we're talking about Carl Honoré's book *In Praise of Slow*, which tells us that we're all living too fast and working too hard, and that we should all just slow down. With me are two journalists, Kim Mayhew and Rob Davis – both workaholics, of course. Kim, what did you think of the book?
KIM I thought it was very interesting and quite funny in places too.
P And what about you, Rob?
ROB Well, as soon as I finished it, I decided that I must take more time off work.
K Yes, me too. Honoré says people should only work 35 hours a week.
P And do you think that's a good idea?
K Yes, definitely. Firstly, a lot of people are unemployed these days, as we know, so if everyone worked fewer hours, it might create more jobs.
R But according to Honoré, people are already working less in some countries. For example, Germans spend 15% less time at work now than in 1980.
P Honoré also believes that we ought to spend more time with our families.
K And that's already happening in some countries too, isn't it? It says in the book that some French employees are allowed to begin their weekend at 3 p.m. on Thursday.
R Yes, and Honoré also says people can get their best ideas when they're doing nothing. Albert Einstein was famous for just looking into space at his office at Princeton University. And you can't say he didn't have a few good ideas!
P Absolutely. Kim, what else interested you about the book?
K Well, I was interested to read that Americans work 350 hours a year more than Europeans, but in some American companies, employees can sleep whenever they want. Apparently they have special rooms where people can go and relax if they're tired.
P Really? If we had one here, I'd be in there every afternoon!
R Actually, by law people in the UK are supposed to have a break every four hours, but a lot don't, of course. I was also surprised to read that 20% of British people work more than 60 hours a week. We work the most hours in Europe and it's certainly not making us happier.
K Yes, and lots of people have to take work home because they're under a lot of pressure to meet deadlines. Apparently 60% of British people who were interviewed said they didn't take all their paid holiday. Now that's just crazy!
R And these days of course we're able to continue working when we're travelling. You know, on the train or on a plane or whatever.
K Yes, the Japanese even have a word for it – karoshi – which means 'death from working too hard'.
P On that happy note, we'll leave it there.

CD1 ▶ 10

ANSWERS 2 I must 3 Are you able to 4 I'm supposed to 5 don't have to 6 Are you allowed to 7 can 8 have to 9 ought to 10 have to 11 mustn't

CD1 ▶ 12

I'm blogging from a busy street food market. | I'm sitting in one of Mexico City's busy parks. | Now I'm writing a book about street food. | We're working in Mexico for a few days. | My blog is becoming more popular every year. | More people are visiting Thailand on holiday these days.

CD1 ▶ 13

[words in pink = weak forms]

MAN How many people do you know who have trouble sleeping at night? For many of us insomnia's part of life, and not being able to get to sleep isn't just annoying, it can also be very dangerous.
WOMAN Yes, and with us today is sleep scientist, Doctor Angela Moore. Welcome to the programme.
ANGELA Thank you.
W Doctor Moore, how much of a problem is this, do you think?
A Well, we know tiredness can cause accidents. More than fifty per cent of road accidents in the USA are because of people driving when they're tired.
M That's amazing!
A Yes, it is, isn't it? And when you think thirty per cent of people in the UK can have problems getting to sleep or staying asleep, and ten per cent have serious insomnia – that's a lot of accidents waiting to happen.
W So how much sleep do you think people are getting these days?
A Well, a hundred years ago, before electricity, people went to sleep when it got dark and woke up when it got light. But now in our twenty-four-hour society we sleep about an hour and a half less than we did a century ago.
W Well, I've got two teenagers and no one can say they're sleeping less!
A I'm sure a lot of parents would say that. Actually, scientists now believe teenagers need about an hour more sleep than adults.
W Really?
A Yes, it's because their bodies are still growing. Of course, teenagers don't need as much sleep as babies and small children – they need the most sleep. It's actually older people who generally need the least amount of sleep.
W That's very interesting.

A   Yes, and another interesting thing about teenagers is their body clock is different, so they naturally want to go to bed and wake up about two hours later than adults.
W   So that's why our children aren't very bright in the morning.
A   And because they have to get up early for school, this means they can feel exhausted when they get there. Recently a school in the north of England decided to start lessons at ten rather than nine. With a later starting time, fewer students missed school and the exam results in English and maths were much better than the previous year.
M   So do you think all schools should start later?
A   Well, that's certainly what a lot of sleep experts think nowadays.
M   So why do we need sleep?
A   We don't really know. Scientists used to think sleep was the only time you had complete rest, but in fact we use about the same amount of energy when we're asleep as when we're sitting on the sofa relaxing.
M   Really? That's very surprising.
A   Yes, and our brains are very active for some of the time we're asleep. Apparently that's when our brains can organise information they've collected during the day.
W   Well, it's been absolutely fascinating talking to you. Thank you for coming in today.
A   My pleasure.

VIDEO 2   CD1 15

Conversation 1
REBECCA   Here you are, Lisa. One sugar.
LISA   Thanks, Rebecca. Where's Harry?
R   Oh, he's having his afternoon nap.
L   Right. You look a bit stressed. Is everything OK?
R   Well, Charlie and I are having a difficult time at the moment.
L   Oh, dear. What's the matter?
R   Harry isn't sleeping very well. He wakes up four or five times every night, which means Charlie and I wake up too, of course. The trouble is, Charlie finds it difficult to get back to sleep, so he's always absolutely shattered the next day.
L   Hmm, I can see why you're upset. That must be really difficult.
R   Yes, it is. And when Charlie gets home from work he's really exhausted and fed up. So we're arguing a lot more than we usually do.
L   Oh, dear. What a shame.
R   What should I do, Lisa?
L   Well, have you tried talking to him about it?

R   Yes, but we just end up having another argument. Then he tells me I'm spending too much money and starts getting really angry at me.
L   Oh, how awful!
R   But I only buy things we need for the house – and for the baby, of course.
L   Perhaps you ought to spend more time together – you know, just the two of you. I think you need at least one evening off a week.
R   Yes, you could be right. I'll talk to Charlie when he gets home.
L   I'd be happy to babysit for you, if you like.
R   Oh, that's very kind of you, Lisa, thanks a lot. Uh oh. Sounds like someone's woken up. Back in a minute.

Conversation 2
ANDY   Charlie? Have you got the file for the Bradley account?
CHARLIE   Oh, er, yeah, here it is.
A   Thanks. Are you OK? You look exhausted.
C   Yeah, I'm fine. Just having trouble sleeping these days, that's all.
A   I'm sorry to hear that. What's the problem?
C   Well, Harry isn't sleeping very well. He wakes us up in the middle of the night then we can't get back to sleep.
A   Maybe you should sleep in separate rooms. You know, just till Harry's sleeping better. Then you won't wake up so often.
C   Well, it's worth a try, I guess. But it's not just that. Rebecca's spending too much money. Not on herself, but she buys lots of things for the house and the baby that we just don't need.
A   Well, why don't you talk to her about it?
C   I've tried that, but we just start arguing again, and then she tells me I'm working too hard, which is probably true. But I've heard that some people are going to lose their jobs soon, and I don't want to be one of them.
A   Yes, I see what you mean. But I really don't think you're going to lose your job. The company needs you.
C   Thanks, Andy, that's good to hear. So what do you think I should do?
A   Well, I'd take her out for a really nice meal, you know, just the two of you. That's what Fiona and I do when we're having problems and it's always really helpful.
C   Yes, that's a good idea. I might try that. Thanks, Andy.
A   No problem. Good luck.
C   Cheers. Actually, I'll call her now.
REBECCA   Hi.
C   Hi honey, it's me. Look, do you think we could get a babysitter this evening?

CD1 16

ANSWERS   2 a 3 b 4 b 5 a 6 b

CD1 18

[pink = weak forms; blue = strong forms]

JO   Which company do you work for?
ED   It's called Getaway Holidays. I work for the owner.
J   Really? I'm thinking of going on holiday soon. Do you think you can get me a cheap flight?
E   Yes, maybe I can. Where do you want to fly to?
J   Well, my brother's working at a hotel in the Caribbean and I'd like to go and see him.
E   Which hotel is he working at?
J   It's called The Island Palace. Do you know it?
E   Yes, I do. How long do you want to go for?
J   About three weeks if I can.
E   OK, I'll see what I can do for you. Text me!

CD1 19

MEGAN   I'm a guide for a company that organises hiking tours in the Rocky Mountains in Canada. I'm actually American, not Canadian, but I've lived in this country for about three years and I really love working here. I've worked in the USA and in Europe and I really enjoyed my time there too, but for me there's nowhere like the Canadian Rockies. A lot of our customers have been hiking before, but when they get back to the hotel they often say it's the best experience they've ever had, which is very satisfying. It's not always an easy job – you have to deal with difficult weather conditions and sometimes it can be quite dangerous. Also I have to put up with a few people who do stupid things. For example, three days ago a guy set off on his own into the mountains without telling anyone. He got lost, then fell and broke his leg. Luckily he had GPS on his phone and we were able to rescue him. Actually, I've just been to Banff to pick him up from the hospital. He can't do any more hiking, of course, but at least he'll have a good story to tell his friends when he gets back home.

CLIVE   My wife and I started working in the hotel industry 19 years ago, but this is the first time we've run a hotel in a touristy place like the Lake District. We've had this place since 2008 and I'm a bit fed up with it, to be honest. Running a tourist hotel is quite stressful, particularly when people complain about things. It can be difficult for tourists to get around in the summer because of all the cars, but I don't know why they complain to me about it! Also some people think they can check in and out whenever they want. We have to clean the rooms, of course, so if guests don't check out on time it makes life very difficult for us. Another problem is that one of us always has to be here. For example, my wife's gone to see some friends off at Manchester airport, so I have to stay and look after the hotel. And because we're open all year, it's difficult for us to have a holiday together. We've been away a few times, but each time there was a problem at the hotel so we had to come back early. But this December we're closing the hotel and going to South America – we're really looking forward to it.

CD1 20

I've worked in the USA and in Europe. | We've been away a few times. | I've lived in this country for about three years. | We've had this place since 2008. | My wife's gone to see some friends off. | I've just been to Banff to pick him up from the hospital. | This is the first time we've run a hotel in a touristy place.

CD1 22

1   They lived in Egypt for ten years.
2   We've opened a restaurant.
3   I've decided to stay here.
4   You lost a lot of money.
5   She's visited a lot of interesting places.
6   He phoned all his friends.

CD1 23

ANSWERS   2 came 3 moved 4 opened
5 've lived 6 've just opened 7 've had
8 arrived 9 've visited 10 's just gone
11 've been 12 was 13 haven't had

CD1 24

I've been /bɪn/ working here for /fə/ six months. | How long have /əv/ you been /bɪn/ travelling? | Scott's been /bɪn/ writing books since 2006. | He's written five books so far. | They haven't been /bɪn/ playing golf for /fə/ long. | How long has /əz/ he had that car? | I've known Zak since we were kids. | We've been /bɪn/ waiting for /fə/ two hours.

CD1 25

PRESENTER   Good afternoon and welcome to *Take a Break*. Today we're taking a look at the rise in voluntourism around the world. I'm here with Alison Armstrong from the travel website voluntours.net. Alison, first of all, can you tell all our listeners what voluntourism is?
ALISON   Well, er … it's when people go to another part of the world on holiday, or on a longer trip, and volunteer to work for free in the place they're visiting. And at the moment it's one of the fastest-growing types of tourism in the world.
P   And what kind of holidays are we talking about?
A   They can be almost anything, really. Typical examples are helping to build a school in Asia, planting trees in a national park in Australia, or perhaps working on an organic farm in Spain.
P   And what sort of people go on these holidays?
A   Oh, all sorts of people. These days a lot of students take a gap-year – that is to say, a year off between school and university – and about twenty-five per cent of people in the UK take a year off work between the ages of seventeen and twenty-five. These young people often want to travel the world and do something useful at the same time.
P   But it isn't just young people going on these holidays, is it?
A   Oh no, absolutely not. There's a huge increase in the number of volunteers in their thirties and forties, and also a lot of retired people too.
P   And why do you think this type of holiday's becoming so popular?
A   Well, we get so much information about all the problems in the world these days and a lot of people want to do something practical to help. It's also a great way to get to know the people and culture of the place you're visiting.
P   Yes, that's a good point.
A   And a lot of older people want more from their holiday than just sitting on a beach or going on guided tours. But it can be difficult to meet local people when you stay in tourist hotels, and eat in tourist restaurants.
P   OK, but do the volunteers really help the countries they visit?
A   If the holiday's well organised, yes, definitely. Tourists still have to pay to go on these holidays, of course, and some of that money is used to help the local community. The tourists also do useful work while they're there and local people enjoy sharing their culture with people from different countries.
P   And what about the tourists? Do they have a good time?
A   Yes, most of them do, and a lot of people say that it's the best holiday they've ever had. If you read some of the blogs on our website, you'll find that for many people, voluntourism is a life-changing experience.
P   Well, it seems like everybody wins. Perhaps I should take my family on one of these holidays next year. Alison, thanks very much for coming in today.
A   Not at all.

VIDEO 3   CD1 26

REBECCA   Mmm, these samosas are nice. Try one.
ELLA   Mmm, yeah, they're delicious.
CHARLIE   So, are you two looking forward to your trip to India?
MIKE   Yeah, we can't wait.
R   Where are you flying to?
M   New Delhi. It was the cheapest flight we could get.
E   You've been to Delhi, haven't you?
R   Yes, we went there about 18 months ago.
M   Well, maybe you can give us some tips.
C   Sure. What do you want to know?
E   Well, firstly, do you know any good places to stay?
C   Um, well, there are lots of good hotels in Connaught Place – that's right in the centre of New Delhi.
R   Yes, the place we stayed in is called The Raj Hotel. It's not too expensive and very comfortable. You can book rooms online.
M   Great, thanks. We'll check it out. And what's the best way to get around?
R   In Delhi it's probably best to use rickshaws. They're quicker than taxis, and quite cheap.
E   OK.
C   And to travel to other cities I'd recommend the trains. They're a lot safer than the buses, especially at night.
E   Hmm, that's good to know. So what should we go and see – are there any good museums?
R   Oh no, don't bother going to the museums. They're not that interesting and there are much better things to see in Delhi.
C   Yeah, but you should definitely see the Red Fort in Old Delhi. It was built in the 17th century and it's absolutely huge.
M   Right, the Red Fort in Old Delhi. What else is worth visiting?
R   Well, there's the Jami Masjid, of course. That's well worth seeing. It's the biggest mosque in India and it's only a few minutes from the Red Fort.
E   OK, that sounds good.
C   And there's a much older fort about half an hour from the centre.
R   Yes, but it isn't really worth visiting, I don't think.
M   OK. And what about places outside Delhi?
C   Well, it's probably already on your list, but you really must go to Agra to see the Taj Mahal. It's only three hours away by train – you can do it in a day if you start early.
E   Yes, we're planning to go there. And, er, what about the food? Do you know any good places to eat in Delhi?

159

C Yes, there are lots of really good restaurants in Connaught Place. Oh, what was the name of that place we used to go to?
R Oh, yes, I know the place you mean … I think it's called The Shanti.
C Yes, that's right. It's only a few minutes from the Raj Hotel and the food there was amazing!
M Thanks, that's really useful. Er, have you got any other tips?
R Well, only drink bottled water, of course. And don't drink anything with ice in it. Ice is usually made with tap water, which isn't very safe.
E Yes, I've heard that before.
C And I wouldn't eat any salads because they're often washed in tap water too.
M Yes, that sounds like good advice.
R All this talk of India is making me want to come with you.
C Yeah, me too. Perhaps we can ask Lisa and Daniel to babysit for a month!
E Oh look, here comes our food.

CD1 30

she threw her shoes into the crowd → While she was /wəz/ doing an encore, she threw her shoes into the crowd. | the manager came over and /ən/ congratulated me → While I was /wəz/ playing my last track, the manager came over and /ən/ congratulated me. | all the fans were /wə/ singing along → It was /wəz/ a fantastic atmosphere and all the fans were /wə/ singing along. | dancing and /ən/ having a good time → All the clubbers were /wə/ dancing and /ən/ having a good time. | go to a lot of /əv/ gigs → I used to /tə/ go to a lot of /əv/ gigs. | play at /ət/ friends' parties → I used to /tə/ play at /ət/ friends' parties.

CD1 31

PAUL What are you working on at the moment, Josie?
JOSIE I've been making a TV series called *Modern Adventurers*.
P That sounds interesting.
J Yes, it's fascinating. The first episode is about a man called Ed Stafford, who became the first person to walk the length of the River Amazon in 2010.
P Wow, that sounds like hard work. How long did it take him?
J About two-and-a-half years.
P You're joking! Why didn't he go by boat?
J Very funny. But that's the point of the series. Why do some people go on these crazy adventures? Just to be the first person to do something?
P Good question. So did this guy – what was his name again?
J Ed Stafford.
P Right. So did Ed Stafford walk the Amazon on his own?
J No, he set off with a friend called Luke Collyer. They'd planned to do the whole walk together, but Luke went home after 68 days.
P I'm not surprised. I wouldn't last 68 minutes!
J No, me neither. Anyway, a Peruvian guide called Cho joined the expedition after Luke had gone back to the UK. Cho had planned to walk with Ed for only five days, but ended up staying with him until the end.
P And what did they eat?
J They mainly lived on rice and beans, which they bought in villages and carried with them. But they also went to parts of the forest that nobody had ever been to before. So they sometimes ran out of food and had to eat whatever they could find.
P So did they just disappear into the jungle for two-and-a-half years?
J No, not really. Every day Ed wrote his blog or uploaded a video of his journey onto his website, and of course he also read messages that people had sent him.
P So how far did he walk in total?
J Well, the River Amazon is about 4,000 miles long, but Ed calculated that he'd walked about 6,000 miles.
P I hope he took some insect repellent.
J Well, if he did, he didn't take enough. He says that during the trip he got 200,000 mosquito and ant bites.
P Really? That's amazing!
J Yes, and he also got 600 wasp stings and 12 scorpion stings.
P Ouch! So what did he do when he'd finished the journey?
J He flew back to England, had a rest, and then a few weeks later he ran four marathons in 27 hours!
P Wow! This guy makes me feel exhausted just hearing about him.
J Well, if you think he's extreme, the second programme is about another modern adventurer called Martin Strel. He was the first person to …

CD1 32

Luke had /əd/ gone back to /tə/ the UK → Cho joined the expedition after Luke had /əd/ gone back to /tə/ the UK. | people had /əd/ sent him → He also read messages that /ðət/ people had /əd/ sent him. | he'd walked about six thousand miles → Ed calculated that /ðət/ he'd walked about six thousand miles. | the whole walk together → They'd planned to /tə/ do the whole walk together. | nobody had /əd/ ever been to before → They went to /tə/ parts of the forest that /ðət/ nobody had /əd/ ever been to before. | he'd finished the journey → So what did he do when he'd finished the journey?

CD1 34

1 I had a bad day. I'd had a bad day.
2 John had arrived early. John arrived early.
3 She made a mistake. She'd made a mistake.
4 Tom had thought it was wrong. Tom thought it was wrong.
5 The couple had asked for a bigger room. The couple asked for a bigger room.
6 We told him the news. We'd told him the news.

CD1 35

ANSWERS 2 became 3 had already tried 4 swam 5 took 6 'd broken 7 swam 8 had ever done 9 travelled 10 swam 11 arrived 12 'd been

CD1 36

PRESENTER … and with the weekend just around the corner, I have with me /j/ in the studio Gabrielle Wallace, from the /j/ excellent website londonfornothing.com, to tell us how to /w/ enjoy London for free.
GABRIELLE Hi there.
P Welcome to the programme, Gabrielle. To /w/ a lot of people, London appears to be /j/ a very /j/ expensive city to visit.
G Well, it can be, but there /r/ are /r/ actually /j/ a lot of things you can do /w/ in the city for free.
P Such as?
G Well, of course you don't have to pay to visit many /j/ of London's museums or /r/ art galleries, such as the British Museum or the National Gallery.
P Right.
G And if you'd prefer to wander /r/ around the city /j/ on your /r/ own, you can download free walking tours onto your phone. My favourite is the tour /r/ of the /j/ area /r/ around London Bridge, which is really /j/ interesting. And all the tours come with a free downloadable map so you don't get lost.
P OK. And is there /r/ anywhere you can hear some free music?
G Yes, there /r/ is, actually. For /r/ example, there's free jazz at the National Theatre six days a week, and if you go to the Royal Opera House at lunchtime on Mondays, you can enjoy some free /j/ opera.
P Really? I didn't know that.
G Yes, and you can also go /w/ and see /j/ a radio /w/ or TV programme being recorded. I've seen a few TV comedies and chat shows being made, and they're /r/ always great fun – and the /j/ audience always gets in for free.
P And how do you get tickets?

G You normally have to /w/ apply /j/ online. There /r/ are various websites that specialise in free tickets.
P Right. And what about more /r/ unusual days out?
G Well, you can visit the Houses of Parliament, of course. Anyone can queue /w/ up and go /w/ in for free, and then you can watch a live debate from the public gallery.
P Hm, I'm sure that would be very /j/ interesting.
G Yes, it can be, and it's worth going just to go /w/ inside the building, which is very /j/ impressive, of course. But if you want to go /w/ on an official tour, you have to pay, /j/ unfortunately.
P Right.
G And you can also go /w/ and watch a trial at the /j/ Old Bailey, which is the biggest criminal court in the country. If you get a good case, it can be /j/ absolutely fascinating. But don't forget to take some ID with you.
P And what about if you have to /w/ entertain children for the /j/ afternoon?
G Well, why not take them to /w/ a city farm? There /r/ are /r/ about thirteen in the city, and most of them are free. And at all of these places, children are /r/ allowed to feed the /j/ animals, play with the rabbits, or whatever.
P Gabrielle, thank you for coming in to see /j/ us today. For free, obviously.
G Obviously!

VIDEO 4 CD1 ▶ 38

COMMENTATOR And he's just outside the box. He shoots! It's just wide. And there goes the whistle for half time here at Old Trafford …
CHARLIE That'll be Rebecca and Lisa.
DANIEL Just in time for the second half.
C Hi, honey. We're watching the football.
LISA Hello, you two. Good match?
D Yeah, United are winning two-one.
REBECCA Oh, that's wonderful news. I'm pleased you haven't wasted your afternoon.
C Rebecca isn't very keen on football.
R Well, I just think that most football fans are really rude and aggressive.
C Well, some of them can be quite aggressive at times, I agree, but it's not as bad as it used to be when I was a boy. There was a lot more football violence then.
D Yeah, I agree. On the whole, most fans just want to see a good game and have fun.
C It's not much fun when your team loses, though, is it?
D Yeah, that's true.

L Well, it's the players I have a problem with, not the fans. I can't believe how much they get paid. Some of them get over £200,000 a week, just for kicking a ball around. It's ridiculous.
D Well, I agree that footballers tend to earn rather a lot of money, but you have to remember that football is part of the entertainment industry. Hundreds of millions of people are watching this match all around the world. That's why footballers get paid so much, because so many people want to see them play.
C Yeah, singers and film stars get paid millions every year too, but you don't hear people complaining about that.
R Well, I wouldn't mind so much if they behaved themselves. But every week you read stories about famous footballers getting into fights in nightclubs or um crashing their Porsche into a tree and things like that. That's not very sensible behaviour, is it?
C I agree. But generally speaking, most footballers are just normal people and never get into any trouble. It's only a few who are a bit crazy.
L Well, maybe. But I don't understand why men take football so seriously. Who wants to spend their weekends watching a group of millionaires kicking a ball around? I mean, it's only a game!
D Well, perhaps some people can take it a bit too seriously. But what was it someone once said? "Football isn't a matter of life and death – it's much more important than that."
R Very funny. Anyway, I just don't want Harry growing up and becoming obsessed with football, like you two are.
C Too late. Look what Daniel's bought Harry.
L Daniel!
D Well, you have to get them when they're young. Otherwise he might end up supporting Manchester City!
R Oh, I give up!
L Anyway, are you coming next door to help me with the washing machine? It still doesn't work.
D I'd love to, but the second half is just about to start.
R Come on. Let's leave the boys in peace.
L Yeah, it's hard having three children to look after, isn't it?

CD1 ▶ 41

1 /ɔː/ en**or**mous, sn**or**ing, g**or**geous, b**or**ing, unf**or**tunately, unif**or**m
2 /ə/ c**or**rect, inf**or**mation, g**or**illa, mot**or**bike, mirr**or**
3 /ɜː/ w**or**st, w**or**th, homew**or**k

CD1 ▶ 42

TIM OK, let's start with the first place we saw. What did you think of the terraced house in Bishopston?
JO Yeah, I thought it was nice. It seemed slightly bigger than where we live now.
T No, I think it's the same size as our house. It just seemed bigger because it didn't have any furniture in it.
J Yes, you're probably right. I thought the back garden was lovely, and it had a new kitchen.
T Yes, I liked the kitchen too. And it's the least expensive place we've seen so far.
J Yes, that's true.
T Mm. OK, so what about the detached house in Redland?
J Well, it's one of the oldest houses we've looked at, and I like old houses, they've got a lot of character. It's got more space than the other two places.
T Yeah, and it's got a garage, which is useful. But it's quite a long way from the station, which might be a problem.
J Yes, you could be right. And it's a little further away from the city centre than we wanted to be.
T Mm. OK. And what did you think of the flat in Hotwells?
J Well, it's not as big as the other two places.
T Yes, that's true. But it is a flat, not a house. Actually, it was a lot more spacious than I'd expected.
J Yes, it was, wasn't it? I think that's because of those enormous windows.
T Yes, I suppose so. It was different from anything else we've seen.
J And it had the most amazing view. You know, all the way down the river.
T Yes, that was fantastic, wasn't it?
J But it's got the worst kitchen I've ever seen. The cupboards were falling off the wall! And it hasn't got a garden.
T So that's a no, then.
J Yes, I think so. It's just not right for us.
T OK. So what about the other two places? Do you want to go and see either of them again?
J Well, the house in Redland was nice, but the back garden was far smaller than I'd expected, you know, for a detached house. It's as small as the one we've got now.
T And it was much noisier than the other two. It's on a very busy road.
J Yes, that's true.
T That might be a problem, especially at night.
J Right. So you thought the first place we saw was better?

T You mean the house in Bishopston? Yes, I think so. It's very similar to where we live now, so all our furniture will fit in OK.
J And it's a bit less expensive than the Redland house.
T OK, let's go back and see it again tomorrow. Then we can decide.
J Right. I'll give the estate agent a ring. Have you got their number?

CD1 43

It seemed slightly bigger than /ðən/ where we live now. | It's not as /əz/ big as /əz/ the other two places. | It was /wəz/ a lot more spacious than /ðən/ I'd expected. | It's very similar to /tə/ where we live now. | It's the same size as /əz/ our house. | The back garden was /wəz/ far smaller than /ðən/ I'd expected. | It was /wəz/ different from /frəm/ anything else we've seen. | It was /wəz/ much noisier than /ðən/ the other two. | It's as /əz/ small as /əz/ the one we've got now.

CD1 44

TIM Right, what's next?
JO What about this old laptop?
T Actually, I'm going to give it to my brother. He says it'll be fine for his kids to use. He's picking it up tomorrow evening after work.
J Yeah, OK.
T So that goes in …
J … the 'give away' pile, with the books.
T And what about that old printer?
J Oh, I think we should throw that out. It doesn't work any more so we can't really give it away.
T Right. So which pile?
J Put it next to that old TV and the videos.
T And what about these old letters? I don't know why you've kept them. You'll never read them again.
J Hmm … Yes, you're probably right. OK, I'll throw those away.
T Right.
J And what shall we do with all these old photos?
T Oh, I'm in the middle of going through those.
J But we never look at them any more.
T I know, but that's because they're not in order or anything. I'm going to sort out the rest of them at the weekend. Then we can get rid of the ones we don't want.
J OK, so we're keeping these for now.
T Yes. So … that pile.
J Yes, the one with the suitcase and the lamp. And can we throw out your old CDs?
T Sorry, I don't really want to get rid of those.

J But you'll never listen to them again. You only listen to music on your MP3 player these days.
T Yeah, but I want to copy the CDs onto the laptop. Then I can get rid of them.
J Fine, put them in the 'keep' pile. You really don't like throwing things away, do you?
T That's not true. I'm definitely going to get rid of this awful jumper. It's really ugly.
J Er, that was a birthday present from my mother.
T Oh, was it? Er, OK. I should probably keep it, then.
J Not if you're not going to wear it.
T OK, I'll put it in the 'give away' pile. We can take it to a charity shop.
J And what about your old tennis racket? You've got to throw that out.
T Actually, I'm going to give that to Julia next door. She's going to start taking tennis lessons.
J You're joking! That old thing? It's twenty years old! It's going to break the first time she uses it.
T Oh, it's fine for a nine-year-old.
J Right, what's next? What about these curtains?

CD1 45 CD1 46

1 I'm going to sort out the living room tomorrow.
2 It's going to rain in a few minutes.
3 I'll put away all the stuff we want to keep.
4 I think he'll become famous one day.
5 We're having some friends round for dinner on Saturday.

CD1 47

ANSWERS 1 he'll use 2 I'll throw 3 He's coming 4 I'll put 5 I'm going to start 6 it'll look 7 we're meeting 8 I'll finish

TIM Ok. See you later. Bye.
JO Bye, darling. Right, now he's gone I can start doing this properly. Let's throw out those smelly old trainers, for a start. And that broken tennis racket. Oh, and I'm definitely keeping all my old love letters!

CD1 48

ASHLEY My birthday's on um January 1st, you know, New Year's Day. So it's … I mean, it's always a bit strange because people kind of forget about my birthday. It's kind of like – Happy New Year! – oh, and er by the way, happy birthday, Ashley! The best … er my most memorable birthday was in 2000, you know, the beginning of the new millennium. We all … er me and some friends went to London to watch the fireworks by the river. Apparently there were like three million people there that evening! The atmosphere was absolutely brilliant and it sort of felt as if three million people had all come to my birthday party!

JEAN Well er my most memorable birthday was last year because I was … um I was a hundred years old! You see, my husband died um 13 years ago, but er you know life goes on, doesn't it? And it was … um I had a really lovely day. My two daughters organised a party for me and um I didn't have to do a thing. All my family were there, you see, including my four grandchildren and my um seven great-grandchildren. There weren't … they didn't put 100 candles on the cake, though, it wasn't big enough for that! And er I got lots of lovely birthday cards, including um one from the Queen with a special birthday message inside, which was wonderful.

RUBY I'm er … I'm a twin, you see, and so every birthday is my sister Daisy's birthday too. I never … um I didn't enjoy birthdays very much when I was a kid because you know I always had to like share them with my sister. And we … um we only had one cake between the two of us! After we grew up Daisy moved to Ireland so we like stopped having birthday parties together. And I really missed her – I mean, it just wasn't the same. Anyway, last year it was our 30th so Daisy and I had an old-fashioned birthday party at our parents' house, you know, with balloons and er party games and um ice cream and stuff. And it … um it was the best birthday party I've ever had! And er we both had our own birthday cakes with our names on, which was fantastic!

STUART Well, I don't like … er I hate getting older, so I just sort of pretend that it's a normal day. People send me … um I still get a lot of birthday cards, which is kind of annoying. But the best … er my most memorable birthday must be my 40th when my brother organised a surprise party for me. I mean, it was nice of him, I suppose, but um I wasn't very happy about it at the time. He had … um he'd invited some of his friends along, including um a woman called Patricia, who I thought was you know absolutely gorgeous. Anyway, to cut a long story short, Patricia and I spent the whole evening talking and um we started going out together soon afterwards. So er birthdays can be good sometimes, I suppose!

VIDEO 5 CD2 1

KATHARINA Excuse me?
LISA Can I help you?
K Er, yes, I hope so.
L What do you need?
K Um, I'm sorry, I've forgotten what it's called. It's a thing for making soup.
L Is this what you're looking for? A saucepan?

K No, it's a type of machine. It's … er you put food and water in, then er you turn it on and it cuts up the food.
L Do you mean a blender?
K Oh yes, that's right. A blender.
L OK, the blenders are over there, on the top shelf.
K Oh, OK, OK, thanks a lot.
L Is there anything else you need?
K Um, yes, er I don't know what it's called in English. Um, it's stuff for getting marks off your clothes.
L Do you mean washing powder?
K No, it's a type of liquid. Um, you use it when you get coffee or wine on your shirt.
L Oh, you mean stain remover. That's on the second floor, in the Home Laundry department.
K Thanks very much. What's it called again?
L Stain remover.
K Thank you for your help. Goodbye.
L Goodbye.
LISA Hello again. Did you find what you were looking for?
KATHARINA Oh, yes, thanks. But I'm still looking for one or two other things.
L Well, can I help at all? What is it that you need?
K I … I can't remember what they're called, but you use them to mend your clothes. Um, they're made of metal and they've got a hole in the end.
L Oh, you mean needles.
K Yes, that's right, needles.
L They're over there, near the escalator. You'll find all sorts of different types of cotton there too.
K Oh yes, I can see them. Thanks a lot.
L Can I help you with anything else?
K Um, yes, just one more thing. Um … I'm sorry, I don't know the word for them. Er, you wear them when it's cold outside.
L Do you mean gloves, you know, you wear them on your hands?
K No, you wear them on your ears. They look like headphones.
L Oh, you mean ear muffs. They're on the ground floor, in the accessories department.
K Right. Um, what are they called again?
L Ear muffs.
K OK, well, thank you very much for all your help.
L No problem. Have a nice day.
K You too.

CD2 4

1 /dʒ/ **j**ourney, ve**g**etable, **J**uly, dan**g**erous
2 /j/ **y**our, **y**ear, **y**et, on**i**ons
3 /juː/ **u**sually, h**u**ge, barbec**ue**, m**u**sic

CD2 5

ADAM Hello?
LILY Hi, Adam.
A Hi, Lily. How are things?
L Oh, um not too bad, I suppose. But now the kids are at school, I've been wondering what to do with my time. I get bored being at home all day on my own.
A So, er what choices do you have?
L Well, I could go back to teaching, but I'm thinking of doing another degree instead.
A Really? Wow!
L Well, if I start teaching again, I'll be exhausted after a year. And I don't know if I want to work in a school all day and then look after three children when I get home.
A What will you study if you do another degree?
L I'd like to do fashion design. You know I've always been interested in that kind of thing. I've talked to a few colleges and I don't think it'll be a problem getting in.
A Well, that's good. But you might not get in this year if you don't apply soon. It's already June.
L Yes, I know.
A What does Jack think?
L Well, he's worried about the money side of things. You know how expensive university fees are nowadays. But unless I do it soon, I'll be too old.
A Well, have you asked Mum and Dad? They might lend you some money.
L Yes, that's a good idea. I'll ask them before they go on holiday.
A Anyway, I don't think you should worry about the money. I think you should do what will make you happy.
L Yes, you're probably right. As soon as I make up my mind, I'll let you know. So, how are things with you?
A Yeah, good thanks. Actually, I've just been offered a new job.
L Really? Where?
A Beijing.
L Really? Wow, that's fantastic news! What's the job?
A The same as I'm doing now, sales manager. They want me to set up a new sales team there.
L So, are you going to take it?
A I don't know. I'm not sure I want to live on the other side of the world.
L Oh, I'm sure you'll enjoy it when you get there.
A Maybe. I've got a meeting with my boss on Monday about it. I'll make a decision after I talk to him.
L Well, I think you should take the job. You might never get this kind of opportunity again.
A But I can't speak a word of Chinese.
L Well, why don't you do an intensive course before you go? I'm sure the company would pay for it.
A Yes, that's not a bad idea.
L Have you talked to Mum and Dad about this?
A Er, no, not yet.
L Well, don't worry. I won't say anything until you decide what to do. I know they'll want you to go, though.
A Yes, probably. Anyway, I'll call you when I know what I'm doing. So, how's Billy getting on at his new school?

CD2 6

I'll be exhausted after a year. → If I start teaching again, I'll be exhausted after a year. | if you do another degree → What will you study if you do another degree? | if you don't apply soon → You might not get in this year if you don't apply soon. | I'll be too old → But unless I do it soon, I'll be too old. | I'll let you know → As soon as I make up my mind, I'll let you know. | until you decide what to do → I won't say anything until you decide what to do.

CD2 7

you want them to be happy and successful → If you have children, you want them to be happy and successful. | they don't develop in other ways → If children study all the time, they don't develop in other ways. | they shouldn't put too much pressure on them → If parents want their children to be happy, they shouldn't put too much pressure on them. | praise the effort they make → If you want to help your children, praise the effort they make. | they can feel like they're failures → If you criticise children for not getting good grades, they can feel like they're failures.

CD2 9

1 If my children work hard, they get good grades.
2 If you fail the exam, you have to take it again.
3 I'll text you if there's a problem.
4 We'll call you if we don't get there on time.
5 If she doesn't call me, I worry.
6 If I see him, I'll say hello.

CD2 10

EDWARD Charlotte, are you very superstitious?
CHARLOTTE No, not really. Why do you ask?
E I'm reading a fascinating book called *The History of Superstitions*. Did you know that in Britain, people think that seeing a black cat is good luck, but in nearly every other country in the world it's bad luck?

C That's quite strange, isn't it?
E Yes, I thought so too. And do you know why breaking a mirror is seven years' bad luck?
C No, why?
E Well um the Romans believed that life started again every seven years. If a mirror broke, then people thought the last person who looked at it was very ill and would continue to be ill for the next seven years of their life – you know, until they got a 'new life'.
C OK then – my uncle always carries a rabbit's foot around with him. Why would a rabbit's foot be lucky?
E Hang on, lucky charms are here somewhere – yes, here it is – er, rabbits were believed to help families grow their crops because they lived in the fields and had lots of babies. So they became a sign of fertility and good luck.
C Hmm. Not so lucky for the rabbit, though.
E Yeah, true. So, what superstitions do you believe in?
C Well, let me think … Oh, I touch wood – but everyone does that, don't they?
E Ah, that's an interesting one. According to this book, thousands of years ago, people used to believe that good spirits lived in the trees and that touching wood called on these spirits and protected people from danger.
C That's interesting. I also do that thing with salt, you know, throw it over my shoulder. I've no idea why, though.
E Ah, that's in here too … Yes, here it is. Apparently hundreds of years ago salt used to be very expensive and valuable, and was mainly used as a medicine, so spilling it was a really bad thing to do. You throw it over your left shoulder – or the right one if you live in Argentina or Italy – into the faces of the evil spirits behind you, to stop them hurting you.
C Hmm, sounds like an interesting book.
E Yes, it is. You can borrow it when I've finished, if you like.
C Yes, please. Thanks a lot.

VIDEO 6 CD2 11

IAN Right, are we ready to start? OK, as you know, we're planning to hold a festival in the summer to celebrate the 200th anniversary of our village. Now, we've never done anything like this before, so I'm happy to hear everyone's opinions and suggestions.
REBECCA Perhaps the first thing to discuss is what sort of entertainment we want.
LISA Yes, that seems a good place to start.
DUNCAN May I make a suggestion?
I Yes, of course, Duncan.
D How about having some live music? We could put up a stage on the village green for the weekend.

L Yes, that sounds like a good idea. Who shall we get to play?
R We could hire some professional musicians.
I I'm not sure about that. For one thing, they could be quite expensive.
D What about charging people five pounds each to get into the festival? That would raise quite a lot of money.
R Sorry, I don't think we should do that. I think the festival should be free for everyone.
L Yes, I agree. A lot of people won't come if they have to pay.
D Well, we could ask bands to play for free. There are lots of local bands who'd love to play at a festival, I'm sure.
R Yes, we could put an ad in the local paper and on the website.
I Well, it's definitely worth a try. But we'll still need to raise some money to pay for the stage and the lights, that sort of thing.
L I've got an idea! Let's have a festival raffle and ask people to buy raffle tickets when they come in. Then we can use the money we make to pay for the festival.
D Yes, that's not a bad idea.
R Can I make a point here?
I Of course.
R If we have a raffle, we'll need to buy prizes. So we might not make enough money to pay for the festival.
D Well, why don't we ask local businesses to donate the prizes for free? It would be good advertising for them.
I Yes, that could work. OK, what else could we do?
L Have you thought of asking the school to put on a musical in the daytime?
R That's a brilliant idea! Parents would love that.
I OK. I'll talk to the head teacher this week. And what about food and drink?
D Why don't we make all the food ourselves?
L I'm not sure that's a good idea. I think people in the village will want to enjoy the festival, not make sandwiches all day.
I Well, we can just have stalls selling burgers, chips, sandwiches and stuff – every festival has those.
D Er, can I just say something here?
I Sure, go ahead.
D As it's a village festival, I think we need to involve the people who live in the village in the festival a bit more.
I OK. So how can we do that?
D I suggest we have some competitions, you know, the best cake, the biggest vegetables, the most beautiful pet, that kind of thing. People always love those.
I Yes, that's a great idea! OK, let's just go over what we've got so far.

CD2 14

1 /eɪt/ decor**ate**, don**ate**, cre**ate**, medit**ate**, appreci**ate**, gradu**ate** (verb), separ**ate** (verb)

2 /ət/ consider**ate**, immedi**ate**, clim**ate**, pir**ate**, chocol**ate**, gradu**ate** (noun), separ**ate** (adjective)

CD2 15

Listening Test (see Teacher's Book)

CD2 16

I didn't have a clue how to /tə/ sing opera. | She's very good at /ət/ encouraging people. | I found it impossible to /tə/ breathe and /ən/ sing at /ət/ the same time. | I was /wəz/ useless at /ət/ learning languages at /ət/ school. | I was /wəz/ able to /tə/ give a good performance. | I had no idea how to /tə/ do any magic tricks. | He knows how to /tə/ do some really amazing tricks. | I found some of /əv/ the tricks quite easy to /tə/ learn. | I'm no good at /ət/ doing card tricks. | I managed to /tə/ do all the tricks without messing them up.

CD2 17

JUDY I run a company that makes personalised gifts. Basically people send us their photos online and we put them on posters, T-shirts, calendars, mouse mats, that kind of thing. All of our customers order online. If the internet didn't exist, I wouldn't have a business. The most important part of the company is our website because that's how everyone places their order. We'd lose a lot of customers if our website crashed. It's a very cheap business to run, but one thing I don't like about it is that I never talk to customers any more, it's all just online order forms and emails. I'd like to talk to a real customer again, you know, face-to-face.

WESLEY I've owned this café for 12 years and I'd say that the internet is essential for my business. There's an art college across the road and the students come in here all the time, you know, just to have a coffee and check their email or whatever. If we didn't have WiFi, this place would be empty. They don't even need a password to log on. But it does mean people talk less than they used to. Sometimes I look round and nobody's talking to each other, they're all online in their own little worlds. If they turned off their computers, they might make some new friends. But it also means they stay longer and spend more money, so I can't complain, I suppose.

FRANK I'm the sales manager for a sports equipment company and like most people I couldn't live without the internet – or my laptop. I've got all my personal stuff on there and a lot of information about the company too. If I lost my laptop, I'd probably lose my job! One thing that's changed because of the internet is that a lot of my meetings are online nowadays. In some ways they're great, because they save a lot of time. But of course this means I hardly ever travel for work any more. I used to enjoy visiting other parts of the world and staying in nice hotels. If we didn't have so many online meetings, I could get out of the office more often.

CD2 18

I'd probably lose my job → If I lost my laptop, I'd probably lose my job! | I wouldn't have a business → If the internet didn't exist, I wouldn't have a business. | this place would be empty → If we didn't have WiFi, this place would be empty. | if our website crashed → We'd lose a lot of customers if our website crashed. | they might make some new friends → If they turned off their computers, they might make some new friends. | I could get out of the office more often → If we didn't have so many online meetings, I could get out of the office more often.

CD2 20

1 If I have enough money, I'll buy a new laptop. If I had enough money, I'd buy a new laptop.
2 If you opened that attachment, it'd crash your computer. If you open that attachment, it'll crash your computer.
3 I'd give you a lift if I had time. I'll give you a lift if I have time.
4 You'll see them if you get there early. You'd see them if you got there early.
5 If they study harder, they'll pass their exams. If they studied harder, they'd pass their exams.
6 If we moved house, we'd miss our friends. If we move house, we'll miss our friends.

CD2 21

ANSWERS   1 I'd 2 didn't 3 was 4 could 5 don't 6 I'll 7 misses 8 I'll 9 wouldn't 10 knew 11 give 12 I'll

CD2 22

[words in pink = weak forms]
GARY Here are your drinks. We were lucky to get a table, weren't we?
JENNY Yes, it's always quite busy in here after work.
SIMON Cheers.
G&J Cheers.
G So how was the meeting?
J Oh, it was quite boring, actually. Marcus went on about sales figures and cutting costs and stuff like that.
G Right. Did you go to the meeting, Simon? Simon?
J Oh, don't worry about him, he's probably updating his Facebook page. Saying something fascinating like 'in pub with people from work' or whatever.
S Just because I'm online, it doesn't mean I can't hear you.
G I can see why they don't allow people to go on Facebook in the office.
J Yeah, what did Marcus call it? 'Social not-working.'
G So how often do you go on Facebook, Simon?
S Oh, I don't know. About ten or fifteen times a day, probably.
G Really?
S Yeah. All of my friends are on it and I like to know what's happening to them.
G Are you on Facebook, Jenny?
J Yes, but I don't check it very often any more. I used to do it all the time – it's very addictive. But I was spending hours and hours on it and it wasn't as much fun as it used to be. And in the end, you're still just sitting on your own in front of a computer screen.
G Yeah, I see what you mean.
J Actually, I thought it was damaging my friendships. I always knew what my friends were doing, so I never phoned them up for a chat or arranged to meet up with them. There didn't seem to be a reason to. Now I only check it once a week and try to meet up with friends face-to-face more often.
S So how many friends do you have?
J Do you mean real friends or Facebook friends?
S Er, Facebook friends.
J Oh, I don't know. About a hundred, I think.
S Is that all? I've got … um, let's see … seven hundred and sixty-two. And even my sister's rabbit's got over two hundred friends.
G Which means your sister's rabbit is twice as popular as Jenny.
S Exactly. Computers never lie.
J Very funny.
S What about you, Gary? Are you on Facebook?
G No, I'm not, but I'm on Twitter.
J Oh, right. Do you tweet a lot?
G No, but I like reading tweets from film stars and footballers and people like that.
S And what about YouTube?
J Yeah, I love YouTube. I can spend hours watching videos of baby animals.
S Yeah, women love that sort of thing. My favourite YouTube videos are the ones of people having hilarious accidents.
G Well, my wife posts videos of the children so our relatives can watch them.
S Yeah, that's the wonderful thing about the internet. You can use it to share videos of your kids …
J … or to tell your Facebook friends it's your turn to buy the drinks?
S What? Oh, yeah, OK then. Same again?

VIDEO 7 CD2 25

Conversation 1
CHARLIE Hello, Tanya. Have you got a minute?
TANYA Hello, Charlie. Yes, of course. Take a seat.
C Thanks.
T Right. How can I help?
C I just wanted to talk about next week's meeting with Sunspot Hotels. As you know, they're very important clients and we need everything to go perfectly.
T Yes, absolutely. Right. Jack and Melissa Johnson from Sunspot are flying over from the States on Monday.
C Can you tell me when they're arriving?
T They're arriving in London from New York at … let's see … 15.23.
C Good. Do you know whether we've booked them a hotel room?
T Yes, we have. Jenny's booked them into the Holiday Inn near the airport.
C Fine. And the meeting's on Tuesday morning, is that correct?
T Yes, it is.
C Could you tell me what time it starts?
T It starts at 10 and should finish about 12.30. Then you and I are taking them for lunch at the Rose and Crown. You know, that lovely old pub by the river.
C That's a good choice. And what about all the other people attending the meeting?
T Jenny emailed everyone about it last week.
C I think it's important that Barry Mackenzie should be there. He knows more about the American market than anyone else. Have you any idea if he's been invited?
T Er, I'm not sure.
C Well, perhaps you could check.
T Yes, I will.
C Do you think we should email everyone again? You know, just to remind everyone.
T OK, I'll do that myself this afternoon.
C Great. OK, perhaps we should talk about our presentation. Do you want to talk about the new products, or shall I?

Conversation 2
CHARLIE Hi, darling, I'm home.
REBECCA Hello. Good day at work?
C Yes, not bad, thanks. Mm, that smells good.
R Don't get excited. It's for Harry, not for you. You haven't forgotten about his first birthday party on Saturday, have you?

165

C   No, of course not. What time does it start?
R   At 3 o'clock, but some people have said they'll be a bit late.
C   Right. Are your parents coming?
R   Yes, of course they are. They wouldn't miss their grandson's first birthday!
C   When are they arriving?
R   On Friday. It's a long way to come and they wanted to make a weekend of it.
C   Right. They're not staying here, are they?
R   No, we thought it would be easier if they didn't.
C   Have we booked them a hotel room?
R   Yes, I did it this afternoon.
C   OK. So, how many people are coming?
R   Er, I'm not sure yet. Some people haven't replied.
C   Should we email everyone again?
R   Yeah, good idea.
C   What about your uncle Bob?
R   What about him?
C   Has he been invited?
R   Of course. I know you don't get on with him, but he's family. Just try not to get into an argument with him this time.
C   I will. Perhaps you can ask him not to break my TV this time too.
R   That was an accident. Anyway, come and see what I've got Harry for his birthday.

CD2 26

1   Could you tell me what time it starts? (a)
2   Have you any idea if he's been invited? (b)
3   Can you tell me when they're arriving? (a)
4   Do you know whether we've booked them a hotel room? (b)
5   Do you think we should email everyone again? (b)

CD2 29

[words in pink = weak forms]

ANN   Hi, Tom. What are you doing at the moment?
TOM   I'm trying to download an attachment, but my laptop keeps crashing. Do you think it's got a virus?
A   Maybe. Perhaps the software's a bit out of date. When did you last update it?
T   I can't remember. And it slows down every time I try to send an email.
A   I think it's time to get yourself a new computer.
T   I was thinking exactly the same thing!

CD2 30

Tsunamis are /ə/ caused by earthquakes under the ocean. | They can /kən/ also be caused by a landslide or a volcano erupting. | About a quarter of /əv/ a million people were /wə/ killed. | Droughts often happen because all the trees have /əv/ been /bɪn/ cut down. | A lot of /əv/ towns and /ən/ cities on the coast will be flooded. | It's possible to /tə/ predict which places are /ə/ going to /tə/ be hit by an earthquake. | This increase in temperature is being caused by man-made climate change.

CD2 31

VAL   Hi, James.
JAMES   Hello, Val. Hi, Pete. Come in.
PETE   Hi.
V   Are you ready to go?
J   Er, not quite. Do you want a coffee? I've just put the kettle on.
V   Yes, sure. You get ready, we'll make it.
J   OK. Oh, there's a bit of pasta left if you're hungry.
V   Er, no thanks, we've just eaten. Well, I've found some coffee, but there's no sugar.
P   There's some in that jar by the toaster.
V   Oh yes.
P   Hm. There's enough milk for two cups, but not enough for three, I don't think.
V   It's OK, I'll have it black.
J   And can someone feed the cat? There are plenty of tins of cat food in the cupboard. He has one small tin.
V   Sure. Here you go, kitty. James, where do you put your recycling?
J   Er, in the bin.
V   What, the rubbish bin?
J   Yes, that green one over there.
V   You should recycle things like tin cans. Too much rubbish is just thrown away when a lot of it could be made into something useful.
J   Yeah, you're probably right. I never recycle anything, I'm sorry to say.
P   Well, you're not the only one. Hardly any people in our building recycle stuff. Did you know that Germany recycles over 70% of its rubbish, but in the UK it's still only about 40%?
J   Hm, that's not much, is it?
V   No, it isn't. And there aren't enough places to recycle in this city. And did you know that on average, every person in the UK throws away seven times their own body weight in rubbish every year?
J   Really? Wow!
V   Well, it's never too late to start. There's a lot of stuff in your bin that could be recycled. Look, there's loads of paper and several plastic bottles. The bottles can be made into clothes and the paper is used to make toilet paper. And all these empty cat food tins can be recycled and the metal used for making fridge parts.
J   You seem to know a lot about all this.
P   Well, there's plenty of information on the internet. But it takes time to change people's habits. People are naturally lazy, I think.
V   Yes, too many people just don't make the effort. But the government should do more too. In Germany people have to recycle their rubbish – it's the law. They should do that here too, I think.
J   Yes, I suppose you're right. I've got a few friends who recycle things like you do, but most people I know just throw everything away. But in future I'll recycle what I can.
P   Come on, we're late.
J   Let me get my coat. Won't be a second.
V   We made a little progress there, I think.
P   Yes, I think so. But I think he should recycle that coat. It looks like his cat sleeps on it!

CD2 32   **CD2 33**

1   I think there's a bit of milk in the fridge.
2   We haven't got enough bags of crisps.
3   There's hardly /j/ any food in the cupboard.
4   He's got a lot of tins of cat food.
5   We need to get a few packets of biscuits.
6   There's lots of coffee /j/ and plenty /j/ of cups.

CD2 34

BEVERLY   A British tourist has been attacked by /j/ a shark off the coast of Texas, making it the /j/ eighth shark attack in America this year. We now go /w/ over live to /w/ Andrew /w/ Evans for /r/ a special report. Andrew, I /j/ understand that the man didn't do /w/ anything unusual to cause this attack.
ANDREW   Yes, that's right, Beverly. Mark Skipper, a 49-year /r/ old man from Oxford, was just swimming on his own quite close to the beach when he was attacked.
B   How badly was he hurt?
A   Well, we don't have much information yet, but we know that his leg was bitten quite badly. He was immediately taken to hospital and we're waiting to hear how he's doing.
B   So /w/ Andrew, why /j/ are the sharks coming in so close?
A   Well, Ryan Williamson, who works for the Texas Parks and Wildlife Department, believes that the /j/ increase in shark attacks is because of what they call dead zones. These are /r/ areas in the /j/ ocean where there /r/ isn't enough oxygen, so /w/ all the fish die.
B   So there /r/ aren't any fish for the sharks to /w/ eat.
A   Exactly. Many /j/ of these dead zones are /r/ actually quite close to the coast, so the sharks come in closer /r/ and closer looking for food.

B So what turns_an_area_/t/_of the_/j/_ocean_into_/w/_a dead zone?
A I'm_afraid_it's_us, Beverly, people. There's too much pollution_in the sea_/j/_and_it's killing_all the fish. And these dead zones cover fairly large_areas – the one we're talking_about here, for_/r/_example, covers_about 5,800 square miles.
B And_are these dead zones_only_/j/_around the US coast?
A No, they're not. According to the United Nations, there_/r/_are_/r/_over four hundred dead zones_around the world – that's nearly three times_as many_/j/_as there were five years ago.
B So_/w/_is the wildlife department_in Texas now saying that people shouldn't go swimming?
A No, they_/j/_aren't telling people to stay_/j/_out of the water, but they've_advised holidaymakers not to go swimming early_/j/_in the morning or_/r/_in the_/j/_evening, because those_are the times when sharks feed.
B Thank you, Andrew_/w/_Evans, for that report.

VIDEO 8 CD2 35

REBECCA So, how can I help?
LISA Well, Daniel's asked me to go on a hiking holiday in the Lake District with him.
R Oh, right. That sounds fun.
L Er, yes, maybe. Anyway, he wanted me to look at his old tent to see if it's still OK.
R Well, I wouldn't like to be on top of a mountain in that. If I were you, I'd buy a new tent.
L Yes, maybe you're right. You and Charlie have been hiking a few times, haven't you?
R Yes, we used to go quite a lot before Harry was born.
L Well, could you give me some advice? I've never been hiking before and I'm a bit nervous about it.
R Yes, of course. Well, firstly, make sure you take plenty of warm clothes. It can get really cold at night in a tent.
L OK.
R And it's a good idea to take some waterproof clothing in case it rains. Which it probably will – this is England, after all.
L Yes, Daniel's going to lend me his waterproof jacket. And I've already got a rucksack, a camping stove and a warm sleeping bag.
R Great! And make sure you wear comfortable walking boots. Don't wear new boots or else you'll get blisters on your feet.
L Yes, I've got some old boots that are very comfortable.

R OK, that's good.
L And what about food? What should we take?
R Well, dried food and pasta is good because it isn't very heavy to carry. You can camp by a river and use the water to cook with.
L OK. That's really useful, thanks. What else do you think we should take with us?
R Well, you'd better take a torch in case you have to walk in the dark. And you'll need it when you're camping too, of course. And take some spare batteries for your torch and your camera.
L That's a good idea. I hadn't thought of that.
R And don't forget to take a map. It's easy to get lost in the mountains, particularly in bad weather.
L Right. And what should we do if we get lost?
R Well, you can try to use the GPS on your phone, but you can't always get reception, so it's worth taking a compass, just in case. And whatever you do, don't lose sight of each other. If the weather is bad, you and Daniel must stay together at all times.
L Right, thanks. That's really helpful.
R Oh, and be careful when you're crossing rivers. They can be more dangerous than they look.
L Yes, we will. Do you think it's a good idea to tell someone where we're going?
R Yes, definitely. And when you expect to get back. Then, if you're not back on time, someone can come and look for you.
L Right. That sounds like good advice.
R Oh, and one more thing.
L What's that?
R Watch out for wolves. There are quite a few in the Lake District, and you don't want one of those coming into your tent at night.
L Wolves? Are you serious?
R No, don't worry, I'm only joking. The most dangerous thing in the mountains is always the weather.
L And Daniel's cooking, probably.
R Right, I'd better go and pick up Harry from his grandparents. See you later.
L Thanks, Rebecca. See you!
R Bye!

CD2 38

1 /ɪə/ h**ear**, n**ear**, f**ear**, b**eer**, volunt**eer**, engin**eer**, ch**eer**
2 /eə/ sc**ared**, nightm**are**, softw**are**, sp**are**, st**airs**, f**air**, h**air**
3 /ɜː/ **ear**ly, **ear**n, h**ear**d, m**ur**der, t**urn**, f**ur**ther, b**ur**glar

CD2 39

ANSWERS 1 A surgeon 2 An operating theatre 3 Asthma 4 A specialist 5 The A&E department 6 An allergy

CD2 40

MOIRA DIXON Hello, I'm Moira Dixon, and here are today's main news stories. World leaders have met to discuss the global economy at the World Trade Summit in Hamburg. EU Finance Ministers have asked for more help from the World Bank for countries that are having problems paying off their debts. Outside the conference hall, thousands of people have taken part in a demonstration to protest against the World Bank's economic policies. The demonstration began peacefully, but soon turned violent as protesters tried to enter the conference hall and were stopped by police. At least forty people have been arrested and six police officers have been taken to hospital.
A new report on the environment has just been published. The report shows that the UK has failed to meet its targets to reduce CO_2 emissions. However, environment minister Jack Clarke told reporters that some progress has been made.
JACK CLARKE We haven't met our targets yet, that's true, but we've made good progress. The amount of CO_2 produced by the UK has already been reduced by 2.7% in the last three years, which will help reduce global warming. But we could – and we should – do better, and I'm sure that we will.
MD Over 1,500 ancient gold and silver objects have been discovered by a retired teacher in Wales. 72-year-old Gareth Jones found the treasure five days ago while he was walking around his brother-in-law's farm with a metal detector. Experts say the find, which includes coins, swords and items of jewellery, dates back to the 7th century and could be worth over £10 million. One of the UK's leading archaeologists, Professor Geoffrey Baxter, says that the government needs to act fast to make sure the treasure stays in public hands.
GEOFFREY BAXTER Some of the items still haven't been examined, but this is already the most important archaeological discovery this century. But why haven't we heard anything from the government yet? It's important that these pieces are kept for the nation and eventually put on display in the British Museum. If the government doesn't act soon, some of them might end up in private collections.

CD2 42

1. A new survey has /həz/ just been /bɪn/ published.
2. The government has /həz/ just published a new survey.
3. Three people have /həv/ been /bɪn/ taken to hospital.
4. The police have /həv/ taken three people to hospital.
5. The government hasn't met its targets yet.
6. The targets haven't been /bɪn/ met yet.
7. The pay offer has /həz/ already been /bɪn/ rejected.
8. The workers have /həv/ already rejected the pay offer.

CD2 43

ANSWERS 1 has been rejected 2 has just confirmed 3 has been called off 4 have found 5 have been discovered 6 has just arrived 7 has already sold 8 've/have just heard 9 has been taken 10 has been described

CD2 44

INTERVIEWER Welcome back. With me in the studio is Dr Miriam Richards, who's a psychologist at the University of Pennsylvania and has just published a new report on the psychology of lying.
MIRIAM Hi there.
I Now, Dr Richards, why exactly do we lie?
M Well, put simply, we lie because we want to control what other people think of us, and how we see ourselves. The main reasons we lie are to avoid arguments, to protect ourselves from harm or danger, to save face – you know, so that we don't look stupid in front of other people – and of course just to get what we want in life.
I And does everybody lie?
M Yes, I would say that everyone lies at some time or other. And anyone who says that they don't is obviously a liar!
I And how can we tell that someone is lying to us?
M Well, it's often easier to look at the person's body language than to listen to what they're saying. For example, when someone is lying, they'll often avoid eye contact. However, very good liars might make more eye contact than usual to try and make you think they're telling the truth.
I Really?
M Yes, and they often smile a lot too – but they won't be real smiles, of course.
I So how can you tell if a smile is real?
M Well, a real smile uses the muscles around the eyes, but a fake smile doesn't. So if you can't tell if someone's really smiling, then look at their eyes, not their mouth.
I Are there any other ways you can tell if someone is lying?
M Oh yes. When we tell the truth, our eyes tend to move to the right, because the left side of the brain, which stores facts, controls the right side of the body.
I I see.
M Yes, and when we're lying, the right side of the brain, which controls imagination, makes the eyes go left.
I Hmm, that's interesting.
M Yes, and people tend to look up when they're telling the truth, because they're getting information from their brain. If they start lying, they'll look down or straight ahead. When they go back to telling the truth, their eyes will go up again.
I I've also been told that people put their hands over their mouths when they're lying. Is that true?
M Yes, it is. People also touch their noses a lot when they're lying, because that covers the mouth too.
I That's fascinating. And what about white lies?
M Well, of course most people tell white lies when they don't want to hurt people's feelings, for example, er, saying a meal was delicious when it was awful. But some people can also train themselves to become expert liars, like, er, politicians, for example.
I Dr Richards, thanks for coming in to talk to us today.
M My pleasure. And I really mean that!

CD2 46

1. My aunt is 40 today. (1st British)
2. I saw a girl walking across the park. (1st American)
3. Why can't you ask your mother? (1st American)
4. My brother's got a lot of cars. (1st British)
5. The water isn't very hot. (1st British)
6. This party's better than I thought. (1st American)

CD2 47

ANSWERS 2 feeling 3 allergic 4 eaten 5 back 6 taking 7 symptoms 8 look 9 temperature 10 prescription

VIDEO 9 CD2 48

Conversation 1
DOCTOR Hello, Mr Philips. Take a seat.
MR PHILIPS Thank you.
DR Now what seems to be the problem?
MR P I'm not feeling very well. I've got a terrible stomach ache and I keep throwing up.
DR Have you had any diarrhoea?
MR P No, I haven't.
DR How long have you been feeling like this?
MR P Since um late last night.
DR Do you know if you're allergic to anything?
MR P No, not that I know of.
DR What have you eaten recently?
MR P Well, my two children cooked dinner for my wife and me last night. It was our wedding anniversary, you see, and they wanted to surprise us.
DR That was a nice thought. What did you have?
MR P Well, I'm not sure what it was, actually. Some sort of er seafood and pasta dish. They spent a long time cooking it, so you know I felt I had to eat it. It wasn't very nice, to be honest. My wife hardly ate any, so I ate hers too.
DR OK, I think you've got food poisoning. The best thing to do is to rest and don't eat anything for the next 24 hours. After that you can eat things like bread or rice, but no milk or cheese.
MR P Right.
DR And drink lots of water, or black tea with a little sugar in.
MR P OK. Do I need to make another appointment?
DR No, I'm sure you'll be fine, but come back if you're not feeling better in two days.
MR P Thanks a lot.
DR And maybe tell your children that you want to go to a restaurant next year.
MR P Yes, I will. Goodbye.
DR Goodbye.

Conversation 2
DOCTOR Hello, Mr Green. Please sit down.
MR GREEN Thanks. Achooo!
DR What seems to be the problem?
MR G Well, I haven't been feeling very well recently. My chest hurts and I keep getting really bad headaches.
DR Have you been taking anything for them?
MR G Yes, paracetamol, but er it didn't really help much.
DR Have you got any other symptoms?
MR G Yes, I can't stop sneezing. Achooo!
DR Yes, I can see that. And how long have you been feeling like this?
MR G Oh, let me see, it's three days now.
DR Right, let me have a look at you. Say "aaaah".
MR G Aaaah …
DR That's fine, thanks. I'm just going to take your temperature. … Yes, you've got a bit of a temperature, but nothing serious. I think you've got a virus. You need to stay in bed and rest for two or three days.
MR G Do I need a … a …
DR A what?
MR G ACHOOO!
DR Bless you!
MR G Thanks. Do I need some antibiotics? I'm allergic to penicillin, by the way.

DR   No, antibiotics don't work with viruses, but I'm going to give you something stronger for the headaches.
MR G   Oh, right.
DR   Here's a prescription for some painkillers.
MR G   Thanks a lot. How often should I take them?
DR   Every four hours. If you're not better in three days, then come back and we'll do some blood tests.
MR G   Thank you, doctor.
DR   Not at all. Goodbye.
MR G   Bye.
DR   Right, who's the next patient? AchOOO! Oh no …

CD2 50

/ɔː/ sort, ought, bought, brought, fought, thought
/ʌ/ stuff, enough, rough, tough
/əʊ/ grow, though, although
/aʊ/ shout, drought
/uː/ too, through
/ɒ/ off, cough

CD3 1

PEGGY   Hello?
LEO   Hi, Mum.
P   Oh, hello darling. How are you?
L   I'm OK, thanks. Did you get the message I left yesterday?
P   Oh, dear, yes I did. I was supposed to call you back, wasn't I? Sorry, Leo, I was out all day. Hope it wasn't important.
L   No, it's OK. It's just that, well, Karen and I wondered if you had any special plans for your wedding anniversary this year. You know, as it's your 25th and all that.
P   Er, well, we were going to spend our anniversary in the cottage in Wales where we had our honeymoon, but it was already booked. Tom was supposed to book it months ago, but he forgot. So the short answer is no, no plans.
L   Right. Karen and I want to organise a party for you. It was going to be a surprise party, but we can't organise it without you.
P   What a lovely idea!
L   Actually, we want to invite all the people who came to your wedding so we borrowed some of your old wedding photos. But we haven't got a clue who most of them are.
P   Well, we've lost touch with most of them. 25 years is a long time.
L   What about the best man?
P   Oh, Derek Bradley. Yes, he and his wife, Brenda, were our closest friends back then. She was my bridesmaid. They moved to New York just after our wedding. We were going to visit them later that year, but we didn't go for some reason. Haven't heard from them in, oh, er 15 years or so. I've no idea how to get in touch with them.
L   Well, if you let me have all the information you've got, I'll try to get hold of as many people as I can.
P   Well, let's see. I'm still in touch with Trevor Jones and his wife, Sheila – they met at our wedding, you know. And then there's Jane Lewis. We used to share a flat together. I think I still have a phone number for her somewhere …

CD3 2

We were /wə/ going to /tə/ spend our anniversary in Wales. | It was /wəz/ going to /tə/ be a surprise party. | We were /wə/ going to /tə/ visit them later that year. | I was /wəz/ supposed to /tə/ call you back. | Your father was /wəz/ supposed to /tə/ book it months ago. | We were /wə/ supposed to /tə/ leave a message.

CD3 3

KAREN   You look lovely with your hair up, Mum. And I love that red dress.
PEGGY   Thank you, Karen. Have you seen your father?
K   Not for a while, no. Anyway, how are you feeling?
P   A bit nervous, actually. And where's Leo?
K   I'm not sure. He could be picking people up from the station.
P   Oh, right.
K   Who's that, Mum? The woman in the flowery skirt with wavy hair and glasses.
P   That's Brenda Bradley. She was my bridesmaid.
K   That's right. That can't be her real hair colour, though, can it? It looks dyed to me.
P   Yes, I think it is. She used to be fair, I think. She must be going grey.
K   And who's the woman with the blonde hair in the blue suit? Is that Jane Lewis?
P   Yes, it might be. Hang on, she's spotted us.
JANE   Peggy! Gosh, it must be, what, 15 years since I last saw you.
P   Hi, Jane. You look fantastic!
J   Thank you. You too. Um, where's Tom?
P   Good question. He must be talking to some guests in the other room. Er so, anyway, what are you doing these days?
LEO   Karen!
K   Ah, there you are. Have you seen Dad?
L   No, why?
K   Mum's looking for him.
L   Well, he must be around somewhere. He may want to be on his own for a bit. You know, it's a big thing, this party.
K   Yes, maybe. … Hey, who's that?
L   Who?
K   Him – the guy in the dark suit with curly hair and the moustache. It could be the guy that moved to New York, er, what's his name, Derek something?
L   No, that isn't Derek Bradley. He's the tall guy over there, the one in the grey suit.
K   With the beard?
L   Yeah.
K   Oh, right.
L   And that's his son, Nick, next to him, with the flowery tie and glasses.
K   Look, the man with the curly hair is coming over.
TREVOR   Hi, you must be Peggy's daughter.
K   Yes, that's right, I'm Karen. Hi. And this is my brother, Leo.
L   Nice to meet you.
T   Hi, I'm Trevor Jones. Thanks very much for inviting us, it's a wonderful party.
K   Glad you're having a good time.
T   Have you met my wife, Sheila?
K   Er, no, not yet.
T   She's over there – the one with red hair in the dark brown dress. We first met at your parents' wedding, you know …
K   Haven't you found him yet, Mum?
P   No, I haven't.
K   Maybe he's having a secret cigarette somewhere.
P   Oh, don't be silly. He can't be having a cigarette. He stopped smoking months ago. Ah, Leo, there you are. Where's your father? He should be here talking to the guests.
L   Well, he might be in the bathroom.
P   Yes, perhaps. Go and check, will you, Leo?
L   Sure, won't be a minute. … Yes, he's in there. He's practising his speech in front of the mirror. He says he'll be out in a few minutes.
P   Oh, honestly, he must know that speech by now. We spent hours going over it last night. Go and get him, will you? I'm going back to join the party.
L   Sure. I'm glad we only have to do this every 25 years!

CD3 6

PRESENTER   Today I'm talking to Wendy Robinson, whose new book, *I Do*, is a history of wedding traditions.
WENDY   Hello.
P   Wendy, first_of all, we shoul[d] star[t] with the most_obvious question. When di[d]_our ancestors star[t] getting marrie[d] to each other?
W   Oh, weddings have been aroun[d] since the beginning of civilisation, bu[t] they haven'[t] always been as peaceful as they are now. In parts of Europe aroun[d] two thousan[d] years ago, if there weren'[t]_enough single women in the village, men often went_an[d] kidnappe[d]_a woman from another village.

169

P   Really?
W   Yes, and the man always took a close frien[d] with him to help with the kidnapping, which is where the tradition of the 'bes[t] man' comes from.
P   That's interesting.
W   That's also why the bes[t] man stands nex[t] to the groom during the wedding ceremony, so he could protec[t] the bride if her family trie[d] to come an[d] take her back.
P   Well, I'm please[d] tha[t] things have move*d* on a bi[t] since then. An[d] wha*t* abou[t] wedding rings? Where di[d] they originate?
W   Tha[t] tradition was starte[d] by the Ancien*t* Egyptians. An[d] the wedding ring is always worn on the thir[d] finger of the left han[d] because the Ancien*t* Egyptians believe[d] the vein of tha[t] finger was the 'vein of love' an[d] ran directly to the heart.
P   Oh, right. An[d] wha*t* abou[t] wedding cakes?
W   Well, they've been aroun[d] since Ancien[t] Greek an[d] Roman times. The Greeks use[d] to throw small cakes a[t] the bride an[d] groom, while the Romans use[d] to break a cake over the bride's head. Both of these were symbols of fertility – you know, to help the bride have lots of children.
P   An*d* am I righ*t* in thinking that's why people throw confetti too?
W   Yes, exactly. Guests use[d] to throw wheat, rice or nuts coate*d* in sugar over the happy couple to help them have children, an*d* also to wish for a successful harvest. Now, of course, people ten[d] to throw confetti instead.
P   OK, so then the happy couple go on their honeymoon. Where di[d] tha[t] tradition originate?
W   Well, one theory says this starte*d* in Babylonia abou[t] 4,000 years ago. After the wedding the bride's father gave his new son-in-law all the mead – that's beer made from honey – the man coul[d] drink. This was drunk for the nex[t] month – an*d* as the calendar was base*d* on the moon, this perio*d* of time after the wedding became known as the honeymoon.
P   An*d* in the UK, women are traditionally allowe[d] to propose to men on the 29th February. Why is that?
W   Ah, this dates back hundreds of years, when the leap year wasn'[t] recognise[d] by law. For this reason, women believe[d] tha[t] they didn'[t] have to follow the usual traditions, so they fel[t] they coul*d* ask their men to marry them.
P   An[d] wha*t* abou*t* other traditions, such as …

VIDEO 10 CD3 8

Conversation 1
REBECCA Morning, Ella. Sleep well?
ELLA Yes, like a log. What's the time?
R   About 11.30.
E   Really? I've been asleep for nearly 12 hours!
R   Well, I'm sure it'll take a few days to recover. It's a long flight from Delhi.
E   Yeah, it took about 11 hours, and we didn't sleep at all on the plane. Mike's still fast asleep. I'm starving. Can I make myself some breakfast?
R   Yes, of course you can. Help yourself. You know where everything is.
E   Thanks. And thanks a lot for letting us stay, Rebecca. That's really kind of you.
R   No problem. Stay as long as you like, it's nice to have the company. Is there anything else you need?
E   Er, well, all our clothes are absolutely filthy from all the travelling. May I use your washing machine?
R   Actually, I was just going to put some washing in. I need some clean clothes for Harry. But you can use it later if you like.
E   Great, thanks.
R   So what are your plans?
E   Well, I need to look for a job, actually. We spent all our money on the India trip.
R   You could talk to Charlie. Apparently they need a new PA in the office.
E   Really? That's interesting. I'll talk to him about it later. It's much colder here than in Delhi. Do you mind if I borrow a jumper?
R   No, not at all. They're in the bottom drawer in our bedroom. Pick whichever one you like.
E   Great, thanks a lot. Be back in a minute.

Conversation 2
CHARLIE Oh, Mike, what's it like to be back in the UK?
MIKE Well, it's quite strange, actually. We were only in India for a month, but it feels like we were away for a year. But it's very nice to be back.
C   And when are we going to see your photos?
M   Oh er they're all still on our camera at the moment. Er, is it OK if I use your laptop to upload some photos?
C   Sorry, I left mine at work. But I'm sure Rebecca will let you use hers.
M   Thanks a lot. Then I can show them to you and Rebecca later, if you like.
C   Yeah, good idea. We could do it after dinner.
M   Oh, I have another big favour to ask you. Would you mind if I borrowed your car some time this week? My brother lives about 20 miles away and I haven't seen him for ages.
C   Sorry, it's only insured for Rebecca and myself. But we can drop you at the station whenever you like.
M   No problem, I just thought I'd ask.
C   Is there anything else you need?
M   Er, do you think I could use your landline to call my parents? I said I would phone them today and I don't have any credit left on my mobile.
C   Yes, of course. Go ahead. The phone's in the front room, by the window.
M   Thanks a lot.
C   While you do that, I'll get Rebecca's laptop so you can upload those photos.
M   Thanks.

CD3 9

ANSWERS   2 a 3 b 4 a 5 a 6 b

CD3 12

ROB Hi, Sue. What␣are you doing␣at the weekend?
SUE We're planning to go␣/w/␣away.
R   Really? Where␣are you␣/w/␣off to?
S   We're␣/r/␣off to Dublin for␣/r/␣a wedding. We have to check␣in␣at ten, so we're setting␣off␣at eight.
R   Well, this weekend␣I'm going to tidy␣/j/␣up my␣/j/␣office. I've been putting␣it␣off for␣/r/␣ages, but␣I really need to sort␣it␣out.
S   So␣/w/␣are you going to be␣/j/␣in␣all weekend?
R   Yes,␣I␣/j/␣am. Do you want me to look␣after your cat while you're␣/r/␣away?
S   That'd be great, thanks. See you␣/w/␣on Monday!

CD3 13

GABI Hello, On The Box. Can I help you?
FIONA Hello. Um, can I speak to Max Foster, please?
G   I'm afraid he's in a meeting all day. I'm his PA, Gabi. Can I take a message?
F   Er, yes, probably. My name's Fiona Robbins, and I'm er going to be in your new TV drama *Undercover*.
G   Oh yes, of course. You're going to be Kat, aren't you?
F   That's right, yes. Anyway um I'm afraid I can't come to the meeting on Monday.
G   Oh, dear. Why's that?
F   Well, um I'm in hospital. I was in a car accident and I've broken my leg.
G   Oh, how terrible!
F   Yes, I won't be able to walk on it for a month, or so they tell me.
G   Poor you! That must be awful!
F   Well, it's quite painful, yes. But I've already had one operation. It went quite well, I think.
G   Well, that's good news, at least.
F   Yes, I suppose so. And I'm having another operation on Friday. I hope it's going to be OK.

G Oh, I'm sure it is.
F Thanks. Anyway, about *Undercover*. I still want to be in the programme, of course, but I don't know what to do.
G Well, they're going to start filming soon, I think.
F Yes, I know.
G Well, um, you must talk to Max. And the sooner, the better, really. Um, can he call you tomorrow?
F Yes, please. He can call me on my mobile, which is 07700 900348.
G Er, yes, of course.
F Thanks. Look, I'm really sorry about this.
G Don't worry. I'll ask Max to call you back in the morning.
F OK.
G And get well soon!
F Thanks a lot. Bye.
G Bye.

CD3 14

GABI Hello, Max.
MAX Morning, Gabi. Any messages?
G Yes, quite a few, actually. Um, we've got a problem.
M Oh, what's that?
G Fiona Robbins called. You know, the actress who's going to be Kat in *Undercover*.
M Uh huh …
G Well, she's broken her leg.
M You're joking!
G No, really, it's true. She said that she'd been in a car accident.
M Oh no! That's the last thing we need.
G Yes, I know. But she's being looked after very well, I think. She told me that she'd already had one operation.
M Well, that's good news, I guess.
G Yes, I think so. And she said that she was having another operation on Friday.
M Did she say when she'd be able to work again?
G Not exactly. But she said she wouldn't be able to walk on it for a month.
M Oh, I don't believe it! Does she realise how serious this is?
G Yes, I think so. She sounded quite worried about it.
M Not her leg – the fact that we're going to lose our lead actress!
G Anyway, she told me she couldn't come to the meeting on Monday.
M No, obviously not. What was she thinking of?
G Well, I don't think she planned to be in a car crash.
M No, I suppose not. What else did she say?
G She said she still wanted to be in the programme.
M What, in a wheelchair? She's supposed to be an undercover cop!
G Yes, I know.
M So what did you tell her?
G I told her they were going to start filming soon.
M Good. So she knows that we have to find someone else.
G Well, er, not exactly.
M What do you mean?
G I told her that she had to talk to you. Here's her mobile number.
M Right. While I'm doing this, find someone else to play Kat. I want three people here for auditions first thing tomorrow morning.
G Sure, will do. Before you go, you had some other messages too.
M Who from?
G Well, Mr Hall said he …

CD3 16

GABI Sure, will do. Before you go, you had some other messages too.
MAX Who from?
G Well, Mr Hall said [h]e had to talk to you.
M OK, I'll call [h]im later. What's [h]is number?
G **H**e only gave me **h**is mobile number. Here it is.
M What does [h]e want, anyway? I talked to **h**im last week.
G Apparently **h**is wife wants [h]er script back.
M Well, send it to **h**er – it was rubbish anyway. What's next?
G Er … Carl told me **h**e was going to be in New York next week.
M Why is [h]e going to New York? **H**e should be going to L.A. That man's an idiot. I'll call [h]im later.
G And Sid said that [h]e hadn't understood your email. Maybe you should call [h]im back.
M OK, I will. Is that it?
G Er, not quite. Who's next? Um, oh yes, Linda Wise said she couldn't come to Monday's meeting.
M Did she say why?
G Yes, she's hurt [h]er back again.
M Typical. I told [h]er to see a doctor. She just won't listen.
G And Mrs Lee told me the designs would be ready on Monday.
M Well, that's some good news, at least.
G Yes, I told [h]er you'd be pleased. What's next? Oh, Ted Black said [h]e was having a party on Saturday.
M Who on earth is Ted Black?
G You know, the film producer. I told [h]im you'd be there.
M Oh no! You know I can't stand [h]im.
G **H**e said [h]e wanted to talk to you about a new project.
M Fine. Is that all?
G And there's er one more.
M What's that?
G Your ex-wife told me she'd sold the house.
M What?! Get [h]er on the phone – now!

CD3 17

GABI I'm sorry, I don't know what you're talking about.
EVA We've been watching you for a while, you know. We've got it all – phone conversations, emails, text messages, bank statements, the lot.
G You're joking! You mean you're a cop?
E Got it in one, mate. And I hope you like prison food, because unless you start giving me some names, you're going to be eating it for the next ten years.
MAX Thank you very much um Eva. That was very good. Thanks, Gabi.
G No problem. See you later.
M Now, Eva, I'd like to ask you a few questions.
E Sure, go ahead.
M Are you working at the moment?
E Er, not at the moment, no.
M Do you have any acting work in the next three months?
E Well, maybe. I've had some auditions for other TV programmes, but I'm still waiting to hear back from them.
M And what was your last acting job?
E I played a nurse in an episode of *Ward Six* recently – you know, the TV hospital soap. I got hit by a car and ended up as a patient in the hospital I worked in. I died at the end of the episode. But it was a very challenging part.
M OK, that sounds good. What other parts have you had recently?
E Before that, well, I was a schoolteacher in a film called *Flowers in Winter*. I had the lead role in that. It was quite a demanding role, but very rewarding too. The film's coming out next month, I think.
M Right. And where did you study acting?
E I trained at the London School of Drama for three years.
M Really? Hm, that's good. And the last question. Are you available to start next week?
E Next week? Yes, I think so.
M OK, that's about all. Thanks for coming in. We've got your number, haven't we?
E Yes, it's on my CV – or you can call my agent.
M Fine. We'll let you know by the end of the day. Have you got any questions?
E Yes, I've got a couple, actually. Who are the other actors in *Undercover*?

CD3 18

JOE So, how did it go?
EVA Oh, quite well, I think. It was quite stressful, though. I had to read from the script, then Max, the producer, interviewed me.
J What did he ask you?
E First he asked me if I was working at the moment.
J And how did you deal with that?
E Well, um I couldn't tell him I was a waitress working part-time in a café, could I? So I said no. Then he asked what my last acting job had been, so I told him about *Ward Six*.
J That's good. It shows you're a working actress – well, some of the time, anyway.
E Very funny. He also asked if I had any acting work in the next three months.
J And what did you say?
E I told him about the other auditions and said I was very hopeful. That was the best thing to say, don't you think?
J Yes, probably.
E Oh, and he wanted to know where I'd studied acting.
J Uh-huh.
E So I told him about the drama school, of course.
J Did he ask anything else?
E Er … let me think … yes, he asked me what other parts I'd had recently.
J You told him about *Flowers in Winter*, I hope.
E Of course. Then … guess what?
J What?
E He wanted to know whether I was available to start next week!
J Next week?! So you've got the part?
E Er, no, not exactly – he said he'd let me know by the end of the day. But I have a good feeling about this, I really do.
J Well, I really hope you get it. Will you still love me when you're famous?
E No, I'll start going out with a good-looking man who's got a well-paid, glamorous job!
J Hey!

CD3 20

EVA Hello?
MAX Hello, is that Eva West?
E Yes, it is.
M This is Max Foster from On The Box.
E Oh, er, yes, hi!
M Good news! You've got the job!
E Really? Oh, that's wonderful, thank you!
M No problem. Can you come to a meeting on Monday?
E Er, yes, of course. What time?
M Be at our offices at ten. The director and all the other actors will be here too.
E Yes, of course.
M Oh, and one more thing. Don't accept any more work. This is a full-time job and you'll be busy for the next three months, at least.
E No, of course not. Thanks again. Bye.
M Bye.
E Wow! I've got the job!
JOE Congratulations! That's brilliant!
E Yes, I can't believe it! A TV series … and I'm the main character!
J So what did he say?
E Well, he asked me to come to a meeting on Monday. He wants me to meet the director and the other actors.
J That's great!
E Yes, he told me to be at their offices at ten.
J Excellent. Did he say anything else?
E Yes, he told me not to accept any more work. This is going to last three months, at least.
J Fantastic! So what's your character's name again?
E Kat. I don't know much about her yet, but it sounds like a really challenging part. Apparently she's an undercover cop …

CD3 21

DARREN [Are you] Sure this is the place, Glenn?
GLENN Yeah. [The] Warehouse on Tudor Street. [At] Seven thirty.
D [It] Looks closed to me. [Do you] Want a cigarette?
G No, thanks, mate. [I] Gave up last week.
D Yeah, right. [Have you] Heard from Kat recently?
G Not since four. She'll call if she needs to. They're late.
D Only five minutes. Maybe they're stuck in traffic or something.
G Maybe. Let's wait a few more minutes.
D Yeah, OK. ¹**We'll wait and see what happens.**
G I'm getting a bad feeling about this.
D Me too. ²**Why don't we call Kat?** Where is she tonight, anyway?
G [She's] Out on a date.
D A date? You're joking. Who with?
G The son, Dom. [She] Thought she could get some information out of him.
D Information. Right.
G [Have you] Got a cigarette?
D [I] Thought you said you'd given up.
G That was last week. ³**Oh, don't forget to turn the camera on when they arrive.** We need this on film.
D Yeah, I know. Where are they?
RUPERT Hendrik. At last. I said seven thirty.
HENDRIK Sorry I'm late, Rupert. [I] Had a bit of a problem finding it. Why didn't we meet at the warehouse, like we usually do?
R [The] Cops are watching me, that's why.
H What?!
R They've put an undercover cop in the gallery. [A] Girl called Kat.
H You're joking.
R Do I look like I'm joking? That's why I called you back this afternoon from a payphone and told you to meet me here instead.
H [Are you] Sure you weren't followed?
R No, the cops went to the warehouse. Idiots. So, [have you] got the statues?
H [They're] In the van. ⁴**I'll put them in your car myself, if you like.**
R Hang on a minute. Are the diamonds inside them?
H [Of] Course they are.
R They'd better be. Or we'll both end up dead.
H Hey, relax. All I want is the money. Er … where is it, by the way?
R [It's] In the bag. Two million, used ten-pound notes, just like we agreed.
H Perfect. Hey, Rupert, when this is all over, ⁵**would you like to come and visit me in Amsterdam?**
R [I] Don't think that's a good idea. But if this works, ⁶**I'll definitely buy some more of your statues.** Now help me carry this one …
KAT I've locked up the gallery, Gloria. Here are the keys.
GLORIA Thanks. Um, Kat, before you go, can I talk to you in the office?
K Of course.
G After you. … Put your hands on your head. Now!
K What's going on?
G I have a gun pointing at your head. ⁷**If you turn around, I'll kill you.**
K Gloria, there must be some mistake.
G There's no mistake, 'Kat' – if that is your real name. We know you're a cop, so let's stop playing games, shall we?
K What are you talking about? Of course I'm not a cop. Whatever gave you that idea?
G I saw you bugging our phone the other night. Now if you don't start telling me the truth, I'll put a bullet between your pretty little ears.
K OK, you're right. ⁸**I work for the SCS.** We know what you and Rupert have been doing. But if you help us, I'll make it easier for you.
G ⁹**I'm not going to help the police.** I'd rather go to prison.
K They've probably arrested Rupert already, you know.
G I don't think so. We're one step ahead of you. Now sit down and shut up.
DOM Kat, are you there? Kat?
G ¹⁰**Don't say a word.**
D Kat, the taxi's waiting … where are you? Kat?

VIDEO 11 CD3 22

ELLA Hello, Getaway Holidays. How can I help you?
MR KRANE Hello, my name's Bob Krane. Can I speak to Tanya Wilson, please?
E I'm sorry, she's out of the office all day. Would you like to leave a message?
MR K Er … yes, if you don't mind.
E Sorry, what did you say your name was again?
MR K Bob Krane.
E Is that Crane with a C?
MR K No, with a K.
E Right, thank you. And what was the message?
MR K Um, well, your company wants to send customers to our hotels here in Florida and I'd like to meet with her when I come to the UK next week to discuss a contract.
E OK. Shall I ask her to call you?
MR K Actually, I'm flying to London Heathrow on Thursday on other business. I'm only in the UK for 48 hours, so perhaps Tanya could meet me at a hotel near Heathrow for lunch on the day I arrive. I'm on … er, let's see, British Airways flight BA614 from Miami, which arrives at Heathrow at 11.15 a.m.
E Sorry, I didn't get all of that. Could you say it again, please?
MR K Yes, British Airways flight BA614 from Miami, which arrives at Heathrow at eleven fifteen.
E Flight BA614 from Miami.
MR K That's right.
E And it arrives at eleven fifty.
MR K No, not eleven fifty, eleven fifteen.
E OK, Mr Krane, I'll let her know as soon as she gets in tomorrow.
MR K Thank you very much. Bye.
E Goodbye.
ELLA Hello, Getaway Holidays. Can I help you?
ANDY Hi, it's Andy. How are things?
E Oh, hello Andy. Er, fine, I think. There's a lot to learn, though.
A I'm sure you'll be fine. If you're not sure about anything, just ask Charlie.
E Yes, I will. Anyway, aren't you supposed to be on holiday in Morocco?
A Yes, I am, but I'm not leaving till tomorrow, and there are a couple of things I didn't have time to do before I left on Friday.
E Well, can I help?
A Yes, if you don't mind. Firstly, could you call Rupert Nielson at The Times and tell him that the meeting on Wednesday has been cancelled.
E Do you mean this Wednesday, the twelfth?
A No, next Wednesday, the nineteenth.

E And could you tell me his surname again?
A Nielson.
E Is that spelt N-i-e-l-s-e-n?
A No, it's N-i-e-l-s-o-n.
E Right. Got it.
A And could you check that all our sales reps have been invited to the sales conference?
E Er, are you talking about the UK sales conference?
A No, the European one. It's in Lisbon next month.
E OK. I'll check they've all been invited.
A Thanks a lot.
E Is there anything else I can help you with?
A No, that's all, I think. But if you have any problems, give me a call on my mobile.
E Er, I haven't got your number.
A Oh, right hang on. It's um, 07700 900372.
E Sorry, I didn't quite catch that. Can you give it to me again, please?
A Sure. 07700 900372.
E Thanks. I won't call unless I have to. Have a great holiday!
A Will do. And good luck with the new job! Bye.
E Bye.
A Thanks for waiting. City centre please.

CD3 25

1
ELLA Is that Crane with a C?
MR KRANE No, with a K.
2
ELLA Do you mean this Wednesday, the twelfth?
ANDY No, next Wednesday, the nineteenth.
3
ELLA Is that spelt N-i-e-l-s-e-n?
ANDY No, it's N-i-e-l-s-o-n.
4
ELLA Er, are you talking about the UK sales conference?
ANDY No, the European one.

CD3 26

1
A Hello, [1]can I help you?
B Yes, can I speak to Mr Smith, please?
A Do you [2]mean Ron Smith?
B No, Ed Smith.
2
A Can you call Gary on extension 223 and remind him about the meeting?
B Sorry, I didn't [3]get all of that. Did you [4]say extension 233?
A No, extension 223.
B And are you [5]talking about today's meeting?
A No, tomorrow's meeting.
3
A Sorry, I didn't quite [6]catch that. Can you [7]give me your address again?

B 23 Jerrard Street, SE19.
A Is [8]that Gerrard [9]with a G?
B No, it's [10]with a J.
4
A Sorry, [11]what did you say his name was again?
B It's Trevor Martyn.
A And is that [12]spelt M-a-r-t-i-n?
B No, it's M-a-r-t-y-n.
A And do you [13]want to talk to him [14]about this year's conference?
B No, next year's conference.

CD3 28

1 /ʃən/ reception, collection, promotion, prescription, education, invitation, conversation, information, organisation, pronunciation, examination
2 /ɪdʒ/ message, village, language, damage, sausage, luggage, package
3 /tʃə/ future, miniature, temperature, manufacture

CD3 29

1
JULIET We've been standing here for nearly twenty minutes.
LENNY Yes, I know. But I'm sure one will be along soon.
J I wish we had a car.
L Yeah, me too, but you know we can't afford one, not until I find a job.
J Yeah, I know, I'm just saying. If we had a car, I wouldn't spend half my life waiting for buses.
L Oh look, here's one. See, I told you.
2
AMANDA Do you fancy a drink? Sally and I are off to the pub.
RYAN Oh, I wish I could come with you. But I have to stay and finish this report.
A Can't you do it tomorrow?
R No, Brian wants it before he goes home. He's off to New York in the morning.
A Well, if you finish it in the next hour or two, give me a call.
R Yes, I will. I could really do with a drink. Anyway, have a good time. Now, where was I?
3
JASON Are you enjoying this film?
TINA No, it's rubbish, isn't it? Actually, I'm sick of sitting here watching telly in this freezing cold flat.
J Yeah. I wish I was on a beach somewhere, you know, relaxing in the sunshine.
T Yeah, we could really do with a holiday, couldn't we? It's a shame we're so broke.
J Do you fancy going for a walk?
T No, I can't be bothered. Let's see what else is on.

4

MOLLY You look nice. I can't remember when I last saw you in a suit.
PATRICK Thanks. But I wish we didn't have to go to this party. I don't really feel up to it.
M Oh, you can't miss your sister's birthday. Anyway, you'll enjoy it when you're there.
P Yes, I suppose so. But let's not hang around for too long after dinner.
M No, of course not. So, which of these dresses should I wear?
P Er … I don't mind, it's up to you.
M The red one, I think … or maybe the green one.

5

DYLAN Are you off?
BARBARA Yes, I'm meeting Jackie at the station in a few minutes.
D Well, give her my love.
B Will do. I wish you were coming to the theatre with me.
D You know I'm not really into musicals. Anyway, I've got to finish marking all these exams.
B OK. I'll see you later.
D Have a good time. Bye.

CD3 30

ANSWERS 1 could 2 wasn't/weren't
3 didn't have to 4 had 5 were staying
6 was/were 7 could 8 didn't have to
9 liked 10 was/were sitting

CD3 31

CAROL The most important moment in my life was um the day I met Owen. An old friend was having a party, but the weather was so bad that I nearly didn't bother going. Just think, if I'd stayed at home, I wouldn't have met my husband. Anyway, my friend introduced me to Owen and we got on really well. He was only in London for a few days – he's American, you see – and he was supposed to fly back to Boston the following day. But the next morning Owen called me to say that Heathrow airport was closed because of ice and snow. He'd have flown home that day if the weather hadn't been so bad. Anyway, he invited me out for lunch and we got to know each other a bit better. He flew home the next day, but by that time we were already madly in love. We got married two years later – and the rest, as they say, is history.

ANTHONY For me the, um … probably the biggest turning point in my life was when I lost my job. I was working for an advertising agency, but they got into financial trouble and had to get rid of some people, including me. I got quite depressed at first, but I was getting fed up with working for a big agency anyway. So I decided to start my own online design company. If I hadn't lost my job, I wouldn't have started my own business, but it's been really successful. I've always fancied working from home, and so I moved to the country and bought a nice little cottage. I wouldn't have left London if I'd stayed with the ad agency. I don't get as much money as I used to, but I'm much happier than I was then.

MICHELLE Well, for me it's probably the day I won my first race. When I was a kid I used to get into trouble a lot at school, and the only thing I enjoyed was running, which I was always quite good at. Then one day my dad took me to the local athletics club. When we got there I found out that he'd entered me for the 400 metres! I was really nervous, but I won by over two seconds. That was the turning point for me. If I hadn't won that race, I'd never have become a serious athlete. I started training really hard and three years later I managed to get into the British youth athletics team. I've got better as I've got older and now I want to compete in the next Olympics. So, yeah, running's changed my life. If I hadn't started doing this, I'd have got into a lot more trouble, I'm sure of that.

CD3 33

1 They'd have come to the party if they'd wanted to.
2 If you'd left a message, I'd have called you back.
3 He wouldn't have sold his car if he hadn't lost his job.
4 If I hadn't been so tired, I'd have gone out last night.
5 If he hadn't moved to New York, he wouldn't have met his wife.

CD3 34

if they'd wanted to → They'd have /əv/ come to the party if they'd wanted to. | I'd have /əv/ called you back → If you'd left a message, I'd have /əv/ called you back. | if he hadn't lost his job → He wouldn't have /əv/ sold his car if he hadn't lost his job. | I'd have /əv/ gone out last night → If I hadn't been so tired, I'd have /əv/ gone out last night. | he wouldn't have /əv/ met his wife → If he hadn't moved to New York, he wouldn't have /əv/ met his wife.

CD3 35

[words in pink = weak forms]

PRESENTER Hello and welcome to the programme. Stories of superheroes have entertained us for nearly eighty years, and one of the most popular of these is Spider-Man. Today I'm talking to the author Robin Baker, whose new book, *Superhero*, tells the story of Spider-Man's creator, Stan Lee. Welcome to the programme, Robin.
ROBIN Thank you.
P Robin, what can you tell us about Stan Lee's early life?
R Well, his real name was Stanley Lieber, and he started working for a company called Timely Comics when he was sixteen. Twenty years later the company – which was now called Marvel Comics – was almost broke, so Lee was asked to invent some new superheroes.
P Which characters did he create?
R First he created a comic called *The Fantastic Four*, which was very successful and saved the company. This was followed by *The Incredible Hulk*, *The X-Men*, and then, er, *Spider-Man*.
P Where did the idea for Spider-Man come from?
R Well, according to Stan Lee himself, he was in his office trying to come up with a superpower for a new character he'd just created. While he was sitting there, he was watching a fly walking up a wall. Then he thought, wouldn't it be great if my character could walk up walls like an insect? So Spider-Man was born. Actually, he nearly called him Insect-Man.
P Really?
R Yes, but he thought it just didn't sound right. Then he tried Crawling-Man, Mosquito-Man … and then finally Spider-Man.
P And Spider-Man was rather different to earlier superheroes, wasn't he?
R Yes, absolutely. The character Peter Parker – who's Spider-Man, of course – was a typical young guy. He had problems with girls, he missed appointments, he couldn't pay the rent, that kind of thing. So um even though he had these amazing superpowers, he was still a normal guy with all the problems young people usually have.
P How did he get his superpowers?
R Well, in the original comic Peter Parker was bitten by a radioactive spider at a science museum. This gave him his super strength and his "spider sense", which is his ability to sense danger. And of course he er can also climb up the sides of buildings, which is very useful!
P As we've all seen in the films.
R Yes, indeed. And a funny little fact is Stan Lee often appeared in his characters' movies – usually as a hot-dog seller.
P Robin, thanks very much for coming in to talk to us today.
R My pleasure.

CD3 37

Listening Test (see Teacher's Book)

Phonemic Symbols

Vowel sounds

/ə/	/æ/	/ʊ/	/ɒ/	/ɪ/	/i/	/e/	/ʌ/
f<u>a</u>ther <u>a</u>go	<u>a</u>pple c<u>a</u>t	b<u>oo</u>k c<u>ou</u>ld	<u>o</u>n g<u>o</u>t	<u>i</u>n sw<u>i</u>m	happ<u>y</u> eas<u>y</u>	b<u>e</u>d <u>a</u>ny	c<u>u</u>p <u>u</u>nder

/ɜː/	/ɑː/	/uː/	/ɔː/	/iː/			
h<u>er</u> sh<u>ir</u>t	<u>ar</u>m c<u>ar</u>	bl<u>ue</u> t<u>oo</u>	b<u>or</u>n w<u>al</u>k	<u>ea</u>t m<u>ee</u>t			

/eə/	/ɪə/	/ʊə/	/ɔɪ/	/aɪ/	/eɪ/	/əʊ/	/aʊ/
ch<u>air</u> wh<u>ere</u>	n<u>ear</u> h<u>ere</u>	t<u>our</u> m<u>atu</u>re	b<u>oy</u> n<u>oi</u>sy	n<u>i</u>ne <u>eye</u>	<u>eigh</u>t d<u>ay</u>	g<u>o</u> <u>o</u>ver	<u>ou</u>t br<u>ow</u>n

Consonant sounds

/p/	/b/	/f/	/v/	/t/	/d/	/k/	/g/
<u>p</u>ark sou<u>p</u>	<u>b</u>e ro<u>b</u>	<u>f</u>ace laugh	<u>v</u>ery li<u>v</u>e	<u>t</u>ime whi<u>t</u>e	<u>d</u>og re<u>d</u>	<u>c</u>old loo<u>k</u>	<u>g</u>irl ba<u>g</u>

/θ/	/ð/	/tʃ/	/dʒ/	/s/	/z/	/ʃ/	/ʒ/
<u>th</u>ink bo<u>th</u>	mo<u>th</u>er <u>th</u>e	<u>ch</u>ips tea<u>ch</u>	<u>j</u>ob pa<u>g</u>e	<u>s</u>ee ri<u>c</u>e	<u>z</u>oo day<u>s</u>	<u>sh</u>oe a<u>c</u>tion	televi<u>s</u>ion

/m/	/n/	/ŋ/	/h/	/l/	/r/	/w/	/j/
<u>m</u>e na<u>m</u>e	<u>n</u>ow rai<u>n</u>	si<u>ng</u> thi<u>n</u>k	<u>h</u>ot <u>h</u>and	<u>l</u>ate hel<u>l</u>o	ma<u>rr</u>y <u>wr</u>ite	<u>w</u>e <u>wh</u>ite	<u>y</u>ou <u>y</u>es

Irregular Verb List

infinitive	Past Simple	past participle
be	was/were	been
become	became	become
begin	began	begun
bet	bet	bet
bite	bit	bitten
blow	blew	blown
break	broke	broken
bring	brought /brɔːt/	brought /brɔːt/
build /bɪld/	built /bɪlt/	built /bɪlt/
buy	bought /bɔːt/	bought /bɔːt/
can	could /kʊd/	been able
catch	caught /kɔːt/	caught /kɔːt/
choose	chose /tʃəʊz/	chosen
come	came	come
cost	cost	cost
cut	cut	cut
do	did	done /dʌn/
draw /drɔː/	drew /druː/	drawn /drɔːn/
drink	drank	drunk /drʌŋk/
drive	drove	driven
eat	ate	eaten
fall	fell	fallen
feed	fed	fed
feel	felt	felt
find	found	found
fly	flew /fluː/	flown /fləʊn/
forget	forgot	forgotten
get	got	got (US: gotten)
give	gave	given
go	went	been/gone
grow /grəʊ/	grew /gruː/	grown /grəʊn/
hang	hung	hung
have	had	had
hear	heard /hɜːd/	heard /hɜːd/
hide	hid	hidden
hit	hit	hit
hold	held	held
keep	kept	kept
know	knew /njuː/	known /nəʊn/
learn	learned/learnt	learned/learnt
leave	left	left
lend	lent	lent

infinitive	Past Simple	past participle
let	let	let
lie	lay	lain
lose /luːz/	lost	lost
make	made	made
meet	met	met
pay	paid /peɪd/	paid /peɪd/
put	put	put
read /riːd/	read /red/	read /red/
ride	rode	ridden
ring	rang	rung /rʌŋ/
run	ran	run
say	said /sed/	said /sed/
see	saw /sɔː/	seen
sell	sold	sold
send	sent	sent
set	set	set
shake	shook /ʃʊk/	shaken
shoot	shot	shot
show	showed	shown
sing	sang	sung /sʌŋ/
sink	sank	sunk
sit	sat	sat
sleep	slept	slept
speak	spoke	spoken
spell	spelled/spelt	spelt
spend	spent	spent
split	split	split
spread	spread	spread
stand	stood	stood
steal	stole	stolen
strike	struck	struck
swim	swam	swum /swʌm/
take	took /tʊk/	taken
teach	taught /tɔːt/	taught /tɔːt/
tell	told	told
think	thought /θɔːt/	thought /θɔːt/
throw /θrəʊ/	threw /θruː/	thrown /θrəʊn/
understand	understood	understood
wake	woke	woken
wear	worn	worn
win	won /wʌn/	won /wʌn/
write	wrote	written

Cambridge Dictionary

Make your words meaningful

Free, trustworthy, corpus-informed dictionaries, grammar reference and language learning resources.

Definitions, audio, translations and grammar

Written especially for learners of English, our definitions are clear and easy to understand. You'll also find American and British English audio pronunciations for each word, grammar advice, lots of example sentences, and translation dictionaries in more than 20 languages.

Optimised for smartphones

Perfect for looking up definitions, checking grammar and listening to pronunciations on the move. Cambridge Dictionary is as easy to use on a mobile phone as it is on a tablet or laptop.

Always up to date

Follow our blog to find out about new words and to get advice on grammar, vocabulary, phrasal verbs and idioms. Join us on Facebook, Twitter and Instagram for our Word of the Day and to become part of our community.

Personalised for you

Create and share personalised wordlists, quiz yourself and be the first to receive information about new features by signing up for Dictionary +Plus.

- @cambridgewords
- @cambridgewords
- @cambridgedictionariesonline
- Cambridge Dictionary

dictionary.cambridge.org